Means and Ends

The Revolutionary Practice of Anarchism in Europe and the United States

by

ZOE BAKER

Means and Ends: The Revolutionary Practice of Anarchism in Europe and the United States
© 2023 Zoe Baker
This edition © 2023 AK Press (Chico / Edinburgh)

ISBN 978-1-84935-498-1
E-ISBN 978-1-84935-499-8
Library of Congress Control Number: 2022948753

AK Press   AK Press
370 Ryan Avenue #100   33 Tower Street
Chico, CA 95973   Edinburgh, EH6, 7BN
USA   Scotland
www.akpress.org   www.akuk.com
akpress@akpress.org   akuk@akpress.org

The addresses above would be delighted to provide you with the latest AK Press
catalog, featuring several thousand books, pamphlets, audio and video products, and
stylish apparel published and distributed by AK Press. Alternatively, visit our websites
for the complete catalog, latest news and updates, events, and secure ordering.

Cover design by John Yates | www.stealworks.com
Cover photographs (top) courtesy of Centro Studi Libertari /
Archivio Giuseppe Pinelli, Milan, Italy (bottom) courtesy of Abel
Paz Fund, Anselmo Lorenzo Foundation Archive (CNT)

Printed in the United States of America on acid-free, recycled paper

DEDICATION AND ACKNOWLEDGMENTS

This book is dedicated to the vast number of anarchist workers whose names do not appear in history books but who nonetheless played a vital role in the struggle for universal human emancipation.

This work, which began as a PhD thesis submitted to Loughborough University, greatly benefited from feedback provided by Ian Fraser, Alexandre Christoyannopoulos, Paul Raekstad, Jesse Cohn, Shawn P. Wilbur, Mark Leier, David Berry, Kenyon Zimmer, Danny Evans, James Yeoman, Ruth Kinna, and Constance Bantman. Thanks to my editor Charles Weigl for making the book much nicer to read. Any errors are my responsibility.

Contents

"The coincidence of the changing of circumstances and of human activity or self-changing can be conceived and rationally understood only as revolutionary practice. . . . The philosophers have only interpreted the world, in various ways; the point is to change it."

—KARL MARX, *THESES ON FEUERBACH* (1845)

Introduction

The history of capitalism and the state is the history of attempts to abolish them and establish a free society without domination and exploitation. Revolutionary workers in the nineteenth and early twentieth centuries believed that another world was possible. It is still possible today. One of the main social movements that attempted to overthrow capitalism and the state during the nineteenth and early twentieth centuries was anarchism. Members of the historical anarchist movement not only attempted to change the world but also produced an elaborate body of ideas that guided their actions. This book is concerned with explaining what their ideas were. Historians sometimes unearth old ideas from the past because they are an interesting way of gaining insight into a different time and place. This is not my principal motivation. I wrote this book because I want to live in a society in which everyone is free. I am convinced that, if we are to achieve this goal, it is important to know the history of previous attempts to do so. My hope is that, through learning about how workers in the past sought to emancipate themselves, workers alive today can learn valuable lessons and develop new ideas that build on the ideas of previous generations.

How to define anarchism is a contentious topic and will be discussed in depth in chapter 1. For the purposes of this book, it will be understood as a form of revolutionary antistate socialism that first emerged as a social movement in late nineteenth-century Europe within the International Workingmen's Association between 1864 and 1872 and the subsequent Saint-Imier International between 1872 and 1878. During and after its birth as a social movement, it spread rapidly to North America, South America, Asia, Oceania, and parts of Africa through transnational networks, print media, and migration flows. I will focus exclusively on anarchist collectivists, anarchist communists, and anarchists without adjectives who were agnostic about the nature of the future society but advocated the same strategy as anarchist collectivists and anarchist communists. I do not claim that this is the one true form of anarchism. It is only the kind of anarchism I am focusing on.

Anarchism so understood is one of the largest movements in the history of socialism. According to the historian Benedict Anderson, "international anarchism . . . was the main vehicle of global opposition to industrial capitalism, autocracy, latifundism, and imperialism" during the late nineteenth century.[1] Even the hostile Marxist historian Eric Hobsbawm is forced to concede that, between 1905 and 1914, "the main body of Marxists" belonged to increasingly reformist social-democratic political parties while "the bulk of the revolutionary left was anarcho-syndicalist, or at least much closer to the ideas and the mood of anarcho-syndicalism than to that of classical marxism."[2] The vast amount of theory that the anarchist movement produced can be broken down into five main elements:

1. A theoretical framework for thinking about humans, society, and social change.
2. A set of ethical principles that form the value system of anarchism.
3. An analysis and critique of existing social relations and structures in terms of their failure to promote these ethical principles.
4. A vision of alternative social relations and structures

that are achievable and would actually promote these ethical principles.

5.   A series of strategies (which are consistent with the ethical principles) for abolishing existing social relations and structures in favor of the proposed alternative social relations and structures.

Fully explaining each aspect of anarchist theory, and how these ideas changed over time and varied around the world, goes far beyond the scope of what a single book can hope to achieve. The aim of this book is narrower. I shall rationally reconstruct the revolutionary strategies of anarchism within Europe and the United States between 1868 and 1939. It is important to note that this exclusive focus on one part of the world is an artificial construction. The real historical anarchist movement was constituted by transnational networks that operated at a global scale and enabled ideas and people to flow between continents. The movements in different countries were so interconnected that a complete history of anarchism in Europe and the United States necessarily includes the history of anarchism in Latin America, Asia, Africa, and Oceania—and vice versa. The true history of anarchism can only be written as a global history. My book is a contribution toward this global history but only covers a small fragment of it.[3]

In order to rationally reconstruct the revolutionary strategies of anarchism, it is necessary to explain the other four main elements of anarchist theory—theoretical framework, value system, critique of existing society, and vision of a future society—in depth. This is because what anarchists thought about strategy can only be understood within the context of anarchist theory as a whole. Although anarchists developed revolutionary strategies to abolish a variety of different oppressive structures, I shall primarily focus on their strategies to abolish capitalism and the state since this is what most anarchist texts discuss. I shall, when it is relevant, include anarchist views on how to abolish patriarchy, but it should be kept in mind that anarchist men, who were the majority of published anarchist authors, did not give this topic sufficient attention. When explaining anarchist ideas, I will write in the past tense because, for the purposes of this book, I am focused on anarchism during one time period. Many of the ideas I describe are still believed by anarchists today and are not exclusive to the past, such as a commitment to anticapitalism.

I shall throughout this book refer extensively to, and quote from, a number of major anarchist authors who lived in Europe or the United States between 1868 and 1939. This includes, but is not limited to, Michael Bakunin (1814–1876), Élisée Reclus (1830–1905), Peter Kropotkin (1842–1921), James Guillaume (1844–1916), Carlo Cafiero (1846–1892), Errico Malatesta (1853–1932), Émile Pouget (1860–1931), Ricardo Mella (1861–1925), Luigi Galleani (1861–1931), Max Baginski (1864–1943), Voltairine de Cleyre (1866–1912),[4] Emma Goldman (1869–1940), Alexander Berkman (1870–1936), Rudolf Rocker (1873–1958), Luigi Fabbri (1877–1935), and Charlotte Wilson (1854–1944). I shall supplement the quotations from major anarchist authors with quotations from sources collectively produced by the movement. These will include programs, congress resolutions, and manifestos of formal organizations or affinity groups. In order to maintain a consistent style, all quotes are rendered using American-English spelling.

A key factor determining which authors I have chosen to include within this book is the fact that I can only read English. This is a significant limitation given that the majority of anarchist primary sources within Europe and the United States were originally written in languages other than English—mainly French, Italian, German, Spanish, Russian, and Yiddish—and have yet to be translated.[5] As a result, there are authors who were historically important but whose ideas I cannot examine in any depth due to lacking access to them, such as the Yiddish-speaking anarchist Saul Yanovsky or the Dutch anarchist Domela Nieuwenhuis. Even with authors who have been translated into English, such as Reclus, I often only have access to a small amount of their total output. It should therefore be kept in mind that generalizations I make about anarchism are based on the primary sources available in English, and these represent a small fragment of the total texts produced by the historical anarchist movement.

I shall be quoting anarchist authors at length, rather than only rephrasing their ideas in my own words, because, in order to understand what anarchists thought historically, a modern reader must understand them on their own terms and so through their own language and exact ways of conceptualizing or expressing their ideas. Doing so will not only help ensure that my explanation of anarchist theory corresponds to what anarchists actually thought, but will also bring many obscure and not well-known passages to the reader's attention. Although I shall sometimes have to, for the sake of clarity and consistent terminology, introduce new language when summarizing anarchist ideas in my own words, this shall only ever represent a change in language and not a change in ideas. I shall, in addition, attempt to use the same language as historical anarchists as much as possible. Throughout this book, I shall not be arguing that anarchist theory was correct or interjecting with my own personal views on which anarchist authors or ideas were best. I will instead only be concerned with establishing and explaining what anarchist authors themselves thought.

Through quoting these anarchist authors, I shall be rationally reconstructing the ideas of different thinkers into a coherent system of thought. A rational reconstruction is a reorganization of a set of ideas that highlights the logical relations between its different elements.[6] A rational reconstruction of a political theory, in other words, not only explains what its exponents claim about various topics, such as how they think about society or the forms of action they advocate to change society. A rational reconstruction also makes the logical connections between the different elements of a political theory explicit, such as how their social theory underpins their choice of tactics. It is necessary to rationally reconstruct anarchist ideas in this manner for two main reasons. First, the vast majority of anarchist texts are short articles, speeches, or pamphlets. Even texts that were published as books are often compilations of previously published articles. Given this, an understanding of what an anarchist author thought can only be reached through assembling the many different ideas they espoused in different places. Bakunin, for example, wrote several sentences and paragraphs about freedom within texts concerned with a more general topic, but did not write an extended essay or book devoted solely to the subject of freedom. In order to establish what Bakunin thought about freedom, one must assemble a collection of short sentences and paragraphs made by him in several different texts. Even when an anarchist author did write about a topic in more detail, it is still necessary to combine different texts together because the positions advocated in one short article can be misunderstood or misrepresented when not connected to the claims made in other short articles. The ideas of the anarchist movement can likewise only be understood by assembling the ideas of a large number of different authors.

Second, a key reason why anarchist authors wrote political theory was that they aimed to spread revolutionary ideas to workers and inspire them to rise up against their oppressors. This led anarchists to write in a style that was accessible to a wide readership, but could also make their arguments appear simpler than they actually were. For example, on numerous occasions anarchist authors do not explicitly lay out the conceptual connections between their different beliefs. Even when anarchist authors do claim that certain ideas are connected, they do not always explain why this is the case or only explain briefly. Given this, it is necessary to rationally reconstruct anarchist ideas in order to build up the interconnected conceptual system that anarchist authors often left implicit or did not explain in sufficient depth.

The technique of rational reconstruction is usually applied to explaining the ideas of a single individual author, such as Marx or Descartes. Such efforts must be sensitive to the fact that an individual author changed their mind or developed their ideas over time. It would therefore be a mistake to unthinkingly place ideas from one period of their life alongside ideas from another period simply because they were written by the same person. This issue becomes greater when rationally reconstructing the ideas of an international social movement over several decades. Assembling together the ideas of a large number of different authors is straightforward when explaining ideas that all anarchists advocated, such as the abolition of capitalism and the state, but is more complicated when examining areas where anarchists disagreed with one another, an idea significantly changed over time, or a whole new idea emerged during a specific historical moment and did not exist prior to this. A rational reconstruction of the ideas of anarchism as a social movement must be sensitive to the fact that anarchist theory was not a single unchanging monolith, but a cluster of different tendencies in dialogue and debate with one another.

While this study will utilize the conceptual rigor of philosophy to summarize the arguments of anarchist authors, it will not examine these ideas in a historically anachronistic manner as if they existed outside of time and space. To truly understand the political theory of historical anarchism it is necessary to understand what these authors intended to mean and communicate to their audiences and how their texts were, independently of these authorial intentions, understood by readers at the time. This requires locating texts within a specific linguistic context—inherited assumptions from previous thinkers, ongoing debates and discussions, how certain words were used at the time, etc.—and the wider social, economic, and political world that these ideas were produced within and in reaction to—the social relations through which the production and consumption of goods were organized, what kinds of domination the ruling classes engaged in, how the oppressed classes resisted and struggled against their rulers, and so on.[7]

A comprehensive study of anarchism that fully contextualizes its ideas within their historical moment goes far beyond the scope of this book. I shall, instead, be focusing on a single main context: the history of the anarchist movement itself. This will include not only the theoretical debates within the movement, but also its various actual attempts at overthrowing capitalism and the state in favor of an anarchist society. This is because the revolutionary strategy of anarchism was articulated by members of a social movement in order to be put into action. It is furthermore the case that the ideas different anarchist authors proposed were developed in response to the ongoing experiences of class struggle, such as the various actions of different working-class social movements, state repression of anarchist movements, and debates within anarchist organizations about how to act in a specific moment. In order to include this context, I shall combine a detailed textual interpretation of primary sources available in English with the secondary literature on the history of different anarchist movements in Europe and the United States.

There are three limitations to this approach. First, the product of such a rational reconstruction will not correspond precisely to each individual author's viewpoint and will contain propositions that some of the authors I cite may have objected to, because they disagreed with other anarchists on the topic. To minimize this issue, I shall, when it is relevant, point out when a view was distinct to a specific author and when there are important exceptions to a generalization.

Second, this rational reconstruction will not exactly correspond to what the workers who composed the bulk of the anarchist movement thought. These workers were, after all, not automatons who blindly repeated word for word the ideas expressed by the major authors of anarchism. They had thoughts of their own about what anarchism was, and about what anarchists should do. They may have, in addition to this, disagreed with my interpretation of the authors I cite, not noticed features of these texts that I have, noticed features that I have failed to, and in general gained different ideas from reading these texts than I have. It is furthermore the case that I will have read texts that individual workers within the movement were unfamiliar with, and they would have read, or if they were illiterate had read to them, texts that I am unfamiliar with.

It is difficult to find out what these anarchists thought because the majority of anarchists were not published authors and instead developed ideas through face-to-face conversations with their comrades. German anarchists in New York, to give one example, would discuss politics in a wide variety of locations, ranging from anarchist-run beer halls to singing societies to family picnics in the park.[8] The contents of these conversations have unfortunately been largely lost when those who experienced and remembered them died, since only a tiny fraction of them were ever recorded in writing. Given this, it should be kept in mind that it is often unclear whether a major anarchist author is expressing ideas that they themselves came up with or is merely repeating ideas that were developed through countless face-to-face discussions between anarchist workers. Influential anarchist authors themselves routinely pointed out that they were repeating ideas collectively developed within working-class social movements. To give one example, Malatesta wrote in 1899 that "the anarchist socialist program is the fruit of collective development which, even ignoring its forerunners, lasted several decades, and which no one individual could claim to have authored."[9]

Third, my reconstruction of anarchist political theory draws upon a small number of women authors. This is because, although large numbers of women played a significant role in the late nineteenth- and early twentieth-century anarchist movement, most published anarchist authors appear to have been men.[10] Of those anarchist authors who were women, many of them cannot be included in my rational reconstruction since either they lived outside of Europe and the United States, such as the Chinese anarchist He-Yin Zhen, or they have not been translated into English, such as the Yiddish-speaking anarchist and doctor Katherina Yevzerov.[11] Nor can my reconstruction, due to its focus on texts, include the perspectives of those women who were active within the anarchist movement but did not (as far as I am aware) have their ideas published by the anarchist press. This includes such individuals as the militant Concha Pérez, who took up arms in the Spanish revolution of 1936 and fought against fascists in Barcelona and on the Aragon Front.[12]

Despite these shortcomings, a rational reconstruction of the ideas that can be found in the major theorists of anarchism who lived in Europe and the United States will provide a useful synthesis for thinking about the ideas that were prominent within the anarchist movement during the period I am examining. It should be kept in mind throughout that this reconstruction is primarily based on sources written by a small list of people who, despite exerting great influence on the movement, should not be conflated with the movement as a whole. Given this, when I write that "anarchists thought x" or "anarchism holds that y," I am not committing myself to the strong position that every person within the anarchist movement held these views, since this is not something I could possibly know. I am instead using these phrases as shorthand for the more modest claim that the major anarchist authors, newspapers, and programs of organizations I cite did adhere to these views.

The central argument of this book is that the reasons anarchists gave for supporting or opposing particular strategies were grounded in a theoretical framework—the theory of practice—which maintained that, as people engage in activity, they simultaneously change the world and themselves. This theoretical framework was the foundation for the anarchist commitment to the unity of means and ends: the means that revolutionaries proposed to achieve social change had to be constituted by forms of activity that would develop people into the kinds of individuals who were capable of, and were driven to, (a) overthrow capitalism and the state, and (b) construct and reproduce the end goal of an anarchist society.

The structure of this book is as follows. In chapter 1, I define anarchism in depth. In chapter 2, I explain anarchism's theoretical framework—the theory of practice. With this in place, I rationally reconstruct anarchism's value system, critique of existing society, and vision of a future society in chapter 3. The core ideas on strategy that were in general shared by the anarchist movement are described in chapter 4. Chapter 5 reconstructs the anarchist critique of state socialism. Chapters 6 and 7 provide an overview of the two main schools of anarchist strategy: insurrectionist anarchism and mass anarchism. Chapters 8 and 9 expand the discussion of mass anarchism by explaining the history, theory, and practice of one of its main forms: syndicalist anarchism, which is a kind of revolutionary trade unionism. Chapter 10 continues the discussion of mass anarchism by describing the history and theory of organizational dualism, which was the idea that anarchists should simultaneously form mass organizations open to all workers and smaller organizations composed exclusively of anarchists. Chapter 11 summarizes the main ideas of anarchist political theory and reaffirms my central argument that the revolutionary strategy of anarchism was grounded in the theory of practice.

CHAPTER 1

Defining Anarchism

Overviews of anarchism often begin by claiming that it is incredibly broad, incoherent, and inherently difficult to define.[1] Being difficult to define is not a unique feature of anarchism. It is a general problem facing the intellectual historian because, as Friedrich Nietzsche wrote, "only something which has no history can be defined."[2] That is to say, the reason why one can define hydrogen in terms of essential and unchanging necessary and jointly sufficient conditions is that it lies outside of history and so does not vary within and between human societies. What hydrogen is does not change between tenth-century France and twentieth-century Alaska. This remains true even though how humans have understood or thought about hydrogen has changed over time. But the same is not true of things that are historical in the sense of being inherently connected to and concerned with human activity, such as Christianity or anarchism.

Such historical entities have a beginning and boundaries that distinguish them from other parts of human existence, but the elements that compose them nonetheless change over time. Christianity, for example, emerged during the first century CE and was characterized by a set of beliefs and practices that made it different from other religions. It was subsequently modified numerous times during its history, such as by the invention of Catholicism and Protestantism. Historical entities are fluid and ever-changing because they are produced by and are about humans who are themselves constantly changing as they engage in activity within constantly evolving social structures. At any given moment in history, people will think and act differently in response to the same wider context. The consequence of this is that, as people articulate distinct perspectives, argue with one another, and act to ensure that their understanding remains dominant or becomes so, they also produce competing and contradictory versions of the same historically produced entity. Over time, this process of contestation causes the widespread version of a historically produced entity to change as some elements arise to prominence or fade into obscurity, whole new elements are added, and other elements are removed. There is no one true version of a historically produced entity. Instead, there is only what elements do or do not compose it according to different individuals or groups of people at the various stages of its development.

This should not be mistaken for the claim that there are no characteristics that distinguish one historically produced entity from another. Christianity may be a constellation of disparate elements that changes over time, but it is nonetheless distinct from the religion of the Aztecs. Nor does Nietzsche's view entail that all definitions of a historical entity are equally good and cannot be better or worse than another definition. A person who defined Christianity as a religion that believes in a single God would be failing to construct a useful definition, because it includes belief systems that should be excluded, such as other monotheistic religions like Islam, and fails to specify the distinct elements that compose Christianity historically and within modern society, such as the belief that Jesus was resurrected.

Nietzsche's views on historically produced entities have several consequences for thinking about how to define anarchism. Although anarchism will have an origin and some conceptual boundaries that have historically demarcated it from other ideologies, there will not be a single, unified body of thought called *anarchism*. At a given historical moment, there will be a series of distinct individuals or groups of people who all happen to call themselves anarchists and are in a process of contestation with one another over what anarchism means or should mean. Since what anarchism means is historically variable, the best we can expect from a definition is that it provides a snapshot of how specific individuals or groups of people understood anarchism at a given moment of its historical development. Such a definition may be rendered incomplete by unexpected developments within anarchism, such as whole new elements arising or previously important elements fading into obscurity. The point is not to establish what anarchism truly means once and for all, but to construct a definition of anarchism that is useful for investigating a particular historical period, topic, or type of anarchism.

There are two main views on what anarchism is. Transhistoricists generally define anarchism as referring to any political theory in history that advocates the abolition of the state, or systems of rulership in general, in favor of a free stateless society without rulers.[3] In response to this way of thinking about anarchism, historicists have argued that anarchism should instead be defined as a historically specific form of antistate socialism that first emerged in nineteenth-century Europe and rapidly spread, during and after its birth as a social movement, to North America, South America, Asia, Oceania, and Africa through transnational networks, print media, and migration flows.[4]

The disagreement over when to date the birth of anarchism partly stems from the fact that how modern authors think about the history of anarchism has been shaped by the earliest historiographies of anarchism, which were written in the late nineteenth and early twentieth centuries by members of the anarchist movement. These anarchists, like modern historians of anarchism, disagreed with one another about how anarchism should be defined and when anarchism first emerged. Some authors defined anarchism transhistorically. Peter Kropotkin, for example, remarked in 1913 that "there have always been anarchists and statists" and claimed to have found "anarchist ideas among the philosophers of antiquity, notably in Lao Tzu in China and in some of the earliest Greek philosophers."[5] This view was shared by Rudolf Rocker, who wrote in 1938 that anarchists advocate the abolition of "all political and social coercive institutions which stand in the way of the development of free humanity" and that, given this, "anarchist ideas are to be found in every period of known history."[6]

Other anarchists adopted a historicist account of anarchism in which it referred exclusively to a historically specific form of antistate socialism that first emerged in the nineteenth century as a response to the oppression of capitalism and the state. In 1884, Charlotte Wilson claimed that "Anarchism is a new faith" and "the name assumed by a certain school of socialists" who advocated the simultaneous abolition of capitalism and the state.[7] Decades later, Errico Malatesta wrote in 1925 that there was a distinction between "Anarchy," which is a cooperative society without oppression and exploitation, and "Anarchism," which "is the method of reaching anarchy, through freedom, without government."[8] The latter "was born" when people "sought to overthrow" both "capitalistic property and the State" and therefore did not exist prior to this.[9]

Importantly, this was not an exclusively European perspective. The Chinese anarchist Li Yaotang, who wrote under the pen name Ba Jin, argued in 1927 that "Anarchism is a product of the mass movement . . . not an idle dream that transcends time. It could not have emerged before the Industrial Revolution, and . . . the French revolution."[10] To him, it shared nothing with Daoism and the ideas of Lao Tzu. The Japanese anarchist Kubo Yuzuru likewise wrote in 1928 that "Anarchism originated from the fact of the struggle of the workers. Without that, there would be no anarchism."[11]

Given my commitment to Nietzsche's way of thinking about definitions, I shall be taking a historicist approach and defining anarchism as a historically specific form of antistate socialism that first emerged in nineteenth-century Europe. It is of course the case that the idea of a free stateless society existed before people in nineteenth-century Europe decided to start calling themselves anarchists. The Chinese Daoist Bao Jingyan argued in the third century that the state was created by the strong to oppress the weak, and became the means through which the wealthy reproduced the servitude of the poor. He thought that prior to the rise of states there existed a free, harmonious society with "neither lord nor subject" and claimed that it would be better if the state ceased to exist. Although his one surviving text proposed no strategies to achieve this goal, he did believe that the poor would revolt against the wealthy.[12] Even within Europe one can point to earlier authors who advocated the abolition of the state and property in favor of a free society based on communal ownership, such as the radical Christian Gerrard Winstanley in the seventeenth century.[13]

The history of anti-statist thought includes not only a long list of dead authors, but also the large numbers of people who have lived in, or do live in, stateless societies around the world. This is something that historical anarchists were themselves aware of.[14] The available anthropological evidence indicates that these people do not live in stateless societies by chance. They have, just like people who live under states, developed political philosophies about the kind of society they want to live in, and intentionally implemented these ideas throughout the course of their lives. They are aware that someone could establish themselves as ruler of the group and have, within the limits established by their ecological and social context, consciously and deliberately created social structures to prevent this from happening. This generally goes alongside an awareness of nearby societies with states. A striking illustration of this point is that, on numerous occasions, stateless societies have been created by people who have deliberately fled processes of state formation or expansion, such as stateless societies in the uplands of Southeast Asia.[15]

Members of stateless societies have developed a variety of complex social relations and arrangements in order to realize their conscious political goals and ethical values. These include: making collective decisions through consensus, between all involved; ensuring that leaders lack the power to impose decisions on others through coercion and must instead persuade people to act in a certain way, through oratory skill alone; and utilizing various forms of social sanction to respond to behavior that threatens the freedom or equality of the group, such as bullying, being greedy, issuing orders, taking on airs of superiority, engaging in acts of physical violence, and so on. These social sanctions include, but are not limited to, criticism, gossiping, public ridicule, ignoring what they say, ostracism, expulsion from the group, and even, in some extreme cases, execution.[16]

The many different forms of stateless societies that have existed, and continue to exist, around the world should not be romanticized and viewed as utopias. Even societies without a state or a ruling class can contain other kinds of oppressive social relations, such as the oppression of children by adults or women by men. Nor should the stateless societies that anthropologists have studied be viewed as straightforward windows into the past or living fossils of what human life was like prior to the emergence of states. The members of these societies do not live in the paleolithic or the neolithic but the modern world. Their social relations have been shaped by, and are part of, modern history, including the history of colonialism.[17] Matters are only made more complicated by the fact that a significant number of stateless societies move between very different forms of social organization on a seasonal basis.[18]

In claiming that "anarchism" refers to a form of anti-state socialism that first emerged in nineteenth-century Europe, I am not denying the existence of other political philosophies that have advocated a free, stateless society prior to, in parallel with, or after the emergence of anarchism. Although this book aims to demonstrate the intellectual sophistication of historical anarchist political theory, I also believe that modern anarchism can greatly improve through engaging with these other political traditions and learning valuable insights and lessons from them. My point is only that the term "anarchism" should not be used to refer to any political theory in history that advocates the abolition of the state, or systems of rulership in general, in favor of a free stateless society without rulers.

This is motivated by two main reasons. First, throughout the history of socialism, multiple theorists and social movements have advocated the long-term goal of abolishing the state and all systems of class rule in favor of a society of free producers, such as Louis Auguste Blanqui or all of Marxism.[19] If a transhistoricist wishes to label such figures as Bao Jingyan an "anarchist" due to their advocacy of a free stateless society without rulers, then they must, in order to be consistent, also refer to Blanqui and all of Marxism as "anarchists." Doing so would be a mistake given that self-identified anarchists opposed these other forms of socialism on the grounds that they, unlike anarchists, advocated the conquest of state power as a means to achieve human emancipation. This includes not only individuals who anarchists had polemical debates with, such as Karl Marx and Friedrich Engels, but also leaders of states who were responsible for the imprisonment, deportation, murder, and repression of anarchists, such as Vladimir Lenin, Leon Trotsky, and Joseph Stalin. Given this, any definition of anarchism must include strategies to achieve social change within its criteria and cannot define anarchism solely in terms of its goal.

The second reason to reject transhistorical definitions of anarchism is that they are historically anachronistic. The many different people who have advocated the abolition of the state or rulership throughout human history did not refer to themselves as "anarchists" or belong to a social movement that called itself "anarchist." At no point did they establish a historically contingent configuration of elements that were understood by people at the time to be what "anarchism" is. An author like Winstanley will not tell a historian anything about what "anarchism" as a historically produced entity means. A study of Winstanley's 1649 *The True Levellers Standard Advanced* instead informs a historian about the political ideology that Winstanley understood himself to be an advocate of: the Diggers. To categorize Winstanley as an "anarchist " is to anachronistically impose a later category onto him rather than understand him on his own terms.[20]

Although adopting a historicist approach significantly limits the scope of who can be considered an anarchist, it is not sufficient to develop a useful definition of anarchism for the purposes of studying it as a coherent political theory. This is because, during its history as a concept, people with fundamentally different commitments have called themselves anarchists and engaged in processes of contestation with one another over what anarchism is or should be. A brief and condensed summary of this history is as follows.

From Anarchy to Anarchism

The term "anarchist" was sometimes used as an insult during the English Civil War and the French Revolution.[21] It did not refer to a distinct political ideology until it was adopted by antistate socialists in the nineteenth century within the context of industrialization, and the rise of capitalism and the modern nation-state (henceforth referred to as the state) as a global economic and political system. The earliest known occurrence of this was in 1840, when the French socialist Pierre-Joseph Proudhon declared himself an "anarchist" in his book *What is Property?* He defined "*Anarchy*" as "the absence of a master" and argued that the "highest perfection of society is found in the union of order and anarchy."[22] It is important to note that Proudhon was not consistent with his vocabulary and sometimes used the word "anarchy" to signify chaos and disorder.[23] On other occasions, Proudhon labeled himself an advocate of "mutuality," "mutualism," and "the mutualist system."[24] This was a term that Proudhon borrowed from a previously existing social movement among silkworkers in Lyon.[25]

During the 1840s, Proudhon advocated the abolition of capitalism and the state in favor of a decentralized market socialist society in which the means of production and land were owned in common. In such a society, workers, either as individual producers or voluntary collective associations, would possess, but not own, the means of production and land that they personally used or occupied. To possess a resource was to have the right to control it. As a result, Proudhon envisioned a society where workers self-managed the organization of production and exchanged the products of their labor with one another.[26] This was to be achieved through a process of gradual and peaceful social change. From the late 1840s onward, Proudhon advocated the strategy of workers forming cooperatives with the aid of loans provided by a people's bank, at low or no interest. He thought that, over time, these cooperatives could grow in number, trade with one another, and take on more and more social functions until socialism as a society-wide economic system had been established.[27]

Between the 1840s and 1860s, Proudhon's version of anti-state market socialism influenced a number of individuals in the United States and Europe who also came to refer to themselves as mutualists.[28] Although these mutualists agreed with Proudhon's broad vision of socialism and his strategy of forming cooperatives funded by loans from a people's bank, they also had ideas of their own, were influenced by other authors such as Josiah Warren, and argued with one another about a wide variety of topics.[29] Some of those influenced by Proudhon adopted the language of "anarchy" and "anarchist." For example, in France the journalist Anselme Bellegarrigue wrote and published a short-lived journal called *Anarchy, A Journal of Order* in 1850. In the first issue of the journal he wrote, "I am an anarchist," and insisted that "anarchy is order, whereas government is civil war."[30] Around the same time a young Élisée Reclus, who would go onto become an important geographer and member of the anarchist movement, wrote an unpublished essay in order to clarify his thoughts. In it, he advocated the abolition of economic competition and "the tutelage of a government" in favor of socialism and "the absence of government . . . anarchy, the highest expression of order."[31]

An especially significant contribution was made by Joseph Déjacque, who was born in France and moved to the United States in the early 1850s. He not only repeated Proudhon's language of "anarchy" and "anarchist" but was also the earliest known person to self-identify as an advocate of "anarchism." Déjacque was the first person to use the word "libertarian" as a synonym for "anarchist" as well. In the August 18, 1859, edition of his paper *Le Libertaire*, he defined "anarchism" as the abolition of government, property, religion, and the family in favor of liberty, equality, solidarity, and the right to work and love.[32] In contrast to Proudhon and mutualism in general, Déjacque advocated the long-term goals of common ownership of the products of labor, distribution according to need, and the emancipation of women from patriarchy.[33]

In order to achieve these goals, the ruling classes had to be overthrown. Déjacque proposed that this could be achieved via the violent strategy of mass armed insurrections and small secret societies assassinating capitalists and governors.[34] Although Déjacque advocated the abolition of government, he thought that, given the current ideas and abilities of workers, a revolution would not establish anarchy immediately. There would instead be a period of transition in which decisions were made by workers themselves through universal and "direct legislation" within "the most democratic form of government."³⁵ Déjacque's proposed democratic government was constituted by self-governing communes of 50,000 people in which laws were passed by majority vote and government administrators were elected and recallable. The police were to be randomly selected by lottery and rotated over time such that everyone would engage in policing and there would be "no police outside the people."³⁶ Those who broke the law would be subject to trial by jury and an elected magistrate. A person found guilty by an unanimous decision of the jury would not be executed or imprisoned—since the "prison" and the "scaffold" were "government monstrosities"—but would instead only be subject to "moral or material reparation" or "banishment."³⁷ Over time, people would develop new and better ways of organizing society until government had been completely abolished and anarchy had been realized.

In parallel to these ideological developments, various organizations were formed by the working classes to achieve their emancipation and foster cooperation between workers of different countries.³⁸ In September 1864, this culminated in the founding of the International Workingmen's Association (henceforth referred to as the First International) at a meeting in St. Martin's Hall, London. The International included a wide variety of different kinds of socialists, and this led to a great deal of debate about what aims and strategies the organization should adopt. At the 1869 Basel Congress, the majority of delegates voted in favor of the collective ownership of land as a goal. This was opposed by a minority of mutualists who, while advocating the collective ownership of the means of production, thought that land should be individually owned by those who occupied it. The socialists who advocated the collective ownership of land referred to themselves as collectivists or advocates of collectivism. Some collectivists continued to think of themselves as mutualists.³⁹

During this period, a tendency emerged within the collectivist wing of the International that rejected participation in parliamentary politics and attempting to achieve socialism via the conquest of state power. They, despite being influenced by Proudhon, dithered from mutualism and advocated revolutionary trade unionism and the simultaneous abolition of capitalism and the state through an armed insurrection, which would forcefully expropriate the capitalist class.[40] This tendency referred to itself, and was referred to by others, using a variety of labels. This included not only *collectivist* but also *federalist, revolutionary socialist,* and *anarchist.* Between the mid-1870s and early 1880s, the labels of *anarchist* and *anarchism* became increasingly prominent until they were the dominant terms for this social movement.[41] A number of individuals and groups continued to also use alternative language, such as *autonomist, libertarian, libertarian socialist,* and *libertarian communist.*[42]

The anarchist tendency within the First International was primarily located within Italy, France, Belgium, Spain, and the Jura region of Switzerland. It began to form a distinct social movement during a series of congresses held in Spain (Barcelona June 1870, Valencia September 1871), Switzerland (La Chaux-de-Fonds April 1870, Sonvilier November 1871), and Italy (Rimini August 1872). During these congresses, delegates passed resolutions that rejected the strategy of achieving socialism via parliamentarism specifically and the conquest of state power in general. From November 1871 onward, congress resolutions were passed that opposed Marx and Engels's attempt to convert the General Council of the First International, which was supposed to perform only an administrative role, into a governing body that imposed state-socialist decisions and policies on the organization's previously autonomous sections. Marx and Engels thought this was necessary due to their false belief that Bakunin was secretly conspiring to take over the International and impose his anarchist program onto it.[43]

The conflict between the opponents and supporters of the General Council culminated in the International's September 1872

Hague Congress.[44] During this congress, resolutions were passed by majority vote that expelled the anarchists Bakunin and James Guillaume from the International, relocated the General Council from London to New York, and committed the organization to the goal of constituting the working class into a political party aimed at the conquest of political power. Marx and Engels achieved this majority by nefarious means. This included requesting blank mandates from various sections that did not specify who the delegate was or how they should vote. These blank mandates were then sent to supporters of the General Council. In multiple instances, these supporters even had their travel expenses paid for by Marx and Engels in order to ensure that they attended the congress. Several of the groups that issued blank mandates or pro–General Council mandates did not really exist as actual sections of the International, and had been created for the sole purpose of issuing a mandate at Marx and Engels's request. The resolutions of the Hague Congress were subsequently rejected by the Jura, French, Belgian, Italian, Dutch, English, and Spanish sections of the International on the grounds that they had been passed by a fake majority and violated each section's autonomy to determine its own strategy and program.[45]

Shortly after the end of the Hague Congress, delegates representing the Spanish, French, Italian, Jura, and American sections of the International met at a congress in Saint-Imier, Switzerland. In organizing this congress, which was held on September 15 and 16, 1872, the sections did not think they were forming a new distinct organization that split from the First International. They were rather, from their point of view, merely reorganizing or reconstituting the International on its original federalist basis. In order to avoid confusion, I shall refer to this organization as the Saint-Imier International but it should be kept in mind that this is anachronistic.[46]

During this congress, the delegates voted in favor of four resolutions. The first resolution rejected every resolution of the Hague

Congress and the authority of the new General Council in New York. The second resolution declared a pact of mutual defense, solidarity, and friendship between the sections that attended the meeting and any section that subsequently wished to join. This pact consisted of a commitment to be in regular correspondence with one another and to stand in solidarity with any section whose freedom was violated by either government repression or the impositions of an authoritarian General Council. The only distinctly anarchist resolutions were the third and fourth. They advocated a social revolution that abolished capitalism and the state simultaneously and established the free federation of free producers. This transformation of society was to be achieved by workers themselves organized within trade unions and autonomous communes. It was proposed that workers in the present should build toward the social revolution by organizing strikes. These forms of class struggle were advocated because they caused workers to develop an awareness of their distinct class interests, taught workers to act for themselves, and increased the power of workers against capitalists. Strikes prepared workers for the social revolution and established, or expanded, the systems of organization through which workers could successfully overthrow the ruling classes and reorganize production and distribution. The resolutions rejected the strategy of attempting to achieve socialism via the conquest of state power, because it would result in workers being dominated and exploited by a new minority of rulers who actually exercised state power, rather than the abolition of all systems of class rule.[47]

For several members of the historical anarchist movement, anarchism did not exist during the 1840s and 50s. Instead anarchism, as they understood it, first emerged within the First International and Saint-Imier International. In 1922, Luigi Fabbri referred to "the whole fifty-year history of anarchism" and so dated the birth of anarchism to 1872.[48] A similar position was articulated by Malatesta on numerous occasions. In 1899, he wrote that "we, anarchist socialists, have existed as a separate party, with essentially the same program, since 1868, when Bakunin founded the *Alliance* . . . and we were the founders and soul of the anti-authoritarian wing of the 'International Working Men's Association.'"[49] In 1907, Malatesta claimed that "the first anarchists" belonged to "the international."[50] He later wrote that "Anarchism was born" with the adoption of the resolutions of the Saint-Imier Congress in September 1872 and thereby transitioned from the "individual thought of a few isolated men" into "the collective principle of groups distributed all over the world."[51]

It should nonetheless be kept in mind that the Saint-Imier International was not an exclusively anarchist organization. The founding congress was attended by anarchist delegates representing Spain, France, Italy, and the Jura region of Switzerland, but it also included the delegate for America, Gustave Lefrançais, who, despite being a survivor of the Paris Commune, was not strictly speaking an anarchist. The organization soon grew to include a minority of state socialists from England, Germany, and Belgium. This led to a series of heated debates about strategy and the vision of the future society at the 1873, 1874, and 1876 congresses.[52]

The pluralist nature of the organization can be seen in the fact that the founding 1872 resolutions declared that each section had the right to decide for itself what form of political struggle they engaged in and that it was "presumptuous," "reactionary," and "absurd" to impose "one line of conduct as the single path that might lead to its social emancipation."[53] This position was reaffirmed at the 1874 congress, where the delegates voted unanimously in favor of a res-olution that each section should decide for itself whether or not to engage in parliamentary struggle. It was not until the final 1877 Ver-viers Congress of the Saint-Imier International, which was attended by delegates representing anarchist groups in France, Switzerland, Italy, Germany, Spain, Belgium, Greece, and Egypt, that the dele-gates were exclusively anarchist due to state socialists having left the organization. Anarchist-led sections in Argentina, Mexico, and Uruguay had affiliated with the Saint-Imier International but did not send delegates to the congress due to the distance.[54]

During the Verviers Congress, the anarchist delegates passed a series of resolutions that completely separated them from state socialism and thereby established anarchism as a fully distinct social movement, rather than one tendency within a pluralist International.[55] The anarchist delegates declared that their goal was the self-abolition of the proletariat through an international social revolution that overthrew capitalism, via the forceful expropriation of the ruling classes. They proposed that the private property of capitalism should be replaced by the collective ownership of land and the means of production by federations of producers themselves, rather than state ownership and control of the economy. To achieve this, they advocated revolutionary trade unionism and rejected forming political parties that engaged in parliamentary politics.[56]

In many respects, the Verviers resolutions were almost the same as the resolutions adopted five years previously at Saint-Imier. There was one crucial difference. The delegates at Saint-Imier had qualified their critique of achieving socialism via the conquest of state power with a commitment to different views on political struggle coexisting within the same pluralist International. The resolutions of Verviers were, in comparison, actively hostile to state socialism. They declared that society is divided into two main classes with distinct class interests: workers and capitalists. The state exists to defend the interests of capitalists and economic privilege in general. As a result, the state, irrespective of which political party wields its power, cannot be used to abolish class society and will instead reproduce it. The goal of emancipation can only be achieved by workers themselves directly engaging in class struggle.[57] Given this: "Congress declares that there is no difference between *political* parties, whether they are called socialist or not, all these parties without distinction forming in its eyes one reactionary mass and it sees its duty as fighting all of them. It hopes that workers who still travel in the ranks of these various parties, instructed by lessons from experience and by revolutionary propaganda, will open their eyes and abandon the way of politics to adopt that of revolutionary socialism."[58]

The theory and practice of the anarchist movement were not invented by a single founding father who developed the ideology in full and then transmitted it to workers. Anarchism was instead cocreated over several years by an international social network that formulated its common program through a process of debate and discussion in newspapers, pamphlets, books, formal congresses, informal meetings, and letters between key militants. This social network was mostly composed of workers, such as Jean-Louis Pindy and Adhémar Schwitzguébel, and a few formally educated individuals from privileged backgrounds, such as Bakunin and Carlo Cafiero.[59] This point was understood by later anarchists. In 1926, the Group of Russian Anarchists Abroad declared that "anarchism was born, not of the abstract deliberations of some sage or philosopher, but out of the direct struggle waged by the toilers against Capital, out of the toilers' needs and requirements, their aspirations toward liberty and equality. . . . Anarchism's leading thinkers: Bakunin, Kropotkin, and others, did not invent the idea of anarchism, but, having discovered it among the masses, they merely helped refine and propagate it through the excellence of their thinking and their learning."[60]

How Collectivists Became Anarchists

The history of how anarchism as a social movement arose is not only the history of how its program was formulated. It also includes the history of how, and why, a tendency within the First International came to refer to themselves as "anarchists" in the first place. It is

necessary to establish in detail how this happened because it clar-
ifies the relationship between the anarchism of Proudhon, who in
1840 was the first person to self-identify as an anarchist, and the
anarchism of the social movement that emerged from the late 1860s
onward. In 1880, Kropotkin claimed that:

> When in the heart of the International there rose up a party
> that fought against authority in all its forms, that party first
> took on the name of the federalist party, then called itself
> *anti-statist* or *anti-authoritarian*. At that epoch it even avoided
> assuming the name of anarchist. The word *an-archy* (as it
> was written then) might have attached the party too closely
> to the Proudhonians, whose ideas of economic reform the
> International then combated. But it was precisely to create
> confusion that the adversaries of the anti-authoritarians took
> pleasure in using the name.[61]

Nonetheless, as Kropotkin noted, anarchists came to accept the
name. As he pointed out in 1910, "the name of 'anarchists,' which
their adversaries insisted upon applying to them, prevailed, and
finally it was revindicated."[62]

One potential problem with Kropotkin's narrative is that
Bakunin first publicly called himself an "anarchist" in August 1867 in
"The Slavic Question," which was printed in the Italian paper *Freedom
and Justice*. He wrote in response to Pan-Slavists that "they are uni-
tarians at all costs, always preferring public order to freedom and I
am an anarchist and prefer freedom to public order."[63] Crucially, this
was written before Bakunin had even joined the First International
in June or July 1868.[64] A few years later, Bakunin referred to himself
as an "anarchist" in private in his 1870 letter to Sergei Nechaev and
his unsent October 1872 letter to the editors of *La Liberté*.[65]

Bakunin continued to use this language in his published
1873 book *Statism and Anarchy*. In it, he labeled the opponents of

German state communists as "anti-state socialists, or anarchists" and endorsed what he called "the *anarchist* social revolution."[66] He wrote that "we revolutionary anarchists are proponents of universal popular education, liberation, and the broad development of social life, and hence are enemies of the state and of any form of statehood. . . . Those are the convictions of social revolutionaries, and for them we are called anarchists. We do not object to this term because we are in fact the enemies of all power, knowing that power corrupts those invested with it just as much as those compelled to submit to it."[67]

It is difficult to determine how much impact Bakunin's decision in *Statism and Anarchy* to refer to himself and the movement he belonged to as "anarchist" had on the language of anti-state socialists within the Saint-Imier International. This is because *Statism and Anarchy* was the only major revolutionary socialist text written by Bakunin in Russian, rather than French, and almost all of the 1,200 copies that were printed in Switzerland were smuggled to St. Petersburg and distributed among Russian revolutionary circles.[68] In other texts, Bakunin used different language. For example, in "The Paris Commune and the Idea of the State," which was written in 1871 and published posthumously in 1878, he referred to the movement he belonged to as "collectivists" and "revolutionary socialists."[69] Even in *Statism and Anarchy* he also referred to anarchists as "revolutionary socialists."[70]

It is rare to find other examples of people identifying as "anarchists" between 1867–1871. One notable example is the September 1871 declaration of principles written by the Geneva Section of Socialist Atheists. Its members referred to themselves as "Anarchists" who sought the abolition of the state and "the autonomy of the individual and of the commune," which were to be achieved without "participation in politics, for to destroy the state, we cannot use the same means as those who support it."[71] On other occasions, the term "anarchist" was used to refer to federalist

systems of organization, rather than a specific ideology or movement. For example, on December 31, 1871, the Spanish section of
the First International reprinted the Jura Federation's "Sonvilier
Circular" with their own preface. This preface claimed that the
First International had an "anarchist constitution," despite the fact
that the constitution was not committed to what would soon be
regarded as core anarchist principles, such as the abolition of the
state or abstention from parliamentary politics.[72]

The fact that people did not widely refer to themselves as "anarchist" during this period is demonstrated by the resolutions of the
September 1871 London conference of the First International. The
resolutions forbid sections from designating "themselves by sectar-
ian names such as Positivists, Mutualists, Collectivists, Communists,
etc.," but did not include "Anarchists" within the list.[73] If the label
"anarchist" was already being widely used by anti-state socialists in
late 1871, Marx and Engels, who wrote the resolutions, would have
included the term in their list of forbidden section names, especially
since they did include the anti-state socialist label "collectivist." That
the term "anarchist" was not widely used in early 1870s Switzerland
is confirmed by Kropotkin's eyewitness testimony in his autobiography. He recalled that, in early 1872, when he visited the Swiss
sections of the First International, "the name 'anarchist' was not
much in use then."[74] In 1899, Malatesta similarly remembered that,
around 1868, "Bakunin came onto the scene, bringing with him the
ideas that would later be called anarchist."[75] Anarchists in Italy initially just referred to themselves as socialists, because they were the
first socialist movement in the country.[76]

The adoption of the term "anarchist" became increasingly common in the build up to and aftermath of the First International's
September 1872 Hague Congress. In Spain, Francisco Tomás wrote,
on September 8, 1872, that the First International was divided
between two main factions:

one founded in unitary and centralist principles, and the other in the principles of anti-authoritarianism and federalism. The former has as its aim the organization of the International as a political party and as its purpose the conquest of political power. The latter has as its aim the organization of all workers to demolish all the institutions of this corrupt society and the abolition of political-legal-authoritarian conditions providing a free worldwide federation of free associations of free producers. The Spanish Federation is in the ranks of the latter, that is, anarchist collectivism.[77]

This is not to say that all anti-state socialists adopted the term "anarchist" when the Saint-Imier International was founded in September 1872. There was a great deal of debate and discussion around labels. Reclus, who first publicly called himself an anarchist in March 1876, argued in 1878 that the terms "anarchy" and "anarchist" should be adopted by the movement due to the etymology of the words, and the fact that supporters and opponents were already using the words to refer to them. This is an argument Reclus would not have felt the need to make if there was already a consensus within the movement about the terms.[78]

One of the main opponents of the term was Guillaume. Although he had declared his socialism to be "an-archist" in August 1870, he had changed his mind by January 1872. He wrote: "We have been wrong to use, without closely examining it, the terminology of Proudhon, from which we drew those famous words, *abstention* and *an-archy*. . . . As to the word *anarchy*, I have never liked it, and I have always asked that it be replaced by *federation of autonomous communes*."[79] Guillaume rejected "anarchist" because of its negative connotations and preferred to continue to use the term "collectivists," which had been used during the First International's congresses in Brussels (1868) and Basel (1869) to refer to advocates of the collective ownership of land.[80] The first usage of the word "collectivism" had itself, according to Guillaume, been in the early September 1869 issue of his paper *Le Progrès*.[81] In 1876, Guillaume wrote in the *Bulletin of the Jura Federation*:

> The words *anarchy* and *anarchists* are, in our eyes and in those of many of our friends, words we should stop using, because they only express a negative idea without giving any positive theory, and they lend themselves to unfortunate misrepresentations. No "anarchist program" has ever been formulated, as far as we know. . . . But there is a *collectivist* theory, articulated in the congresses of the International, and that's the one we associate with, as do our friends from Belgium, France, Spain, Italy and Russia.[82]

The label "anarchist" became increasingly common despite Guillaume's opposition. In December 1876, Malatesta and Carlo Cafiero wrote a letter to the *Bulletin of the Jura Federation* in which they reported that the Italian section of the Saint-Imier International was committed to an "anarchist, collectivist, revolutionary program."[83] In his history of the International, Guillaume revealed that the *Bulletin of the Jura Federation* did not consciously adopt the label "anarchist" until April 1877.[84] A few months later, in July, the *Bulletin* referred to itself as belonging to "the revolutionary anarchist party." In August, the French section of the Saint-Imier International held a congress where they adopted what they referred to as a "collectivist and anarchist program."[85]

Even after 1876, the widespread adoption of the terms "anarchist" and "anarchism" did not happen overnight but took several years. As late as 1880, what would become the German-speaking anarchist movement in the United States had yet to adopt the label of anarchism. They instead referred to themselves as social revolutionaries in order to distinguish themselves from parliamentary social democrats. By December 1882, they had altered their language and were now declaring themselves in favor of anarchism.[86] The widespread decision to adopt this language in the 1880s appears to have occurred independently of Déjacque's previous usage of the term during the 1850s. The available evidence indicates that Déjacque was not widely known among anarchists until the 1890s. This can be seen in the fact that Max Nettlau's first article on Déjacque was only published in 1890 in the German anarchist paper *Freiheit*.[87] Jean Grave's republication of Déjacque's book *L'Humanisphère* did not occur until 1899.[88] In 1910, Kropotkin referred to this text as having been only "lately discovered and reprinted."[89]

The social movement that emerged within the First International came to adopt the labels "anarchist" and "anarchism" through a complex and contingent historical process. This, in turn, raises the question: why did they end up adopting these words? They could, after all, have invented a new term or continued to use other terms, such as federalist, collectivist, or revolutionary socialist. A clue to this puzzle can be found in the September 3, 1876, edition of the *Bulletin of the Jura Federation*. An article distinguished between "those whose ideal is a popular state" and "the fraction that is called anarchist," rather than the fraction that calls itself anarchist.[90] A month later, the editor of the paper, Guillaume, gave a speech at the October 1876 Berne Congress of the Saint-Imier International. In it, he claimed that they were usually called "anarchists or Bakuninists" by their political opponents.[91]

Two of their main political opponents were Marx and Engels. Throughout their correspondence during the 1870s they usually referred to the collectivists as "Bakuninists."[92] This label was rejected by the collectivists because, as Malatesta explained in 1876, "we do not share all the practical and theoretical ideas of Bakunin" and "follow ideas, not men . . . we reject the habit of incarnating a principle in a man."[93] Bakunin himself agreed. He wrote in his 1873 resignation letter from the Jura Federation that "the 'Bakuninist label' . . . was

thrown in your face" by "our enemies," but "you always knew, perfectly well, that your tendencies, opinions and actions arose entirely
consciously, in spontaneous independence."[94]

The other term Marx and Engels publicly used during the early
1870s was "anarchists." To take a few examples: in their May 1872
pamphlet *Fictitious Split in the International*, they labeled the Jura
Federation's "Sonvilier Circular" as "the anarchist decree"; Engels
described the Italian section of the Saint-Imier International as
"anarchists" in his July 1873 article, "From the International"; they
sarcastically referred to "Saint-Michael Bakunin" as an "anarchist"
and his ideas as "the anarchist gospel" in *The Alliance of Socialist
Democracy and the International Workingmen's Association*, which
was published between August and September 1873.[95]

It is important to note that Marx and Engels referred to the
Jura Federation as "anarchists" in May 1872, which was prior to
most collectivists referring to themselves with the term. A key reason why Marx and Engels referred to the self-described federalists,
collectivists, or revolutionary socialists as "anarchists" was because
they wrongly believed their views to be a simple rehashing of
Proudhon. In November 1871, Marx wrote a letter to Friedrich Bolte
in which he claimed that Bakunin's views were "scraped together
from Proudhon, St. Simon, etc." and that Bakunin's "main dogma"
was "(Proudhonist) abstention from the political movement."[96] In
January 1872, Engels described Bakunin's ideas as "a potpourri of
Proudhonism and communism" in a letter to Theodor Cuno.[97]

The decision by individuals within the movement to adopt the
"anarchist" label was not inevitable and occurred to a significant
extent by chance. They could have continued to call themselves
the federalist, collectivist, or revolutionary socialist movement.
Guillaume could have successfully persuaded a large number of people to not refer to themselves as anarchists. They could have called
themselves Bakuninists or invented a whole new label. One of the
main reasons they adopted the term "anarchist" was that they were

borrowing language from Proudhon. But this was not the only reason. Other people within the First International, in particular Marx and Engels, choose to call them "anarchists" due to the belief that they had the same politics as Proudhon. This led to a situation where the federalists, collectivists, or revolutionary socialists had to decide if they were going to adopt the label as their own.

It should not be automatically assumed that Proudhon and the collectivists of the First International belonged to the same political tradition because they both called themselves "anarchists." It cannot be assumed that the collectivists would have ever used the term in such large numbers if it had not been imposed on them by their political opponents, and if there had been no feud with the General Council. If they are to be viewed as belonging to the same political tradition, it must be because of the ideas, rather than just the language that they held in common.

It is true that both Proudhon and the collectivists advocated the abolition of capitalism and the state in favor of the free federation of free producers.[98] Anarchists like Bakunin and Kropotkin were deeply influenced by Proudhon.[99] The fact that Proudhon and the collectivists were both anti-state socialists does not, however, entail that they belonged to a single political tradition. Malatesta remarked in 1897 that although "Proudhon . . . first popularized, though amid a thousand contradictions, the idea of abolishing the State and organizing society anarchically," it was "Bakunin to whom we anarchists of today trace most directly our lineage."[100] Bakunin had himself been careful to describe the politics of First International collectivism as being "the widely developed and pushed to the limit Proudhonism," rather than a mere repetition.[101] He was deeply critical of what he took to be aspects of Proudhon's thought.[102] In *Statism and Anarchy* he asserted that "there is a good deal of truth in the merciless critique" Marx "directed against Proudhon."[103] He described his own politics as "the anarchic system of Proudhon broadened and developed by us and freed from all its metaphysical,

idealist and doctrinaire baggage, accepting matter and social economy as the basis of all development in science and history."[104]

One of the main topics on which the collectivists differed from
Proudhon was strategy. This is extremely important because, as
noted above, socialists who called themselves "anarchists" were not
distinguished from other kinds of socialism by advocating the abolition of the state. This was a long-term goal of several different kinds
of state socialists, including Blanqui, Marx, and Engels. Anarchism
must be defined in terms of both its goal and the strategies it proposed to reach this goal.

Proudhon, like mutualists in general, rejected the idea of transforming society through violent insurrection while nonetheless
viewing himself as a revolutionary. During the late 1840s, as already
mentioned, he held that capitalism and the state could be gradually
abolished through a process of workers forming cooperatives that
would, with the aid of loans provided by a people's bank at low or
no interest, grow in number, trade with one another and take on
more and more social functions until socialism as a society-wide
economic system had been established. The collectivists, in contrast, viewed Proudhon's strategy to achieve fundamental social
change as misguided, since cooperatives would be out-competed
by larger capitalist businesses (aided by government economic
intervention); become like capitalist businesses due to pressure
from market forces; or merely improve the living conditions of a
small number of workers. If a cooperative movement became so
successful that it was a genuine threat to ruling class power, then
it would simply be crushed by state violence. According to collectivists, class society could only be abolished through the working
classes launching a violent armed insurrection that smashed the
state and forcefully expropriated the means of production and land
from the ruling classes.[105]

This key difference on strategy could justify three distinct ways
of conceptualizing anarchism: (a) Proudhon and the collectivists

represent subdivisions within anarchism as a single political tradition; (b) Proudhon was an anarchist and the collectivists were
not anarchists due to diverging from Proudhon; (c) Proudhon was
not an anarchist and the term "anarchism" should only be used to
refer to the social movement that emerged in the First International.
These three potential conceptualizations of Proudhon's relationship to anarchism rest on the implicit premise that there is one true
anarchism that Proudhon is or is not a part of. There is no one true
anarchism. There is instead a series of distinct "anarchisms" that
arose during the nineteenth century as different people at different
historical moments articulated what they thought the words "anarchist" and/or "anarchism" meant or should mean.

In 1840, the term "anarchist" picked out Proudhon's political
theory for the simple reason that Proudhon decided to call himself an anarchist. The term was subsequently used by a variety of
socialists in the 1840s and 1850s to refer to the goal of a society without government or authority. This included Déjacque referring to
his ideas as "anarchism" in the late 1850s while advocating what he
regarded as a democratic government during the transition to a fully
stateless society. Between 1868 and 1880, what the words "anarchist"
and "anarchism" were understood to mean changed. This occurred
due to an international social network within the First International
and Saint-Imier International who were influenced by Proudhon,
developing a distinct revolutionary political theory that they called
anarchism but could have continued calling federalism, collectivism,
autonomism, or revolutionary socialism.

What matters for the purposes of studying anarchism as a historical concept is that Proudhon's anarchism and the anarchism of
the movement are viewed as distinct entities. Whether one chooses
to conceptualize this as: (a) different phases of a single political tradition, or (b) a new political tradition developing out of a previous
one does not change the differences between them. These are only
alternative ways of viewing the differences. Given my focus on the

revolutionary strategy of anarchism, I shall from now on be using
the term "anarchism" to refer exclusively to the theory and practice
of the anarchist movement, and not its intellectual precursors that
can be found during the 1840s and 1850s.

The Anarchist Movement

Who did and did not belong to the anarchist movement is itself
a controversial topic. This is because the social movement that
emerged within the First International and the Saint-Imier International between 1864 and 1878 was not the only group of people
to adopt the term during this period. In parallel to these developments, a small group of mutualists in the United States continued
to advocate anti-state market socialism achieved through gradual
peaceful means. From the early 1880s onward, they consciously
adopted Proudhon's label of "anarchist" as their own.[106] Although
they were largely an American phenomenon, they did also gain a
few adherents in Europe.[107]

This led to a situation in which two forms of anti-state socialism, which had both been influenced by Proudhon's ideas and
referred to themselves as "anarchists," coexisted with one another.
On the one side, anarchist collectivists and anarchist communists,
and on the other side, individualist anarchists. The fact that they
fundamentally disagreed with one another on such topics as their
visions of a future society and strategies to achieve social change led
to further contestation over what "anarchism" should mean. Both
sides sometimes argued that they alone were the true anarchists,
and their opponents were fake, pseudo, or inconsistent anarchists.
The influential individualist anarchist Benjamin Tucker, for example, gave a talk at the Boston Anarchist Club in November 1887. He
drew a distinction between "real Anarchists like P. J. Proudhon,
Josiah Warren, Lysander Spooner" and "miscalled Anarchists like

Kropotkine," who had wrongly "usurped the name of Anarchism for its own propaganda."[108] The German individualist anarchist John Henry Mackay shared this attitude and argued that anarchism and communism were incompatible with one another.[109]

Similar remarks can be found among anarchist communists. The English paper *Freedom* published an editorial in 1892 that argued that "individualists," such as Tucker, "are not Anarchists" because they advocate market competition and so "lack the fundamental principle of Socialism and Anarchism—solidarity."[110] Reclus wrote in an 1895 letter that "the only resemblance between individualist anarchists and us is that of a name."[111] In 1914, Kropotkin argued that "an Individualist, if he intends to remain Individualist, cannot be an Anarchist" because "Anarchy necessarily is *Communist*."[112]

On other occasions, there were attempts at tolerance, cooperation, and even combining collectivist/communist anarchism and individualist anarchism together. To give a few examples, Kropotkin and Rocker included individualist anarchists in their summaries of anarchist history.[113] The American bookbinder Dyer D. Lum advocated the broad goal of American individualist anarchists—stateless market socialism—achieved via the strategy of anarchist collectivists and anarchist communists—trade unionism and armed insurrection.[114] The anarchist paper *The Alarm*, which Lum edited, published both individualist anarchist and anarchist-communist authors. In 1889, the anarchist-communist Johann Most reacted to this by verbally attacking Lum for publishing individualist anarchist views and insisted that, as a result of this, German workers should cancel their subscriptions to the paper.[115] In response to these kinds of conflicts, Max Nettlau argued in 1914 that anarchist communists and individualist anarchists should cease to be dogmatic and learn to coexist and cooperate with one another, rather than "being divided into little chapels."[116] This idea was repeated in the 1920s, when Sébastian Faure and Vsevolod Mikhailovich Eikhenbaum, who wrote under the pen name Voline, attempted to form anarchist

federations that would unite individualist anarchists, anarchist communists, and anarcho-syndicalists into a single organization and
develop a new form of anarchism that would be a synthesis of each
tendency's best ideas.[117]

This topic is only made more complicated by the fact that
what "individualist anarchism" even meant varied between contexts. Within Italian anarchism, a tendency developed during the
1880s and 1890s that referred to itself as "individualist anarchism."
In contrast to other self-described individualist anarchists, it was
committed to the goal of anarchist communism, opposed formal
organization, and advocated the strategy of individuals engaging
in robberies, assassinations, and bombings.[118] This distinction can
be seen in Malatesta's 1897 remark that there are "the individualist
anarchists of Tucker's school" and "the individualist anarchists of
the communist school."[119]

The different varieties of individualist anarchism in Europe
and the United States also changed over time. For example, during
the 1890s, the individualist anarchist writer Mackay popularized
the previously obscure German philosopher Max Stirner. These
ideas, in turn, influenced wider circles of individualist anarchists
when editions of Stirner's 1844 book *The Unique and Its Property*
appeared in multiple languages from the early 1900s onward, including English, Italian, French, and Russian.[120] Mackay went so far as to
rewrite the history of anarchism and claim that Stirner, who never
referred to himself as an anarchist, was one of its main founders
alongside Proudhon.[121]

The fact that several different and incompatible tendencies
adopted the language of "individualist anarchism" is important for
understanding Malatesta's various remarks on the topic. In 1897,
he critiqued "those who, in calling themselves individualists, see
that as justification for any repugnant action, and who have about
as much to do with anarchism as the police do with the public
order they boast to protect."[122] In response to such self-appointed

"individualist anarchists," Malatesta had argued a year earlier that, since "we cannot stop others adopting whatever title they choose," our only option is to "differentiate ourselves clearly from those whose notion of anarchy differs from our own."[123] In 1924, Malatesta continued to claim that some self-appointed "individualist anarchists" were not in fact anarchists, while advocating tolerance toward "individualists" who "are really anarchists."[124] He even recommended a book by the French individualist anarchist E. Armand and described him as "one of the ablest individualist anarchists."[125]

Given this history, there is no neutral and uncontested definition of the anarchist movement. What people in the nineteenth and early twentieth century took anarchism to mean was a product of ongoing debates and discussion between groups who all claimed to be anarchists but had conflicting and incompatible views on both what anarchism meant and who was and was not a genuine anarchist. Although it is impossible to find a neutral and entirely uncontested definition of anarchism, it is possible to pick out contingents that represented one side within the process of contestation over what anarchism meant and to view anarchism from their point of view.

For the purposes of this book, anarchism will be defined as a form of revolutionary anti-state socialism that first emerged as a social movement in late nineteenth-century Europe within the First International between 1864 and 1872 and the subsequent Saint-Imier International, which included anarchist groups in Europe, South America, and Egypt, between 1872 and 1878. I will focus exclusively on anarchist collectivists, anarchist communists, and anarchists without adjectives who advocated the same strategy as anarchist collectivists and anarchist communists.

I will not examine the ideas of the intellectual precursors of the anarchist movement who wrote during the 1840s and 50s, such as Proudhon, or the individualist anarchists who operated in parallel with anarchist collectivists and anarchist communists from the 1880s onward. This is motivated by the fact that both Proudhon and individualist anarchists advocated distinct visions of a future society and strategies to achieve the abolition of capitalism and the state. Examining the ideas proposed by every single individual or movement who called themselves anarchists in the nineteenth and early twentieth centuries is not possible within the limited space of this book. I am not committing myself to the strong view that Proudhon and the individualist anarchists were not anarchists. My definition of anarchism only specifies the kind of anarchism I will be examining, and does not claim to establish the one true version of anarchism.

CHAPTER 2

Theoretical Framework

To understand anarchist political theory, one must first understand the theoretical framework that anarchists used for thinking about humans, society, and social change. This is the theory of practice.[1] It is important to note that the theory of practice was often implicit in anarchist texts and not laid out in great detail. The vast majority of anarchist texts were short articles or pamphlets that focused on other topics, such as why capitalism should be abolished or concrete discussions about how to achieve anarchist goals. In addition, anarchist authors did not, in general, feel the need to write an explicit and detailed statement of their social theory's foundational premises because it was already accepted as the common ground that underpinned their theorizing. A rational reconstruction of the theory of practice has to be made by piecing together different brief statements that anarchist authors made, and then supplementing these brief statements with my own examples in order to clearly illustrate what they thought.

Materialism and Human Nature

Anarchists were, in general, materialists in the broad sense that they viewed matter as the fundamental building block of reality.[2] This materialism went alongside the view that the natural world must be conceptualized as a process that undergoes changes over time, rather than as a static entity. For Bakunin, the universe is the "infinite totality of the ceaseless transformations of all existing things."[3] Cafiero similarly referred to the "continuous processes of transformation" that occur to the "infinity of matter" that constitutes the universe.[4] The natural world so understood included human society. As Malatesta noted, "the social world" is "nothing but the continuing development of natural forms."[5]

Anarchists thought that the natural world, which included society, must be conceptualized as a totality or whole. This totality was constituted by interconnected parts that stand in relation to, and mutually shape, one another. Bakunin thought that the universe was a "totality" in which "each point acts upon the Whole" and "the Whole acts upon every point."[6] As a result, he viewed the purpose of science as establishing the "related connections and mutual interaction and causality that really exist among real things and phenomena."[7] Reclus wrote that individuals living in society "are part of a whole" and that when "groups of men encounter one another, direct and indirect relations arise."[8] Kropotkin similarly held that the goal of his history of the French Revolution was "to reveal the intimate connection and interdependence of the various events that combined to produce the climax of the eighteenth century's epic."[9]

Society, this totality of interconnected and mutually determining parts, changes over time due to the action of humans. According to Bakunin, "history is made, not by abstract individuals, but by acting, living and passing individuals. Abstractions advance only when borne forward by real men."[10] For Rocker, since "every social process . . . arises from human intentions and human goal-setting and occurs within the limits of our volition" it follows that "history is . . . nothing but the great arena of human aims and ends."[11] Anarchist social theory rested on a particular understanding of what humans

are, what human activity is, and how human activity both shapes
and is shaped by society.

Anarchists viewed humans as unchanging and changing at the
same time. They are unchanging in that there are certain characteristics that all humans across all societies have in common: they
need food, water, and sleep to survive; reproduce through sex; have
brains; are social animals who communicate through language;
experience emotions; and so on.[12] As Rocker wrote: "We are born,
absorb nourishment, discard the waste material, move, procreate
and approach dissolution without being able to change any part of
the process. Necessities eventuate here which transcend our will. . . .
We are not compelled to consume our food in the shape nature
offers it to us or to lie down to rest in the first convenient place, but
we cannot keep from eating or sleeping, lest our physical existence
should come to a sudden end."[13]

One of the distinguishing characteristics of humans as a species
is their consciousness. Bakunin argued that, since this is the product
"of the cerebral activity of man" and "our brain is wholly an organization of the material order . . . it follows that what we call *matter*,
or *the material world*, does not by any means exclude, but, on the
contrary, necessarily embraces the ideal world as well."[14] With this
consciousness, humans think about themselves, other people, the
world in which they live, and worlds that they have imagined. They
make plans for the future and reflect on past events. They direct
and alter their behavior. In short, humans are able to mentally stand
apart from their immediate experience and make their own life an
object of their thought.[15] According to Reclus, "humanity is nature
becoming self-conscious."[16] Cafiero wrote that "the feeling of one's
self is without doubt the dominant sentiment of the human soul.
The awareness of one's being, its development and betterment,
the satisfaction of its needs, these make up the essence of human
life."[17] Each individual human always possesses a particular form
of consciousness, by which I mean the specific ways in which they

experience, conceptualize, and understand the world in which they live. I will refer to this as "consciousness" for short.

Since these characteristics are constant across all humans, they must stem from certain basic facts about human biology. Human biology and the natural environment are the starting points for human activity and the parameters in which it occurs. Crucially, human nature was not viewed by anarchists as a fixed, entirely static entity or an abstract essence that exists outside of history. They distinguished between the fundamental raw materials of human nature that constitute all humans and what these materials are shaped into during a person's life within a historically specific society. Bakunin distinguished between innate "faculties and dispositions" and "the organization of society" that "develops them, or on the other hand halts, or falsifies their development."[18] Given this, "all individuals, with no exception, are at every moment of their lives what Nature and society have made them."[19]

Kropotkin, who was a geographer, similarly thought that "man is a result of both his inherited instincts and his education."[20] Although there are "fundamental features of human character" that "can only be mediated by a very slow evolution," the extent and manner in which these characteristics are expressed, Kropotkin claimed, is a result of a person's social environment and the forms of activity they engage in.[21] One of these fundamental characteristics with a strong biological basis, he believed, was the tendency for humans to cooperate with one another and engage in mutual aid in order to survive. Yet he also held that "the relative amounts of individualist and mutual aid spirit are among the most changeable features of man."[22]

Similar views were expressed by other anarchist authors. Emma Goldman declared that "those who insist that human nature remains the same at all times have learned nothing. . . . Human nature is by no means a fixed quantity. Rather, it is fluid and responsive to new conditions."[23] The extent to which anarchists thought that the expression of human nature was malleable or plastic can be seen in the fact that several anarchists claim that there is an infinite number of different kinds of person. Malatesta, for example, wrote that in an anarchist society "the full potential of human nature could develop in its infinite variations."[24]

This was not to say that humans could transform themselves into anything they wanted. The nature of the raw materials that constitute humans places definite limits on what they can be shaped into. Humans cannot morph their arms into wings or lay eggs like a chicken. This is because, although a human can become an incredibly wide variety of different things during the course of their finite existence, the scope is predetermined by the kind of animal they are. As Rocker wrote, "man is unconditionally subject only to the laws of his physical being. He cannot change his constitution. He cannot suspend the fundamental conditions of his physical being nor alter them according to his wish."[25]

Stereotypes of anarchists depict them as having naive conceptions of human nature in which it is imagined that humans are innately good and kind. In reality, anarchists held that humans were defined by two main distinct tendencies: struggle/strife and sociability/solidarity.[26] Malatesta thought that humans possessed both the "harsh instinct of wanting to predominate and to profit at the expense of others" and "another feeling which draws him closer to his neighbor, the feeling of sympathy, tolerance, of love."[27] As a result, human history contained "violence, wars, carnage (besides the ruthless exploitation of the labor of others) and innumerable tyrannies and slavery" alongside "mutual aid, unceasing and voluntary exchange of services, affection, love, friendship and all that which draws people closer together in brotherhood."[28] This position was shared by Kropotkin, who wrote in his *Ethics* that there are "two sets of diametrically opposed feelings which exist in man. . . . In one set are the feelings which induce man to subdue other men in order to utilize them for his individual ends, while those in the other set induce human beings to unite for attaining common ends by common effort: the first answering to that fundamental need of human nature—struggle, and the second representing another equally fundamental tendency—the desire of unity and mutual sympathy."[29]

The Theory of Practice

One of the main processes that modifies and develops the raw materials of human nature is human activity itself. This makes fundamental social change possible. If humans are conscious creatures who are able to modify themselves significantly through activity, then how humans are today is not inevitable or fixed but something that they can consciously change themselves. Human activity is conceptualized by anarchist social theory in terms of practice. By practice I mean the process whereby people with particular consciousness engage in activity—deploy their *capacities* to satisfy a psychological *drive*—and through doing so, change the world and themselves simultaneously.

A *capacity* is a person's real possibility to do and/or to be, such as playing tennis or being physically fit. It is composed of two elements: (a) a set of external conditions which enable a person to do and/or be certain things, and (b) a set of internal abilities which the person requires in order to be able to take advantage of said external conditions. For example, a person's capacity to play tennis consists of external conditions like a tennis court, a tennis racket, someone to play against, and so on. Internally, it consists of abilities such as being able to hold a racket, hit a ball, and know the rules of the game. In the absence of either the external or internal conditions, a person lacks the real possibility to achieve the doing of playing tennis and therefore lacks the capacity to play. A *drive*, in comparison, is a person's particular desires, intentions, motivations, goals, values, or concerns—such as wanting to play tennis.[30]

Anarchists used a variety of different terms to describe this process. They mostly referred to the deployment of "capacities," "powers," or "capabilities" in order to satisfy "drives," "urges," "wants," "desires," or "needs."[31] Malatesta, for example, wrote that "social life became the necessary condition of man's existence, in consequence of his capacity to modify his external surroundings and adapt them to his own wants, by the exercise of his primeval powers in co-operation with a greater or less number of associates. His desires have multiplied with the means of satisfying them, and they have become needs."[32] In order to avoid confusion, I shall generally refer to capacities and drives.

As humans exercise their capacities to satisfy their drives, they continually develop and shape their existing capacities and drives, while also developing entirely new ones. A person who frequently plays the guitar will become better at playing a particular chord and finds their preexisting motivation to play grows. They learn whole new guitar techniques and discover drives that they did not have when they started, such as the desire to play heavy metal. As Alexander Berkman wrote, "the satisfaction of our wants creates new needs, gives birth to new desires and aspirations."[33] Were they to stop playing, their capacity to play guitar would diminish over time along, perhaps, with their inclination to do so. Capacities and drives are not fixed or static, but are rather in constant motion as human action maintains, alters, erodes, destroys, and creates them over time. When humans produce anything, they engage in an act of double-production. They simultaneously produce a particular thing, such as a good or service, and the capacities and drives exercised, developed, or created during the activity of production itself. When people engage in practice, they are also changing themselves. This theory can be seen in Kropotkin's advocacy of "teaching which, by the practice of the hand on wood, stone, metal, will speak to the brain and help to develop it" and thereby produce a child whose brain is "developed at once by the work of hand and mind."[34]

Engaging in practice not only affects a person's capacities and drives, but also has a significant impact on their consciousness. Learning music theory will not only, for example, make us better at reading sheet music or acquire the motivation to learn more about the subject. It also changes how we experience, conceptualize, and understand music—or life in general—such as noticing a feature of a song or thinking of oneself as a person of culture and sophistication.

This is not to say that anarchists viewed the process of development as automatic or predetermined. Different people can develop different drives in response to the exact same kinds of practice. One person might eat dark chocolate and want to consume it daily, while another wants to avoid it at all costs. Two people can read the same book and develop distinct thoughts and feelings in response to it. Despite this, generalizations can still be made, such as the fact that people socialized to reproduce patriarchal gender roles will in general do so or that the activity of being a member of the Ku Klux Klan or the police (or both) will, in general, bring out the worst in someone.

This theory of practice can be clearly seen in the writings of Bakunin. He wrote that "all civilization, with all the marvels of industry, science, and the arts; with all the developments of humanity—religious, esthetic, philosophic, political, economic, and social" was created by humans through "the exercise of an active power . . . which tends to assimilate and transform the external world in accordance with everyone's needs."[35] Bakunin thought that, as humans exercise their capacities, they develop them. Whereas "ants, bees, beavers, and other animals which live in societies do now precisely the same thing which they were doing 3,000 years ago," humans have developed their powers such that they have invented new technology and gone from living in "huts" and using bows or spears to building "palaces" and manufacturing guns and artillery.[36]

Such processes of development are, of course, not an entirely individual matter. Humans are, in Malatesta's words, "a social animal whose existence depends on the continued physical and spiritual relations between human beings," which are "based either on affinity, solidarity and love, or on hostility and struggle."[37] Humans experience life immersed in the actions, emotions, and ideas of other people, which in turn conditions and alters how people develop as individuals. A child will be taught to read and write by adults who are already literate, while a dancer may develop the desire to dance in a new style after watching a ballet performance. We adopt a particular perspective on the world due to reading books written by other people or by thinking with concepts that have been collectively produced and reproduced by our culture.[38]

What capacities, drives, and consciousness people develop varies across social and historical contexts. The capacity to sail a longboat and the drive to die heroically in battle so that you will go to Valhalla developed from living as a warrior in a ninth-century Norse society. These traits are not widespread in modern Nordic societies because people are no longer engaging in that sort of Viking practice. Instead, people engage in practices that develop their capacity to assemble flat-pack furniture or their drive to go to melodic death metal concerts. The social and historical situation in which one lives also determines how universal aspects of human nature are experienced. For example, the universal drive of hunger may be experienced as hunger for beef burgers in a modern North American fast food restaurant, but as hunger for seal meat in a nineteenth-century Inuit house.

Anarchist authors emphasized these points again and again. They generally conceptualized human history in terms of a series of economic periods characterized by specific kinds of technology and ways of organizing production. Their descriptive model held that humans had gone from living in hunter-gatherer societies to living in ancient agricultural societies based on slavery, feudal agricultural societies based on serfdom, and finally modern industrial societies based on wage labor.[39] This view of history included an awareness of the fact that European colonialism, and so the development of industrial societies, involved the enslavement of Black people.[40] Anarchists were also aware that hunter-gatherer societies existed at the same time as industrial societies.[41]

Anarchists inherited the broad model of human history as a series of economic stages from the French and Scottish Enlightenment and read it in early anthropology.[42] Although the specifics of this model are outdated in light of the latest research, they nonetheless highlight what anarchists thought about capacities, drives, and consciousness. Different economic systems were constituted by specific kinds of practice, such as hunting with a bow and arrow as a nomad, collecting the harvest as a peasant, or working in a car factory as a wage laborer, and so developed distinct characteristics within people. This way of thinking can especially be seen in anarchist discussions of drives. Luigi Galleani, for example, thought that when a human develops themselves they acquire "a series of ever-more, growing and varied needs claiming satisfaction."[43] These "needs vary, not only according to time and place, but also according to the temperament, disposition, and development of each individual."[44] He wrote,

> A farmer who lives in an Alpine valley, in the present conditions of his development, may have satisfied all his needs—eaten, drunk, and rested to his heart's content; while a worker who lives in London, in Paris, or in Berlin, may willingly give up a quarter of his salary and several hours of his rest, in order to satisfy a whole category of needs totally unknown to the farmer stranded among the gorges of the Alps or the peaks of the Apennine mountains—to spend an hour of intense and moving life at the theater, at the museum or at the library, to buy a recently published book or the latest issue of a newspaper, to enjoy a performance of Wagner or a lecture at the Sorbonne.[45]

The social environment in which capacities, drives, and consciousness develop is itself produced by practice. Society is the totality of social relations that individual and collective actions continuously constitute, reproduce, and transform. As Bakunin noted, "the real life of society, at every instant of its existence, is nothing but the sum total of all the lives, developments, relations, and actions of all the individuals comprising it."[46] Kropotkin likewise held that "humanity is not a rolling ball, nor even a marching column. It is a whole that evolves simultaneously in the multitude of millions of which it is composed. . . . The fact is that each phase of development of society is a resultant of all the activities of the intellects which compose that society; it bears the imprint of all those millions of wills."[47] An implication of this, as Malatesta saw, is that social action "is not the negation, nor the complement of individual initiative, but it is the sum total of the initiatives, thoughts and actions of all the individuals composing society: a result which, other things equal, is more or less great according as the individual forces tend toward the same aim, or are divergent and opposed."[48]

Imagine a group of hunters who cooperate to find and kill animals for food. During this process, these hunters produce social relations among themselves, such as the most experienced member leading the hunt or everyone singing a song in victory afterward. The social relations that collective practice produce, in turn, determine the nature of the practice, since the practice is itself performed through these social relations. How hunters hunt both produces the social relation of singing songs in victory and is altered by this social relation. Importantly, collective practice is not necessarily friendly or egalitarian practice. The slave master owns and controls the slave. They nonetheless both engage in the collective practice of a cotton plantation, albeit in very different roles.

This interplay between practice producing social relations and practice being performed through social relations results in the formation of relatively stable and enduring social structures. These social structures simultaneously enable and constrain practice. They enable it by developing in people the necessary internal abilities, drives, and consciousness for practice and by producing many of the external conditions that the exercise of the internal abilities is pre-conditioned on. They teach people how to hunt and they organize the manufacture of hunting equipment. Social structures constrain practice by imposing limits and exerting pressure on which and how capacities are deployed, what drives are satisfied, and the direction in which new capacities, drives, and consciousness are developed. A hunter is unlikely to develop the desire to become a vegetarian.

Social structures are relatively stable, but they are not fixed entities. They are processes reproduced over time by the practice of humans, who are continually modifying themselves through action, and being modified by the action of others. In Bakunin's words, "every man . . . is nothing else but the result of the countless actions, circumstances, and conditions, material and social, which continue shaping him as long as he lives."[49] Berkman also emphasized the manner in which people are shaped by simultaneous three-way interactions between social structures, consciousness, and their actions: "the life we lead, the environment we live in, the thoughts we think, and the deeds we do—all subtly fashion our character and make us what we are."[50]

These changes to the humans that compose the social structure can, in turn, lead to the modification of the social structure itself. The group of hunters who sing songs to celebrate could, over time, become primarily concerned with their music and sing more often during hunts. They could even create a whole new social structure, such as deciding to form a band. As Rocker noted, "every form of his social existence, every social institution . . . is the work of men and can be changed by human will and action or made to serve new ends."[51]

The kinds of practice that people within social structures engage in is significantly determined by the social structure in question, due to its enabling and constraining aspects. People engage in the practices that turn them into people capable of, and driven to, reproduce the social structure itself. In Malatesta's words: "Between man and his social environment there is a reciprocal action. Men make society what it is and society makes men what they are."[52] Given this, "man, like all living beings, adapts and habituates himself to the conditions in which he lives, and transmits by inheritance his acquired habits. Thus being born and having lived in bondage, being the descendant of a long line of slaves, man . . . believed that slavery was an essential condition of life, and liberty seemed to him an impossible thing."[53] Social structures that consistently shape people in this manner come to be dominant structures when they underpin the reproduction and relative stability of the society in which they are embedded.

Anarchist authors disagreed with one another about which dominant structures played the most important role in history or contemporary society. They also had distinct views on how to conceptualize the manner in which dominant structures interact with, shape, and mutually constitute one another. A significant number of historical anarchists endorsed various forms of economic determinism. Malatesta, who would later reject economic determinism, wrote in 1884 that, since "man's primary need and the essential prerequisite of existence is that he is able to eat, it is only natural that the character of a society is determined primarily by the manner in which man secures the means of survival, how wealth is produced and distributed."[54] He went so far as to claim that *the economic question is fundamental* in Sociology" and "other matters—political, religious, etc.—are merely its reflections, perhaps even the shadows it casts."[55] If "political institutions and moral sentiments derive their raison d'être from economic conditions," then it followed that *economic inequality is the source of all moral, intellectual, political, etc. inequalities."[56]

Anarchists who advocated economic determinism appear to have done so due to the influence of inaccurate interpretations of

Marx's theory of history, which were popularized by socialist parties at the time. In 1887, the American anarchist Albert Parsons claimed that "the mode and manner of procuring our livelihood affects our whole life; the all-pervading cause is economic . . . and social institutions of every kind and degree result from, grow out of, and are created by the economic or industrial regulations of society."[57] The fact that Parsons was influenced by Marx can be seen in the fact that he quotes large sections of Marx's *Capital* and *Manifesto of the Communist Party*.[58] Parsons was not unique in this respect. Rocker claimed that, in London during the 1880s, "the Jewish anarchists at that time and for some time after accepted the idea of economic materialism" and "the Marxist conception of history."[59] Malatesta noted in 1897 that, prior to the period in which anarchists discarded the mistakes of Marxism, they had been "more consistent or even more orthodox advocates" of Marxist theory "than those who professed to be Marxists and, perhaps, than Marx himself."[60] Elsewhere, he claimed that in Italy during the early 1870s, "though none of us had read Marx, we were still too Marxist" due to the influence of Bakunin's views on political economy and history.[61] The Italian anarchist Cafiero subsequently read Marx while in prison and published a summary of Marx's *Capital* in 1879, which Marx himself approved of.[62]

Bakunin had a somewhat ambivalent attitude toward what he regarded as Marx's social theory. In 1872, he simultaneously praised Marx for drawing attention to the importance of economic factors in history, while arguing that Marx wrongly ignored "other elements in history, such as the effect—obvious though it is—of political, judicial and religious institutions on the economic situation."[63] This included the manner in which the temperament of specific cultures, which were "the product of a host of ethnographic, climatological and economic, as well as historical causes . . . exert a considerable influence over the destinies and even the development of a country's economic forces, outside and independent of its economic conditions."[64] Rocker and Kropotkin later developed a model in which a range of social structures—economic, political, religious, cultural etc.—were taken to mutually determine one another but no social structure or causal factor was thought to be necessarily primary. Which causal factor played the most important role varied among different moments and so could only be established through empirical investigation on a case-by-case basis.[65]

Irrespective of where anarchists stood on the question of economic determinism, they thought in terms of multicausal explanations in which events were the products of the relations between several social structures. Goldman, for example, insisted in 1910 that "it would be one-sided and extremely superficial to maintain that the economic factor is the only cause of prostitution. There are others no less important and vital," such as gender relations or cultural norms around sex.[66] Rocker similarly argued that "all social phenomena are the result of a series of various causes, in most cases so inwardly related that it is quite impossible clearly to separate one from the other. We are always dealing with the interplay of various causes."[67]

This commitment to multicausality accompanied the view that dominant structures do not ever include or exhaust all the elements that constitute a particular society. Rather, they exist alongside a wide variety of less influential or smaller social structures that are constituted by and reproduced through distinct kinds of practice and their accompanying capacities, drives, and consciousness. These smaller social structures include ways of life as diverse as Romanticism, punk, Scientology, and the microstructure of a particular family. It is because of the existence of these less influential or smaller social structures that it is possible for alternative practices to emerge and modify or replace existing dominant structures. As Kropotkin argued, even within capitalist societies based on hierarchical social relations, production for profit, and economic competition, there are also numerous instances of people organizing horizontally to satisfy each other's needs and engage in mutual aid. Such voluntary associations are "the seeds" of a "new life."[68] I will describe these forces that are fundamentally at odds with existing dominant structures as *radical*: if universalized they would transform society and replace one dominant structure with another. The drive to not oppress women, for instance, is radical within a patriarchal society because its universalization is incompatible with the ongoing existence of patriarchy.[69]

Anarchists held that a crucial factor in the modification or replacement of dominant structures are the attempts by both dominant and oppressed groups to shape society in their interests. Kropotkin noted that "history is nothing but a struggle between the rulers and the ruled, the oppressors and the oppressed."[70] Malatesta likewise held that "through a most complicated series of struggles of every description, of invasions, wars, rebellions, repressions, concessions won by struggle, associations of the oppressed united for defense and of the conquerors for attack, we have arrived at the present state of society."[71] Such conflicts between the oppressors and the oppressed are conflicts over how practice, and so the development of capacities, drives, and consciousness, is organized. They are, in short, struggles to determine what kinds of humans society produces.

Ultimately, according to anarchists, to change society, it is necessary to engage in forms of practice that develop radical capacities, drives, and consciousness and thereby replace existing dominant social structures with alternative social structures that produce fundamentally different kinds of people. This, of course, raises the question: why did anarchists think society should be changed, and what did they want it changed into?

CHAPTER 3

Values, Critique, and Vision

Anarchists were antistate socialists. They sought the emancipation of humanity and the abolition of all structures of domination and exploitation through the self-emancipation of the working classes. This position was grounded in a set of ethical principles that forms the value system of anarchism, an analysis and critique of existing social relations and structures in terms of their failure to promote these ethical principles, and a vision of alternative, achievable social relations and structures that promote these ethical principles.

The Value System

Anarchism's central ethical value is that individuals should lead free lives. Although anarchists focused on the freedom of the individual, they did not conceptualize this freedom in terms of an isolated, abstract entity who stands outside of society. For anarchists, an individual can, given the kind of animal that humans are, only be free if they belong to a community of equals bonded together through relations of solidarity.[1] As the Black anarchist Lucy Parsons's put it, "emancipation will inaugurate liberty, equality, fraternity."[2] Anarchists viewed the values of freedom, equality, and solidarity as interdependent such that they cannot be understood in isolation from one another. The realization of one of these values can only be achieved through the realization of all three at once.

Anarchists conceptualized freedom in two main ways: not being subject to domination or having the real possibility to do and/or to be. Although anarchist authors consistently valued both of these things, they did not all label them as freedom. Wilson, for example, defined freedom as nondomination, while at the same time arguing that having the real possibility to do and/or to be is important for human development and flourishing.

Freedom as nondomination holds that individuals are free if and only if they are not subordinate to someone who wields the power to impose their will on them. If a person is subject to the arbitrary power of another then, even if it is not currently being exercised, they are being dominated. To be free is to be able to live in accordance with one's own will, rather than being subject to the will of another.[3] In 1869, Bakunin claimed that freedom consists in "the full independence of the will of the individual with respect to the will of others."[4] In the same text, he defines "freedom" as "independence ... with respect to all laws that other human wills— collective and isolated [from the collectivity] impose."[5] During his subsequent 1871 lectures to Swiss members of the International, he said that "the negative condition of freedom is that no person owe obedience to another; the individual is free only if his will and his own convictions, and not those of others, determine his acts."[6] In 1870, Bakunin explicitly connected this idea with nondomination when he advocated "*self-determination*" and "*the fullest human freedom in every direction, without the least interference from any sort of domination.*"[7]

The same position was expressed by other anarchist authors. Wilson referred to the "impulse in men to dominate their fellows, i.e., impose their will upon them and assert their own superiority."[8] She advocated the abolition of domination in favor of freedom such that every person had an equal claim to "direct his life from within by the light of his own consciousness," rather than be subordinate to "the will of any other individual or collection of individuals."[9] Galleani similarly defined "the broadest individual autonomy" in terms of "absolute independence from any domination by either a majority or a minority."[10]

According to the real possibilities view of freedom, an individual becomes more free as what they can do and/or be increases, that is, the activities they can perform and the states they can experience. The possible beings and doings available to a person, and so the extent to which they are free, are a product of (a) the external conditions within their social and natural environment and (b) their internal abilities, which enable them to take advantage of external conditions. In order to have the real possibility to read *The Very Hungry Caterpillar*, a child must, among many other requirements, know how to read (internal ability), live in a society where *The Very Hungry Caterpillar* is produced, and possess a copy of the book (external conditions). As they grow older, they become better at reading (development of internal ability) and acquire a greater number of books (expansion of external conditions). This marks an increase in their freedom, since their range of possible beings and doings has increased. They can now become an expert on the history of the potato or read the *Poetic Edda*.

An individual's freedom is restricted when obstacles decrease the number of real possibilities open to them. A slave owner who prevents their slaves from reading, further limits what possibilities they have and thereby makes them even less free. Such obstacles do not have to be directly established by the threat or exercise of violence. The cultural norm that homosexuality is unnatural and immoral can, by itself, limit a person's opportunity to be gay, due to them internalizing these ideas and sensitizing them to the judgement of others. Crucially, though, obstacles can be removed or overcome. For instance, slaves can rise up and kill their slave masters, or gay people can gain the confidence to be themselves, and not care what homophobes think.

This emphasis on having the actual means to lead a specific kind of life can be seen in Malatesta's claim in 1884 that "true freedom is not the right but the opportunity, the strength to do what one will" and in his observation, decades later, that "freedom is a hollow word unless it is wedded to ability, which is to say, to the means whereby one can freely carry on his own activity."[11] Yet, people's real possibility to do and/or to be can be restricted through domination by others. Malatesta also wrote that freedom "presupposes that everybody has the means to live and to act without being subjected to the wishes of others."[12] As a result, he advocated "the complete destruction of the domination and exploitation of man by man."[13]

Malatesta was not the only anarchist to define freedom as a person's real possibility to do and/or to be. In 1927, Berkman distinguished between "negative liberty," which is freedom from something, and "positive freedom," which is "the opportunity to do, to act."[14] Two years later, he wrote that "freedom really means opportunity to satisfy your needs and wants. If your freedom does not give you that opportunity, then it does you no good. Real freedom means opportunity and well-being. If it does not mean that, it means nothing."[15] His comrade Goldman similarly wrote in 1914 that "true liberty . . . is not a negative thing of being free from something. . . . Real freedom, true liberty is positive: it is freedom to something; it is the liberty to be, to do; in short, the liberty of actual and active opportunity."[16]

All anarchists thought that one of the main reasons why freedom is valuable is that it is a prerequisite for full human development in the sense of people improving their internal abilities in multiple directions and, in so doing, truly realizing their potential. Rocker claimed that "freedom is not an abstract philosophical concept, but the vital concrete possibility for every human being to bring to full development all the powers, capacities, and talents with which nature has endowed him."[17] Goldman argued that "authority stultifies human development, while full freedom assures it."[18] Elsewhere she declared that "only in freedom can man grow to his full stature. Only in freedom will he learn to think and move, and give the very best in him. Only in freedom will he realize the true force of the social bonds which knit men together, and which are the true foundations of a normal social life."[19]

The same position was articulated by anarchists who defined freedom in terms of nondomination. Wilson thought that "the creed of Anarchism is the cultus of Liberty, not for itself, but for what it renders possible. Authority, as exercised by men over their fellows, it holds accursed, depraving those who rule and those who submit, and blocking the path of human progress. Liberty indeed is not all, but it is the foundation of all that is good and noble, it is essential to that many-sided advance of man's nature, expanding in numberless and ever-conflicting directions."[20]

Although anarchist authors used different definitions of freedom, they agreed that not being dominated, having the real possibility to do and/or to be a broad range of things, and developing oneself as a human, were all valuable. This is because they feed off one another. In order to develop one's internal abilities in multiple directions, a person must have the real possibility to do so, and in order to have this real possibility they must, among other things, not be subject to domination that deprives them of these real possibilities.

Anarchists held that the freedom of the individual, however defined, is only possible in and through society. Humans are by nature social animals and so cannot achieve freedom outside of a social context. To quote Bakunin, "man completely realizes his individual freedom as well as his personality only through the individuals that surround him, and thanks to the labor and the collective power of society. . . . Society, far from decreasing his freedom, on the contrary creates the individual freedom of all human beings. Society is the root, the tree, and liberty is its fruit."[21] Furthermore, "being free for man means being acknowledged, considered and treated as such by another man, and by all the men around him. Liberty is therefore a feature not of isolation but of interaction, not of exclusion but rather of connection."[22]

For anarchists, in order for a society to be free over an extended period of time, it must be structured so that it both enables the freedom of the people who comprise it and prevents individuals from being able to oppress others. The social structures and relations that ensure the ongoing freedom of individuals are necessarily egalitarian ones. Anarchists thought that freedom and equality are so interconnected that it is in practice impossible to have one without the other. Bakunin wrote, "I am a convinced supporter of *economic and social equality*, because I know that, outside that equality, freedom . . . will never be anything but lies."[23] Kropotkin echoed this sentiment: "to have the individual free, they must strive to constitute a *society of equals*."[24]

It is apparent that anarchists advocated equality, but it is not yet clear what exactly they meant by the term. My interpretation is that anarchists conceptualized equality as the *equality of freedom*, or as Malatesta phrased it, the "equal freedom for all."[25] This is the idea that society should be structured such that there is, as far as is possible, equality of self-determination and equality of opportunity. Equality of self-determination was connected with nondomination, while equality of opportunity was connected to human development and the real possibility to do and/or to be.

Equality of self-determination was conceptualized as having two components. First, each individual is equally free to live in accordance with their own will, unless they subject another person to their will through coercion—because doing so would establish a relation of domination, and thereby violate the equal freedom of all. As Berkman put it, "you are to be entirely free, and everybody else is to enjoy equal liberty, which means that no one has a right to compel or force another, for coercion of any kind is interference with your liberty."[26] Malatesta similarly argued that anarchists advocate "freedom for all and in everything, with no limit other than the equal freedom of others: which does not mean . . . that we embrace and wish to respect the 'freedom' to exploit, oppress, command, which is oppression and not freedom."[27]

Second, organizations are structured in a horizontal, rather than hierarchical, manner such that there are no divisions between rulers who make decisions and subordinates who do as instructed and lack decision-making power. In horizontal organizations, each member has an equal say in collective decisions and so codetermines the organization with every other member.[28] According to Malatesta, this kind of equality emerges from the fact that individuals within a group have three choices. Either they "submit to the will of others (be enslaved) or subject others to his will (be in authority) or live with others in fraternal agreement in the interests of the greatest good of all (be an associate)."[29] Anarchists choose to be associates.

These two components of equality of self-determination can be seen in Bakunin's remark that domination must be prevented by not giving anyone the opportunity, which should be achieved *"by the actual organization of the social environment, so constituted that while leaving each man to enjoy the utmost possible liberty it gives no one the power to set himself above others or to dominate them, except through the natural influence of his own intellectual or moral qualities,* which must never be allowed either to convert itself into a right or to be backed by any kind of political institution."[30]

Equality of opportunity, or what Bakunin termed *"equality at the outset,"* was understood by anarchists to refer to a situation in which each individual had equal access to the external conditions necessary for the real possibility to do and/or to be, such as food, healthcare, and education.[31] According to Malatesta, anarchists "call liberty the possibility of doing something," and, in order for this to be realized, society must "be constituted for the purpose of supplying everybody with the means for achieving the maximum well-being, the maximum possible moral and spiritual develop-ment."[32] In the opinion of Berkman, "far from leveling, such equality opens the door for the greatest possible variety of activity and devel-opment."[33] It would, in other words, result in an expansion of human development.

Anarchists held that freedom and equality are generally main-tained over time by solidarity between individuals and groups.[34] By *solidarity*, anarchists meant two different kinds of social relation. The first consisted in individuals cooperating with one another in pursuit of a common goal. This is the concrete means through which the external conditions necessary for people to exercise capacities and satisfy drives are established, such as the organization of a school where children can develop and transform themselves or the coordination of an economy that provides the materials a school needs. As Kropotkin noted, a free society "could not live even for a few months if the constant and daily co-operation of all did not uphold it."[35] According to Malatesta, "liberty," in the sense of one's real possibility to do and/or to be, "becomes greater as the agree-ment among men and the support they give each other grows."[36]

The second kind of solidarity anarchists advocated was indi-viduals forming reciprocal caring relationships, in which each individual acts to ensure the ongoing freedom and equality of those around them. Malatesta praised solidarity in the sense of "affection, love, friendship and all that which draws people closer together in brotherhood."[37] For him, "*solidarity*, that is, harmony of interests and sentiments, the sharing of each in the good of all, and of all in the good of each, is the state in which alone man can be true to his own nature. . . . It causes the liberty of each to find not its limits, but its complement, the necessary condition of its continual exis-tence—in the liberty of all."[38] In short, anarchists understood that, in order to be free, an individual needs positive social relationships, such as loving parents, a supportive teacher, and good friends. For anarchists, such reciprocal caring relationships could only genuinely occur between equals who horizontally associate with one another. As Reclus wrote, "between him who commands and him who obeys ... there is no possibility of friendship" since "above is either pitying condescension or haughty contempt, below either envious admiration or hidden hate."[39]

Critique of Existing Society

Equipped with this value system, anarchists critiqued existing society on the grounds that it systematically fails to promote freedom, equality, and solidarity. They understood that society is not the way it is merely because of the negative personality traits of some bad rulers. Rather, it is the consequence of the fundamental structure of society and the forms of practice that constitute and reproduce it over time. As Malatesta explained to a jury while on trial in 1921, "social wrongs do not depend on the wickedness of one master or the other, one governor or the other, but rather on masters and governments as institutions; therefore, the remedy does not lie in changing the individual rulers, instead it is necessary to demolish the principle itself by which men dominate over men."[40]

Anarchists are best known for advocating the abolition of the state. While it is true that anarchists are anti-statists, it must also be emphasized that they do not view the state as the main oppressive social structure, or the singular root cause of social problems. Anarchists in the late nineteenth and early twentieth centuries critiqued three main dominant structures: capitalism, landlordism, and the state. The structures of economic oppression (capitalism and landlordism) and political oppression (the state) were taken to constitute an interconnected global social system that I shall call *class society.* For the sake of brevity, I will focus on the anarchist opposition to capitalism and the state and not discuss landlordism in the sense of feudal or semi-feudal economic relations.

Anarchists viewed capitalism as a social system constituted by: (a) private ownership of land, raw materials, and the means of production; (b) wage labor; and (c) production of commodities for profit within a competitive market. Under capitalism, society is divided into two main economic classes: a minority of capitalists and landowners who privately own land, raw materials, and the means of production; and a majority of workers who do not own private property and who sell their labor to capitalists and landowners. The labor of workers produces goods and services that are sold by capitalists and landowners on the market in order to generate profit and thereby expand their wealth. Workers, in comparison, receive only a wage, which they then use to buy the necessities of life—food, shelter, and clothing—and thereby reproduce themselves.[41]

The terms *working class* and *proletariat* are sometimes used only to refer to industrial wage laborers who engage in manual labor, especially within factories. Anarchists often used these words in a much broader sense. In 1884, Malatesta wrote that humanity is divided "into two castes: one caste of haves, born with an entitlement to live without working; the other of proletarians whose lot from birth is wretchedness; subjection; exhausting, unrewarded toil."[42] He defined a worker as "anybody plying a useful trade who does not exploit another person's labors."[43] Anarchists who claimed that society was divided into two main economic classes did not think that there were no subdivisions within the working class or proletariat broadly construed. They generally distinguished between urban wage laborers, rural wage laborers, artisans, and landless peasants.

Which specific classes anarchists referred to varied depending upon the context they were writing in. In 1873, Bakunin wrote that

"Italy has a huge proletariat. . . . It consists of 2 or 3 million urban factory workers and small artisans, and some 20 million landless peasants."[44] He went onto claim that "the Slavic proletariat . . . must enter the International en masse [and] form factory, artisan, and agrarian sections."[45] As capitalism developed, and the number of artisans dramatically declined due to their inability to compete with large-scale industry, anarchists updated their language and began to refer only to urban wage laborers, rural wage laborers, and landless peasants. In 1926, the Group of Russian Anarchists Abroad, who came from a society where peasants were still the majority of the population, claimed that capitalist society is split into "two very distinct camps . . . the proletariat (in the broadest sense of the word) and the bourgeoisie."[46] The proletariat so understood included "the urban working class" and "the peasant masses."[47]

Berkman, in an analysis for a predominantly North American audience, adopted a narrower definition of the working class or proletariat in 1929. He defined them as those people employed by capitalists in a range of industries—in mills and mines, in factories and shops, in transportation, and on the land.[48] For him, "the working class consists of the industrial wage earners and the agricultural toilers" or "farm laborers."[49] Berkman only used the word "peasant" in descriptions of classes in Russia and continental Europe and consistently framed them as being distinct from "the proletariat" or "workers." When Berkman referred to wage laborers and peasants as a group, he did so with such expressions as "the toilers" or "the masses." Artisans, who were defined as skilled, self-employed laborers who own their own tools and small workshops, only featured as part of Berkman's description of how the development of capitalism forced them to become wage laborers.[50]

In this book, I will use the phrase *the working classes* to refer to urban wage laborers, rural wage laborers, artisans who did not exploit anybody else's labor, and landless peasants. It should be kept in mind that these categories are not necessarily mutually exclusive.

A person born into the peasantry could, for example, work as a wage laborer in a city during one season, and as a small farmer in the countryside during another.[51]

Anarchists advocated the abolition of capitalism because it is based on the oppression and exploitation of the working classes. Wage laborers allegedly choose to sell their labor to capitalists and landowners, but only do so because they have no other option. Under capitalism, a small minority owns the land, raw materials, and the means of production. Workers own personal possessions, such as their hat or sewing kit, but they do not own private property like a factory or mine. As a result, the majority of the population lacks the means to survive independently through their own labor. In order to gain access to the goods and services they need to survive—such as food, clothing, and shelter—workers have to purchase them with money. Given their social position, the only realistic way to earn this money is to sell their labor to capitalists and landowners in exchange for a wage.[52] Workers choose to engage in wage labor in the same manner that a person might choose to hand over their possessions to an armed robber. The robbery victim makes this choice because the only realistic alternative is being attacked. Workers similarly sell their labor to capitalists and landowners because the only realistic alternative is extreme poverty, homelessness, starvation, and so on. It is an involuntary decision forced upon workers by the fundamental structure of capitalist society.[53]

Wage labor is not only involuntary. It is based on a relationship of domination and subordination in which capitalists and landowners have the power to command workers to do as instructed. Malatesta described capitalism as a society in which "a few individuals have hoarded the land and all the instruments of production and can impose their will on the workers, in such a fashion that instead of producing to satisfy people's needs and with these needs in view, production is geared toward making a profit for the employers."[54]

Goldman similarly wrote that, under capitalism, workers "are sub-ordinated to the will of a master."[55]

The economic ruling classes also determine what forms of labor workers engage in and so the kind of capacities, drives, and consciousness they develop during the process of production itself. Workers lack control over the kind of people they develop into. They engage in forms of labor that maximize profit but actively harm them. The process of capitalist production produces not only goods and services, but also broken people unable to develop in a positive direction and fulfill their human potential. This point was frequently made by anarchists through the metaphor of workers being turned into machines.[56] Wilson thought that capitalism had a tendency to transform workers into a "steam-engine with wages for coal."[57] For Goldman, each worker became "a mere particle of a machine, with less will and decision than his master of steel and iron. Man is being robbed not merely of the products of his labor, but of the power of free initiative, of originality and the interests in, or desire for, the things he is making."[58] As a result, workers are reduced to being "living corpses without originality or power of initiative, human machines of flesh and blood who pile up mountains of wealth for others and pay for it with a grey, dull, and wretched existence for themselves."[59]

Under capitalism, labor is but one commodity for sale. Capitalism is a market economy in which "the whole economic life of society . . . [is] regulated by the *competition* and *profit* principle."[60] The negative consequences of this are numerous. Capitalists hire a small number of workers and force them to work long hours in order to reduce costs, maximize profit, and out-compete rival companies. Improvements in technology make workers unemployed rather than enabling them to work less. Companies produce more commodities than they can sell and are then forced by this over-production to close down and fire their workforce. This, in turn, leads to regular economic crises. Even when the capitalist market is operating more smoothly, it is based on an irrational organization of production in which a vast number of human needs that society has the means to fulfill are not satisfied because there is no profit in doing so, such as housing homeless people or adequately feeding poor people. On the international scale, economic competition, alongside a range of other factors like ambition and greed, results in states engaging in colonialism, imperialism, and war in order to find new markets, establish monopolies, maximize capital accumulation, and serve the interests of capitalists in their respective countries, especially those involved in the manufacturing of weapons, ammunition, warships etc.[61]

According to anarchists, the oppression and exploitation of capitalism is maintained over time by the violence of the modern state.[62] Bakunin claimed that "the historical formation of the modern concept of the state" occurred "in the mid-sixteenth century" and consisted in an ongoing process of "military, police, and bureaucratic centralization."[63] This process of state formation occurred due to the requirements of "modern capitalist production," which needed "enormous centralized states" in order to subject "many millions of laborers to their exploitation."[64]

Kropotkin later expanded upon this narrative by arguing that, the modern state developed as "a mutual insurance company formed by the landlord, the military, the judge, the priest, and later on the capitalist in order to assure each of them authority over the people and the exploitation of [their] poverty."[65] As a result, "the State, as a political and military power, along with modern governmental Justice, the Church, and Capitalism appear in our eyes as institutions that are impossible to separate from each other. In history these four institutions developed while supporting and reinforcing each other. . . . They are linked together by the bonds of cause and effect."[66] Rather than positing a one-sided perspective in which the modern state was created by capitalism, anarchists held that the modern state and capitalism cocreated one another.[67]

Through an analysis of the modern state (henceforth referred to as the state) as an actually-existing social structure, anarchists came to define it in terms of both its functions and its particular organizational forms and characteristics. The primary function of the state is to reproduce the power of the economic ruling classes through violence. For Malatesta, its "essential function is always that of oppressing and exploiting the masses, and of defending the oppressors and exploiters," and, even when it performs other functions—such as acknowledging certain legal rights, maintaining roads, and organizing healthcare—it does so "with the spirit of domination" and remains a committed defender of the economic ruling classes.[68] The same point was made by Reclus, who held that "the present function of the state consists foremost of defending the interests of landowners and the 'rights of capital.'"[69]

The capitalist state performs its essential function through many different means. Most obviously, it enforces private property rights. In Malatesta's words, "the landowners are able to claim the land and its produce as theirs and the capitalists are able to claim as theirs the instruments of labor and other capital created by human activity" because "the dominant class . . . has created laws to legitimize the usurpations that it has already perpetrated, and has made them a means of new appropriations."[70] The state, in addition to this, aids the economic ruling classes by establishing monopolies, subsidizing private companies, repressing social movements via the police and prisons, and maintaining an army in order to keep "the people in bondage" and conquer "new markets and new territory, to exploit them in the interests of the few."[71]

The state can nonetheless not be defined solely in terms of its essential function. The state as a really existing institution is also characterized by a specific organizational form. Actual states are institutions that (i) perform the function of reproducing the power of the economic ruling classes; (ii) are hierarchically and centrally organized; (iii) are wielded by a minority political ruling class who sit at the top of the state hierarchy and possess the authority to make laws and issue commands at a societal level that others must obey due to the threat or exercise of institutionalized force.[72]

This definition of the state was mostly clearly expressed by Kropotkin and Malatesta. According to Kropotkin, the state "not only includes the existence of a power situated above society, but also of a *territorial concentration* and a *concentration of many functions in the life of societies in the hands of a few*. . . . A whole mechanism of legislation and of policing is developed to subject some classes to the domination of other classes."[73] The state is therefore the "perfect example of a hierarchical institution, developed over centuries to subject all individuals and all of their possible groupings to the central will. The State is necessarily hierarchical, authoritarian—or it ceases to be the State."[74] Malatesta, in comparison, wrote that

> For us, the government is the aggregate of the governors, and the governors—kings, presidents, ministers, members of parliament, and what not—are those who have the power to make laws, to regulate the relations between men, and to force obedience to these laws. . . . In short, the governors are those who have the power, in a greater or lesser degree, to make use of the collective force of society, that is, of the physical, intellectual, and economic force of all, to oblige each to do the said governors' wish. And this power constitutes, in our opinion, the very principle of government, the principle of authority.[75]

Given this, anarchists did not define class solely in terms of a person's relationship to the means of production. Class is also about a person's relationship to the means of institutionalized coercion. Those who directly controlled state power, such as politicians, monarchs, heads of the police, etc., were taken by anarchists to constitute a distinct political ruling class with interests of their own. As Malatesta wrote, while "the State is the defender, the agent, and the servant of the propertied class," it "also constitutes a class by itself, with its own interests and passions. When the State, the Government, is not helping the propertied to oppress and rob people, it oppresses and robs them on its own behalf."[76] This is not to say that these two classes are mutually exclusive. An individual can, for example, be a capitalist and a politician at the same time.

Anarchists opposed the state, to quote Bakunin, because it "is placed by its very nature and position above and outside the people and must inevitably work to subordinate the people under rules and for objectives foreign to them."[77] In short, it *means coercion, domination by means of coercion.*"[78] Through this domination, the state not only prevents the working classes from living in accordance with their own wills, but also hinders their development as people and limits their real possibility to do and/or to be. It oppresses humanity in two main ways: either directly by physical violence, or indirectly, by enforcing private property rights and thereby depriving the majority of the population of access to the means of existence such that they are forced to work for the economic ruling classes.[79] In so doing, the state violates the equal freedom of all and promotes social relations of strife over solidarity because, "*so long as political power exists, there will be persons who dominate and persons dominated, masters and slaves, exploiters and the exploited.*"[80]

Anarchists thought that this critique of the state applied not only to monarchies and dictatorships but also democratic republics in which a segment of the political ruling class were elected by the citizenry. Even if a state was somehow genuinely democratic, in the sense that it was one in which the majority ruled, it was still a state and so incompatible with freedom, equality, and solidarity. All states are social structures in which those who rule have the power to impose decisions on everyone within a given territory via institutionalized methods of coercion, such as the legal system, police, prisons, and the army. The rule of the majority would, even if it was preferable to the rule of the few, result in the domination of various minorities due to them being subject to this coercive power.[81] In a fundamentalist Christian society, for example, majority rule would most likely result in laws oppressing atheists, scientists, and gays. Anarchists did not, however, think that actual states have ever been based on majority rule. They consistently described them as institutions based on minority rule by a political ruling class in their interests and the interests of the economic ruling class. Malatesta, to give one example, wrote in 1924 that "even in the most democratic of democracies it is always a small minority that rules and imposes its will and interests by force."[82] As a result "Democracy is a lie, it is oppression and is in reality, oligarchy; that is, government by the few to the advantage of a privileged class."[83]

Although capitalism and the state were two of the main social structures anarchists sought to abolish, they were not the only ones. Wilson concluded that "the solution of the social problem can only be wrought out from the equal consideration of the whole of the experience at our command, individual as well as social, internal as well as external."[84] Kropotkin similarly thought "that the whole of the life of human societies, everything, from daily individual relationships between people to broader relationships between races across oceans, could and should be reformulated."[85] As a result, anarchists understood that humans are oppressed by a myriad of other social structures that must also be abolished if the values of freedom, equality, and solidarity are to be truly realized. These included racism,[86] patriarchy,[87] homophobia,[88] hierarchically organized religion,[89] and authoritarian modes of education.[90] Some anarchists, such as Reclus, went beyond a singular focus on human emancipation and advocated vegetarianism, animal liberation, and the protection of the natural environment.[91]

Unfortunately, a significant number of anarchists failed to put the theoretical opposition to racism, sexism, and homophobia into practice or, on occasion, even support it in theory. To give a few examples:

Bakunin was an antisemite,[92] most male anarchists were sexist toward women in the movement,[93] and some anarchists opposed Goldman giving talks on homosexuality for fear it would damage the reputation of the movement to discuss "perverted sex-forms."[94]

Vision of an Alternative Society

Anarchists argued that capitalism and the state should be abolished in favor of a society in which humanity as a whole was free, equal, and bonded together through relations of solidarity. They called this society anarchy. In advocating anarchy as their ultimate end goal, anarchists were not using the term in the sense of a disorganized and chaotic society, a war of all against all. They were instead referring to a stateless, classless, and nonhierarchical society. In 1897, Malatesta wrote that "anarchy signifies *society organized without authority*, authority being understood as the ability to *impose* one's own wishes" on others through "coercion."[95] A few years later in 1899, Malatesta defined "Anarchy" as "a society based on free and voluntary accord—a society in which no one can force his wishes on another and in which everyone can do as he pleases and together all will voluntarily contribute to the well-being of the community."[96]

Anarchist authors outlined visions of what anarchy would look like in numerous texts. They did not view themselves as utopians in the style of Charles Fourier who elaborated incredibly detailed blueprints of what a postcapitalist society would look like. Bakunin himself explicitly critiqued "Fourierists" for wrongly assuming "that it was theoretically and *a priori* possible to build a social paradise in which all of future humanity could recline. They had not realized that while we may well define the great principles of its future development we must leave the practical expression of those principles to the experience of the future."[97] This way of thinking was shared by Malatesta, who wrote in 1891 that anarchists cannot, "in the name of

Anarchy, prescribe for the coming man what time he should go to bed, or on what days he should cut his nails!"[98] Such practical questions can only be answered by those who actually live in and self-managed the future classless society. All any present-day anarchist can do is desire "that a society be constituted in which the exploitation and domination of man by man are impossible" and "indicate a method" to achieve this.[99] By this, Malatesta meant that anarchists should:

1. envision anarchy as a society that successfully instantiates certain social conditions, such as people being free from domination, people having access to the external conditions that are necessary to develop themselves, or social relations being infused with a sense of solidarity.

2. articulate general anarchist methods of organization and association that could successfully actualize these conditions, such as each person in a group having a vote, smaller groups federating together to form larger groups, or organizations electing instantly recallable mandated delegates to perform administrative tasks.

According to this view, anarchists could not know with absolute certainty how, say, the education of children would be organized under anarchy, but they were in a position to indicate the method through which it would be organized. Parents, teachers, and other adults interested in the positive development of children would come together as equals within general assemblies to "meet, discuss, agree and differ, and then divide according to their various opinions, putting into practice the methods which they respectively hold to be best" and, in so doing, establish through a process of experimentation what the best system of education was.[100] How anarchy was organized would "be modified and improved as circumstances were modified and changed, according to the teachings of experience."[101] It was for this reason that Malatesta saw anarchist ideals as "the experimental system brought from the field of research to that of social realization."[102]

Some anarchist authors did articulate detailed models of how an anarchist society would function. They generally focused on how workers should reorganize production and distribution during a revolution and, as a result, largely discussed practical issues. The Russian anarcho-syndicalist Gregori Maximoff, for example, developed proposals for how an anarchist revolution could reorganize agriculture, cattle rearing, fishing, hunting, manufacturing, forest management, mining, construction, transportation, healthcare, sanitation, and education. These proposals largely specify (a) how organizations should be structured, make decisions, and coordinate with one another; (b) what kind of organization is responsible for a specific aspect of the economy; and (c) general principles that should be implemented, such as the abolition of rent or both men and women receiving an education.[103]

The theorists of anarchism were not naive and understood that it would not be possible to establish anarchy as an ideal during or immediately after the abolition of capitalism and the state. Cafiero distinguished between anarchy today and anarchy in the future: "Anarchy today is indignation, deadly hatred and eternal war against every oppressor and exploiter on the face of the earth. . . . But tomorrow, once the obstacles have been overcome, anarchy will be solidarity and love—complete freedom for all."[104] He thought it would take a significant amount of time to achieve full anarchy. This can be seen in his claim that one generation would fight in the revolution and the next generation would work toward full anarchy in a postrevolutionary world. He wrote that contemporary anarchists would:

> perhaps perish in a skirmish or during the first shots of the great day; some perhaps will be fortunate enough to see the first dawning of humanity's great event. In all cases, we shall fall satisfied. Satisfied with having contributed to the certain

ruin of this unjust, cruel and rotten world, whose collapse will bury us in the most glorious tomb ever made for a fighter.

Other men will be born from the very entrails of the fertile revolution and take on the task of carrying out the positive, organic part of anarchy.

For us—hatred, war and destruction; for them—love, peace and happiness.[105]

Malatesta, in comparison, conceded that "some comrades" mistakenly "expect Anarchy to come with one stroke—as the immediate result of an insurrection which violently attacks all that which exists and replaces it with institutions that are really new."[106] These comrades, he said, were wrong, because the full achievement of anarchy requires that "all men will not only not want to be commanded but will not want to command . . . [and] have understood the advantages of solidarity and know how to organize a plan of social life wherein there will no longer be traces of violence and imposition."[107] Such a significant transformation of individuals and social structures would take a long time to achieve.

Malatesta thought that society immediately after the abolition of capitalism and the state "would not be Anarchy, yet, or it would be only for those few who want it, and only in those things they can accomplish without the cooperation of the non-anarchists."[108] The development toward anarchy would be a product of "peaceful evolution" in which anarchist "ideas . . . extend to more men and more things until it will have embraced all mankind and all life's manifestations."[109] For Malatesta, "Anarchy cannot come but little by little—slowly, but surely, growing in intensity and extension. Therefore, the subject is not whether we accomplish Anarchy today, tomorrow or within ten centuries, but that we walk toward Anarchy today, tomorrow and always."[110]

Similar points were made by other anarchist authors. Berkman argued that the "revolution is the *means* of bringing Anarchy about but it is not Anarchy itself. It is to pave the road for Anarchy, to establish conditions which will make a life of liberty possible."[111] Maximoff likewise thought that, during the process of abolishing capitalism and the state, there would be a transitional phase that laid the foundations from which anarchy would eventually arise. As a result, he was careful to distinguish between the "communal structure, which is the transitory step" and "the structure of full communism and anarchy."[112]

Anarchists, in other words, viewed the abolition of capitalism and the state as an act that created the preconditions for the achievement of anarchy and moved society closer to it but would not alone create anarchy as an ideal, universal social system. The task of anarchists during and immediately after the social revolution was to establish the basic forms of organization and association that would exist under anarchy and thereby establish the social conditions from which anarchy could emerge. In order to clearly differentiate these basic social structures from anarchy, I shall refer to the totality of these social structures as an anarchist society.

Anarchists generally envisioned an anarchist society as having four main components.[113] These were:

1. Humanity as a whole collectively owns land, raw materials, and the means of production. The division of society into economic classes is abolished such that there are no longer workers or proletarians but only people who engage in acts of production and consumption. Those who occupy or use a piece of land, raw materials, or the means of production on a daily basis directly control and self-manage the relevant sphere of production or distribution. Individuals can only own possessions they personally use without exploiting the labor of others. In other words, humanity owns the watch factory, those who labor in the watch

factory directly control and self-manage watch production, and individuals own their personal watches.

2.   Workplaces and communities are self-managed by
the people who constitute them through general
assemblies in which everyone involved has an equal
say in collective decisions.[114]

3.   Markets and money are replaced by a system of
decentralized planning.

4.   The rigid capitalist division of labor is abolished such
that people do a combination of mental and phys-
ical labor, and unsatisfying labor is either removed,
automated, or shared among producers. Individuals
would still specialize in specific skills, such as learning
how to drive a train or build a house, but they would
not be limited to one sphere of activity such that
they only drove trains or built houses. This would go
alongside a significant reduction to the length of the
working day, such as four hours instead of ten.

In an anarchist society, "the relations between its members are
regulated, not by laws . . . not by any authorities—whether they
are elected or derive their power by right of inheritance—but by
mutual agreements, freely made and always revocable, as well as
[social] customs and habits, also freely accepted."[115] Such statements are not advocating a society in which people are free to do
absolutely anything, including acts that oppress others. Anarchists
argued that, if a person imposes their will on another via violence or
coercion, they are engaging in an act of domination and should be
prevented from doing so, by force if necessary. Such force, providing
it is proportionate and does not reconstitute the state, would not
be a form of authority or a violation of the equal freedom of all. It
would rather defend the freedom of all in a manner compatible with
the goal of anarchy.[116]

Collective decisions within an anarchist society would be made within workplace and community assemblies via either unanimous agreement, majority vote, or a combination of the two.[117] Malatesta personally thought that in an anarchist society, "everything is done to reach unanimity, and when this is impossible, one would vote and do what the majority wanted, or else put the decision in the hands of a third party who would act as arbitrator."[118] This is not to say that an anarchist society was based on the rule of the majority over the minority. Anarchists believed in free association and so held that decisions should not be imposed on others via the exercise or threat of violence. Given this, they rejected both the rule of the minority over the majority and the rule of the majority over the minority. Within a free association that makes collective decisions via majority vote, the majority and minority positions would coexist with one another when this was possible. If a collective decision required everyone involved to agree on a single course of action, such as when the next meeting would take place or what color a room would be painted, then minorities would voluntarily defer to the majority decision. If the minority strongly disagreed with this decision then they were free, not only to persuade others of their point of view, but also to leave and voluntarily disassociate. This freedom of association also included the freedom of majorities to voluntarily dissociate from minorities, such as a person who constantly shouted at and bullied other people during meetings being expelled from a group.[119]

Although anarchists thought that collective decisions should be made in general assemblies, they also understood that it is often necessary or practical for an individual, or small group of people, to complete a specific task. As Malatesta wrote, "in every collective undertaking on a large scale there is need for division of labor, for technical direction, administration, etc."[120] In such circumstances, anarchists proposed that general assemblies would elect mandated delegates to complete a task or perform a role, such as corresponding with other groups, editing a newspaper, or drawing up plans for a new public transportation system. These delegates would not be governors who wielded authority, since they did not have the right to command others and force people to obey them. Decision-making power would remain in the hands of the general assembly who elected them and retained the right to recall delegates, give them new instructions, accept or reject their suggestions, and so on.[121]

In an anarchist society, decision-making would flow "from the bottom upwards and from the circumference inwards, in accordance with the principle of liberty, and not from the top downwards and from the center outwards, as is the way of all authority."[122] Within such a society, "the free association of all" would establish "a social organization" structured "from the low to the high, from the simple to the complex, starting from the more immediate to arrive at the more distant and general interests."[123] Anarchists envisioned a decentralized and bottom-up system of decision-making in which workplace and community assemblies made their own decisions about how they operated at a local level. They then associated with one another via free agreement in order to form a network capable of achieving coordination and cooperation on a large scale. As will be explained in more detail in Chapters 6 and 7, there were two main positions on how to achieve large-scale coordination and cooperation during both the struggle against class society and the reproduction of an anarchist society. Antiorganizationalists, who appear to have been in the minority during the period I am examining, argued that coordination should only be achieved through free agreements between groups that were nodes of informal social networks. Galleani, for example, endorsed "a society functioning on the basis of mutual agreement" between "free social groupings," while rejecting formal organizations that had administrative committees, congresses, and constitutions.[124]

Organizationalists, in comparison, also advocated the establishment of formal federations.[125] These federations took three main forms: federations of producers belonging to the same branch of production; federations of all the workplace assemblies, regardless of industry, in a given geographical area; and federations of community assemblies in a given geographical area. Federations are free associations of autonomous groups that are formed in order to achieve shared objectives. Within a federation, these autonomous groups are formally linked together through a common program, a bottom-up organizational structure, and the various agreements made at meetings and congresses. In an anarchist society, the basic unit of a federation would be a group in which collective decisions were made in a general assembly. The different assemblies in a given area would voluntarily associate with one another to form a local federation. The local federations in a given region would then voluntarily associate with one another to form a regional federation. The regional federations would associate to form a national federation and the national federations of the world would form an international federation. Federations of federations were often called confederations. Although organizationalist anarchists advocated creating national confederations before and during a social revolution, it is likely that, in a stateless society without borders, new labels would be used to refer to a federation of this size.[126]

Federations would enable coordination at various scales. Collective agreements between different groups would be made at regular congresses held at local, regional, national, and international levels, each attended by delegates from smaller groups comprising the federation. Proponents of federations disagreed about whether resolutions passed at congresses by majority vote should be binding on every individual or group involved in the decision-making process, or on only those who voted in favor of the majority position.[127] Between congresses, the day-to-day administration of a federation would be organized by a committee composed of elected delegates. What tasks these administrative committees performed would vary depending upon the kind of federation but would include such things as facilitating the exchange of information between sections, publishing bulletins on behalf of the federation, or compiling statistics.

The delegates of a federation, in contrast to representatives in capitalist parliaments, are not granted the power to make decisions independently and impose them on others. They can only act as spokespeople for the group that elected and mandated them on what to say and how to vote. If they fail to implement the group's mandate, they can be instantly recalled and replaced by a newly elected delegate. The same principle would apply to delegates who perform other roles for the federation, such as the members of the administrative committees. As Kropotkin explained, within a federation, the members of a local group discuss "every aspect of the question that concerns them," reach a decision, and then "choose someone and send him to reach an agreement with other delegates of the same kind."[128] At this meeting "the delegate is not authorized to do more than explain to other delegates the considerations that have led his colleagues to their conclusion. Not being able to impose anything, he will seek an understanding and will return with a simple proposition which his mandatories can accept or refuse."[129] Malatesta similarly claimed that "the respective delegates would take their given mandates to the relative meetings and try to harmonize their various needs and desires. The deliberations would always be subject to the control and approval of those who delegated them."[130]

All anarchists, regardless of where they stood on the topic of federations, did not think that workplace and community assemblies would be the only organs of self-management in an anarchist society. Kropotkin, for example, advocated a society constituted by an "interwoven network, composed of an infinite variety of groups and federations of all sizes and degrees, local, regional, national, and international—temporary or more or less permanent—for all possible purposes," including not only production and consumption but also "communications, sanitary arrangements, education,

mutual protection," and "the satisfaction of an ever-increasing number of scientific, artistic, literary and sociable needs."[131]

The forms of organization and decision-making that anarchists
advocated were not invented by isolated theorists imagining abstract
social possibilities from their studies. The anarchist vision of a future
society was instead the generalization of the forms of association
that working-class social movements had themselves developed and
implemented during the course of the class struggle. As Kropotkin
argued, "Anarchy" is an "ideal society" based upon *the study of
tendencies already emerging in the evolution of society.*"[132] One of the
main tendencies Kropotkin focused on was the labor movement. He
noted that the anarchist vision of a future society was "worked out,
in theory and practice, from beneath" by workers themselves within
the local sections, national federations, and international congresses
of the First and Saint-Imier Internationals.[133] This occurred through a
process of workers collectively generating ideas via discussion, dialogue, and drawing upon their knowledge of a specific trade or region.
They not only made proposals about how the future society should
be organized, but based these proposals on their own experiences
of participating in "a vast federation of workers groups representing
the seeds of a society regenerated by social revolution."[134]

Although anarchists agreed that land, raw materials, and the
means of production should be owned in common by humanity as
a whole, they disagreed about how the products of labor should be
distributed in an anarchist society. Anarchist collectivists argued
that the products of labor should be owned by those who produced them so that, as they saw it, each producer enjoyed the full
product of their labor.[135] Bakunin, the most famous anarchist collectivist, proposed in 1868 that society should be structured such
that it "allows each to share in the enjoyment of social wealth—
which in fact is produced only by labor—only to the extent that
he has contributed his own to its production."[136] Anarchist collectivists within the First International did not initially specify how

the products of collective labor would be distributed to those who produced them and argued that the question would be resolved in various ways by communities themselves depending upon their circumstances.[137] For example, at the 1877 Verviers Congress of the Saint-Imier International, Spanish anarchist collectivists advocated a society based on the collective ownership of the means of production and land, which "gives autonomy to each community of producers and each receives according to his production."[138] They did not, however, specify how this system of distribution would actually be organized.

A more concrete proposal was made by the anarchist collectivist Guillaume in 1874. He reaffirmed the collectivist position that each community should decide for itself how to distribute the products of labor, while suggesting a system of labor vouchers in which individuals receive a certain number of vouchers per hour of work or per type of work performed and then use them to acquire items at stores. Once the postrevolutionary society had stabilized and abundance was achieved, he thought this should be replaced by the principle of "from each according to ability, to each according to needs."[139]

From 1876 onward, a number of prominent anarchists, including Malatesta, Cafiero, and Reclus, rejected anarchist collectivism in favor of anarchist communism. This soon came to be the dominant position within the anarchist movement, although anarchist collectivism continued to be advocated by a significant segment of anarchists in Spain during the 1880s. Anarchist communism was seen as a society in which each person voluntarily contributes to production according to their abilities and the products of labor are collectively owned by humanity as a whole and distributed according to need. This would, during and immediately after the social revolution, be organized through a system of rationing. Once the economy was sufficiently developed and stable, rationing would be abolished in favor of free access to the products of labor. In contrast to Guillaume, who had previously proposed distribution according to need as the long-term goal, anarchist communists rejected the idea of distribution via labor vouchers as an intermediary system.[140]

Over time, the debate between anarchist collectivists and anarchist communists became increasingly hostile, most notably in Spain during the 1880s where it was entangled with wider strategic debates.[141] In response, Fernando Tarrida del Mármol and Ricardo Mella formulated the idea of "anarchism without adjectives" in 1889. They argued that it was not possible for people living in class society to know with certainty which specific system of distribution would best realize anarchist values after the revolution. As a result, anarchists existing under capitalism should adopt a nondogmatic stance whereby collectivism and communism would coexist in the postrevolutionary society and the argument over which system was superior would be settled through actual experimentation in different economic arrangements. Until this had occurred, anarchists could make proposals about how they personally thought the economy would best be organized, but they would not be in a position to identify as either collectivist or communist. So long as anarchists lived within class society, they should simply call themselves anarchists who advocated socialism and not add to this label any particular adjective denoting a future system of distribution.[142]

This position would go onto influence some anarchists outside of Spain. A notable example is the American anarchist de Cleyre, who was initially an individualist anarchist and advocate of market socialism. Her perspective on anarchism changed due to her four-month visit to England and Scotland in 1897. During her lecture tour, she met and conversed with a variety of anarchist communists. This included both groups of English, Scottish, French, Spanish, and Jewish anarchist workers, and prominent anarchist authors and public speakers, such as Kropotkin, Nettlau, Grave, and Louise Michel. De Cleyre claimed that one of the most impressive people she met was Tarrida del Mármol, the advocate of anarchism without adjectives.[143] From at least 1900 onward, she advocated a

stateless socialist society in which the means of production were
owned in common, while referring to herself as an anarchist without
economic label attached. In contrast to early Spanish advocates of
anarchism without adjectives, de Cleyre claimed that experiments
in different socialist economic arrangements would not only set-
tle the debate between collectivists and communists. It would also
establish an answer to the largely American debate between proponents of market socialism and advocates of a planned economy.[144]

For Kropotkin, who played a significant role in theorizing and
popularizing anarchist communism, it was important to describe
the nature of the future society, because how one envisions the
future shapes how one acts in the present. A socialist who envisions
a society based on producers owning and self-managing the means
of production themselves will act differently, both under capitalism
and during a revolution, from a socialist who envisions a society
based on the state owning and managing the means of production
through a vast bureaucracy. They each have a different vision and
so will act differently to try and create very different worlds.[145] This
perspective can be seen in Kropotkin's 1913 remark that the anarchist vision of a future society "soon separated the anarchists in
their means of action from all political parties, as well as, to a large
extent, from the socialist parties which thought they could retain
the ancient Roman and Canonical idea of the State and carry it into
the future society of their dreams."[146]

If the achievement of anarchy required that the working classes
engage in forms of practice that actually produce an anarchist society, such as establishing workplace or community assemblies, then
the working classes must first develop both the awareness of what
an anarchist society would look like and the motivation to create
such a society. As Kropotkin wrote, "no struggle can be successful
. . . if it does not produce a concrete account of its actual aim. No
destruction of what exists is possible without, during the struggles
leading to the destruction and during the period of destruction

itself, already visualizing mentally what will take the place of what you want to destroy."[147]

The role of anarchist authors like Kropotkin or Cafiero was to articulate and spread this vision among the working classes, and thereby instill in them the radical drives that were necessary for achieving an anarchist society. Anarchists had to decide not only on "the *aim* which we ourselves propose to attain" but must also "make it known, by words and deeds, in such a way as to make it notably popular, so popular that on the day of action it will be on everybody's lips."[148] In outlining these visions of what an anarchist society would look like, anarchists did not think that they were establishing the permanent means through which society would be organized after the social revolution. Instead, they assumed that people living in a future anarchist society would develop new and better ways of organizing that they had not considered, and had not even been in a position to conceive.[149]

The Problem of Socialist Transformation

Anarchists not only advocated the abolition of capitalism and the state in favor of an anarchist society. They also constructed effective strategies for how to set about achieving their goals. One of the central problems that their strategies had to overcome was that both the abolition of class society in favor of an anarchist society and the day-to-day reproduction of an anarchist society require the bulk of the population to have developed a vast array of different capacities, drives, and consciousness, such as the ability to make collective decisions in general assemblies, the desire to not dominate or exploit others, and the understanding that capitalism and the state make people unfree. The dominant structures of class society, however, produce people fit for the reproduction of that oppressive and unequal society, rather than its abolition. Class society cannot, by itself, produce the kinds of people that an anarchist revolution and an anarchist society need.

Such individuals would arise in a properly functioning anarchist society due to the forms of practice they engaged in on a daily basis, such as participating in a workplace assembly or being taught how to horizontally associate as a child. These are exactly the kinds of people that anarchist social movements need in order to succeed. Anarchists, unfortunately, live in a class society. They therefore have a problem: in order to transform society they need transformed people. In order to have transformed people, they need a new society. How then could anarchist social movements effectively transform society? This problem was succinctly expressed by Malatesta:

> Between man and his social environment there is a reciprocal action. Men make society what it is and society makes men what they are, and the result is therefore a kind of vicious circle. To transform society men must be changed, and to transform men, society must be changed. Poverty brutalizes man, and to abolish poverty men must have a social conscience and determination. Slavery teaches men to be slaves, and to free oneself from slavery there is a need for men who aspire to liberty.... Governments accustom people to submit to the Law and to believe that Law is essential to society; and to abolish government men must be convinced of the uselessness and the harmfulness of government.[150]

Despite the self-reproducing nature of dominant structures, social change remains a possibility. This is because existing society is not solely the product of the "will of a dominating class" but is also "the result of a thousand internecine struggles, of a thousand human and natural factors acting indifferently, without directive criteria."[151] Social structures are not fixed monoliths, but webs of interconnected processes that "contain organic contradictions and are like the germs of death, which, as they develop, result in the dissolution of institutions and the need for transformation."[152] This can be seen in the history of class struggle, which contains numerous examples of the oppressed and exploited choosing to rebel against, modify, and sometimes overthrow, self-reproducing social structures. Given this, anarchists who "are besieged and buffeted on every side by hostile realities" must not "accept everything, and defer to everything because this is the situation in which history has placed us," but should instead choose to "combat these realities" and thereby change what reality is.[153] De Cleyre said much the same. She argued in 1910 that, although humans are shaped by their circumstances, they are also at the same time "an active modifying agent, reacting on its environment and transforming circumstances, sometimes slightly, sometimes greatly, sometimes, though not often, entirely."[154]

It is therefore possible for one segment of society to choose to engage in actions that, given the theory of practice, would simultaneously change social relations and themselves, constructing new social structures. To quote Mella,

> We must realize that we will not suddenly find ourselves, one day, with men made in accordance with the future, suitable to realize the content of new ideals. And we must surrender to the evidence that, without the continual and growing exercise of individual faculties, without the habit of autonomy, as broad as possible, free men or at least men in conditions to be free will not be made so that the social deed changes the face of things. External and internal revolutions presuppose one another and should be simultaneous in order to be fruitful.[155]

For example, workers choose to go on strike and win. In so doing, they change social relations—wages increase and workers gain more power over their bosses—and change people—workers learn how to organize a strike, acquire an increased sense of solidarity with one another and see the economy in a fundamentally different way. During the course of the strike, they construct a new social structure that did not exist before—a trade union. Long-term participation in this trade union would, in turn, cause workers to develop their capacities, drives, and consciousness in new directions. This would make the organization of new actions possible, such as strikes that mobilize workers in multiple industries. These kinds of action could continue and multiply over time as increasingly large numbers of workers engage in the process of simultaneously transforming social relations and themselves. This would eventually culminate in a shift from workers only modifying the dominant structures of class society, to workers abolishing them and replacing them with new ones. The anarchist solution to the problem of socialist transformation was, in short, that the working classes could become capable of, and driven to, overthrow capitalism and the state, and establish and reproduce an anarchist society through engaging in revolutionary practice. As Malatesta put it, "progress must advance contemporaneously and along parallel lines between men and their environment."[156]

CHAPTER 4

Anarchist Strategy

Anarchists in the nineteenth and early twentieth centuries argued that one must not merely critique existing institutions or aspire for a better society. One must also form social movements that engage in class struggle against the ruling classes and thereby bring about fundamental social change. To quote Bakunin, "neither writers, nor philosophers, nor their books, nor socialist journals, would reconstitute a socialism that was alive and vigorous. It is only through enlightened revolutionary instincts, through collective will and through the real organization of the working masses themselves that the latter has a real existence, and when instinct, will and organization are lacking the best books in the world will be nothing more than empty theories and powerless dreams."[1] In order to engage in effective action and achieve their goals, working-class social movements had to be guided by an overarching strategy that was both appropriate to their situation and capable of actually bringing about an anarchist society. As Kropotkin succinctly put it, "theory and practice must become one if we are to succeed."[2]

A crucial aspect of anarchist theory was, therefore determining what methods of action to engage in. According to Malatesta, "to be able to act, to be able to contribute to the realization of one's cherished ideas, one has to choose one's own path. In parties, as more generally in life, the questions of method are predominant. If the idea is the beacon, the method is the helm."[3] It is for this reason that "we are anarchists in our goal... but we are anarchist in our method too."[4] Elsewhere Malatesta defined anarchism as "the method of reaching anarchy, through freedom, without government."[5]

Anarchists understood that creating appropriate methods of action was not a matter of inventing abstract strategies fit for all times and places, and following them as if there were an instruction manual for producing a revolution. Anarchism, to quote Kropotkin, contains "no ready-made recipes for political-cooking."[6] Building an anarchist society requires action within a specific context and, since this context varies according to time and place, it follows that, in Goldman's words, "the methods of Anarchism . . . do not comprise an iron-clad program to be carried out under all circumstances" but "must grow out of the economic needs of each place and clime, and of the intellectual and temperamental requirements of the individual."[7] As Malatesta wrote, "the problem facing us anarchists, who regard anarchy not so much as a beautiful dream to be chased by the light of the moon, but as an individual and social way of life to be brought about for the greatest good of all . . . is to so conduct our activities as to achieve the greatest useful effect in the various circumstances in which history places us. One must not ignore reality, but if reality is noxious, one must fight it, resorting to every means made available to us by reality itself."[8]

Despite anarchist methods of action varying depending upon the historically specific context, there were common views on strategy and social change that pervaded the anarchist movement. These were: (a) the advocacy of social revolution, the unity of means and ends, prefiguration, direct action; the spirit of revolt; and (b) the rejection of attempting to achieve social change via the conquest of state power. In this chapter, I shall explain the first group of topics and then, in chapter 5, I shall turn to the anarchist critique of conquering state power. Throughout both chapters, I shall demonstrate that anarchists advocated the strategies they did due to their beliefs about what forms of practice constituted them and how these practices would simultaneously transform people and social relations.

Social Revolution

Anarchists held that the abolition of class society could "only be achieved by means of a revolutionary movement" instigating a social revolution.[9] It is common for modern academics who study the history of revolutions to define a "revolution" as necessarily involving the transformation of the state from one form into another.[10] Anarchists wanted to abolish the state, rather than seize its power, and so did not define a social revolution in such a state-centric manner. They attempted to create a social revolution that fundamentally transformed "the foundations of society, its political, economic and social character" and so was distinct from a statist revolution in which there is "a mere change of rulers, of government."[11]

This fundamental transformation of society required, according to Kropotkin, "completely reconstructing all relationships" between people, from the relationships within a household, factory, or village to those between urban and rural areas.[12] The same idea was expressed by Wilson, who advocated "a revolution in every department of human existence, social, political and economic."[13] Anarchists did not limit the scope of revolutionary transformation to the public sphere of the community or workplace. For the revolution to be meaningful, it had to also transform the so-called private sphere of sexual relationships, parent-child relationships, housework, and so on. Goldman, to take one example, argued that the compulsory social relations of marriage should be replaced by free love in which "love can go and come without fear of meeting a watch-dog," and neither partner acts or views themselves as the owner, controller, and dictator of the other.[14] The extent to which some anarchists viewed emancipation within the private sphere as essential can be seen in Kropotkin's insistence that "a revolution, intoxicated with the beautiful words Liberty, Equality, Solidarity would not be a revolution if it maintained slavery at home. Half humanity subjected to the slavery of the hearth would still have to rebel against the other half."[15]

Although anarchists sometimes claimed that the social revolution should be "spontaneous," the majority of anarchists did not expect it to appear suddenly without any planning and preparation. Nor did anarchists think that the social revolution would occur independently of anarchists influencing other workers through words and deeds. They instead meant that the social revolution should not be imposed on society by a revolutionary elite acting in the name of the people. For a revolution to be "spontaneous" in this sense of the term was for it to be voluntarily launched and self-determined by workers themselves. A worker acted spontaneously when they acted of their own volition, even if their actions were inspired by the actions of those around them.[16] Anarchists were, in other words, committed to the famous words of the 1864 preamble to the statutes of the First International: "the emancipation of the working classes must be conquered by the working classes themselves."[17] This line from the preamble was consistently repeated by anarchist authors or rephrased in slightly different language, such as Malatesta's remark that "we anarchists do not want to *emancipate* the people; we want the people to *emancipate themselves*."[18]

The necessity of a social revolution emerged from the fact that a ruling class had never in history given up their power voluntarily. In every instance, it had required violence or at least the threat of it.[19] Although anarchism aimed at, to quote Malatesta, "the removal of violence from human relations," the vast majority of anarchist authors advocated revolutionary violence as a means to overcome the violence that defended and maintained class society.[20] This revolutionary violence took two main forms: the forceful expropriation of the economic ruling classes and the violent destruction of the state. In 1884, Malatesta advocated "an armed, violent revolution" that would "smash the army and police" and achieve the "forcible expropriation of property owners" and "the abolition of all political authority."[21] This position emerged from an awareness that, as Malatesta explained in 1892, "the means we employ are those that circumstances make possible or necessary . . . we have to make our fight in the world as it is, or else be condemned to be nothing but fruitless dreamers."[22] Class society is violently enforced by "powerful military and police organizations which meet any serious attempt at a change with prison, hanging, and massacre. . . . Against the physical force that blocks our way there is no appeal except to physical force."[23]

The same position was consistently advocated by Kropotkin over several decades. In 1877, he endorsed "the expropriation and suppression of the bourgeoisie."[24] A few years later in 1881, he wrote that workers must "seize all of the wealth of society, if necessary doing so over the corpse of the bourgeoisie, with the intention of returning all of society's wealth to those who produced it, the workers."[25] In 1906, he claimed that in order to achieve "the complete destruction of Capitalism and the State, and their replacement by Anarchist Communism" it was necessary to engage in "armed struggle against the dominating order" and expropriate the ruling classes.[26] In 1913, he argued that "economic emancipation" required "smashing the old political forms represented by the State."[27] A year later, he wrote that "two things are necessary to be successful in a revolution . . . an idea in the head, and a bullet in the rifle! The force of action—guided by the force of Anarchist thought."[28] The extent to which Kropotkin was a proponent of violence against the forces of state repression can be seen in the fact that, in 1877, he attended a demonstration in Switzerland armed with a gun. He was ready, in his own words, to "blow out the brains" of the police if they attacked.[29] In the wake of the 1905 Russian revolution, when he was in his sixties, Kropotkin practiced shooting with a rifle in case he returned to Russia and needed to participate in street fighting.[30]

Malatesta and Kropotkin were not unique in this respect. Countless other anarchists can be quoted making the exact same points.[31] Adolph Fischer claimed in 1887 that "only by the force of arms can the wage slaves make their way out of capitalistic bondage," "expropriate the privileged," and achieve "the abolition of political authority, the state."[32] Rocker insisted in 1920 that "we already know that a revolution cannot be made with rose-water. And we know, too, that the owning classes will never yield up their privileges spontaneously. On the day of victorious revolution the workers will have to impose their will on the present owners of the soil, of the subsoil and of the means of production."[33] In order to do so, workers would also have to demolish the state, since it is "the fortress" that violently maintains the power of the ruling classes.[34]

The forms of violence that anarchists advocated and engaged in covered a wide spectrum of behavior and varied among different contexts. It included, but was not limited to, riots; fighting the police with fists, sticks, and stones; assassinating class enemies; and engaging in armed conflict with the military. This is not to say that anarchists who advocated revolutionary violence agreed with one another on which forms of violence were ethically acceptable or strategically advisable. Johann Most wrote several articles during the 1880s in which he actively encouraged anarchists to engage in violent acts of vengeance against the ruling classes.[35] Malatesta, in comparison, argued in the 1890s that although anarchists should use violence to overthrow systems of oppression, they should not engage in violence to achieve revenge.[36]

A significant number of anarchists saw potential dangers in revolutionary violence. In 1896, Malatesta argued that "let us have no unnecessary victims, not even in the enemy camp . . . a liberating revolution cannot be born of massacre and terror, these having been—and ever so it shall remain—the midwives to tyranny."[37]

Kropotkin similarly wrote in 1892 that "slaughtering the bourgeois so as to ensure that the revolution succeeds is a nonsensical dream" since "organized and legalized Terror . . . serves only to forge chains for the people" and "lays the groundwork for the dictatorship of whoever will grab control of the revolutionary tribunal."[38] Even Most told an audience in Baltimore that "we are revolutionists not from love of gore" but "because there is no other way to free and redeem mankind."[39]

In the popular imagination, revolutions are typically equated with violent acts of destruction, such as fighting the police and army or storming parliament. Anarchists advocated these acts, but they did not reduce the social revolution to them. For them, the social revolution was above all an act of creation. The old world had to be destroyed only because this was a prerequisite to the construction of a new social order. In 1873, Bakunin claimed that although "the real passion for destruction . . . is far from sufficient for achieving the ultimate aims of the revolutionary cause . . . there can be no revolution without widespread and passionate destruction, a destruction salutary and fruitful precisely because out of it, and by means of it alone, new worlds are born and arise."[40] For anarchists like Berkman, a revolution "*begins* with a violent upheaval," but this is only "the rolling up of your sleeves" before "*the actual work*" of revolution occurs, namely "the reorganization of the entire life of society."[41]

As Kropotkin noted, the "first skirmish" of a social revolution, when the people rise up in insurrection, "is soon ended, and it is only after the overthrow of the old constitution that the real work of revolution can be said to begin."[42] This did not mean that violence was not an important aspect of launching and defending the social revolution. Kropotkin predicted that a revolution would most likely result in a civil war, due to the ruling classes launching a counterattack against the working classes.[43] Anarchists were instead drawing attention to the fact that the core of the social revolution was people internalizing anarchist ideas and reconstructing and reorganizing society according to them. The social revolution, in other words, rested on the simultaneous transformation of social structures and of the people who constituted, produced, and reproduced them. It required a change not only in how society was organized, but also a corresponding change to what drives and capacities people exercised and developed. Above all, for anarchists like Goldman, it required people to develop revolutionary consciousness, such as a "sense of justice and equality, the love of liberty and of human brotherhood."[44] This aspect of the social revolution would continue long after the ruling classes had been successfully overthrown.

Therefore, anarchists did not expect the social revolution to occur quickly. Kropotkin predicted in 1885 that "it is not by a revolution lasting a couple of days that we shall come to transform society in the direction posed by anarchist communism. . . . It is a whole insurrectionary period of three, four, perhaps five years that we must traverse."[45] During and after this insurrectionary period, society as a whole would be restructured not from the top down by means of government decree but from the bottom up by millions of workers, in both urban and rural areas, reorganizing their workplaces, communities, and households according to anarchist ideas. Fabbri went further and noted in 1922 that "however extensive and radical a revolution may be, before it manages to be victorious completely and worldwide not one but many generations must elapse."[46] In other words, anarchists viewed "the social revolution" as a "process" that stretched over an extended period of time.[47]

Anarchists divided the process of social revolution into moments of destruction and construction.[48] The working classes would destroy the old world by overthrowing and abolishing the state and expropriating land, raw materials, the means of production, and the necessities of life, such as warehouses of food and clothing or apartment blocks, from the ruling classes.[49] The working classes would build the new society on the ruins of the old by establishing the communal ownership of these things, building organs of self-management—workplace and community assemblies—and, through these, organizing the ongoing reproduction and restructuring of society. As noted in the previous chapter, most anarchists thought that in order to coordinate production, distribution, and revolutionary activity on a large scale, these assemblies should establish formal local federations that would, in turn, federate together to form regional, national, and ultimately, if the social revolution goes as hoped, international federations. A minority of anarchists opposed the establishment of formal federations and argued that large-scale coordination should only be achieved through free agreements between groups that were nodes of informal social networks.

The defense of the social revolution would be achieved through the formation of worker militias, rather than through the seizure of state power. These worker militias would act as organs of class power. As early as 1868, Bakunin, who had previously joined the barricades during the 1848 revolution in Paris and Prague and an 1849 insurrection in Dresden, argued that revolutionaries must "organize a revolutionary force capable of defeating reaction," which would include the "federation of the Barricades."[50] This view was repeated in 1870, when he wrote that, during an anarchist revolution, workers would be "armed and organized" in order to coordinate "common defense against the enemies of the Revolution."[51] Decades later in 1922, Malatesta advocated "the creation of voluntary militia, without powers to interfere as militia in the life of the community, but only to deal with any armed attacks by the forces of reaction to reestablish themselves, or to resist outside intervention by countries as yet not in a state of revolution."[52] Berkman similarly argued in 1929 that "the armed workers and peasants are the only effective defense of the revolution."[53]

Advocating workers' militias was not limited to the writings of famous anarchist authors. It can also be seen in the resolutions of anarchist organizations. The resolutions passed at the Spanish National Confederation of Labor's (CNT) May 1936 Zaragoza

Congress acknowledged "the necessity to defend the advances made through the revolution" from both "foreign capitalist invasion" and "counterrevolution at home."[54] This would be achieved through arming the populace with an array of weapons including not only pistols and rifles but also "planes, tanks, armored vehicles, machine-guns and anti-aircraft cannon," creating a workers' militia of "all individuals of both sexes who are fit to fight," which would coordinate its action via their local "commune" and the "Confederation of Autonomous Libertarian Communes."[55] Anarchists put this theory into practice and formed workers' militias to defend the revolution during the Russian revolution and civil war of 1917–23, and the early phases of the Spanish revolution and civil war of 1936–39.[56]

The manner in which anarchists described the social revolution can give the false impression that they thought it would occur all at once and imagined that, to pick a country at random, all or most of France would simultaneously rise up, overthrow the ruling classes and build an anarchist society. This interpretation ignores that Kropotkin routinely pointed out that the social revolution would most likely: (a) occur alongside a parallel statist revolution launched by republicans or state socialists; (b) develop out of a statist revolution or a series of smaller insurrections; and (c) begin with local uprisings in particular regions, such as Paris, or by particular groups of people, such as miners, and spread to the rest of the country (and hopefully the world) as people in other regions and industries heard of these uprisings and were inspired to join the emerging revolutionary process.[57]

As has already been mentioned, anarchists held that these uprisings, and the social revolution at large, should involve the forcible expropriation of the ruling classes. They thought that any social revolution that did not engage in expropriation would be doomed to failure. If a social revolution were to succeed, the population as a whole must be fed, clothed, and housed. If this did not happen, workers would never support the social revolution, because it does not improve their lives directly or causes a decline in living conditions. Without the support of the masses, the social revolution would fail and reactionaries would be able to restore class society with the promise of bringing stability. Anarchists, in other words, understood that "it is not enough to cherish a noble ideal. Man does not live by high thoughts or superb discourses, for he needs bread as well."[58] It is essential that, once a social revolution begins, people immediately expropriate and redistribute food, clothing, and housing among the population. The expropriation of the means of production and land would, in turn, enable the working classes to produce the necessities of life needed to sustain the population over a longer period of time and prevent food shortages from defeating the social revolution.[59]

Several anarchists in the late nineteenth century predicted that, even if a country were able to achieve this, the social revolution would likely fail unless it occurred internationally. Guillaume argued in 1874 that "the Revolution cannot be confined to a single country; on pain of death, it is obliged to subsume into its movement, if not the whole world, then at least a considerable portion of the civilized countries."[60] No country can be entirely self-sufficient and were the states neighboring a country in revolution to impose a blockade, let alone invade, then "the Revolution, being isolated, would be doomed to perish."[61] Kropotkin shared this concern and developed a detailed response to the problem of economic isolation in his famous 1892 book *The Conquest of Bread*. He attempted to demonstrate in exhaustive detail how a country could reorganize production and distribution during a revolution with the use of the technology and productive capacities of the time, such as through the extensive use of green houses in urban areas.[62] Decades later, Berkman witnessed the blockade that was imposed on the 1917 Russian revolution by capitalist states. In 1929, he wrote in response to these experiences that "the revolution is *compelled* to become self-supporting and provide for its own wants."[63]

The anarchist fear that an isolated revolution would be defeated, alongside their commitment to universal human emancipation, led them to place a great deal of importance on opposing the patriotism and nationalism of the state and fostering internationalism among the working classes. Bakunin understood that "a real and definite solution to the social question can be found only on the basis of an international solidarity of workers of every land," because "no isolated local or national workers' association, even one based in the largest of European countries, can ever triumph in the face of a formidable coalition of every privileged class, of every wealthy capitalist, and of every state in the world."[64] To overcome this coalition of reaction, workers had to achieve "the unity of all local and national bodies" through the formation of "one universal association—the great *International Workers' Association of every land*."[65] This point was reiterated by Rocker decades later when he argued that "the effective basis . . . for the international liberation of the working class" will only be laid "when the workers in every country . . . come to understand clearly that their interests are everywhere the same, and out of this understanding learn to act together."[66]

The outcome of this internationalism would, to quote Malatesta, be workers coming to view "the whole world as our homeland, all humanity as our brothers and sisters."[67] Under capitalism, this internationalism would be grounded in an understanding of the working class's shared interests, such that any "worker, the oppressed, Chinese or Russian or from any other country, is our brother, just as the property-owner, the oppressor, is our enemy, even if he is born in our home town."[68] This belief in working-class internationalism led anarchists in Europe and the United States to form multiethnic and multiracial social movements or organizations. The aptly named International Group of San Francisco brought together Russian, Jewish, Chinese, Polish, French, Italian, and Mexican anarchists in order to organize discussion groups, lectures, picnics, dances, plays, concerts and dinners.[69] In 1931, the paper *L'Emancipazione*, which was collectively produced by members of the group, declared its goal to be "overcoming all race hatred for the solidarity of all peoples, [and] the destruction of all borders: to inaugurate the true and sincere pact of human solidarity."[70]

Numerous other examples can be found in the history of anarchism in the United States, which was largely a social movement of immigrants. Anarchists played a key role, alongside other socialists, in the founding of the Industrial Workers of the World (IWW) at a convention in 1905. The constitution of the IWW, in contrast to other trade unions at the time, included an explicit commitment to organizing all workers, regardless of their gender, race, ethnicity, or nationality. This was reflected in the IWW's subsequent organizing campaigns, which included the formation of interracial unions among Black and white timber workers in the South and Northwest, and Black and white dockworkers on the Philadelphia waterfront. The IWW's multiethnic and interracial character can also be seen in the fact that French, Spanish, Italian, Mexican, Finnish, Swedish, Romanian, Bulgarian, Ukrainian, Russian, Jewish, Japanese, and African American anarchists participated within the trade union as members of local sections, organizers of strikes, and editors of, or writers for, newspapers. On the West Coast, Japanese anarchists, including Takeuchi Tetsugoro, translated IWW literature into Japanese, published a bilingual newspaper to promote the IWW, and organized 2,000 Japanese grape pickers via the Fresno Labor League. In September 1909, the Fresno Labor League held a joint rally with the local branch of the IWW, which was primarily composed of Mexican and Italian workers. After the organization dissolved in 1910, many members joined the local branch of the IWW and went on to organize hundreds of Mexican and Japanese orange pickers in 1918.[71]

For anarchists, this commitment to universal human solidarity entailed an opposition to imperialism and colonialism and the support of anticolonial national liberation movements, such as those in

Cuba, India, and Ireland.[72] According to Maximoff, "the Anarchists demand the liberation of all colonies and support every struggle for national independence as long as it is an expression of the will of the revolutionary proletariat and the working peasantry of the nation concerned."[73] This support included the belief that the main goal of national liberation movements—emancipation—could only be achieved through the methods of anarchism, rather than the establishment of a new state. As will be explained in chapter 5, anarchists predicted that if national liberation movements seized state power then they would end up replacing foreign colonial oppressors with a new minority ruling class who oppressed and exploited the majority of the population.

During World War I, anarchist opposition to imperialism was paradoxically used by a small number of authors, including Kropotkin and Grave, to argue that anarchists should support the French Republic against German militarism on the grounds that Germany had launched a war of aggression and, if victorious, would impose autocracy on the rest of Europe. Most anarchists rejected this argument and refused to side with any state in the conflict since it was a war between rival imperialist powers. As the *International Anarchist Manifesto Against War* declared in 1915, "there is but one war of liberation: that which in all countries is waged by the oppressed against the oppressors, by the exploited against the exploiters."[74] This opposition to all states in the conflict coincided with multiple attempts to organize resistance to the war, such as launching campaigns against conscription, which resulted in anarchists experiencing a significant amount of state repression.[75]

Evolution and Revolution

Anarchists did not expect the social revolution to appear out of nowhere. They viewed social change as a single process that could be divided into periods of evolution and periods of revolution.[76] During periods of evolution change is slow, gradual, and partial. Evolutionary change includes such things as certain ideas becoming more popular, small groups of people developing radical capacities and drives, or dominant structures being gradually modified. Over time, this evolutionary change builds up and culminates in a revolutionary period during which change is rapid and large scale, fundamentally altering society. Although periods of evolution are in general much longer than periods of revolution, it does not follow from this that revolutions are short. A revolutionary period could last years if, during this period, it involves ongoing, large-scale change that fundamentally alters society. The French revolutionary period that began in 1789 with the storming of the Bastille, for instance, ended ten years later in 1799 with the seizure of state power by Napoleon Bonaparte.

Evolutionary and revolutionary change were not seen as separate distinct entities but rather fed off and flowed into one another. An evolutionary period would, if events unfolded as anarchists hoped, develop into a revolutionary period. According to Bakunin, revolutions "come about of themselves, produced by the force of things, the tide of events and facts. They ferment for a long time in the depths of the instinctive consciousness of the popular masses— then they explode, often triggered by apparently trivial causes."[77] In turn, they create or open up new pathways for evolutionary change in the future, while at the same time blocking off other avenues. These new evolutions would lead to new revolutionary change in the future, and so on. As Reclus argued, "evolution and revolution are two successive aspects of the same phenomenon, evolution preceding revolution, and revolution preceding a new evolution, which is in turn the mother of future revolutions."[78]

Émile Pouget expressed this same idea in different language. He conceptualized revolution as a single process of social change that includes both gradual modifications to capitalism and the abolition of capitalism in favor of socialism. For him, revolutionary syndicalism "does not regard the Revolution as a future cataclysm for which we must wait patiently to see emerging from the inevitable working-out of events. . . . The Revolution is an undertaking for all times, for today as well as tomorrow: it is continual action, a daily battling without let-up or respite, against the forces of oppression and exploitation."[79] As a result, when the working classes launch an insurrection that forcefully expropriates the capitalist class it will be "the culmination of preceding struggles" in which they had traversed "stages along the road to human emancipation."[80]

Anarchists consistently expressed these ideas about evolution developing into revolution through water-based metaphors. Bakunin wrote in a letter to Reclus that "we are falling back into a time of evolution—that is to say revolutions that are invisible, subterranean and often imperceptible . . . drops of water, though they may be invisible may go on to form an ocean."[81] Guillaume claimed that "it is not in one day that waters rise to the point where they can breach the dam holding them back: the waters rise slowly and by degrees: but once they have reached the desired level, the collapse is sudden, and the dam crumbles in the blinking of an eye."[82] For Berkman, evolutionary change leads into revolutionary change in the same way that water in a kettle gradually heats up until it boils.[83]

This did not mean that anarchists viewed evolution and revolution as natural forces that inevitably propel human subjects toward a better society.[84] Reclus understood that "revolutions do not necessarily constitute progress, just as evolutions are not always directed toward justice."[85] Malatesta similarly held that "there is no natural law that says evolution must inevitably give priority to liberty rather than the permanent division of society into two castes . . . that of the dominators and that of the dominated."[86] These evolutions and revolutions, be they progressive or reactionary, were nothing but the products of humans acting within their historical situation and thereby transforming the world. Mella insisted that "social evolution is constituted by men; these men constitute the means by which it develops."[87] For Malatesta, "human evolution moves in the direction in which it is driven by the will of humanity."[88]

One of the main forms of evolutionary change anarchists engaged in was spreading anarchist ideas through newspapers, pamphlets, books, talks, and demonstrations. Anarchist literature was not exclusively nonfiction and also included poems, songs, short stories, plays, and novels. The majority of anarchist print media was written and edited by workers for free in their spare time after a full day of work. There were a few papers which were run by full-time paid staff, such as Spain's *Solidaridad Obrera* from 1916 onwards, but these were in the minority.[89] Workers who could not read would listen to anarchist texts being read aloud at public meetings, smaller private gatherings, and even at work. Some illiterate workers would deliberately memorize their favorite anarchist articles and then recite them to other workers.[90] The medium of transmitting ideas via face-to-face interaction by itself created a social network of anarchist workers in a specific location. This group of workers could then decide to not only absorb and discuss anarchist theory, but also put theory into practice and take direct action, such as by organizing a strike.

One of the main sources of content for anarchist papers was the vast number of letters that workers sent to editors and publishing groups. These letters usually contained anarchist theory, stories, poetry, calls for solidarity, news of organizing and meetings, and reports of oppressive or scandalous behavior by capitalists and the police. Through writing letters, these correspondents transmitted information and reflections about a local area to the editors of the paper. The editors would, if they deemed it worthy, print the letter in the paper and then send copies to every correspondent they had across the country. Correspondents would distribute the paper to local workers and collect money for both the publishing costs of the paper and solidarity funds that the paper had set up to support striking workers, anarchist prisoners, or widows of dead comrades. The anarchist press was constituted by a social network in which local correspondents were the nodes through which the anarchist press was channeled out to localities, and the thoughts, experiences, and money from localities were channeled back to publishers. During periods when there were no genuinely national formal anarchist organizations in a country, the informal social networks that connected readers, correspondents, editors, and publishers functioned as the organizational structure of the anarchist movement.[91]

Anarchists also spread their ideas through lectures, public debates, and speaking tours. For example, in 1895, the Italian anarchist Pietro Gori went on a vast speaking tour of the United States during which he delivered somewhere between two and four hundred lectures on anarchism in a single year. He began many by singing songs and playing his guitar in order to gather a crowd, before launching into a talk on anarchism, often successfully persuading a number of workers to form anarchist groups.[92] The dual goal of consciousness-raising and organizing was typically facilitated through the distribution of posters, pamphlets, and periodicals at talks. This had the effect that speaking tours established a local archive of anarchist literature wherever they traveled. The new collection of print media could then be used by workers to educate themselves further and become more committed to anarchism once the speaking tour had left the area. Since periodicals included an address to send letters to, the distribution of print media also ensured that new local anarchists had a means to communicate with other anarchists and become part of the social networks that constituted the movement.[93]

This emphasis on spreading ideas was motivated by the awareness that, to quote Lucy Parsons, fundamental social change was preceded by "a long period of education" that developed "self-thinking individuals."[94] The "first task" of anarchists, according to Malatesta, was "to persuade people. We must make people aware of the misfortunes they suffer and of their chances to destroy them. We must awaken sympathy in everybody for the misfortunes of others and a warm desire for the good of all people . . . arousing the sentiment of rebellion in the minds of men against the avoidable and unjust evils from which we suffer in society today, [and] getting them to understand how they are caused and how it depends on human will to rid ourselves of them."[95]

In other words, anarchists sought to bring about a variety of different changes to the consciousness of the working classes. They sought to improve their theoretical understanding of existing society and how it oppresses them, persuade them that an anarchist society is both possible and desirable, instill anarchist values in them, and, perhaps most importantly, motivate them to actually engage in direct action and emancipate themselves. It was for this reason that Kropotkin sought to use his paper *Le Révolté* to inspire workers with hope by documenting "the growing revolt against antiquated institutions," rather than, as many socialist papers did, drive workers to despair and inaction by focusing too strongly on suffering within existing society.[96]

Anarchist newspapers, pamphlets, books, and talks were but one aspect of a wider revolutionary working-class counterculture that the anarchist movement constructed. There are numerous examples of anarchist workers in Europe and the United States organizing plays, poetry scenes, musical performances, dinners, dances, picnics, and public celebrations of key dates in the revolutionary calendar, such as May Day and the anniversary of the Paris Commune. These social events, which constituted a significant amount of day-to-day anarchist activity in the late nineteenth and early twentieth centuries, were not only moments of fun and creativity. They were also instrumental in: (a) drawing workers into a social milieu where they might develop revolutionary consciousness and come to engage in direct action; (b) raising funds for newspapers, strikes, political prisoners, etc.; and (c) forming close social bonds both among anarchist militants and between anarchists and the wider working class in the area. The creation and reproduction of these social networks laid the foundation on which larger acts of revolt and rebellion were organized.[97]

For decades in Spain, workers came into contact with anarchist ideas via cultural and social centers known as ateneos (athenaeums), which were interconnected with the anarchist trade union movement. These ateneos typically featured a café, library, reading rooms, meeting rooms for anarchist and neighborhood groups, and an auditorium for formal debates, public talks, and artistic performances. During periods of state repression when trade unions were forced underground, ateneos were generally able to remain open and thereby ensure the ongoing existence of an anarchist presence within working-class communities. The workers who participated in ateneos organized a wide range of educational and leisure activities in their spare time. This included day schools for working-class children, evening classes for adult workers, theater clubs that would perform radical plays, singing and musical groups, and hiking clubs that allowed poor urban workers to experience the beauty of nature in the countryside and along the coast. Through engaging in these activities, workers developed themselves in multiple directions, such as gaining the confidence to speak before a crowd, learning to read and write, and acquiring an in-depth understanding of why capitalism and the state should be abolished.

A significant number of anarchist militants, especially women, first encountered anarchist ideas and entered into anarchist social networks through their participation in the ateneos when they were children and teenagers. Young people not only received an anarchist education in ateneos, but also gained experiences of anarchist organizing. In 1932, youth groups that had emerged from ateneos in Granada, Madrid, Barcelona, and Valencia formed the Iberian Federation of Libertarian Youth (FIJL). The FIJL, which was an independent organization linked with the CNT, came to be viewed as one of the main pillars of the anarchist movement. On several occasions, the ateneos were the avenue through which workers mobilized to participate in demonstrations and strikes. They were, in short, social spaces that facilitated working-class self-education, recreation, and class struggle.[98]

Unity of Means and Ends

Anarchists did not think that any form of activity could lead to an anarchist society. They argued that working-class social movements should only use means that were in conformity with the ends of creating a free, equal, and cooperative society without domination or exploitation. They advocated the unity of means and ends. In 1881, Kropotkin argued that social movements should establish their "final *objective*" and then "specify a proposed course of action *in conformity with the ends.*"[99] Anarchists like Malatesta often expressed this idea with metaphors of roads and bridges, transit and movement. He wrote,

> It is not enough to desire something; if one really wants it adequate means must be used to secure it. And these means are not arbitrary, but instead cannot but be conditioned by the ends we aspire to and by the circumstances in which the struggle takes place, for if we ignore the choice of means we would achieve other ends, possibly diametrically opposed to those we aspire to, and this would be the obvious and inevitable consequence of our choice of means. Whoever sets out on the highroad and takes a wrong turning does not go where he intends to go but where the road leads him.[100]

Goldman made this same point in 1922 when she argued, in response to the Bolshevik seizure of state power during the Russian

Revolution, that "means cannot be separated from the ultimate aim" because the "means employed, become, through individual habit and social practice, part and parcel of the final purpose; they influence it, modify it, and presently the aims and means become identical."[101] Given this, "revolutionary methods must be in tune with revolutionary aims. The means used to further the revolution must harmonize with its purposes. In short, the ethical values which the revolution is to establish in the new society must be *initiated* with the revolutionary activities of the so-called transitionary period. The latter can only serve as a real and dependable bridge to the better life if built of the same material as the life to be achieved."[102]

Anarchism's commitment to the unity of means and ends was grounded in the theory of practice, which maintained, as we have seen, that as humans engage in activity, they simultaneously transform themselves and the world around them. An anarchist society would be reproduced over time by people engaging in horizontal systems of association and decision-making and, in so doing, continuously creating and re-creating both anarchist social relations and themselves as people with the right kinds of capacities, drives, and consciousness for an anarchist society. These new social relations can only take root if capitalism and the state are abolished through a social revolution and so will have to be created by the people who presently live in, and have been shaped by, class society. It is therefore essential that during the course of the class struggle workers engage in practices that transform them into people who are capable of, and driven to, overthrow class society and establish and reproduce an anarchist society. If social movements make the mistake of using the wrong or inappropriate means then they will produce people who will create a different society than the one they initially intended.

This theory entailed two main commitments. First, a core part of determining what strategies and tactics a social movement should use to achieve their goals is establishing how the forms of

practice that constitute them transform individuals and social relations simultaneously. If a social movement's end goals can only be
achieved through a social revolution, then it must choose means
during an evolutionary period that build toward this. Kropotkin
argued in 1881 that workers should engage in direct struggle against
capital, especially via trade unions and strikes, because of the unity
of means and ends. He wrote,

> A party which proposes a social revolution as its goal, and
> which seeks to seize capital from the hands of its current
> holders must, of necessity, and from this day onward, posi-
> tion itself at the center of the struggle against capital. If it
> wishes that the next revolution should take place against the
> regime of property and that the watchword of the next call to
> arms should necessarily be one calling for the expropriation
> of society's wealth from the capitalists, the struggle must, on
> all fronts, be a struggle against the capitalists.[103]

The second main position entailed by the unity of means and
ends is that social movements must structure organizations and
make decisions in a manner that causes participants to develop
the kinds of radical capacities, drives, and consciousness that are
necessary for producing and reproducing the social relations of the
future society. A social movement organized in a hierarchical and
centralized manner cannot create an anarchist society because it
will not produce the right kinds of people for the task. Participants
will either act in an authoritarian way or be subject to the authoritarianism of others, such as a small group of leaders monopolizing
decision-making power and issuing orders that the membership
then implements. This will result in the development of authoritarian tendencies in individuals and the establishment of authoritarian
social structures that will, in turn, enable authoritarian modes of
practice and constrain antiauthoritarian ones. If a social movement

constituted by these self-reproducing authoritarian social structures were to launch or take over a revolution, the result would not
be an anarchist society. The authoritarianism of the social movement would instead come to characterize society as a whole. Social
movements that aim to create an anarchist society must therefore
be constituted by forms of practice that produce self-determining
people who associate horizontally with one another. In order to do
so, workers must establish social relations in the present that are,
as far as possible, the same as those that would constitute an anarchist society.

The unity of means and ends led anarchists to maintain that,
although violence was necessary to defend the revolution from
counterattack by the ruling classes, it should not be used to force
the working classes into an anarchist society. In Bakunin's words,
"liberty can be created only by liberty, by an insurrection of all the
people and the voluntary organization of the workers from below
upward."[104] As a result, "a revolution that is imposed, either by official decrees, or by force of arms is no longer a revolution but the
opposite of a revolution, because it necessarily provokes reaction."[105]
Malatesta noted that "anarchy cannot be made by force and violent
imposition by a few" and "is only possible when it is understood
and wanted by large popular masses that embrace all the elements
necessary to creating a society superior to the present one."[106] There
is, in other words, an incompatibility between the means of coerc-
ing people into a particular kind of society and the ends of creating
a free society in which people voluntarily self-manage social life.
A genuine social revolution can only occur if the majority of the
population choose to participate within it and reorganize society
themselves.

For anarchists, means and ends are not only interconnected in
so far as the means you engage in determine the ends you arrive at.
They are also identical in the narrow sense that both the means and
the ends of anarchism are freedom. As Fabbri wrote, "the libertarian

notion of revolution" holds that "freedom is also a means as well as an end."[107] Anarchist actions, in other words, create freedom and are instances of freedom at the same time. This can be seen by connecting the anarchist conceptions of freedom discussed in chapter 3 to revolutionary practice. When the working classes collectively struggle against the ruling classes, they are not only fighting for a distant postcapitalist society in which humanity will finally be free. They are also rejecting domination in the present by choosing to act in accordance with their own wills, rather than obeying the wills of their masters and remaining subservient. When the working classes create organizations and social relations in which they horizontally relate to one another, they are both struggling for a future free society and creating a freer society in the here and now by expanding their real possibilities of experiencing a different kind of life and becoming a different kind of person. When the working classes engage in collective struggles or participate in horizontal social structures, they are developing themselves and becoming more free than they were before.

Such a view was not inconsistent with the fact that the majority of anarchists thought violence was necessary to overthrow the ruling classes and defend the social revolution. Using violence to abolish the power of violent oppressors is not a negation of freedom but rather an affirmation of it. As Malatesta put it, "in order to fight our enemies, and fight effectively, we do not need to deny the principle of freedom," since a commitment to freedom entails "the right to resist any violation of freedom, and to use brute force to resist, when violence is based upon brute force and there is no better way to successfully oppose it."[108] Anarchists wish to use violence to expropriate the economic ruling classes "not because freedom is a good thing for the future, but because it is always good, today as much as tomorrow, and the owners deprive us of it by depriving us of the means of exercising it."[109] Anarchists, likewise, wish to use violence to overthrow the political ruling classes "because governments are the negation of freedom and we cannot be free without having overthrown them."[110]

Prefiguration

The anarchist commitment to the unity of means and ends led them to argue that working-class social movements should establish horizontal social relations that are, as far as is possible, the same as those that would constitute an anarchist society. In so doing, workers attempt to construct the world as they wish it to be during their struggle against the world as it is. They also create, through experimentation in the present, the real methods of organization and association that people in the future might use to achieve the states of affairs that characterize an anarchist society. Kropotkin, for example, argued in 1913 that anarchists "have to find, within the practice of life itself and indeed working through their own experiences, new ways in which social formations can be organized . . . and how these might emerge in a liberated society."[111]

During the second half of the twentieth century, this idea was called *prefiguration* or *prefigurative politics*. It should be kept in mind that this term was not used by anarchists historically.[112] Nonetheless, anarchist organizations generally prefigured the future anarchist society in two ways. First, by embodying the kinds of organizational structure and methods of deliberation and decision-making that a future society would contain. Second, by performing the kinds of functions that organizations in a future society will carry out. Although a social revolution would mark a dramatic shift in social life, there would be no such dramatic shift in anarchist methods of organization and association. The methods would remain the same. What would change is the context and the conditions under which these methods are applied and so the extent to which they can be fully put into practice.

Anarchist organizations built within class society thus have a dual function. In the present they bring people together in order to directly satisfy unmet drives and struggle effectively against capitalism and the state. Through participating in anarchist organizations, workers simultaneously attempt to achieve concrete goals and develop their radical capacities, drives, and consciousness. A tenant union might not only organize a rent strike that wins a reduction in rent or prevents an eviction. The participants could also learn how to make collective decisions in general assemblies and act for themselves through their own direct action. At the same time, they might realize that tenants have shared class interests that are opposed to the class interests of landlords. During the course of the struggle, they begin to understand that society could be organized without landlords, and they may come to aspire for an economic system in which everyone has free access to housing. In changing the world, workers at the same time change themselves.

During a revolutionary period, anarchist organizations would take on new roles and serve as the inspiration for emerging anarchist social forms and/or transform from organizations that struggle against class society into organizations that run a classless society.[113] At such a point, they would not only be the dominant structures through which society was generally organized. They would also continually produce and reproduce individuals who want to and are able to freely associate as equals.

The strategy of prefiguration was not original or exclusive to the anarchist movement. From the 1840s onward, a tendency within the French socialist movement had proposed the formation of workers' cooperatives as organizations that would grow in number under capitalism until they displaced capitalist firms and became the nodes of a socialist society.[114] During debates within the First International, this idea was extended to the First International itself, including the trade unions affiliated to it. The Belgian Internationalist César De Paepe, who was a collectivist but not an anarchist, proposed in his

February 1869 article "The Present Institutions of the International in Relation to the Future" that "the International already offers the model of the society to come and . . . its various institutions, with the required modifications, will form the future social order."[115] For De Paepe, "the International contains within itself the seeds of all the institutions of the future. Let a section of the International be established in each commune; the new society will be formed and the old will collapse with a sigh."[116] The influence these ideas had on the developing anarchist movement can be seen in the fact that the article was republished in April 1869 in *Le Progrès*, which was edited by Guillaume, and in May 1869 by the official organ of the Romance Federation of the First International, *L'Égalité*, which Bakunin wrote for and edited at the time.[117]

One of the earliest anarchist endorsements of prefigurative politics occurred when, on November 12, 1871, the Jura Federation issued the "Sonvilier Circular" in response to Marx, Engels, and their supporters converting the General Council of the First International into a governing body that imposed state-socialist decisions and policies on the organization's previously autonomous sections.[118] As part of their critique of the actions of the General Council they stated that

> the society of the future should be nothing other than the universalization of the organization with which the International will have endowed itself. We must, therefore, have a care to ensure that that organization comes as close as we may to our ideal. How can we expect an egalitarian and free society to emerge from an authoritarian organization? Impossible. The International, as the embryo of the human society of the future, is required in the here and now to faithfully mirror our principles of freedom and federation and shun any principle leaning toward authority and dictatorship.[119]

Anarchists, in short, thought that building prefigurative organizations was essential because of the unity of means and ends. As
Bakunin wrote, a few months after the "Sonvilier Circular" was published, "the fashion and form of one's organization arises from and
flows as a consequence from the nature of one's aims."[120] Kropotkin
likewise argued in 1873 that revolutionaries must reject social relations within "the revolutionary organization" that contradict the
ideals for which it has been formed, relations such as "a hierarchy
of ranks which enslaves many people to one or several persons" or
"inequality in the interrelations of the members of one and the same
organization."[121]

This was important because, as Malatesta explained, "the abolition of government and capitalism is feasible only once the people,
organizing themselves, are equipped to perform those social functions performed today—and exploited to their own advantage—by
rulers and capitalists."[122] To this end, anarchists like Goldman proposed that workers in the present should attempt "to prepare and
equip themselves for the great task the revolution will put upon
them" by acquiring "the knowledge and technical skill necessary
for managing and directing the intricate mechanisms of the industrial and social structure of their respective countries."[123] Anarchist
organizations that prefigured the future anarchist society were the
concrete means through which workers would learn to self-manage
their lives and thereby become equipped to create a self-managed
society. As Mella wrote in 1911,

> The proletariat continues acquiring the capacity for coopera-
> tion and management precisely outside of political action. In
> workers' associations, *especially in those where political prac-
> tices do not govern*, workers are gaining the power of initiative,
> management practices, habits of freedom and direct inter-
> vention in common affairs, ease of expression and mental
> assurance, all things whose development is void in political

entities that have as a base the delegation of powers, and, therefore, the subordination and discipline, and obedience to the elected. In social associations, initiatives come from below and from below come ideas, strength, and action. In this way, free men are made and are released to walk.[124]

Decades later in 1932, the Spanish anarchist Isaac Puente argued that just as a child learns to walk or ride a bicycle by trying and failing until they succeed, so too would workers learn to produce and reproduce an anarchist society through experiments in horizontal forms of association. He wrote, "living in libertarian communism will be like learning to live. Its weak points and its failings will be shown up when it is introduced. If we were politicians we would paint a paradise brimful of perfections. Being human and being aware what human nature can be like, we trust that people will learn to walk the only way it is possible for them to learn: by walking."[125]

Anarchists argued with one another about which prefigurative organizations should be built and how these organizations should be structured. Antiorganizationalists advocated small affinity groups and informal social networks, while organizationalists advocated, in addition to this, large formal federations, such as trade unions. Some anarchists advocated forming intentional communities and workers' cooperatives, while other anarchists rejected this strategy.[126] One area where anarchists generally agreed was on the need to construct emancipatory schools. Anarchists of all varieties founded or participated in schools in Spain, Italy, France, England, the United States, and elsewhere. These schools lasted for varying lengths of time, ranging from one or two years to over four decades, in the case of the Modern School of New York, which opened in 1911, relocated to Stelton, New Jersey in 1915 and finally closed in 1953.[127]

These schools educated children and adults, but also sought to contribute toward fundamental social change. In 1898, a number of prominent anarchists, including Louise Michel, Reclus, Grave, and

Kropotkin, signed an article published in *Les Temps Nouveaux* that advocated the creation of anarchist schools on the grounds that "education is a powerful means of disseminating and infiltrating minds with generous ideas" and so could become "the most active motor of progress," acting as "the lever that will lift up the world and will overthrow error, lies and injustice forever."[128]

One of the most influential anarchist educationalists was Francisco Ferrer, who established a Modern School that taught pupils in Barcelona between 1901 and 1906. He advocated "the establishment of new schools in which, as far as possible, there shall rule this spirit of liberty that we feel will dominate the whole education of the future."[129] Ferrer did not think that teachers would be able to establish a fully emancipatory school overnight. He instead argued that teachers should engage in pedagogical experiments that demonstrated, through a process of trial and error, what approaches to education enabled children to develop themselves and become adults who could think independently and horizontally associate with others.[130] Ferrer's experiments in pedagogy were abruptly ended on October 13, 1909, when he was executed by the Spanish government for a crime he had not committed: orchestrating a week-long working-class insurrection against army reservists being called up to fight in Morocco. His martyrdom led him to become an internationally known figure and inspired the creation of emancipatory schools around the world.[131]

The theory and practice of anarchist prefigurative politics was largely concerned with the formation and structure of organizations and often did not give sufficient attention to interpersonal relations between people in daily life, especially men and women. In the United States, for example, anarchists only shifted to focusing on prefiguration in daily life in the 1940s, after anarchism had ceased to exist as a mass movement in the country.[132] This is not to say that anarchists prior to this did not think it was important to act like an anarchist in daily life. In 1886, Wilson claimed that anarchists should, in parallel with the formation of mass, working-class social movements, "endeavor to discard the principle of domination from our own lives."[133] Malatesta similarly wrote in 1897 that "we need to start by being as socialist as we can immediately, in our everyday life."[134] Nor is it to say that anarchists in this period never explicitly advocated some forms of prefiguration in daily life. In 1907, the Italian anarchist Camillo Di Sciullo argued that anarchists should, "build a little anarchist world within your family."[135]

The main form of prefiguration in daily life anarchists advocated was free love in the sense of a voluntary sexual relationship between equals that occurred outside of marriage. These relationships were mostly monogamous, although some anarchists did advocate and practice polyamory. Notable examples of anarchists seriously attempting to engage in free love include the relationship between Rudolf Rocker and Milly Witkop and the one between Guy Aldred and Rose Witkop. In both cases, Rocker and Aldred appear to have treated their partner in a nonpatriarchal manner. However, most evidence indicates that the majority of anarchist men did not build the gender and romantic relations of the future society within their own households. They continued to treat women in a patriarchal manner, such as expecting their partner to become a mother who did the vast majority of housework and childcare. This, in turn, often led to anarchist women lacking the free time to properly participate within the anarchist movement.[136] In 1935, the Spanish anarchist Lola Iturbe complained that anarchist men "however radical they may be in cafés, unions, and even affinity groups, seem to drop their costumes as lovers of female liberation at the doors of their homes. Inside, they behave with their compañeras just like common 'husbands.'"[137]

A similar failure occurred in public organizations. The CNT, for example, was formally committed to the goal of a society in which men and women were free and equal, but this was generally not prefigured within the trade union's day-to-day social relations.

Soledad Estorach recalled in an interview that women would attend a meeting but not return due to experiences of sexism. Even trade union sections whose membership were mostly women were represented at congresses by men and only a few women spoke during a trade union's local general assembly. Within the FIJL, teenage boys would laugh at girls when they spoke, or were about to speak, at meetings.[138]

Women in both Europe and the United States responded to patriarchy within the anarchist movement by forming their own groups in order to enable women to more fully participate in the movement, struggling against patriarchal and class oppression simultaneously. The Women's Emancipation Group—founded in 1897 by the Italian anarchists Maria Roda, Ninfa Baronio, and Ernestina Cravello—had around fifteen members. It was based in Paterson, New Jersey, held regular meetings over seven years, printed and distributed antipatriarchal literature, and inspired other anarchist women to form their own groups, such as the Women's Propaganda Group in Manhattan.[139] Anarchist women in Spain similarly formed their own groups in the 1920s. These grew in number until they were formally linked together via the establishment of the national federation Mujeres Libres (Free Women) in 1937 during the Spanish revolution. The organization's significance can be seen in the fact that it mobilized over 20,000 women.[140]

One of Mujeres Libres' most important contributions was taking anarchist ideas on prefiguration and applying them to the emancipation of women. Since the 1860s, anarchists had argued that workers should build organizations that used the same structure and decision-making procedures as an anarchist society because, through participating in them, workers learned how to self-manage their lives and thereby how to create a self-managed society. Mujeres Libres developed this theory by arguing that liberation for women (and the drives, capacities, and consciousness this entailed) was not simply a matter of creating organizations that coordinated action via federations or made decisions via general assemblies. This is because one of the main barriers to women developing themselves through revolutionary practice was sexist treatment by men and women's own internalization of patriarchal norms.

In October 1938, Mujeres Libres explained that one of the main goals of the organization was "to empower women to make of them individuals capable of contributing to the structuring of the future society, individuals who have learned to be self-determining."[141] To achieve this, Mujeres Libres organized educational programs specifically for women. These taught not only basic skills, such as reading and writing, but also courses on "social formation" that focused on how women were capable of developing themselves and had to learn to take initiative and act independently of the men in their lives. Members of Mujeres Libres spread these ideas to the countryside during educational trips where they gave talks to other women. During these talks they explained that mothers could be anarchist militants, that men oppressed women, and that women should act themselves to stop this from occurring.[142] In so doing, they were attempting to build the gender relations of anarchy during both the struggle against capitalism and the state and the formation of an anarchist society, rather than waiting till after the revolution for their emancipation.

Direct Action

The primary means by which the working classes would simultaneously transform themselves and the social world was direct action. Individuals or groups engage in direct action when they act themselves to bring about social change, rather than relying upon intermediaries or representatives to act on their behalf. Direct action, to quote Rocker, encompasses "every method of immediate warfare by the workers against their economic and political oppressors."[143] By "immediate warfare," Rocker meant actions such as strikes, boycotts, industrial sabotage, distributing antimilitarist propaganda and, in certain circumstances, the "armed resistance of the people for the protection of life and liberty."[144] Direct action thus includes nonviolent and violent actions that contribute toward both evolutionary and revolutionary change. The social revolution is in a sense the ultimate form of direct action.

Anarchists initially did not use the term direct action and instead deployed a variety of equivalent phrases.[145] It is difficult to trace, using texts that have been translated into English, when the term direct action was first adopted by the anarchist movement. One early example is Wilson's 1886 advocacy of "direct personal action" in the first issue of *Freedom*.[146] The term direct action appears to have become commonly used due to the emergence and growth of revolutionary syndicalism as a social movement in France between the 1890s and the early 1900s. During this period, revolutionary syndicalists, many of whom were anarchists, consistently advocated and engaged in what they termed direct action. This phrase initially referred to when workers drew on their own strength to personally struggle against capitalism and thereby achieve their own liberation through their own actions.[147]

This perspective can be seen in Émile Pouget's appropriately titled 1907 pamphlet *Direct Action*. According to Pouget, who was both an anarchist and a revolutionary syndicalist, direct action meant that "the working class . . . expects nothing from outside people, powers or forces, but rather creates its own conditions of struggle and looks to itself for its methodology. It means that from now on the *producer* . . . means to mount a direct attack upon the capitalist mode of production in order to transform it by eliminating the employer and thereby achieving sovereignty in the workshop."[148] For Pouget, "direct action is, therefore, merely trade union action . . . without capitalist compromises, without the flirtation with the bosses of which the sycophants of 'social peace' dream . . . without friends in the government and with no 'go-betweens' horning in on the debate."[149]

By the early twentieth century, the term direct action had become a staple of anarchist parlance and was used in a much broader sense than can be found in early revolutionary syndicalist texts. In 1910, Goldman argued that "direct action, having proven effective along economic lines, is equally potent in the environ-ment of the individual. There a hundred forces encroach upon his being, and only persistent resistance to them will finally set him free. Direct action against the authority in the shop, direct action against the authority of the law, direct action against the invasive, meddlesome authority of our moral code, is the logical, consistent method of Anarchism."[150] Goldman applied this idea to abolishing patriarchy and argued that women should emancipate themselves through their own direct action, rather than trying to win the right to vote and elect representatives who would act on their behalf. She declared that a woman's "development, her freedom, her inde-pendence, must come from and through herself. First, by asserting herself as a personality and not as a sex commodity. Second, by refusing the right of anyone over her body; by refusing to bear chil-dren, unless she wants them; by refusing to be a servant to God, the State, society, the husband, the family, etc. . . . by freeing herself from the fear of public opinion and public condemnation. Only that, and not the ballot, will set woman free."[151]

This broader notion of direct action was shared by de Cleyre. During a 1912 lecture in Chicago, she said that "every person who ever had a plan to do anything, and went and did it, or who laid his plan before others, and won their co-operation to do it with him, without going to external authorities to please do the thing for them, was a direct actionist."[152] Equipped with this more expansive definition, de Cleyre illustrated the idea by referring not only to the actions of unionized workers. She also pointed to abolitionists, who helped slaves escape their owners through the underground railroad, and to John Brown, who killed supporters of slavery and attempted to free and arm slaves through the seizure of the federal armory at Harpers Ferry.[153]

Anarchists themselves engaged in a wide variety of different forms of direct action, both small and large scale. These included, but were not limited to, workplace strikes, rent strikes, combative demonstrations, riots, armed uprisings, prison escapes, industrial sabotage, boycotts, civil disobedience, and providing illegal abortions. A few of the more exciting, small-scale examples provide some sense of the range direct action could cover.

Anarchists in Paris organized a socialist removal service that would, under the cover of night, move the possessions of poor families from their apartment before they had paid rent. On at least one occasion, anarchists gagged, tied up, and left a landlord or concierge on his bed in order to achieve this.[154] In 1900, anarchists living in the United States unsuccessfully attempted to free Berkman from prison by digging an underground tunnel through which he could escape.[155] Five years later, anarchists in the Russian empire defended Jewish people during the 1905 pogroms by organizing mobile defense units armed with pistols and bombs.[156] In 1919, nearly 150 anarchists, mostly women, rioted at the docks in Lower Manhattan, New York. This was in response to their family members and loved ones being arrested by the American government and deported to Russia for being anarchists.[157] In September 1923, the Spanish anarchist affinity group Los Solidarios, which included Buenaventura Durruti, stole 650,000 pesetas from the Gijón branch of the Bank of Spain in order to buy weapons for a planned, but never carried out, insurrectionary general strike.[158]

On numerous other occasions, anarchists participated in larger acts of collective direct action carried out by mass movements. In early 1902, Galleani and other anarchists organized a series of meetings among dye workers in Paterson, New Jersey. These culminated in a small strike being launched in mid-April by Italian dye workers.

Over the following weeks the strike massively expanded and, on June 17, a general strike was proclaimed that mobilized around 15,000 dye and textile workers in the city and surrounding area. This expansion of the strike was driven forward by the efforts of anarchist militants who distributed local anarchist papers and organized meetings in Italian, German, and English. On June 18, Galleani gave a speech where he called upon the striking workers to "rise up!" and "answer the legal violence of capital with the human violence of revolt!" A group of between 1500 and 2000 striking dyers then marched into Paterson and proceeded to break the windows and doors of several dye works in order to drive out scabs and to close down production. This soon escalated into an extended gun battle with the police during which Galleani, who was armed with a revolver, received a minor gunshot wound to the face. The strike continued over the following week and ended with workers gaining a general wage increase.[159]

From these examples, it is clear why anarchists advocated direct action. When successful, it either immediately results in a goal being achieved or imposes costs onto the ruling classes, such that they acquire an incentive to give into the demands of workers. A strike stops production and so a capitalist's ability to earn profit. If a capitalist wants to stay in business, and is unable to break the strike, they have no choice but to increase wages, reduce hours of work, improve safety conditions, and so on.

Anarchists advocated direct action not only because it was an effective means for achieving social change but also because it positively transformed those who engaged in it. According to the Austrian anarchist Siegfried Nacht, "it is above all through action that the people can educate themselves. Little by little, action will give them a revolutionary mentality."[160] Pouget held that "direct action has an unmatched educational value: It teaches people to reflect, to make decisions and to act. . . . Direct action thus releases the human being from the strangle-hold of passivity and listlessness. . . . It teaches him will-power, instead of mere obedience, and to embrace his sovereignty instead of conferring his part upon a deputy."[161]

Such a transformation in people was essential for the achievement of anarchist goals. The overthrow of class society and the construction of an anarchist society required the working classes to learn to act for themselves and collectively self-organize and self-determine their lives. This viewpoint was grounded in the theory that there is a connection between means and ends. For Kropotkin, the anarchist vision of a future society "necessarily leads us to develop for the struggle our own tactics, which consist in developing the greatest possible amount of *individual initiative* in each group and in each individual—unity in action being obtained by unity of purpose and by the force of persuasion."[162] The social revolution would, after all, only be successful if the working classes had already, to quote Pouget, "acquired the capacity and will" to transform society and overcome "the difficulties that will crop up" through their "own direct efforts, on the capabilities that it possesses within itself."[163] Direct action in the present "lays the groundwork" for the social revolution since "it is the popularization, in the old society of authoritarianism and exploitation, of the creative notions that set the human being free: development of the individual, cultivation of the will and galvanization for action."[164] It was, as Galleani wrote, "the best available means for preparing the masses to manage their own personal and collective interests."[165]

The Spirit of Revolt

Malatesta wrote in 1889 that "the great revolution . . . will come as the result of relentless propaganda and an exceptional number of individual and collective revolts."[166] He was not simply predicting that revolts would culminate in a social revolution. He was also arguing that revolts are a necessary aspect of the process of social change due to the manner in which they, like all forms of direct action, transform workers who participate in or observe them. He thought that "revolts play a huge part in bringing the revolution about and laying its ground-work."[167] This was because

> it is deeds that trigger ideas, which in turn react with deeds and so on. . . . How ever could those millions of men—brutalized by exhausting toil; rendered anaemic by inadequate and unwholesome food; educated down through the ages in respect for priest, boss, and ruler; forever absorbed in the quest for their daily bread; superstitious; ignorant; fearful—one fine day perform an about face and emerge from their hovels, turn their backs on their entire past of patient submission, tear down the social institutions oppressing them and turn the world into a society made up of equals and brothers—had not a long string of extraordinary events forced their brains to think? If a thousand partial battles had not nurtured the spirit of rebellion in them, plus an appreciation of their own strength, a feeling of solidarity toward their fellow oppressed, hatred for the oppressor, and had not a thousand revolts taught them the art of people's warfare and had they not found in the yearned for victory a reason to ask themselves: what shall we do tomorrow?[168]

Anarchists, in other words, believed that, in order for a social revolution to emerge, an increasingly large number of workers have to choose to engage in acts of revolt that transform them and motivate other workers to rise up against their oppressors. During the early 1880s, Kropotkin argued that this process must be driven forward by anarchist workers engaging in acts that spread, what he called, "the spirit of revolt."[169] According to Kropotkin, this was because the majority of workers will not become anarchists during periods of evolutionary change. Even a mass movement of one million anarchist workers would be a minority in a country of thirty million. Anarchism will only be embraced by workers throughout all of society during a revolutionary period, when vast numbers of previously indifferent people are caught up in a wave of excitement, become open to fundamentally new ways of thinking, and take an active role in reshaping society. This was demonstrated by the fact that, in the eighteenth century, republicanism and the desire to abolish monarchy only became popular in France during the French Revolution itself.[170]

The success of anarchism therefore required establishing how evolution develops into revolution. Kropotkin answer was that "it is the *action* of the minorities, continuous action endlessly renewed that achieves this transformation" to a "revolutionary situation."[171] He predicted that the actions of radical minorities, as individuals and groups, will spread discontent with the existing social system, hatred of the ruling classes, and "reawaken audacity, the spirit of revolt, through preaching by example."[172] The acts of revolt carried out by courageous minorities will receive sympathy and support from workers not yet engaging in revolutionary action and thereby "find imitators," such that, as the first radicals are being imprisoned, "others will appear to continue their work" and "the acts of illegal protest, of revolt, of revenge, will continue and multiply."[173]

Kropotkin thought this would occur due to three interdependent processes: (a) revolutionary ideas will spread among previously indifferent workers who are now forced to pick a side in the ongoing class conflict; (b) workers will join the ongoing insurgency because its successes demonstrate the real possibility of overthrowing the ruling classes who previously seemed invincible; and (c) a vicious cycle of state repression will anger the working classes and provoke more and more acts of revolt. Over time, these acts of revolt will spread and grow in size and number until a full-blown social revolution breaks out.[174]

This social revolution will only adopt an anarchist character if anarchist workers play a key role in the early waves of revolt, because "the party which has done most revolutionary agitation, which has manifested most liveliness and audacity, will get the best hearing on the day when action becomes necessary, when someone must march at the head to accomplish the revolution."[175] A social movement that fails to engage in "revolutionary action in the preparatory period" and make its ideas and aspirations popular among the masses "will have a scanty chance of realizing even the smallest part of its programme. It will be overtaken by the activist parties."[176]

Kropotkin developed this position from his study of how the French Revolution of 1789 arose. He claimed that, in urban areas, a minority of republican revolutionaries spread the spirit of revolt by popularizing their ideas through pamphlets, leaflets, posters, and songs as well as organizing protests where orators spoke, effigies of the ruling classes were burned, and soldiers were attacked if they attempted to break up the demonstration. Over time, this developed the militancy and daring of the masses until demonstrations transformed into riots and riots into a revolution.[177] A similar pattern unfolded in the countryside. According to Kropotkin, "during the whole year of 1788 there were only half-hearted riots among the peasantry. Like the small and hesitant strikes today, they broke out here and there across France, but gradually they spread, became more broad and bitter, more difficult to suppress."[178] By 1789, the mass of peasantry had risen up to overthrow the ruling classes. They did so because they "saw that the government no longer had the strength to resist a rebellion" after "a few brave men set fire to the first châteaux, while the mass of people, still full of fear, waited until the flames from the conflagration of the great houses rose over the hills toward the clouds."[179] The actions of these revolutionary minorities were the catalyst for a chain reaction of uprisings until it became impossible to control the revolution. . . . It had broken out almost simultaneously in a thousand places; in each village, in each town, in each city of the insurgent provinces, the revolutionary minorities, strong in their audacity and in the unspoken support they recognized in the aspirations of the people, marched to the conquest of the castles, of the town halls and finally of the Bastille, terrorizing the aristocracy and the upper middle class, abolishing privileges. The minority started the revolution and carried the people with it.[180]

Kropotkin thought it would "be just the same with the revolution whose approach we foresee. The idea of anarchist communism, today represented by feeble minorities but increasingly finding popular expression, will make its way among the mass of the people."[181] This would be achieved by groups of anarchist workers spreading throughout the populace in order to help organize acts of resistance and rebellion. Such collective struggles would culminate in revolution spreading widely until capitalism and the state had been overthrown. During this process, "what is now the minority will become the People, the great mass, and that mass rising up against property and the State, will march forward towards anarchist communism."[182]

CHAPTER 5

Anarchism and State Socialism

Anarchism as a social movement emerged in parallel with, and opposition to, various forms of state socialism. This included not only Marxism but also those influenced by such figures as Louis Auguste Blanqui, Ferdinand Lassalle, César De Paepe, Paul Brousse, and Jean Allemane. During the late nineteenth century, a number of socialist political parties adopted Marxist programs or at least programs influenced by Marxism, such as the Social Democratic Workers' Party of Austria in 1888 and the Social Democratic Party of Germany in 1891. These social democratic parties contained numerous factions, including people who were not Marxists, and coexisted with political parties committed to other kinds of state socialism, such as the Federation of the Socialist Workers of France, who were known as Possibilists. From 1889 onward, the various state socialist parties of the time were linked together through a loosely organized coalition known as the Second International. This coalition disintegrated from 1914 onward, when the majority of socialist parties in Europe supported their respective nation-states in World War I and voted for war credits. This was followed by the Russian revolution of 1917, during which the Marxist Bolshevik party seized state power and established a one-party dictatorship. These two events led to a split in state socialism and the formation of various national Communist parties, which affiliated with the centralized, Bolshevik-led Third International (Comintern) that had been founded in March 1919. These Communist parties, in contrast to a significant chunk of social democracy, were explicit Marxist parties and became the main rivals of anarchism within international socialism.[1]

The anarchist critique of state socialist strategies was largely articulated in response to the programs, newspapers, congress resolutions, and actions of the various socialist, and later communist, political parties that confronted them. Anarchist authors, in other words, generally focused their energy on refuting the theory and practice of really existing social movements, rather than producing an exhaustive examination of Marx and Engels's various writings on the topic (much of which was not publicly available or easy to obtain at the time). This is not to say that anarchists never argued against Marx and Engels. Anarchist critiques of state socialism frequently mentioned Marx and Engels by name or responded to an idea that Marx and Engels had advocated in their best-known works, such as the *Manifesto of the Communist Party* or *Anti-Dühring*.[2] Yet, even when critiquing the strategy of Marx and Engels, anarchists tended to interpret their ideas through the lens provided to them by socialist political parties at the time, rather than understanding Marx and Engels on their own terms.[3]

According to anarchists in this period, state socialists generally argued that, in order to achieve a stateless, classless society (essentially an anarchist society), the working classes must first conquer state power and use it to overthrow the capitalist class, reconstruct the economy along socialist lines, and defend the revolution from counterattack. The conquest of state power would be achieved by forming political parties that either won state power through parliamentary elections or seized state power via force. The government of the bourgeoisie would be transformed into, or replaced with, a democratic workers' republic that, at least in theory, was based on the genuine self-rule of the working classes. The reconstruction of the economy would take the form of private property being abolished in favor of state ownership of the means of production and land. Production, distribution, and exchange would then be organized through the state. Once the revolution had been successful and a classless society achieved, the state would wither away. Anarchists and state socialists agreed on the ends of a stateless, classless society but proposed different means to achieve it.[4]

Anarchists rejected the strategy of attempting to abolish capitalism via the conquest of state power. This rejection did not stem from abstract arguments about morality, or ignore the harsh facts of real politics. They instead did so for fundamentally strategic reasons that were grounded in the theory of practice. Anarchists argued that, given the unity of means and ends (which was explained in the previous chapter), the conquest of state power was a path that would never lead to a stateless, classless society. This argument applied to both engaging in parliamentarism within the existing bourgeois state and attempting to overthrow the bourgeois state and transform it into, or replace it with, a workers' state. In making this argument, anarchists were not, as is commonly claimed by Marxists, rejecting or ignoring political struggle. Given my focus on explaining what anarchists themselves thought, I shall not examine the complex question of whether or not the anarchist critique of state socialism actually applied to their various opponents, such as Marx and Engels.

Parliamentarism

During the late nineteenth century, various socialist parties were formed in Europe and the United States. These parties generally argued that the abolition of capitalism and establishment of socialism could be achieved, or at least built toward, through the strategy of winning local and national elections and participating in bourgeois parliaments as representatives of the working class. Through this political struggle, socialist parties would simultaneously build up their size and organizational strength, win various reforms via the passing of new legislation, and spread socialist ideas to a large audience. In so doing, they would transform parliament from a mere tool of bourgeois rule into a lever of working-class emancipation. This parliamentary struggle would occur alongside, and as a complement to, various forms of extraparliamentary activity, including demonstrations, the organization of trade unions and strikes, the construction of cooperatives, the spreading of ideas via the socialist press, and the establishment of a working-class counterculture within singing societies, bicycle clubs, reading groups, and the like. Socialist parties generally, but not always, viewed the parliamentary struggle as primary and thought that extraparliamentary activity played a secondary and supportive role. Over time, these various forms of struggle would lead to the development of a mass socialist party that was capable of, and driven to, win state power in response to the economic crises of capitalism.[5]

State socialists disagreed with one another about how to achieve this. Moderate state socialists proposed that if a socialist party won a majority in parliament then they would be able to gradually establish socialism through the passing of new legislation and the achievement of various reforms. Radical state socialists rejected this position and argued that the conquest of state power could not be won by legal and peaceful means. State power could only be forcibly seized by such means as an armed insurrection, coup, or general strike. The majority of radical state socialists did not, however, reject parliamentarism and thought that it could still be used as an effective means to win immediate improvements within capitalism, spread socialist ideas to a large audience, and build up the size and organizational strength of the socialist party.[6]

Anarchists had four main objections to parliamentarism. First, even if socialist parties managed to win majorities in parliament, the economic ruling classes would never allow their power and property to be voted away and abolished via peaceful and legal means. Capitalists and landowners would, if necessary, overthrow any socialist party that attempted to do so. The abolition of capitalism in favor of socialism cannot be achieved via the ballot. It can only be achieved by working-class social movements breaking the law and launching a social revolution to forcibly overthrow their oppressors. Anarchists were aware that radical state socialists agreed with them about this.[7]

Second, anarchists rejected the claim that parliamentarism was a necessary or sufficient condition for winning immediate improvements within capitalism. They argued that workers could achieve immediate improvements through direct action alone. This could be seen not only in the numerous strikes that had successfully won higher wages or reductions to the working day, but also in the fact that direct action had played an important role in the achievement of the right to vote itself, as with the 1893 general strike in Belgium. It was clear that a key factor in the achievement of new legislation was the working classes imposing external pressure on parliament via direct action. If this is the case, then reforms could be won by imposing pressure on liberal, republican, or conservative politicians. It did not specifically require the election of socialist politicians. Such immediate improvements would also most likely be won faster if time, energy, and money devoted to electoral campaigns was instead exclusively used on direct action and the self-organization of the working classes.[8]

In the absence of the working classes imposing external pressure on parliament via direct action, socialist politicians routinely found themselves unable to pass new laws in parliament. Bourgeois politicians from a variety of different parties would put aside their differences in order to vote against motions proposed by socialists.[9] Even if socialist politicians did manage to pass laws in parliament that protected or expanded workers' rights, it did not follow from this that the law would be enforced. As de Cleyre wrote in 1912, "nearly all the laws which were originally framed with the intention of benefiting the workers, have either turned into weapons in their enemies' hands, or become dead letters unless the workers through their organizations have directly enforced their observance. So that in the end, it is direct action that has to be relied on anyway."[10]

A state socialist might reply that, in order to achieve maximum effectiveness, working-class social movements should engage in parliamentary politics and direct action simultaneously. In 1897, Malatesta answered this by pointing out that "the two methods of struggle do not go together and whoever embraces them both inevitably winds up sacrificing any other considerations to the electoral prospect."[11] Ultimately, "the electoral and parliamentary contest amounts to schooling in parliamentarism and winds up making parliamentarists of all its practitioners."[12]

The third anarchist objection to parliamentarism was that it is a form of practice that fails to develop in workers the radical traits necessary for a social revolution. Instead of taking direct action within prefigurative organizations, workers would engage in such activities as voting in elections, campaigning for politicians, and listening to them make various promises. Such forms of activity would produce workers who look to politicians to achieve their own emancipation and who respond to injustices by putting their hopes in the next election, rather than taking direct action themselves.[13] In 1912, De Cleyre claimed that the "main evil" of parliamentary politics was "that it destroys initiative, quenches the individual rebellious spirit, teaches people to rely on someone else to do for them what they should do for themselves, what they alone can do for themselves."[14] Decades later, Rocker was convinced that this is what had occurred. He wrote in 1938 that "participation in parliamentary politics has affected the Socialist labor movement like an insidious poison. It destroyed . . . the impulse to self-help, by inoculating people with the ruinous delusion that salvation always comes from above."[15]

Anarchists thought that this would be especially harmful during a revolutionary situation. Parliamentarism not only leads to workers becoming accustomed to elevating party leaders into positions of power. It also makes them believe in the possibility of good government and the false notion that emancipation can be achieved by simply changing who is in power. In a revolution, workers would thus most likely establish a new government based on minority rule by a political ruling class. This government would then, for reasons that will be discussed later, turn on and repress working-class social movements. A new system of domination and exploitation would arise, rather than a stateless, classless society based on self-management and free association. Given this, a key reason why anarchists rejected participating in electoral politics was because, to quote Malatesta, "we consider any methods that lead the people to believe that progress consists in a change of governing individuals, and revolution in a change of government form, to be dangerous, and directly counter to our purposes."[16]

Fourth, anarchists argued that state socialists were wrong to think that they could enter the existing capitalist state, transform it from within, and use it as a tool to build toward socialism. The capitalist state, which is a hierarchical institution that perpetuates the power of the economic and political ruling classes, would transform them. In 1869, before most socialist parties were formed, Bakunin predicted that working-class politicians would be "transplanted into a bourgeois environment, into a political atmosphere of wholly bourgeois political ideas, will cease to be actual workers and will become statesmen, they will become bourgeois, and perhaps more bourgeois than the bourgeoisie."[17] Later anarchists thought that this prediction had come true. Reclus claimed in 1898 that "socialist leaders who, finding themselves caught up in the electoral machine, end up being gradually transformed into nothing more than bourgeois with liberal ideas. They have placed themselves in determinate conditions that in turn determine them."[18] Kropotkin similarly wrote in 1913 that "as the socialists become a party of government and share power with the bourgeoisie, their socialism will necessarily fade: this is what has already happened."[19]

Anarchists thought this would consistently occur to any socialist party that engaged in parliamentarism due to a set of interlocking processes. Most obviously, socialist politicians would be corrupted by the exercise of state power, the intrigues of parliament, and the financial offers of wealthy patrons. Reclus argued that the state is "a collection of individuals placed in a specific milieu and subjected to its influence. Those individuals are raised up above their fellow citizens in dignity, power, and preferential treatment, and are consequently compelled to think themselves superior to the common people. Yet in reality the multitude of temptations besetting them almost inevitably leads them to fall below the general level."[20] As a result of this, socialist politicians with "the best of intentions" may initially "fervently desire" the abolition of capitalism and the state "but new relationships and conditions change them little by little. Their morality changes along with their self-interest, and, thinking themselves eternally loyal to the cause and to their constituents, they inevitably become disloyal."[21]

Socialist parties that attain power within parliament would, in order to exercise that power, have to become effective managers of the bourgeois state and the national economy. Doing so requires, given the nature of capitalism and the state as social structures, the ongoing reproduction of the domination and exploitation of the working classes. As a result, state socialists in power would inevitably develop interests opposed to the wider working classes and side with capital against labor in order to maintain their own position of rulership and influence. This would especially occur in response to workers engaging in direct action and thereby disrupting the smooth functioning of the economy. In Max Baginski's words: "The politics of parliaments are tailored to serve the needs of the bourgeois, the capitalist world. They administer this world and provide the violent means necessary to guarantee its continued existence: soldiers, police, and courts of law. Whosoever, as a representative of the workers, enters parliament or the government is faced with two choices; either he is superfluous or else he is an active accomplice in the administration and safeguarding of a political order founded on the exploitation of labor."[22]

The leadership of socialist parties would, in addition to this, come to view the interests of their nation-state and the interests of the party as increasingly intertwined because the party exercises power within a specific nation and owes its power to the votes of a national electorate. Thus, socialist parties are, to quote Rocker, "compelled by the iron logic of conditions to sacrifice their Socialist convictions bit by bit to the national policies of the state."[23] This would result in the labor movement being "gradually incorporated in the equipment of the national state" until it had become a social force that maintained the stability and "equilibrium" of capitalism.[24]

Socialist parties would be transformed not only by the corrupting effects of wielding state power but also by the compromises that parliamentary politics forced them to make. During this period, socialist parties typically had a maximum program and a minimum program. The maximum program were its long-term goals, such as universal human emancipation and the abolition of private property. The minimum program consisted of immediate improvements to be won within capitalism through legislation. These typically included such demands as universal suffrage, banning child labor, the eight-hour day, compulsory secular state education, free health care, and freedom of speech, the press, and assembly.[25] Anarchists thought that socialist parties would begin as revolutionary organizations that focused on the attainment of the minimum program but, gradually over time, become reformist organizations that had abandoned the maximum program and mistakenly viewed the minimum program as the essence of socialism.

This would consistently occur because, in order to win elections at both a local and national level, socialist parties must secure as many votes as possible by appealing to as many people as possible, including nonsocialists who would otherwise vote for republican, liberal, or conservative political parties. This would, especially in countries without universal suffrage, include people with class interests that were opposed to those of the working classes, such as small merchants and shopkeepers. Socialist parties, in addition to this, have to ensure that they maintain a legal existence and do not engage in activity that could preclude them from standing in elections or sitting in parliament. The need to appeal to as many voters as possible, alongside the need to operate within the confines of the law, would force socialist parties to: (a) reduce their political program to very minor reforms to capitalist society; and (b) oppose workers within the party, or affiliated trade unions, engaging in militant direct action that might scare voters away.[26] This process only accelerates over time as the socialist party grows in size and attracts, to quote Rocker, "bourgeois minds and career-hungry politicians into the Socialist camp."[27]

In order to achieve these minor social reforms, socialist parties, given the nature of the parliamentary system, would be compelled to form alliances with bourgeois political parties in order to form coalition governments or successfully pass laws in parliament.[28] For Bakunin, one of the most notable examples of the dangers of forming alliances with bourgeois political parties occurred when the Geneva section of the First International supported the 1872 electoral campaign of the lawyer Jean-Antoine Amberny, a member of both the First International and the bourgeois Radical Party. During his campaign, he publicly promised fellow members of the bourgeoisie that the First International in Geneva would not engage in strikes that year and, in so doing, acted against the interests of local construction workers, who were at the time, considering taking strike action in response to reduced wages. The leadership of the Geneva section chose to intervene on the side of Amberny and thereby sacrifice the direct struggle of workers themselves in order to protect the electability of a bourgeois candidate. This included unsuccessfully attempting to persuade construction workers to issue a declaration that they were not planning to go on strike.[29] In response to these events, Bakunin concluded that "whenever workers' associations ally themselves with the politics of the bourgeoisie, they can only become, willingly or unwillingly, their instrument."[30]

Anarchists predicted that the combined effect of these various processes, which are inherent in parliamentarianism as a social structure, would result in socialist parties abandoning their revolutionary ideas and becoming socialist in name only. State socialists at the time proclaimed that the parliamentary struggle was merely a means to the end of constructing the mass revolutionary socialist movements that would abolish class society. Anarchists replied that, given the forms of practice that constituted parliamentarism, what was once a means to an end would become an end in and of itself. Socialist parties would become mere reform movements that defended the status quo and only aimed at the improvement of conditions within the cage of capitalism and the state.[31]

A state socialist might reply that although anarchists are correct about the dangers of parliamentarism, socialist parties could participate in elections and parliament solely as a means to spread their ideas and critique the ruling classes. Anarchists thought such a strategy was mistaken because it ignored the manner in which participation in elections and parliament transforms people and organizations independently of their intentions. In 1928, Berkman noted that state socialists had initially claimed that they only meant to engage in parliamentarism "for the purpose of propaganda," but this "proved the undoing of Socialism" because they had failed to realize that "the means you use to attain your object soon themselves become your object."[32] He explained,

Little by little they changed their attitude. Instead of elec-
tioneering being merely an educational method, it gradually
became their only aim to secure political office, to get elected
to legislative bodies and other government positions. The
change naturally led the Socialists to tone down their revolutionary ardor; it compelled them to soften their criticism of
capitalism and government in order to avoid persecution and
secure more votes. Today the main stress of Socialist propaganda is not laid any more on the educational value of politics
but on the actual election of Socialists to office.[33]

Anarchists thought that their critique of parliamentarism was
confirmed by the history of state socialism. To focus on France, the
socialist Alexandre Millerand joined the bourgeois cabinet of Pierre
Waldeck-Rousseau in 1899 and became Minister of Commerce and
Industry. His colleagues included the Minister of War, Gaston de
Galliffet, who had ordered the murder of a large number of workers during the suppression of the Paris Commune. Once in power,
Millerand attempted to establish compulsory arbitration in industrial disputes and thereby harm the ability of trade unions to engage
in direct action. Pouget responded to this by labeling Millerand a
"prisoner of Capital" who "could not break the mold; he is only a cog
in the machine of oppression and whether he wishes it or not he
must, as minister, participate in the job of crushing the proletariat."[34]
Several years later, in 1906, socialist René Viviani became Minister
of Labor and, under his watch, nineteen workers were killed and
an estimated seven hundred were injured due to state repression
during strike actions. This state repression included forty thousand
soldiers being sent to police a miner's strike in 1906, launched in
response to a mining accident that took the lives of 1,100 miners. In
1910, Aristide Briand, who had once been a socialist and an advocate
of the general strike, joined Viviani in government as Minister of the
Interior. He proceeded to defeat a French railway strike by arresting

the strike committee, declaring a military emergency, and conscripting the railway workers into the army. In so doing, he subjected any worker who refused to work to martial law and the potential punishment of execution for disobeying orders.[35]

In 1914, World War I broke out and the majority of socialist political parties in Europe responded by siding with their respective governments. A minority of state socialists, which grew in size as the war progressed, remained committed to working-class internationalism, opposed all sides in the war, and organized the antimilitarist Zimmerwald Conference in 1915. The majority of the anarchist movement, in comparison, refused to side with any state in the conflict and suffered a significant amount of state repression due to this.[36] Anarchists did not think that socialist political parties abandoned antimilitarism simply due to the treachery or negative personality traits of politicians. Rather, they focused on the manner in which socialist parties had been transformed through the social structures they participated in and the forms of practice that constituted them. Berkman argued in 1928 that "the life we lead, the environment we live in, the thoughts we think, and the deeds we do—all subtly fashion our character and make us what we are. The Socialists' long political activity and cooperation with bourgeois politics gradually turned their thoughts and mental habits from Socialist ways of thinking."[37] This gradual process culminated in socialist parties abandoning their principles and becoming "the handmaiden of the militarists and jingo nationalists" who "sent the toilers to murder each other."[38]

From these and other events, anarchists concluded that their predictions had come true. State socialists who entered parliament in order to work toward the conquest of political power and the abolition of classes had not conquered the state. The state had conquered them, and genuine socialist parties had, gradually over time, become fundamentally bourgeois and opposed to the self-emancipation of the working classes.

Workers' State

Anarchists did not limit themselves to critiquing parliamentarism within the existing bourgeois state. They went further and rejected the strategy of overthrowing the bourgeois state and transforming it into, or replacing it with, a workers' state. They viewed the conquest of state power as a means that would never achieve the ends of a stateless, classless society. To understand why, one must first understand the anarchist theory of the state.

Anarchists argued that, given their in-depth analysis of the state as a social structure both historically and when they were writing, the state is necessarily a centralized and hierarchical institution wielded by a political ruling class. This class possesses the authority to make laws and issue commands at a societal level that others must obey due to the threat or exercise of institutionalized force. Kropotkin was convinced that this was "the essence of every State" and that, if an organization ceased to be structured in this manner, then "it ceases to be the State."[39] Since the state is a centralized and hierarchical institution that rules over an extended territory, it follows that the political power of the so-called workers' state could not in reality be wielded by the working classes as a whole. State power would at best be exercised by a minority of elected representatives acting in the name of the working classes. Bakunin predicted "it is bound to be impossible for a few thousand, let alone tens or hundreds of thousands of men to wield that power effectively. It will have to be exercised by proxy, which means entrusting it to a group of men elected to represent and govern them."[40]

Anarchists thought that there was an inherent connection between the organizational form and function of any social structure. And the organizational form of the state did not develop by accident. The state is structured in a hierarchical and centralized manner because of the function that it performs and was created to perform: establishing and maintaining the domination and exploitation of the working classes by the ruling classes. This applied not only to monarchies and individual dictatorships but also to republics governed by parliaments of elected representatives. A social structure characterized by a specific organizational form cannot be used to perform just any possible function. Centralization and hierarchy enable and result in the rule of a minority over a majority. Therefore, the state cannot be transformed into an instrument of liberation simply by writing a new constitution or electing good people with the right ideas into positions of authority. The minority of governors who actually exercise state power would, even if they were genuine socialists elected by universal suffrage, become tyrants who dominate and exploit the majority of the population.[41]

This would occur due to a specific set of processes. Since the state is a social structure like any other, it follows that it is constituted by social relation and forms of practice that produce and reproduce people with particular capacities, drives, and consciousness. According to Malatesta, "the government is the aggregate of the governors ... those who have the power to make laws, to regulate relations between men, and to force obedience to these laws."[42] This force is exercised via various institutionalized mechanisms of coercion, such as the police, army, courts, and prisons. The exercise of state power is therefore necessarily constituted by social relations of command and obedience, of domination and subordination. The minority of socialists who wield this power will use it to implement their own ideas and further their interests. In so doing, they will inevitably come into conflict with different groups of workers who have ideas and interests of their own. This will especially occur with workers who are other kinds of socialist. Given the vast differences in power, the workers will be compelled to follow the commands of their superiors. If they do not do so and choose to ignore, resist, or rebel against the will of the governors they will be met with violent state repression, including censorship, beatings, arrest, imprisonment, and even execution. The result is always the same: workers would not self-determine their lives or the society in which they lived. They would instead be subject to the will of a governing minority. As Malatesta explained, "a government . . . already constitutes a class privileged and separated from the rest of the community. Such a class, like every elected body, will seek instinctively to enlarge its powers; to place itself above the control of the people; to impose its tendencies, and to make its own interests predominate. Placed in a privileged position, the government always finds itself in antagonism to the masses, of whose forces it disposes."[43]

One might object by arguing that these socialist representatives are workers themselves and so do not form a class distinct from the workers who elected them. Bakunin responded to this argument in 1873. He insisted that the governing minority are "*former* workers, who, as soon as they become rulers or representatives of the people will cease to be workers and will begin to look upon the whole workers' world from the heights of the state. They will no longer represent the people but themselves and their own pretensions to govern the people."[44] In other words, they have transitioned from being members of the working classes to being members of the political ruling class in control of the state. State socialists fail to realize that class is not only about a person's relationship to the means of production. It is also determined by a person's relationship to the means of institutionalized coercion. The so-called dictatorship of the proletariat would therefore not be based on the self-rule of the proletariat. It would, to quote Malatesta in 1897, "be the dictatorship of 'Party' over people, and of a handful of men over 'Party.'"[45]

Anarchists argued that a fundamentally new function—the self-management of social life by producers themselves—requires the construction of fundamentally new social structures. These new organs need an organizational form that actually enables and leads to the realization of the desired function. For this to occur, the organs of self-management have to be developed by working-class social movements themselves engaging in a process of experimentation during the course of the class struggle. According to anarchists, these new organs are, as we have seen, workplace assemblies, community assemblies, and workers' militias linked together through formal federations and/or informal social networks.[46]

If state socialists advocated the destruction of the capitalist state and the creation of a new workers' state that was genuinely nothing but the self-rule of the working classes, then the disagreement with anarchists would largely be a semantic disagreement about how to define a state. In 1897, Malatesta considered the possibility of a social democrat who sincerely wanted to abolish the state:

> If they meant that, even as they capture it, they want to abolish the State ... disband any armed governmental force, do away with all legislative powers ... and promote the organization of society from the bottom up through the free federation of producer and consumer groups, then the entire issue would boil down to this: that they express by certain words the same ideas that we express by other words. Saying *we want to storm the fortress and destroy it*, and saying *we want to seize that fortress to demolish it* means one and the same thing.[47]

He knew, however, that the vast majority of state socialists did not advocate federations of workplace assemblies, community assemblies, and workers' militias—the true organs of worker self-rule—and then simply choose to call these systems of organization a state.[48] In June 1919, Malatesta wrote that the Bolsheviks did not mean by "the dictatorship of the proletariat" merely "the effective power of all the workers intent on breaking down capitalist society" by expropriating the ruling classes and creating social structures in which "there would be no place for a class that exploited and oppressed the producers."[49] If this is what "the dictatorship of the proletariat" meant then "our dissent would have to do only with words."[50] In reality, and judging by their actions, the Bolsheviks meant "a dictatorship of a party, or rather of the heads of a party; and it is a true dictatorship, with its decrees, its penal laws, its executive agents and above all with its armed force that serves today also to defend the revolution against its external enemies, but that will serve tomorrow to impose upon the workers the will of the dictators, to arrest the revolution, consolidate the new interests and finally defend a new privileged class against the masses."[51]

According to state-socialist theory, a workers' state would only exist during the transition from capitalism to a stateless, classless society. The state is the coercive instrument by which one economic class rules over and represses another economic class. A workers' state would be the social structure through which the proletariat ruled over and repressed the bourgeoisie. Exercising this political power, the proletariat would reorganize the economy and establish state ownership and control of the means of production and land. In so doing, they would abolish class. Once class had been abolished, the economic basis for the state would cease to exist, since there would no longer be a division between a class who ruled and a class who was ruled over.[52] The workers' state would, to quote Engels, wither away such that "the government of persons is replaced by the administration of things and by the conduct of processes of production. The State is not 'abolished.' *It dies out*."[53] Once this had occurred, society would be organized via "a free and equal association of the producers."[54]

Anarchists living in the nineteenth century were not convinced by this argument. Decades before the Russian revolution and the emergence of the USSR, anarchists predicted that a workers' state would not die out after the abolition of capitalism. It would instead continuously reproduce itself as a social structure. This is because the forms of practice involved in either exercising or being subject to state power produce people with traits that reproduce the state as a dominant structure, rather than people who will want to and be able to abolish the state. In exercising state power, socialist governors would not only change the world but also change themselves. They would acquire distinct class interests as members of the political ruling class and come to focus on maintaining and expanding their own power over the working classes, rather than allowing it to be abolished in favor of a stateless, classless society.

In 1881, Cafiero declared that any socialist who says "they wish to take over the State in order to destroy it once the struggle is over" is "either seeking to mislead us or are deceiving themselves. . . . No power, no authority in the world has ever destroyed itself. No tyrant has ever dismantled a fortress once he has entered it. On the contrary, every authoritarian organism, every tyranny tends always to spread, to establish itself even more, by its very nature. Power inebriates and even the best can become the worst once they are vested with authority."[55] In short, to quote Bakunin, the "habit of commanding . . . [and] the exercise of power never fail to produce this demoralization: *contempt for the masses, and, for the man in power, an exaggerated sense of his own worth.*"[56]

Anarchists thought this would occur irrespective of people's good intentions due to the manner in which they are shaped by the social structures they constitute and participate in. Malatesta wrote, "it is not a question here of the good faith or good will of this man or of that, but of the necessity of situations and the general tendencies that men exhibit when they find themselves in certain circumstances."[57] Bakunin similarly claimed that those who exercised state power would be transformed by "the iron logic of their position, the force of circumstances inherent in certain hierarchical and profitable political relationships." This would occur regardless of their "sentiments, intentions, or good impulses."[58]

The existence of a state ruled by a minority political ruling class would simultaneously have a dire effect on the working classes in general. Instead of directly self-managing their lives themselves, the working classes would be subject to the rule of a governing minority and so engage in forms of practice that lead them to become accustomed to oppressive social relationships after their supposed liberation. They would learn to obey and defer to their superiors rather than to think and act for themselves. Rather than learning how to associate with others as equals, they would learn to put those in power on a pedestal and venerate them in just the same way that people under capitalism learn to hero worship so-called "captains of industry" or political figureheads like royal families and charismatic presidents. Workers would come to support the ongoing existence of the state and view it as a natural and necessary aspect of human existence that cannot be changed.[59] Authority, to quote Berkman, "debases its victims" and "makes those subject to it acquiesce in wrong, subservient, and servile."[60]

Anarchists predicted that the minority political ruling class in control of the so-called workers' state would, in order to defend and maintain their position of authority, create a new economic ruling class that owed them allegiance and so would protect their class interests. This new economic ruling class would initially appear within the state bureaucracy itself given that the so-called workers' state would own and manage the whole or majority of the economy. Over time, the new economic ruling class would grow in power due to the extreme importance of production and distribution in social life and gradually transform the state into an institution that primarily serves their distinct economic interests. This would culminate in the reintroduction of private property and market capitalism.[61] The state was, to quote Fabbri, "more than an outcome of class divisions; it is, at one and the same time, the creator of privilege, thereby bringing about new class divisions."[62] According to Malatesta, "anyone in power means to stay there, and no matter what the costs he intends to impose his will—and since wealth is a very effective instrument of power, the ruler, even if he personally does not abuse or steal, he promotes the rise of a class around him that owes to him its privileges and has a vested interest in his remaining in power. . . . Abolish private property without abolishing government, and the former will be resurrected by those who govern."[63]

Supporters of workers' states in this period generally believed that state socialism was a necessary transitional phase between capitalism and communism. Anarchists replied that state socialism would ultimately be the transitional phase between capitalism and capitalism. Given the self-reproducing nature of the state, and its tendency to establish new class divisions, it could not be used to achieve a stateless, classless society. Although, as Bakunin noted, state socialists claimed that "this state yoke, this dictatorship, is a necessary transitional device for achieving the total liberation of the people; anarchy, or freedom, is the goal, and the state, or dictatorship the means," they failed to realize that "no dictatorship can have any other objective than to perpetuate itself, and that it can engender and nurture only slavery in the people who endure it."[64] The state would never wither away. It had to be intentionally and violently destroyed.[65]

State Capitalism

From an economic perspective, anarchists also rejected the idea that a state socialist society would be socialist at all. They thought it was more appropriate to label such a society *state capitalism*. The term was used by Lenin and the Bolsheviks in a different sense to refer to the Soviet Republic's New Economic Policy of 1921, in which capitalist markets and small private businesses existed alongside state ownership and management of large-scale industry but were subject to control by a self-proclaimed workers' state. The earlier and broader anarchist usage of the term should not be confused with this.[66] It should also be kept in mind that the anarchist claim that state socialist societies would be instances of state capitalism was distinct from their prediction that state socialism would result in the resurrection of private property and market capitalism. From this perspective, it would begin as one form of capitalism and then later transform into another kind of capitalism.

State socialists aim to establish state ownership of the means of production and land, organize production and distribution through centralized state planning, and have workers become employees of the state. Were this to happen then, a single entity—the state—would own and control the whole or the majority of the economy. Under this system, the economy would, due to the state's centralized and hierarchical nature, be owned and controlled by the minority of people who in fact wielded state power, rather than the working classes they claimed to represent. These workers would, instead of directly owning and controlling the economy themselves through organs of self-management, labor within state-owned workplaces hierarchically managed by state bureaucrats. These bureaucrats would implement the policies decided by the minority ruling class who, even if elected via universal suffrage, actually exercise decision-making power on a day-to-day basis. Under such a system, workers become wage laborers employed by the state and subject to its domination within the workplace in the same manner that they had previously been employed and dominated by individual capitalists and landowners.

This perspective can be seen throughout anarchist texts. Bakunin predicted in *Statism and Anarchy* that the leaders of social- ist parties would, if they seized state power, concentrate "in their own hands all commercial, industrial, agricultural, and even sci- entific production and will divide the people into two armies, one industrial and one agrarian, under the direct command of state engi- neers, who will form a new privileged scientific and political class."[67] In *Modern Science and Anarchy*, Kropotkin claimed that anarchists rejected "the new form of wage-labor which would arise if the State took possession of the means of production and exchange, as it has already taken possession of the railways, the post office, education, national security [*l'assurance mutuelle*], and defense of the territory. New powers, industrial powers . . . would create a new, formidable instrument of tyranny."[68] Kropotkin referred to such a society as "state capitalism" on numerous occasions.[69]

State socialism would therefore lead to a reconfiguration of class society rather than the abolition of classes and the self-management of production and distribution by producers and consumers themselves. The existing economic and political ruling classes—capitalists, landowners, bankers, politicians, judges, generals etc.—would be replaced by or subordinated to a new economic and political ruling class—the socialist party leadership—which exercised power through a single institution: the state. This new economic and political ruling class would, in turn, be aided by a vast array of state bureaucrats who would serve as a managerial class that was subject to the authority of the socialist party leadership but at the same time exercised power over the working classes. In Malatesta's words, "whoever has dominion over things, has dominion over men; whoever governs production governs the producers; whoever controls consumption lords it over the consumer. The question is this: either things are administered in accordance with agreements freely reached by those concerned, in which case we have anarchy, or they are administered in accordance with law made by the administrators, and we have Government, the State, which inevitably turns tyrannical."[70]

Since state socialists sought to seize existing state power, it followed that the managerial class would be largely composed of the same bureaucrats who had previously managed the market-capitalist state. State socialists would transform certain aspects of the state during their seizure of state power, such as writing a new constitution, but the bulk of the state's bureaucratic machinery would remain intact since the state could not function without it. This would occur even if state socialists genuinely wanted to smash the old state bureaucracy and immediately construct a new one. During a revolutionary period, the leaders of the socialist party would not be in the position to replace or fundamentally reorganize the state bureaucracy, especially in societies where most people were illiterate. They would instead be forced by circumstances to use, and massively expand, the previously existing state bureaucracy in order to implement their plans as rapidly and as effectively as possible, nationalizing industry and organizing the economy through central planning.

For Kropotkin, this was no different from when republicans overthrew monarchies. The form of the state was altered, but the state bureaucracy continued to operate largely as before. He wrote that, in France, "the Third Republic, in spite of its republican form of government, remained monarchist in its essence." This was because,

> Those holding power have changed the name; but all this immense ministerial scaffolding, all this centralized organization of bureaucrats, all this imitation of the Rome of the Caesars which has been developed in France, all this formidable organization to ensure and extend the exploitation of the masses in favor of a few privileged groups that is the essence of the State-institution—all that remained. And these cogs [of the bureaucratic machine] continue, as in the past, to exchange their fifty documents when the wind has blown down a tree onto a national highway, and to pour the millions deducted from the nation into the coffers of the privileged. The [official] stamp on the documents has changed; but the State, its spirit, its organs, its territorial centralization, its centralization of functions, its favoritism, its role as creator of monopolies, have remained. Like an octopus, they expand [their grip] on the country day-by-day.[71]

State socialism would therefore not only be a reconfiguration of class society. It would also be an expansion of existing class society in so far as the bulk of the state machinery would continue to operate largely as before and this state machinery would move from organizing only certain aspects of the economy—the post office, trains etc.—to organizing the whole or most of the economy.

Within such a society, the state would, for all intents and purposes, act as a single massive capitalist, since it now performed the various functions that were previously performed under market capitalism by multiple individual capitalists owning and directing different aspects of the economy. As a result, anarchists saw in state socialism not the abolition of classes, but the replacement of individual capitalists competing in a market with a single state capitalist that alone owned, directed, and planned the economy.[72] Bakunin, for example, claimed that under state socialism the state would *"become the sole proprietor* . . . the single capitalist, banker, financier, organizer, the director of all national work and the distributor of every product."[73] According to Kropotkin, state socialists aim to "seize the existing power structures and to retain and strengthen their control over them; in place of all of today's ruling classes (landlords, industrialists, merchants, bankers, etc.) they strive to create one single proprietor—the State—to rule over all land, all works and factories, all accumulated wealth, and to be run by a Parliament."[74] Anarchists rejected this vision and could not "see in the coming revolution a mere . . . replacement of the current capitalists by the State [as sole] capitalist."[75]

Anarchists were also afraid that state socialists would create something much worse than state capitalism ruled by an elected parliament. In centralizing so much economic and political power into the hands of the state, they were creating an institution that could, in turn, be seized by a dictator and used to establish an even more tyrannical society. Kropotkin wrote in 1913 that "as long as the statist socialists do not abandon their dream of socializing the instruments of labor in the hands of a centralized State, the inevitable result of their attempts at State Capitalism and the Socialist state

will be the failure of their dreams and military dictatorship." The
state they created during a period of revolutionary turmoil "would
be the stepping-stone for a dictator, representing the reaction." This
would merely be a repeat of what had already happened after the
French revolutions of 1793 and 1848. In the "centralized State ... created by the Jacobins, Napoleon I found the ground already prepared
for the Empire. Similarly, fifty years later, Napoleon III found in the
dreams of a centralized democratic republic which developed in
France after [the revolution of] 1848 the ready-made elements for
the Second Empire."[76]

It was for these reasons that Kropotkin warned revolutionaries
that the state is, "an octopus with a thousand heads and a thousand
suckers, like the sea monsters of the old tales, it makes it possible
to envelop all society and to channel all individual efforts so as to
make them result in the enrichment and governmental monopoly
of the privileged classes."[77] As a result, "if the revolution does not
crush the octopus, if it does not destroy its head and cut off its arms
and suckers, it will be strangled by the beast. The revolution itself
will be placed at the service of monopoly, as was the [French] revolution of 1793."[78]

For anarchists, these predictions were soon proven true by
the one-party Bolshevik state that was established during the 1917
Russian revolution and the subsequent seizure of this state by
Stalin and his supporters after Lenin's death in January 1924.[79] As
early as June 1919, Malatesta wrote that although "Lenin, Trotsky
and their companions are certainly sincere revolutionaries ... they
prepare the governmental cadres that will serve those that will
come, who will profit from the revolution and kill it. They will be
the first victims of their method, and with them, I fear, will fall the
revolution."[80]

Anarchists who had witnessed the revolution first hand subsequently wrote a number of critiques of the Bolsheviks. This included
Goldman, who was deported from the United States to Russia in

1920. She wrote in December 1922 that the Bolsheviks had succeeded only in creating an "all-powerful, centralized Government with State Capitalism as its economic expression," which was based on "the masking of autocracy by proletarian slogans."[81] The Bolsheviks violently repressed all rival forms of socialism, including anarchists, left socialist-revolutionaries, and Mensheviks, in order to keep power within the Communist Party. Members of the Party "who were suspected of an independent attitude" and challenged the party leadership were expelled.[82] In parallel to this, the organs of self-management that had been created by workers themselves during the revolution—soviets, factory committees, trade unions, and cooperatives—were "either subordinated to the needs of the new State or destroyed altogether."[83] The consequence of this was that "the triumph of the State meant the defeat of the Revolution."[84] This occurred because the "revolutionary methods" of the Bolsheviks were not "in tune with revolutionary aims."[85]

The tragedy of the Russian Revolution demonstrated, according to anarchists, that they had been right and state socialists had been wrong. The liberation of the working classes could only be achieved through them crushing state power and building their own organs of self-management and class power. These arguments have, from an anarchist perspective, only proven stronger with time, given that subsequent state socialist revolutions in China, Cuba, and Vietnam have, like their predecessor in Russia, failed to produce a substantially free and equal society in which the working classes themselves own the means of production and self-manage their lives within both the workplace and wider society, let alone a state in the process of withering away. Despite numerous achievements within certain domains, such as increasing literacy rates or improving healthcare, these societies have not laid the foundations from which a stateless, classless, moneyless society based on distribution according to need could possibly emerge.

Anarchism and Political Struggle

The anarchist rejection of seizing state power has led some
Marxists to assert that anarchists opposed, and so ignored the
need for, political struggle.[86] This argument dates back to Marx and
Engels themselves. Marx wrote in an 1870 letter to Paul Lafargue
that Bakunin thought that the industrial working class "must not
occupy itself with *politics*" and instead "only organize themselves by
trades-unions," and thus making what Marx saw as the fatal error of
allowing "the governments, these great trade-unions of the ruling
classes, to do as they like." Bakunin had, according to Marx, failed to
see "that every class movement as a class movement, is necessarily
and was always a *political* movement."[87] After the First International's
Hague Congress of 1872, Marx gave a speech in which he said that "a
group has been formed in our midst which advocates that the workers should abstain from political activity" and thereby ignored that
"the worker will have to seize political supremacy to establish the
new organization of labor."[88] Engels likewise claimed in an 1872 letter to Louis Pio that anarchists in the First International advocated
the "*complete abstention from all political activity, and especially from
all elections.*"[89]

Anarchists in Marx's time and beyond did not, however, reject
political struggle in and of itself. They rejected one form of political struggle—attempting to conquer state power via elections or
armed insurrection—in favor of a different form of political struggle—engaging in direct action outside of and against the state with
the long-term aim of abolishing it. This position was grounded in
the idea that working-class social movements should only engage
in forms of political struggle that built toward a social revolution
that abolished capitalism and the state, rather than leading workers
away from it. As Malatesta wrote, anarchists embraced "political
struggle" in the sense of "struggle against the government and not
co-operation with the government," because "if you truly want to

overthrow the system, then you must clearly place yourself outside and against the system itself."[90] For many anarchists, this political struggle included engaging in direct action to gain or enforce political liberties that expanded the ability of workers to self-organize, such as freedom of assembly, freedom of speech, and freedom of the press.[91]

The anarchist view on political struggle can be seen in Bakunin's distinction between bourgeois reformist politics and the revolutionary proletarian politics of the anarchist movement. According to Bakunin, "it would be the death of the proletariat, if it were preoccupied exclusively and solely with economic matters" and ignored "political questions."[92] This is because any significant attempt by the working classes to emancipate themselves economically will be met by state violence. In Bakunin's words, *the political question is inseparable from the economic question . . .* politics—the institution and mutual relations of States—has no other object except that of ensuring that the ruling classes can legally exploit the proletariat. So in consequence, the moment the proletariat wishes to free itself, it is forced to consider politics—to fight it and overcome it."[93] The First International would for this same reason, "be compelled to intervene in politics so long as it is forced to struggle against the bourgeoisie."[94] Its task as an organization "is not just some economic or a simply material creative activity, it is at the same time and to the same degree an eminently political process."[95]

The question for Bakunin was not whether we should engage in politics but what form our political interventions should take. He was careful to distinguish between bourgeois politics, which did not aim to achieve the immediate emancipation of workers, and the politics of labor or social revolution, which aimed to abolish the state in order to establish socialism.[96] Given this, "It is not true . . . to say that we completely ignore politics. We do not ignore it, for we definitely want to destroy it. And here we have the essential point separating us from political parties and bourgeois radical Socialists.

Their politics consists in making use of, reforming, and transform-ing the politics of the State, whereas our politics, the only kind we admit, is the total *abolition* of the State, and of the politics which is its necessary manifestation."[97]

Bakunin's distinction between bourgeois politics and revolu-tionary proletarian politics was shared by other anarchists. During the First International's 1872 Hague Congress, which was attended by Marx and Engels, Guillaume claimed that the anarchist idea of politics "was not political indifferentism, but a special kind of politics negating bourgeois politics and which we should call the politics of labor," which sought *"the destruction of political power."*[98] Andrea Costa wrote, with Bakunin's assistance, a program for the Italian section of the Saint-Imier International sometime in late 1872. The program distinguished between the "negative politics" of abolishing ruling-class institutions and the "positive politics" of constructing a new society through the "revolutionary power" of the working classes.[99] Over two decades later, in 1897, Malatesta remarked that "who has outdone us in arguing that the battle against capitalism has to be harnessed to the fight against the State, mean-ing the political struggle? There is a school of thought these days in which political struggle means achieving public office through elections: but . . . logic forces other methods of struggle upon those seeking to do away with government, rather than capture it."[100]

For Malatesta, like Bakunin before him, economic struggles would be transformed into political struggles. He argued that "from the economic struggle one must pass to the political struggle, that is to the struggle against government" because "workers who want to free themselves, or even only to effectively improve their condi-tions, will be faced with the need to defend themselves from the government" that violently protects private property rights and the interests of the economic ruling classes.[101] Workers will be forced to "oppose the rifles and guns which defend property with the more effective means that the people will be able to find to defeat force by force."[102] The manner in which capitalism and the state support and cocreate one another led Malatesta to conclude that the economic struggle against capitalism and the political struggle against the state are so interconnected that they should be viewed as two aspects of a single struggle against the ruling classes, rather than as two separate struggles.[103]

A significant number of anarchists held that politics would be abolished via the social revolution. One Spanish anarchist poem, for example, declared that "politics" would "disappear from the world" via "the establishment of anarchy."[104] Other anarchists, in comparison, thought that politics was not inherently state-centric and would continue to exist, albeit in a very different form, after the abolition of the state. Kropotkin argued that "new forms of economical life will require also new forms of political life, and these new forms cannot be a reinforcement of the power of the State by giving up in its hands the production and distribution of wealth, and its exchange."[105] These new forms of political life must instead be "created by the workers themselves, in *their* unions, *their* federations, completely outside the State."[106] Given this, "The free Commune . . . is the *political* form that the *social* revolution must take."[107]

Different Kinds of Anarchism

Anarchists in this historical period generally shared the basic strategic commitments that have been explained in Chapters 4 and 5. They nonetheless also disagreed with one another about a wide variety of more specific topics. This included such questions as what kind of organizations they should build, what tactics they should engage in, and how anarchists should act to help bring about the social revolution. Broadly speaking the anarchist movement can be divided into two main strategic schools of thought: insurrectionist anarchism and mass anarchism. Insurrectionist anarchism advocated the formation of small, loosely organized groups that attempted to trigger, or at least build toward, a social revolution by engaging in an escalating series of individual and collective violent attacks against the ruling classes and their institutions. Mass anarchism, in comparison, advocated the formation of large-scale formal organizations that struggled for immediate reforms in the present via direct action. They viewed such struggles as the most effective means to construct a mass movement capable of launching a social revolution via an armed insurrection.[108]

The terms insurrectionist anarchist and mass anarchist were not used by anarchists historically and are anachronistic. In Spain during the 1880s, the debate occurred between anarchist communists (insurrectionist anarchists) and anarchist collectivists (mass anarchists). In Italy during the 1890s and 1900s, it occurred between anarchist communists who were either organizationalists (mass anarchists) or antiorganizationalists (insurrectionist anarchists). Given the wide variety of different terms that were used historically, I decided to make things clearer by using the same terminology consistently. This terminology, which was coined by the historian Lucian van der Walt, is potentially misleading and two points of clarification must be made.

First, mass anarchists advocated and engaged in armed insurrections, while insurrectionist anarchists ultimately aimed to create a mass working-class social movement. Second, although one can distinguish between insurrectionist anarchism and mass anarchism these are ideal types and individuals cannot always be neatly categorized into one or the other due to their combining elements of both or only subscribing to certain aspects of the theory in question. The anarchist movement contained a great deal of intellectual diversity and, although some anarchists were dogmatic, there were no rigid barriers between different kinds of anarchism that might, in principle, prevent one kind of anarchist learning from and being influenced by another kind of anarchist. Most Italian anarchists who lived in North Beach, San Francisco, for example, subscribed to multiple publications espousing different kinds of anarchism and interacted socially with anarchists from other tendencies.[109] The distinction between insurrectionist anarchism and mass anarchism should be viewed as a simplification that is helpful for thinking about the major strategic disagreements within the anarchist movement, rather than being a perfect description of the ideological complexity of the anarchist movement. In the next several chapters, I will examine the various forms that anarchism took during the late nineteenth and early twentieth centuries.

CHAPTER 6

Insurrectionist Anarchism

Insurrectionist anarchists advocated the formation of small, loosely organized groups that met to learn and discuss ideas, plan direct action, organize talks and countercultural activities—such as dances and picnics—produce or distribute anarchist literature, and engage in violent acts of revolt against the ruling classes and their institutions.[1] The ultimate aim of these different methods of action was the same: to inspire or evoke a revolutionary upsurge by the working classes. In theory, anarchists advocating, praising, and engaging in violent attacks against the ruling classes and their institutions would provoke or inspire significant segments of the working classes to rise up, which would in turn motivate others to join them in insurrection. This would lead to a chain reaction of uprisings spawning an ever-increasing number of revolts until the working classes had formed a mass movement, forcefully expropriated the ruling classes and abolished capitalism and the state in favor of an anarchist society.[2]

This strategy was advocated by Galleani. He held that "the way to revolution, whose initial phase must be the individual act of rebellion, inseparable from propaganda, from the mental preparation which understands it, integrates it, leading to larger and more frequent repetitions through which collective insurrections flow into the social revolution."[3] Although insurrectionist anarchists favored individual acts of rebellion, they also believed that the social revolution would be brought about by the working classes acting as a mass movement engaging in collective insurrections. Galleani endorsed "the direct and independent action of individuals and masses," including "rebellion, insurrection, the general strike, the social revolution."[4] Cafiero thought that a social revolution would require "the violence of the insurgent masses."[5]

The three main ideas that constituted insurrectionist anarchist strategy in this historical period were an opposition to formal organizations, a rejection of struggling for immediate reforms, and a commitment to propaganda of the deed. This chapter will establish what insurrectionists thought and how they used the theory of practice to justify or reject particular strategies. In particular, it will provide an overview of how the meaning of propaganda of the deed changed over time.

Opposition to Formal Organizations

Insurrectionist anarchists argued that anarchism as a movement should not be organized through large, formal organizations characterized by such things as having a constitution, elected delegates, yearly national congresses that passed congress resolutions, and an official membership. Insurrectionist anarchists were initially in favor of federations because anarchism as a movement developed within the federations of the First and Saint-Imier Internationals. Paul Brousse, for example, was one of the main theorists of propaganda of the deed but also participated in a French anarchist federation that was affiliated with the Saint-Imier International.[6] Similarly, during the 1880s, Most advocated propaganda of the deed, rejected the struggle for immediate reforms, and played a key role in the founding of the American national federation of the International Working People's Association.[7]

From the late 1870s onward, a significant segment of insurrectionist anarchists, such as Cafiero, came to reject formal organizations for strategic reasons, while still advocating federations as a key component of the future anarchist society. Eventually what had been a matter of strategy was transformed into a matter of principle and insurrectionist anarchists came to hold that all formal organizations were fundamentally incompatible with anarchist values and goals. It is difficult to establish how many insurrectionist anarchists there were because, unlike trade unions, they did not keep records of their size.[8]

Despite the fact that some insurrectionist anarchists claimed to reject all organization, they were not against organization in the sense of people coming together to act collectively as a group. Insurrectionist anarchists themselves usually distinguished between *free association*, which they supported, and *organization*, by which they meant formal organization, which they opposed. The Italian anarchist Giuseppe Ciancabilla wrote in 1899 that "organization (not free agreement, nor free association, we mean) is absolutely anti-anarchist."[9] In 1925, Galleani advocated a society based on cooperation, mutual agreement between groups, and *"the autonomy of the individual within the freedom of association."*[10] Yet he also thought that "organizationalists cannot find a form of organization compatible with their anarchist principles."[11] For this reason he opposed "the political organization of the anarchist party," by which he meant a specific anarchist organization, and "the organization of the craft and trade unions."[12]

Critics of insurrectionist anarchism were likewise aware that they did not literally reject all organization. The Spanish anarchist Juan Serrano y Oteiza, who advocated formal organization and revolutionary trade unionism, wrote in 1885 that his opponents within the movement, "do not accept any organization except that of a group, and therefore they do not have organized trade sections, nor do they have local federations, district federations or federations of

trade or trade unions. . . . Their only and exclusive form of organization are the groups or circles of social studies among which there
has not been established any pact or constituted any commission
which can serve as a center of relations between the respective
collective bodies that pursue the same ends."[13] Several years later
in 1890, Malatesta noted that antiorganizationalist anarchists "rack
their brains to come up with names to take the place of organization,
but in actual fact they quite sheepishly engage in organization or
attempts at organization."[14]

Insurrectionist anarchists opposed formal organizations for
two main reasons. First, they held that it made it too easy for the
state to infiltrate, persecute, and surveil the anarchist movement.
In 1874, a group of influential Italian anarchists argued that the
wave of state repression that the Italian section of the Saint-Imier
International had experienced was a product of how they had
primarily organized within a formal public federation. This had
enabled "bourgeois troublemakers and spies" to infiltrate the movement and provide the government with information such that they
could track the activities of anarchists and repress them at "the
opportune moment."[15]

From late 1878 onward, the amount of state repression that
Italian anarchists faced massively expanded. This occurred due to
the Italian ruling classes using an unsuccessful republican assassination attempt against King Umberto I of Italy as an opportunity
to destroy the International once and for all.[16] In 1879, Cafiero
responded to these events by arguing that anarchists should
establish "*secret and firm bonds* between all of us" because formal
organizations "display all our forces to the public, i.e., to the police"
and so reveal "how and where to strike us."[17]

One year later, the Italian state issued the killing blow to the
International in Italy when the high court ruled that any internationalist organization composed of five or more people was an
association of malefactors. This enabled the Italian state to arrest

and imprison anarchists simply for being anarchists, even if they had not planned or engaged in any illegal actions. At the same time, numerous anarchists were subject to searches of their home, suppression of newspapers, dissolution of groups, extreme limitations on their freedom of association and movement, and deportation to, and forcible confinement on, desolate islands near Sicily and southern Italy.[18] It was within this context of state repression that the Italian anarchist paper *La Gazetta Operaia* wrote in July 1887 that "experience teaches that a vast association of a revolutionary character easily offers its flank to the police, therefore to persecution. . . . United and fighting all together under the impetus of a vast association we run the risk of being crushed with a single blow by adversaries stronger than us."[19]

The second reason why insurrectionist anarchists opposed formal organization was that, from their perspective, formal organizations made people unfree and inhibited their membership's ability to act and take initiative.[20] This entailed that formal organizations were incompatible with the unity of means and ends, since they failed to produce the self-determining individuals needed for a successful social revolution and the production and reproduction of an anarchist society. This hostile attitude toward formal organization partly stemmed from the negative experiences anarchists had within the First International due to the actions of the General Council.[21]

Formal organizations were above all thought to mirror the organizational form of the state. In February 1887, the Italian anarchist paper *Humanitas* labeled formal organizations "a state in miniature" and argued that they destroyed "the spirit of initiative in individuals, who expect everything from this organization."[22] In 1925, Galleani similarly claimed that any formal organization "has its programme; i.e., its constitutional charter: in assemblies of group representatives it has its parliament: in its management, its boards and executive committees, it has its government. In short, it is a graduated superstructure of bodies a true hierarchy, no matter how disguised."[23]

According to Galleani, constitutions forced the formal organization to follow a particular set of procedures, rather than what was appropriate or necessary given ongoing events and the nature of the present struggle. Formal avenues for decision-making and action, such as congresses, filtered out original ideas and reaffirmed the orthodoxy of the organization. When workers wanted to take action themselves and implement their own ideas, they were instead instructed to go through the appropriate committee or were informed that a committee had already been set up to handle this task and would take care of matters. Even federations based on delegates were critiqued for leading to a situation in which representatives and those higher up in the organization made decisions that the wider membership accepted out of discipline, regardless of their own opinions and interests. In each case, the organization would take on a life of its own and control its membership.[24]

Galleani rejected the idea that delegates could represent others, even if they had been elected and mandated. This was because "every delegate . . . could represent only his own ideas and feelings, not those of his constituents, which are infinitely variable on any subject."[25] He thought it was impossible to "anarchically delegate to another person one's own thought, one's own energy, one's own will."[26] Galleani also rejected congress resolutions on the grounds that they subordinated the minority to the majority and thereby made people unfree. For Galleani, congresses were only useful and consistent with anarchism if they were just meetings that provided an occasion for individual militants to meet, share ideas, and work together.[27]

As an alternative to large formal organizations, insurrectionist anarchists advocated the formation of small, loosely organized groups. These affinity groups, which were also called circles or clubs, were either more or less permanent cells or were formed for a specific task and dissolved once it was complete. They typically had a membership of between four and twenty members and were given a wide variety of different names, such as Germinal (in honor of Émile Zola's novel), The Termites Libertarian Circle, The Barricade Group, The Right to be Idle Group, and the Revolutionary Propaganda Circle.[28] An 1885 article in Le Révolté claimed that "we do not believe in long-term associations, federations, etc. For us, a group should come together only for a clearly defined objective or short-term action; once the action is accomplished, the group should reform on a new basis, either with the same elements, or with new ones."[29]

Thus, anarchist affinity groups were viewed as superior to formal organizations because the fact that they were loosely structured and composed of a small group of people, who knew and trusted one another, meant that they simultaneously enabled freedom of initiative while also being more effective at avoiding infiltration, persecution, and state surveillance. If an affinity group was infiltrated or repressed by the state then, given its small size, the damage to the anarchist movement was less severe than when the same occurred to a large federation.[30] In 1890, Jean Grave argued in La Révolte that affinity groups accustom "individuals to bestir themselves, to act, without being bogged down in routine and immobility, thereby preparing the groupings of the society to come, by forcing individuals to act for themselves, to seek out one another on the basis of their inclinations, their affinities."[31] Affinity groups were, in other words, thought to prefigure the social relations of an anarchist society and so were constituted by forms of practice that developed individuals with the right kinds of radical capacities, drives, and consciousness for achieving anarchist goals.

This is not to say that insurrectionist anarchists thought that only small groups of people should engage in actions. Massive crowds containing numerous small affinity groups could, for example, riot without belonging to a formal organization. Large groups of people who were participating in an uprising could quickly form mass general assemblies in order to make agreements about what to do next. They could do so without establishing a federation, electing an administrative committee, or passing binding congress resolutions. Nor is it the case that affinity groups were completely isolated entities. Insurrectionist anarchists sought to achieve coordination between different groups via informal social networks, which were usually centered around specific periodicals, rather than through the establishment of a formal federation. This can be seen in the history of the paper *Cronaca Sovversiva*, which was edited by Galleani and based in the United States. It not only spread anarchist ideas and instilled a sense of anarchist identity in its readership, but also connected anarchist groups by publishing their correspondence and announcements in a single place that they all read. This facilitated both the exchange of information and enabled groups to engage in dialogue with one another and make collective decisions.[32]

Some insurrectionist anarchists were so committed to their rejection of formal organizations that they viewed those who advocated them as betraying the core principles of anarchism. This resulted in a great deal of polemical debate that could sometimes even turn violent. In September 1899, the antiorganizationalist anarchist barber Domenico Pazzaglia shot Malatesta in the leg during a meeting at a saloon in West Hoboken, New Jersey, due to Malatesta's advocacy of formal organizations. He responded in a truly anarchist fashion by refusing to tell the police who had shot him.[33]

Rejection of Struggling for Reforms

Insurrectionist anarchism opposed the strategy of struggling for immediate reforms in the present. As the paper *L'Insurrezione* argued in 1881, "anything that facilitates and brings the time of the insurrection nearer, is good; all that keeps it away through maintaining the appearance of progress, is bad. This is the principle that guides us."[34] This rejection of struggling for immediate reforms included not only parliamentary politics, which all anarchists rejected, but also participating within trade unions in order to struggle for higher wages, shorter working days, and improved working conditions. Those insurrectionists who did advocate participating within trade unions did so only when they thought it was a good opportunity to undermine the trade union bureaucracy, spread anarchist ideas, develop the spirit of revolt, and persuade workers that their involvement in the trade union was futile and would not achieve their emancipation. This included the organization of wildcat strikes that were not approved or supported by the trade union's leadership.[35]

Insurrectionist anarchists rejected struggling for immediate reforms for three main reasons. First, they held that reforms did not challenge, but rather rested upon, the ongoing existence of dominant institutions. Social movements that aim to win reforms will therefore end up consenting to and reproducing the existing economic and political system, rather than overthrowing it. They may start out as revolutionary, but the practice of struggling for reforms will, over time, cause radical capacities, drives and, consciousness to decay and be replaced by ones compatible with dominant structures. Reforms that are initially viewed as only a means or stepping stone to revolution will, over time, be transformed into the actual end goals of a movement's activity. For insurrectionist anarchists, this process of revolutionary movements being weakened by the struggle for reforms could be clearly seen in socialist political parties that became less and less radical over time in order to gain votes and pass reformist laws through political alliances with bourgeois parties.[36]

Second, they thought that the ruling classes only conceded reforms to the working classes in order to calm popular discontent. Although reforms might improve people's lives in the short term, they also stabilized class society and thereby perpetuated the suffering and oppression of the working classes. This is because the achievement of reforms can alter the consciousness of workers such that they come to mistakenly believe that the ruling classes are benevolent, view the state as a servant of the people, and put their hopes in politicians and the law. Reforms could, in short, have the dangerous effect of causing workers to desire a better and more humane master, rather than no master at all. According to Galleani, "reforms" are "the ballast the bourgeoisie throws overboard to lighten its old boat in the hope of saving the sad cargo of its privileges from sinking in the revolutionary storm."[37] Given this, reforms should be seen as the byproducts of threats to ruling class power that are granted when "attacks against the existing social institutions become more forceful and violent," rather than being the main immediate goal of political and economic struggle.[38]

Third, insurrectionists tended to subscribe to the iron law of wages, which had been advocated by the political economist David Ricardo and later popularized among socialists by Ferdinand Lassalle, who was one of the main founders of what would become German social democracy. The concept claimed that real wages under capitalism would always tend toward the amount of money required to secure the subsistence of the worker. For Ricardo and Lassalle, this was related to population growth: an expansion of the supply of labor would lead to a decrease in wages, and living costs would increase due to larger families.[39] The insurrectionist anarchists, in contrast, focused on the idea that any increase in wages that workers won through struggle would be canceled out by increases in the cost of living as capitalists and landlords charged more for basic necessities such as food and rent. If this were true, then fighting to win higher wages was futile, a waste of time and energy, since any wage increase would not last.[40]

In place of struggles for immediate reforms, insurrectionist anarchists advocated immediate violent confrontation with dominant institutions. Galleani argued that "tactics of corrosion and continuous attack should be preferred . . . immediate attempts at partial expropriation, individual rebellion and insurrection" or strikes that adopt "an openly revolutionary character" and seek, "through the inevitable use of force and violence, the unconditional surrender of the *ruling* classes."[41] Insurrectionist anarchists held that, instead of waiting for the revolution to happen, it would be better to "start the revolution inside oneself and realize it according to the best of our abilities in partial experiments, wherever such an opportunity arises, and whenever a bold group of our comrades have the conviction and courage to try."[42] These tactics were thought to "exert the most spirited influence over the masses" and would therefore inspire the working classes to rise up.[43]

Propaganda of the Deed

If revolutions were, as an article in *La Révolte* stated in 1890, "the product of a spontaneous explosion of the masses' discontent and anger," then the role of revolutionaries was to ignite this anger.[44] Propaganda of the deed was one of the primary means through which insurrectionist anarchists attempted to spread the spirit of revolt and thereby contribute toward the emergence of a social revolution. Historians of terrorism frequently make the mistake of equating the entire idea of propaganda of the deed with the kinds of high-profile assassination or bombings carried out by anarchists at the end of the nineteenth and the beginning of the twentieth century.[45] The idea of propaganda of the deed did not, however, always refer to the advocacy and practice of individuals attempting to murder the ruling classes in the name of revolution. It underwent a process of development over three decades of theory and practice.

What would come to be called "propaganda of the deed" started out as the view that anarchist ideas could and should be spread through actions, rather than only through written or spoken propaganda. Propaganda of the deed proceeded to undergo two main phases of development. During its first phase, between 1870 and 1880, it largely referred to the practice of anarchists collectively attempting to launch armed insurrections in order to spread their ideas and provoke a popular uprising. This went alongside the view that other forms of collective direct action, such as combative demonstrations, were an effective means of popularizing anarchist ideas and gaining support for the anarchist movement. During its second phase, which lasted roughly from the 1880s to the early 1900s, it transformed into the idea that individual acts of violence, such as assassinating heads of state or bombing crowded opera houses frequented by the wealthy, were a legitimate form of working-class vengeance that would weaken the ruling classes and inspire the working classes to rebel.[46] Both notions of propaganda of the deed shared the idea that revolutionary action by an anarchist minority could successfully spread anarchist ideas and spark a chain of events that would culminate in a social revolution. Where they differed was the kind of action advocated and performed.[47]

Propaganda of the Deed: First Phase

The 1870s began with a series of unsuccessful insurrections. In September 1870, Bakunin and his associates launched a quickly defeated insurrection in Lyon. On the September 26, they issued a program, adopted by a crowd of six thousand, declaring the abolition of the state and the establishment of revolutionary committees for each commune, which were subject to the direct supervision of the people. When they attempted to implement this program two days later, they succeeded in storming the city hall and issuing a variety of decrees only to be forced to flee by late afternoon when municipal authorities called in the army. This was soon followed by an equally unsuccessful second insurrection in Lyon on April

30, 1871, the rapid rise and bloody fall of the Marseille Commune between March 23 and April 4, and the Paris Commune between March 18 and May 28.[48] During the violent repression of the Paris Commune, at least seventeen thousand people were, according to the official government report, executed for having risen up against the ruling classes. Anarchists, in comparison, believed that between thirty and thirty-six thousand people had been slaughtered.[49] The Spanish cantonalist rebellion of July 1873, in which anarchists participated, suffered a similarly violent defeat.[50]

It was within this context of armed conflict with the ruling classes that the idea of propaganda of the deed arose and gained prominence. In 1870, Bakunin remarked that revolutionaries "must now embark on stormy revolutionary seas and . . . spread our principles, not with words *but with deeds, for this is the most popular, the most potent, and the most irresistible form of propaganda.*"[51] The aim of these deeds was to inspire the masses through revolutionary acts. In advocating this strategy, Bakunin does not appear to have been arguing that assassinations were an effective means of changing society. In 1866, he had responded to Dmitry Karakozov's attempt to assassinate the Tsar by writing that "no good can come of regicide in Russia for it would arouse a reaction favorable to the Tsar."[52] For Bakunin it was a mistake to think that "the Gordian knot can be cut with one stroke."[53]

On July 8, 1873, the French anarchist Paul Brousse, who would later become a state socialist, responded to the ongoing cantonalist rebellion by writing an article for the Barcelona paper *La Solidarité Révolutionnaire*.[54] In it, he declared that "revolutionary propaganda is . . . above all made in the open, in the midst of the piled-up paving stones of the barricades, on days when the exasperated people make war on the mercenary forces of reaction."[55] This view, as he would later write in the August 1877 edition of the *Bulletin of the Jura Federation*, rested on the idea of grabbing "people's attention, of showing them what they cannot read, of teaching them socialism by means of actions and making them see, feel, touch. . . . Propaganda by the deed is a mighty means of rousing the popular consciousness."[56] An insurrection that established a socialist commune would have to defend itself but even if it was defeated, like the recent insurrections of the early 1870s, this would not matter in the long run since "the idea will have been launched, not on paper, not in a newspaper, not on a chart" but in the real political practices of the working classes; it would thus "march, in flesh and blood, at the head of the people."[57]

Brousse's insistence on propaganda through insurrection partly developed out of being radicalized by the Paris Commune of 1871. The Paris Commune had, Brousse argued, done more to spread revolutionary ideas in two months of fighting than twenty-three years of traditional written propaganda. This was because, while a person must find, buy, and read a book or newspaper in order to be radicalized by it, an armed insurrection rapidly gains the attention of large numbers of people, including those who cannot read, and puts them in a position where they must take a side in the ongoing struggle.[58] This was not mere speculation on Brousse's part. In Italy, a large number of revolutionaries were driven to socialism by news of the Paris Commune, including future prominent anarchists such as Malatesta, Cafiero, and Costa.[59]

Brousse was not alone in holding that insurrections that establish communes have a powerful transformative effect on popular consciousness. Bakunin had himself made a similar point in his unsent 1872 letter to the editors of *La Liberté*, which was not published until 1910. He wrote in response to the Paris Commune that,

> What makes that revolution important is not really the weak experiments which it had the power and time to make, it is the ideas it has set in motion, the living light it has cast on the true nature and goal of revolution, the hopes it has raised, and the powerful stir it has produced among the popular masses

everywhere, and especially in Italy, where the popular awak-
ening dates from that insurrection, whose main feature was
the revolt of the Commune and the workers' associations
against the State.[60]

Cafiero shared this evaluation. In an unpublished chapter of
his 1881 *Revolution*, he wrote that "the events of the Commune
implanted militant socialism in every civilized land, and the
long-awaited distant goal of the propagandist was reached in an
instant by the brilliant flash of events."[61] Two years later, Kropotkin
said, during his court speech while on trial in Lyon, that, after the
defeat of the Paris Commune, "socialism drew new life from the
blood of its followers. Its ideas about property have been given an
enormous circulation."[62]

Nor was Brousse alone in holding that anarchists should, given
the powerful propaganda effect of the Paris Commune, work
toward the social revolution by launching insurrections that establish new communes. In an August 11, 1877, article in *L'Avant-Garde*,
Kropotkin reacted to the recent violently crushed railway strikes
in the United States by proposing that the strikes would have gone
differently if there had been anarchists present who had sought to
transform the strikes into insurrections that established communes
and forcefully expropriated the ruling classes. Even if these proposed communes had been defeated they would have, like the Paris
Commune before them, served as "an immensely resounding act
of propaganda for socialism."[63] In 1879, Kropotkin argued for this
strategy again by insisting that attempts at social revolution must
perform "the deed of expropriation" because it is "the most powerful way of propagating the idea" among the general populace and
thereby motivating other workers to join the emerging social revolution and expropriate their local economic ruling classes.[64]

Within the historical context of the rise and subsequent violent
defeat of the 1848 revolutions, the Paris Commune of 1871, and the

Spanish cantonalist rebellion of 1873, anarchists thought that they were riding a revolutionary wave and that the social revolution was imminent. In 1883, while on trial in Lyon, Kropotkin declared to the court that "the social revolution is near. It will break out within ten years."[65] This was not a uniquely anarchist perspective. Engels also predicted that a revolution was imminent numerous times during the 1880s and 1890s.[66] Reflecting on this period in 1904, Kropotkin wrote that "revolutionaries and moderates agreed then in predicting that the bourgeois regime, shaken by the revolution of 1848 and the Commune of Paris, could not long resist the attack of the European proletariat. Before the end of the century the collapse would come."[67]

If the revolution was near, then, as Costa wrote in January 1874 (with Bakunin's approval), "the time for peaceful propaganda has passed, it must be replaced by resounding—solemn propaganda of insurrection and barricades."[68] These words were written in the journal of the Italian Committee for Social Revolution (CIRS), a secret association whose membership included key Italian anarchists such as Cafiero, Costa, and Malatesta. The group sought to put theory into practice by launching multiple insurrections simultaneously across Italy, which had recently experienced a wave of strikes, demonstrations, and riots in response to high food prices and unemployment. This strategy was opposed by the majority of delegates of the Saint-Imier International at a meeting on March 18, 1874, on the grounds that socialism was not yet popular enough in Italy for armed insurrections to be launched. Despite lacking international support, the Italian federation nonetheless decided to proceed with its plan. The result was total failure.[69]

None of the insurrections attempted on August 7 and 8, 1874, went as the Italian anarchists had hoped. The people did not rise up in response to CIRS' calls for revolution, which they had announced in a bulletin that had been posted to the walls of various cities. The thousands of revolutionaries that were expected to form armed bands did not turn up. Instead only several hundred assembled, with a mere five turning up to join Malatesta's insurrection in Puglia on the night of August 11. In response, the anarchist militants either quickly disbanded or were soon arrested. Other anarchists were arrested before they could even assemble due to police spies sharing the anarchists' plans with the authorities. Bakunin was forced to shave his beard and escape to Switzerland disguised as a priest.[70]

The insurrections of August 1874 were viewed by Costa, one of the main organizers, as an attempt at propaganda of the deed. In his 1890 memoir, Costa wrote that "the occasion had come if not to provoke the social revolution in Italy, at least to give a practical example that would demonstrate to the people what we wanted and to propagate our ideas with evidence of deeds."[71] Despite the failure of 1874, the Italian Federation of the Saint-Imier International officially adopted propaganda of the deed as a strategy during its congress of October 1876. This was done because, as Cafiero and Malatesta explained in a letter published in the December edition of the *Bulletin of the Jura Federation*, "the Italian Federation holds that the *act of insurrection*, designed to assert socialist principles through deeds, is the most effective method of propaganda and the only one that, without deceiving and corrupting the masses, can delve into the deepest strata of society and draw the cream of humanity into the struggle, backed by the International."[72]

In advocating propaganda through the deed of armed insurrection, Italian anarchists were not advocating something new to Italian politics. The strategy had a prior history in the theory and practice of revolutionary Italian republicanism, which much of the Italian anarchist movement had developed out of.[73] Giuseppe Mazzini and his associates had sought to create a unified Italian republic through a strategy of armed bands of revolutionaries engaging in guerrilla warfare and attempting to "rouse the nation into insurrection."[74] This can be seen in Mazzini's hope that a defeated 1853 insurrection in Milan would have been "the kindling of a universal fire throughout Italy" if it had lasted twenty-four hours.[75] Malatesta later claimed, in 1897, that the early anarchist movement in Italy had believed in, "the youthful illusion (which we inherited from Mazzinianism) of imminent revolution achievable through the efforts of the few without due preparation in the masses."[76]

The attempted insurrections launched by Italian republicans were consistently unsuccessful. They often failed, like the future anarchist insurrections, due to the state knowing of the plots before they were launched.[77] The exception was in 1860, when Giuseppe Garibaldi, a longtime associate of Mazzini, contributed to the unification of Italy by invading Sicily with roughly one thousand poorly armed men and subsequently, after amassing a much larger army of twenty thousand soldiers, capturing Naples.[78] An inkling of the effect that Garibaldi's actions had on the developing socialist movement can be seen in Kropotkin's insistence in an 1897 letter to Maria Isidine Goldsmith that between 1859 and 1860 "Garibaldi's brave campaigns did more to spread the liberal, radical spirit of revolt and socialism right across Europe than anything else."[79]

The strategy of forming armed bands that launched insurrections coincided with some republican revolutionaries unsuccessfully attempting to assassinate monarchs. On January 14, 1858, Felice Orsini and two accomplices tried to assassinate Emperor Napoleon III of France with explosives. The three bombs that were thrown killed eight and wounded at least 156 people but barely harmed the Emperor. On December 8, the soldier Agesilao Milano stabbed and wounded King Ferdinand II of Naples with a bayonet. These republican acts of violence, be they collective revolts or individual attacks, had a profound influence on Italian anarchism.[80] Malatesta remembered in 1932 that "the idea of violence, even in the sense of the individual *attentat*, which many today believe characteristic of anarchism, was inherited by us from democracy. . . . Before accepting the teachings of Bakunin, the Italian Anarchists—Fanelli, Friscia, Gambuzzi—had admired and exalted Agesilao Milano, Felice Orsini, and *coups de main* typical of Mazzini. When they passed over to the International, they were not taught anything in this camp that they had not already learned from Mazzini and Garibaldi."[81]

Italian anarchists were particularly influenced by Carlo Pisacane, whose writings they discovered in the mid-1870s. Pisacane was a socialist influenced by Proudhon and was chief of staff of Mazzini's republican army of 1849.[82] In 1857, shortly before dying in a failed insurrection at Sapri (which he co-organized with Mazzini), he wrote that "ideas spring from deeds and not the other way around . . . conspiracies, plots and attempted uprisings are the succession of deeds whereby Italy proceeds toward her goal of unity. The flash of Milano's bayonet was a more effective propaganda than a thousand volumes penned by doctrinarians."[83]

Undeterred by their previous failure in 1874, the Italian anarchists soon made a second attempt at insurrection, which would come to be known as the Benevento affair. In theory, an armed band of anarchists would roam the Matese mountain range and its surrounding provinces in southern Italy, spreading revolutionary consciousness. One of the insurrection's participants, Pietro Ceccarelli (who had previously participated in Garibaldi's campaigns), explained later in 1881 that they planned "to rove about the countryside for as long as possible, preaching [class] war, inciting social brigandage, occupying small towns and leaving them after having accomplished whatever revolutionary acts we could, and to proceed to that area where our presence would prove more useful."[84] Believing "that revolution must be provoked, we carried out an act of provocation. . . . We were a band of insurgents destined to provoke an insurrection that cannot and must not count on anything but the echo it may find in the population."[85]

Guillaume described the ideas behind this strategy in detail. He wrote,

Our friends in Italy came to the conclusion that, in their country at least, *oral and written propaganda were not enough,* and that, to be clearly understood by the popular masses, especially the peasants, it was necessary to *show* them what could not be made living and real in any theoretical teaching, they had to be taught socialism through *deeds* so that they could see, feel and touch it. A plan was formed for teaching the Italian peasants, by means of a *practical lesson,* what society would be like if it got rid of government and property owners; for this, it would be enough to organize an armed band, large enough to control the countryside for a brief time and go from one commune to another carrying into effect *Socialism through action* before the very eyes of the people.[86]

Again, things did not go according to plan.[87] The Italian state was aware of the plot by mid-February 1877, due to reports from police spies who had infiltrated the anarchist movement. The following month, a member of the group, Salvatore Farina, disappeared after revealing the full details of their plans to the Italian state. Rather than flee the country, the anarchists decided to launch the insurrection at the beginning of April, a month earlier than planned. Doing so did not allow them to escape police repression. Several were arrested before they could even reach the agreed rendezvous point. Those who managed to arrive successfully were forced to flee the area with a fraction of their equipment after discovering and shooting at the four policemen who had them under surveillance. During their escape, they were joined by ten fellow insurgents who had, by chance, eluded the police because they missed their scheduled train. Together the group of only twenty-six anarchists headed for the mountains.

The armed band was low on men, ammunition, weapons, and food. Traveling to nearby large towns to gather supplies was not an option since, as the anarchists soon discovered, the government had already occupied the area with twelve thousand troops. Given these circumstances, the anarchists were only able to enter two small towns, Letino and Gallo. In each case, they did what little they could by burning official documents taken from the town hall, distributing what weapons and money they could find to the local peasants, and giving a speech on the necessity and value of the social revolution. In his speech to the peasants of Letino, Cafiero declared "the rifles and the axes we have given you, the knives you have. If you wish, do something, and if not, go f— yourselves."[88]

According to Brousse, these events had been a practical demonstration that taught the peasants how much contempt they should have for private property and the state.[89] This lesson appears to have had a limited effect, since the peasants of both Letino and Gallo cheered and applauded the anarchists only to return to their daily lives once the band had left. One of the reasons why the peasants did not join the anarchists in insurrection was that they were legitimately afraid of what would happen if they rose up. Malatesta later recalled that a peasant in Gallo had asked him how they could know that the anarchists were not, in fact, undercover police attempting to entrap them. Even if they could be sure that the anarchists were not police, an insurrection was still deeply impractical. As the peasants explained to Malatesta, "the town is in no condition to defend itself, the revolution has not yet erupted on a vast scale, tomorrow the troops will come and massacre us all."[90]

After failing to escape the region due to poor weather conditions, the anarchists took refuge for the night in a farmhouse near Letino. They were soon surrounded by soldiers after being informed on by a local peasant seeking a reward. Fighting was not an option—their weapons and ammunition had been rendered useless by rainfall. Knowing that they would be killed if they resisted the anarchists chose to surrender without a fight. With their arrests the insurrection was over.

Despite this, the insurrection was not a total failure. News of the insurrection and the subsequent trial, during which the defendants gave speeches on anarchism, garnered the International and its revolutionary socialist politics considerable national attention for several weeks. This was probably a contributing factor in the growth of the Italian section of the Saint-Imier International over the following year and a half.[91] Cafiero, perhaps looking for a positive outcome of the failed insurrection he had participated in, later claimed that the Benevento affair had increased demand for Marx's *Capital* to such an extent that a bookseller in Naples was forced to find more copies after having sold out.[92]

Anarchists in Berne, Switzerland, made less ambitious attempts at propaganda of the deed. They attended a demonstration on March 18, 1877, the anniversary of the Paris Commune, and brought red flags with them. The canton had prohibited the public display of the red flag and the previous year's demonstration by social democrats had ended in failure when it was attacked, dispersed, and the red flag was torn up. The aim of the anarchists was to march through Berne defending the flag from attacks by the police. This action was inspired by a Russian demonstration on December 6, 1876, when students and workers had gathered outside Our Lady of Kazan Cathedral after a revolutionary had been killed in prison. At the Russian demonstration, a student carrying a red flag had declared the demonstration's solidarity with all who had suffered in the struggle against Tsarism. The subsequent brutal state repression of the demonstration led to a large increase in public sympathy toward the revolutionaries. The anarchists hoped that their demonstration involving a red flag would have a similar effect and lead to increased sympathy with and support for the Jura Federation, whose membership was in serious decline.

On the day of the protest in Berne, roughly 250 demonstrators, several of whom were armed with sticks and truncheons, assembled themselves into a procession and marched forward with the Swiss anarchist Adhémar Schwitzguébel at their head brandishing a red flag. The demonstration, which was attended by several well-known anarchists including Guillaume, Kropotkin, and the Frenchman Jean-Louis Pindy, was then attacked by police armed with sabers and the anarchists defended themselves. During the struggle six policemen and several protesters were seriously wounded. The anarchists were forced to abandon the original flag but did manage to escape with another red flag and take it to the meeting planned for the end of the demonstration.[93] Kropotkin claimed in letter written to Paul Robin on March 24, that the protest had nonetheless been a success because two thousand people, instead of the expected seventy, had attended the meeting afterward organized by the anarchists. Their act of revolt had gained them "an attentive and in part sympathetic public" since *there is nothing like courage to win over the people*."[94]

In August, Brousse argued that the Berne protest was an act of propaganda of the deed that taught the Swiss working class "that they do not, as they thought they did, enjoy freedom."[95] This lack of freedom was apparent in how the Swiss state responded to the Berne protest. Thirty of the demonstrators were brought to trial and sentenced to periods of imprisonment ranging from sixty days for the two anarchists who had struck policemen with sticks to forty days for Guillaume, thirty days for Brousse, and ten days for the rest. All the foreign participants were expelled from the Berne Canton for three years and with this the movement in Berne lost its leading militants.[96]

Propaganda of the Deed: Second Phase

During its second phase, propaganda of the deed developed into advocating or engaging in assassination and bombings.[97] The transformation occurred in response to a vast array of factors that included: a vicious cycle of anarchists responding to state violence with violent individual attacks that led, in turn, to more state violence and so on; anarchists being influenced by assassinations and bombings carried out by contemporary social movements such as Italian republicans, Russian nihilists, and Irish nationalists; and the nefarious influence of police spies and agent provocateurs. It is difficult to chart the path from collective uprisings into individual acts of violence, partly because it is rarely clear if a particular attack was carried out by a genuine anarchist attempting to implement insurrectionist theory and engage in propaganda of the deed. Attacks were frequently attributed to anarchists by the police or the press (including, sometimes, the anarchist press) with little to no evidence.[98]

The earliest alleged anarchist assassination attempts occurred in 1878 when Max Hödel on May 11 and Dr. Carl Nobiling on June 2 both tried unsuccessfully to kill the Kaiser Wilhelm I of Germany. This was soon followed by Juan Oliva y Moncasi's failed attempt to assassinate King Alfonso XII of Spain on October 25. It is not clear from the available evidence whether either Hödel or Nobiling were genuine anarchists. At best they were socialists with some loose connections to a few anarchist groups.[99] Although Moncasi was a member of the anarchist-led Spanish section of the Saint-Imier International, it is not clear whether he was an anarchist himself.[100]

The first definite anarchist assassination plot occurred in 1880. After guns had failed to kill the Kaiser, the German anarchist August Reinsdorf planned to dig a tunnel under the Reichstag, plant explosives around the building's supports and ignite them while the Reichstag was in session. Reinsdorf made the mistake of explaining his plan in a letter dated September 1, 1880, to his associate Johann Most, a German socialist who, at the time, lived in London, edited the journal *Freiheit*, and had yet to become an anarchist. Oskar Neumann, a spy living in London, heard of the plan and subsequently informed the Berlin police. Reinsdorf was arrested on November 14 while carrying a dagger near the home of the Berlin chief of police, Guido von Madai, whom he planned to assassinate.[101]

This escalation in political practice was mirrored by an escalation in theory. In December 1880, Cafiero wrote an article for *Le
Révolté* in which he repeated the old insurrectionist idea that actions
were an effective means of spreading revolutionary ideas. What had
changed was the scope of acceptable action. Rather than merely
advocating armed bands inspiring a popular insurrection, he now
insisted that anarchists should engage in "permanent rebellion, by
word, by writing, by dagger, by gun, by dynamite . . . we shall use
every weapon which can be used for rebellion. Everything is right
for us which is not legal."[102] He argued that anarchists should immediately engage in violent attacks because "if we go on waiting until
we are strong enough before attacking—we shall never attack, and
we shall be like the good man who vowed that he wouldn't go into
the sea until he had learned to swim. It is precisely revolutionary
action which develops our strength, just as exercise develops the
strength of our muscles."[103] He predicted that if anarchists fought
and died for popular movements then the seeds of socialism they
contained would grow and flower into a revolution. Cafiero, in short,
held that engaging in revolutionary violence would simultaneously
develop the capacities of anarchists and instill radical drives and
consciousness within the working classes.

A few months later, Cafiero wrote a letter to the paper *Il Grido
del Popolo* in which he advocated armed struggle in more detail.
Anarchist militants were to form a group in their area composed of
between six and ten men or women and engage in violent attacks,
including with explosives, against capitalism and the state. He opti-
mistically predicted that their actions "will find echoes all over the
world. Hardly will the actions of one group have begun, when the
whole country will be covered in groups, and action become gen-
eralized. Every group will be its own center of action, with a plan
all of its own, and a multiplicity of varied and harmonic initiatives.
The concept of the whole war will be one only: the destruction of
all oppressors and exploiters."[104]

Propaganda of the deed soon came to be enshrined in the resolutions of the International Social Revolutionary Congress, which
met in London between July 14 and 20, 1881, and was conceived
as an attempt to re-found the International.[105] The congress was
attended by forty-five delegates claiming to represent sixty federations and fifty-nine individual groups with a total membership
of fifty thousand people. One of the most vocal delegates was the
French police agent Égide Spilleux, who operated under the pseud-
onym Serreaux and had successfully infiltrated the movement.[106]
After a significant amount of discussion and debate, the delegates
agreed to adopt the following resolution,

> the International Workingmen's Association deems it nec-
> essary to add "Propaganda by Deed" to oral and written
> propaganda. . . . It is absolutely necessary to exert every effort
> toward propagating, by deeds, the revolutionary idea and to
> arouse the spirit of revolt in those sections of the popular
> masses who still harbor illusions about the effectiveness of
> legal methods . . . Whereas the agricultural workers are still
> outside the revolutionary movement, it is absolutely neces-
> sary to make every effort to win them to our cause, and to
> keep in mind that a deed performed against the existing insti-
> tutions appeals to the masses much more than thousands of
> leaflets and torrents of words, and that "Propaganda by Deed"
> is of greater importance in the countryside than in the cities.[107]

Edward Nathan-Ganz, delegate No. 22 and one of the three
members of the resolution committee appointed to summarize
the proposals that had been put forward during the congress, connected propaganda of the deed to the manufacture of bombs. He
wrote within the resolution that "whereas the technical and chemical sciences have rendered services to the revolutionary cause and
are bound to render still greater services in the future, the Congress

suggests that organizations and individuals affiliated with the International Workingmen's Association devote themselves to the study of these sciences."[108]

Reinsdorf soon decided to follow these proposals and undertake a second attempt at blowing up members of Germany's ruling classes. As he explained in an 1882 letter to an American comrade, only the bomb could "inject the whole bourgeoisie and their slaves with total terror" and achieve "complete and utter revenge" for "all the dirty tricks and atrocities" they committed.[109] This time, Reinsdorf and his associates in the town of Elberfeld planned to use dynamite to kill Wilhelm I, alongside other key members of the German ruling classes, at the inauguration of the Niederwald Monument on September 28, 1883. The assassination failed. Due to a sprained ankle, Reinsdorf was unable to go himself and two of his associates—the saddler Franz Rupsch and the compositor Emil Küchler—went in his place. Küchler made the mistake of ignoring Reinsdorf's instructions to buy a waterproof fuse. The night before the assassination attempt, it rained heavily and the cheaper fuse failed to ignite at the crucial moment. In 1884, Reinsdorf and his group were arrested and put on trial for the attempted assassination of the Emperor. It turned out that one of Reinsdorf's associates, the weaver Carl Rudolf Palm—who had donated forty marks toward Rupsch and Küchler's travel expenses—was in fact a police spy and had been informing on the group from the very beginning. On the morning of February 7, 1885, Reinsdorf and Küchler were executed, with Rupsch having had his death sentence commuted to imprisonment for life.[110]

In parallel to these events, Most, who had known Reinsdorf, moved from London to New York in December 1882 and became an anarchist.[111] During the mid-1880s, Most wrote numerous articles for *Freiheit* which declared that workers should arm themselves with guns, dynamite, poison, and knives in order to violently attack the ruling classes and achieve revenge. For example, in August 1884 he wrote that "Every prince will find his Brutus. Poison on the table of the gourmet will cancel out his debt. Dynamite will explode in the splendid, rubber tyred, coaches of the aristocracy and bourgeois as they pull up to the opera. Death will await them, both by day and by night, on all roads and footpaths and even in their homes, lurking in a thousand different forms."[112] In 1885, Most even published an assassination manual for his readers based on what he had learned working in an explosives factory. It was titled *The Science of Revolutionary Warfare: A Manual of Instruction in the Use and Preparation of Nitroglycerine, Dynamite, Gun-Cotton, Fulminating Mercury, Bombs, Fuses, Poisons, etc.*[113]

This shift to the meaning of propaganda of the deed within anarchist circles did not occur in isolation. Anarchists were influenced by assassinations and bombings carried out by other social movements between the 1850s and 1880s, including Italian republicans, Irish nationalists, and Russian nihilists.[114] One of the most impactful events was Narodnaya Volya (People's Will) assassinating Tsar Alexander II of Russia with explosives on March 1, 1881. In the aftermath of this attack, an increasing number of anarchists came to argue that anarchists should follow Narodnaya Volya's example and organize their own assassination campaign against the ruling classes. It is not a coincidence that the International Social Revolutionary Congress in London passed a resolution advocating propaganda of the deed and the study of chemical sciences to build explosives a few months after the assassination of the Tsar with explosives.[115]

The impact of the Tsar's assassination was clear to anarchists at the time. In 1891, Kropotkin wrote that "when the Russian revolutionaries had killed the Czar . . . the European anarchists imagined that, from then on, a handful of fervent revolutionaries, armed with a few bombs, would be enough to bring about the social revolution."[116] This perspective was echoed by Nettlau. He wrote in 1932 that, during this period, anarchists were inspired by "the example of fortitude and sacrifice set by Russian nihilists" and thought that, due to the assassination of the Tsar, alongside other examples of revolt, insurrection, and state repression, there was a "growing accumulation of acts of violence," which in turn indicated that "a general revolutionary upheaval of a socially destructive type was imminent."[117]

Although the vast majority of anarchist assassinations and bombings were carried out by genuine anarchists acting independently, there are several examples of the police normalizing or encouraging the use of these violent tactics. Louis Andrieux, the prefect of the Paris Police, financed the creation of the anarchist paper *La Révolution Sociale* in September 1880, through his agent Serreaux. The paper, which Serreaux helped to edit, published articles advocating violent attacks and provided the reader with instructions on how to manufacture dynamite. In June 1881, a police agent working for Andrieux played a key role in instigating a small group of anarchists to bomb the statue of the former president Adolphe Thiers, who had ordered the massacre of the Paris Commune a decade earlier. The bomb failed to damage the statue, and left only a black stain. As mentioned earlier, Serreaux attended the International Social Revolutionary Congress in London as a delegate and formed around him a group of supporters that Kropotkin referred to as "*la bande Serreaux*." During the congress, this group advocated propaganda of the deed, a rejection of morality, the study of bomb making, and a repeat of actions like the bombing of the statue of Thiers.[118]

It was not until the 1890s that the new understanding of propaganda of the deed was implemented by anarchists on a grand scale. The manner in which this occurred varied between countries. In Italy, explosives were largely used to damage government buildings, rather than people, and generally did little more than break windows.[119] In Spain and France, by contrast, there were a series of bombings that wounded and killed random civilians who just happened to be in the area. In 1892, François Koenigstein, known more commonly as Ravachol, decided to seek vengeance for the wrongful arrest, torture, and imprisonment of anarchist protesters by the French state. To this end, he bombed the apartment buildings where the judge and prosecutor attorney of the court case lived on March 11 and 27. The bombs injured eight innocent people and failed to wound, let alone kill, their targets.[120]

Several months later, on November 8, Émile Henry left a bomb outside the offices of the Carmaux Mining Company, which had recently crushed a miners' strike. The bomb exploded after being moved to a nearby police station, killing five people. On December 9, 1893, Auguste Vaillant, an unemployed anarchist who was unable to feed his wife and daughter, threw a small nail bomb into France's chamber of deputies in order to call attention to the suffering of the poor. Due to its design, the bomb only slightly wounded several deputies and a few spectators. Despite not having killed anyone, Vaillant was sentenced to death. Seven days after Vaillant was executed, Henry sought revenge and threw a bomb into Paris's Café Terminus on February 12, 1894. His aim was not to target any person in particular but to kill any random member of the bourgeoisie. The explosion killed one and wounded twenty.[121]

Similar events occurred in Spain. On September 24, 1893, Paulino Pallás threw a bomb at Arsenio Martínez de Campos, the Captain General of Catalonia, during a military parade in Barcelona. The bomb, which was thrown in response to the execution of four anarchist militants, killed two people and wounded Campos and twelve soldiers and spectators. Pallás was subsequently executed. Santiago Salvador, who had been converted to anarchism by Pallás, sought revenge for his friend's execution by throwing two bombs down onto the wealthy audience of the Liceu Opera theater in Barcelona during its November 7 performance of *William Tell*. Only one bomb exploded, killing fifteen people and seriously injuring fifty others.[122]

Other anarchists used blades and guns to engage in targeted assassinations. In 1894, Santo Caserio stabbed to death the President of France Sadi Carnot. This was followed by Michele Angiolillo assassinating the Spanish prime minister Antonio Cánovas del Castillo in 1897 and Luigi Lucheni killing the Empress of Austria Elisabeth Eugenie in 1898. Two years later in 1900, Gaetano Bresci killed King Umberto I of Italy with a revolver. In 1901, Leon Czolgosz, who had only recently come into contact with anarchist ideas, shot and fatally wounded the American president William McKinley. On other occasions, anarchist assassins were unsuccessful, such as Berkman's 1892 attempt to kill the capitalist Henry Clay Frick in retaliation for the violent repression of a strike at the Homestead steel works.[123]

Anarchist assassinations and bombings did not end suddenly at the dawn of the new century and continued for several years after. For example, anarchist bomb throwers failed to murder the King of Spain Alfonso XIII during his 1905 visit to Paris and 1906 wedding in Madrid. The explosions from these two assassination attempts injured 124 bystanders and killed twenty-three people. Over a decade later, the anarchist Émile Cottin unsuccessfully attempted to assassinate the French Prime Minister Clemenceau in 1919.[124]

The majority of these attacks were carried out in response to the much greater violence of the ruling classes. A clear example of this is Bresci's assassination of King Umberto I of Italy in 1900. A few years previously, in 1897 and 1898, a wave of protests, demonstrations, strikes, and riots had spread across Italy in response to the spiraling cost of bread, which was the primary source of food for the working classes. This direct struggle included women leading raids on granaries and bakeries in order to expropriate food. Bread prices had risen due to an extremely poor grain harvest in Italy and the Italian state's decision to not lower import duties on foreign grain in order to protect the financial interests of Italian capitalists and landowners. This included the prime minister and finance minister,

who both owned vast amounts of land. The Italian state responded
to the working classes struggle for adequate food with mass arrests,
the mobilization of the army, and the imposition of martial law. On
several occasions, protesters armed with little more than sticks and
stones were wounded or killed by gunfire from soldiers. In the port
of Livorno, two warships even threatened to shell working-class
neighborhoods.

Such threats were not empty. In May 1898, soldiers in Milan
not only responded to thrown rocks with volleys of gunfire. They
also fired artillery at striking workers, who had attempted to defend
themselves by erecting barricades out of little more than furniture,
metal grilles, and trolley cars. Groups of women who attempted
to block the street were met with cavalry charges and trampled
under horses' hooves. A crowd of two thousand students, some of
whom were armed with revolvers, were shot at with cannons. The
names of 264 people were listed as dead victims in local newspapers, though other estimates ranged from four hundred to eight
hundred deaths. King Umberto celebrated this violence by reward-
ing Italy's highest decoration to the commander of the soldiers in
Milan, General Fiorenzo Bava Beccaris.[125] Bresci later claimed that
"when in Paterson I read of the events in Milan, where they even
used cannons, I wept with rage and prepared myself for vengeance.
I thought of the king who awarded a prize to those who carried out
the massacres, and I became convinced that he deserved death."[126]

Such individual acts of violence usually provided an anarchist with the opportunity to engage in propaganda of the word
during their court speech and thereby spread anarchist ideas to a
large audience via the reporting of mainstream newspapers. These
speeches varied in quality and the extent to which they successfully
transmitted anarchist ideas. To give one example, Berkman refused
to be represented by a lawyer and prepared a lengthy court speech
on anarchism. During the trial Berkman's speech was unexpectedly
badly translated from German to English by a court interpreter.

After an hour, the judge abruptly ended the speech and Berkman was unable to complete it. This occurred despite him offering to cut the part on labor and capital and move onto his discussion of the church and the state.[127] Caserio's passionate court speech suffered a similar fate when it was translated into French and quickly read aloud by a court clerk in a monotone voice. His speech nonetheless provides an illustrative example of the manner in which anarchist assassins or bombers justified their violent acts. He declared to the court that anarchists had to respond to the "guns, chains, and prisons" of the ruling classes with "dynamite, bombs, and daggers" in order to "defend our lives" and "destroy the bourgeoisie and the governments."[128]

Anarchists responded to the wave of assassinations and bombings that began in the 1890s in a variety of conflicting ways. Prominent anarchist authors routinely claimed that the individuals who carried out such acts of violence were sensitive or desperate people reacting to the much greater violence of capitalism and the state.[129] A significant segment of the wider anarchist movement labeled the perpetrators as martyrs who acted heroically in the pursuit of social emancipation. In 1895, the English anarchist Louisa Sarah Bevington wrote that "those who did these acts were the very best, the most human, unselfish, self-sacrificing of our comrades, who threw their lives away, meeting death or imprisonment in the hope that their acts would sow the seeds of revolt, that they might show the way and wake an echo, by their deeds of rebellion, in the victims of the present system."[130]

These sorts of statements were part of a broader trend in which the memory of anarchist assassins and bombers were incorporated into anarchist counterculture and took their place alongside other key events of remembrance, such as the anniversary of the Paris Commune. An Italian anarchist group in the United States, for example, named themselves "The Twenty-Ninth of July," after the day Bresci assassinated Umberto.[131] This trend was not universal or always long-lasting. In Spain, several anarchist papers initially praised anarchist assassins and bombers as martyrs, but from 1898 onward, their names rarely appeared in print media.[132]

Anarchists, regardless of what they thought about the individuals who carried out assassinations and bombings, disagreed with one another about whether or not such acts were an effective means of contributing toward positive social change. Galleani wrote articles defending Pallás and Vaillant in December 1893, and publicly recommended a bomb-making manual in 1906 that featured an image of Ravachol on the front cover.[133] Several years later, in 1925, Galleani argued that a wave of individual acts of violence was "*a necessarily intermediary phenomenon between the sheer ideal or theoretical affirmation and the insurrectionary movement which follows it and kindles the torch of the victorious revolution.*"[134] Just as Brousse had previously thought that anarchist-led insurrections transmitted lessons to the people, so too did Galleani think that assassinating monarchs was a powerful means of communication. It taught the oppressed classes that a monarch, who is believed to be picked by God and wields a vast amount of power, can be killed and so is just like any other person. Above all, such individual acts of violence taught workers that they could, if they wanted, free themselves and overthrow their oppressors. For Galleani, no act of rebellion was useless or harmful to the cause.[135]

Other anarchists disagreed and argued that such actions were tactically misguided and immoral when they targeted innocent people. Malatesta opposed Henry's bombing of the Café Terminus as "unjust, vicious, and senseless,"[136] and described Salvador's bombing of the Liceu Opera theater as an act which killed and wounded "needless victims" while achieving "no possible benefit to the cause."[137] In the case of Michele Angiolillo's assassination of the Spanish Prime minister, an act that did not harm any innocent people, Malatesta thought that although the act was morally justifiable, "it is doubtful that his deed served the freedom of Spaniards . . .

it is for reasons of usefulness that, generally speaking, we are not in favor of individual attacks, which have been very common throughout history but almost always have not helped, and have very often harmed, the cause they were intended to serve."[138]

According to the historian Richard Bach Jensen, during the 1890s real or alleged anarchist assassinations and bombings in Europe, the United States, and Australia killed at least sixty people and wounded more than two hundred. Between 1878 and 1914, real or alleged anarchist assassinations and bombings globally (excluding Russia) killed more than 220 people and wounded over 750. Despite such great human costs, which included the needless murder and injury of innocent civilians, the tactic of propaganda of the deed had failed to generate a mass revolutionary movement or inspire large insurrections, let alone ignite the social revolution. It had instead made the social revolution a more remote possibility because it both convinced the political ruling classes, including heads of police, that they were threatened by an international coordinated anarchist conspiracy that had to be destroyed, and it provided them with a political opportunity for directing huge amounts of state repression toward the anarchist movement in particular, and the socialist movement in general. This state repression included the banning of anarchist papers, mass arrests, and laws that criminalized anarchism specifically.[139] Kropotkin neatly summarized the consequences of this state repression in 1907, when he remarked that it had the "effect of thinning our ranks."[140]

Ultimately, it is fair to say that insurrectionist anarchism was unsuccessful, in so far as the main forms of propaganda of the deed they advocated and engaged in failed to inspire the working classes to rise up, and in so doing, form a mass movement capable of overthrowing class society. The strategy of propaganda of the deed can appear to be doomed to failure from a twenty-first century vantage point, equipped with the benefit of hindsight and the lessons of over 150 years of attempts to build socialism. As a result, it is essential to understand insurrectionist anarchists on their own terms, and contextualize their ideas within the time they lived in. The strategy of insurrectionist anarchism did not develop out of nowhere. It was instead a product of anarchists being affected by and responding to their contemporary situation. This included the belief that a social revolution was imminent due to a recent wave of insurrections in multiple countries; being deeply influenced by the actions and ideas of contemporary social movements, such as Italian republicans, Russian nihilists, and Irish nationalists; responding to the much greater violence of the political and economic ruling classes toward the working classes in general and anarchism in particular; and the nefarious influences of police spies and agent provocateurs. Insurrectionist anarchism was nonetheless not the only strategy anarchists developed in response to their context.

CHAPTER 7

Mass Anarchism

Mass anarchists advocated forming, or participating in, large-scale, formal organizations that prefigured the future anarchist society and engaged in collective struggles for immediate reforms in the present. It was held that these collective struggles for reforms would, over time, develop a revolutionary mass movement that was both capable of, and driven to, overthrow capitalism and the state in favor of an anarchist society. The struggle for immediate reforms was, in other words, viewed as the best means to develop the social force that was necessary for launching a successful armed insurrection. Mass anarchists thought this would occur due to workers being transformed by the practice of participating within prefigurative organizations, taking direct action against the ruling classes, and being influenced by anarchists acting as a militant minority within social movements.[1]

Support of Formal Organizations

Mass anarchists advocated building, and participating within, large-scale formal federations that prefigured the kinds of organization that would exist in a future anarchist society. These tended to be federations of trade unions or community groups, whose

membership included both anarchists and nonanarchists, and federations of anarchist militants, which I shall refer to as *specific anarchist
organizations*. The size of organization mass anarchists hoped to
create can be seen in Kropotkin's argument that the victory of the
working classes required "monster unions embracing millions of
proletarians" and the establishment of "an *International Federation
of all the Trade Unions all over the World*."[2]

Large-scale federations were advocated by mass anarchists for
two main practical reasons. First, they held that they were necessary to achieve coordination between, and effective action by, large
groups of people in different areas. In 1870, Bakunin argued that the
self-emancipation of the working classes was impeded by their "lack
of organization, the difficulty of coming to agreements and of acting
in concert."[3] He wrote,

> Certainly, there is sufficient spontaneous strength among the
> people, indubitably the strength of the latter is much greater
> than that of the government and that of ruling classes within
> it; but lacking organization, spontaneous force is no real force.
> It is not in a [fit] state to sustain a protracted struggle against
> forces that are much weaker but much better organized. It is
> on this undeniable superiority of organized force over elemen-
> tal popular force that all the power of the state resides.... Thus,
> the [real] question is not one of knowing if the people are
> capable of an uprising, but rather whether they are ready to
> form an organization which will assure the success of a revolt,
> a victory which is not ephemeral, but durable and definitive.[4]

Given this, Bakunin argued in 1871 that "to make the people's
might strong enough to be able to eradicate the State's military and
civil might, it is necessary to organize the proletariat.... That is
precisely what the International Working Men's Association does"
by organizing workers into federations of trade unions.[5]

This argument was applied not only to the organization of the working classes in general, but also the organization of workers who were anarchist militants. In 1889, Malatesta complained that some anarchists had "attacked the principle of organization itself. They wanted to prevent betrayals and deception, permit free rein to individual initiative, ensure against spies and attacks from the government—and they brought isolation and impotence to the fore."[6] Amédée Dunois similarly claimed at the 1907 International Anarchist Congress in Amsterdam that the anarchist movement in France was disorganized and fragmented into unconnected small groups and isolated individuals. He lamented that,

> Everyone acts in his own way, whenever he wants; in this way individual efforts are dispersed and often exhausted, simply wasted. Anarchists can be found in more or less every sphere of action: in the workers' unions, in the anti-militarist movement, among anti-clericalist free thinkers, in the popular universities, and so on, and so forth. What we are missing is a specifically anarchist movement, which can gather to it, on the economic and workers' ground that is ours, all those forces that have been fighting in isolation up to now. This specifically anarchist movement will voluntarily arise from our groups and from the federation of these groups. The might of joint action, of concerted action, will undoubtedly create it. . . . It would be sufficient for the anarchist organization to group together, around a programme of concrete practical action, all the comrades who accept our principles and who want to work with us, according to our methods.[7]

The second reason why mass anarchists advocated large-scale federations was that they were necessary for developing the kinds of people and social relations that were needed to abolish capitalism and the state and create an anarchist society. In 1892, Malatesta

argued that since "agreement, association, and organization represent one of the laws governing life and the key to strength—today
as well as after the revolution," it follows that the working classes
must be organized prior to the social revolution.[8] This is because
"tomorrow can only grow out of today—and if one seeks success
tomorrow, the factors of success need to be prepared today."[9] This
was especially important given that, as Malatesta explained in 1897,
workers cannot be "expected to provide for pressing needs" during
the social revolution "unless they were already used to coming
together to deal jointly with their common interests."[10] For example,
supplying bread to everyone in a city would have to be organized,
and this required that bakers were "already associated and ready to
manage without masters."[11]

Large-scale, formal organizations were, in short, deemed necessary for both engaging in successful revolts and producing and
distributing goods and services during and after the social revolution. Insurrectionist anarchists were not convinced by such
arguments because they regarded formal organizations as incompatible with the freedom of the individual, and so with anarchism's
commitment to the unity of means and ends. Mass anarchists
replied that formal organizations were both compatible with
freedom and a prerequisite for it. They thought that large-scale
coordination and collective action based on voluntary agreement
expanded a person's real possibility to act and develop themselves
far beyond what an individual could attain by themselves or in a
small group. A worker may have the internal ability to help organize
a large strike across multiple industries but they lack the capacity
to do so when isolated. The external conditions necessary for the
development and exercise of such a capacity only emerge when an
organization like a national trade union is formed that unites workers together, and thereby enables new forms of action.[12]

Mass anarchists also argued that a lack of organizational structures often results in informal hierarchies emerging. Charismatic

individuals can, for example, create a newspaper and use it to steer the anarchist movement in a direction of their own choosing, and transform themselves into a prominent leader. In so doing, they acquire a large amount of influence, and use this to further their own positions and interests in manners that are unaccountable to the wider movement and sometimes even harmful. Formal organizational structures can counter this tendency by creating systems of accountability, such as the editors of newspapers being delegates who are elected and mandated by the members of a trade union.[13]

Mass anarchists were, nevertheless, still anarchists and so opposed to any system of top-down organization based on minority rule and centralization.[14] The conclusions of the 1906 Russian anarchist-communist conference, which were written by Kropotkin, opposed "every form of hierarchical organization that is characteristic of the parties of the State socialists" in which members are "obedient to a central power" and subject to "party discipline and compulsion."[15] This perspective was shared by Baginski who, three years later, rejected "constraining laws that need a centralistic apparatus for their execution," while advocating "a federative association that does not demand subjection from its members, but will rather place understanding, initiative, and solidarity in the place of commands and compulsory, soldierly behavior."[16]

One hierarchical organization that mass anarchists opposed was the bureaucratic trade union. In 1938, Rocker argued that trade unions, in which decisions flow from a small minority of bureaucrats at the top to workers beneath them, should be rejected on the grounds that they are "always attended by barren official routine; and this crushes individual conviction, kills all personal initiative by lifeless discipline and bureaucratic ossification, and permits no independent action."[17] Such top-down systems of decision-making systems were especially harmful because the minority who actually made decisions lacked immediate access to the local information needed to do so. To illustrate this point, Rocker referred to trade unions allied with the Social Democratic Party of Germany, in which strikes had to first be approved by the central committee, which was usually very far away and "not in a position to pass a correct judgement on the local conditions." This meant that workers in a particular area were unable to engage in sudden direct action, and so effectively respond to their immediate circumstances and concerns on the ground.[18] For a state, "centralism is the appropriate form of organization, since it aims at the greatest possible uniformity in social life for the maintenance of political and social equilibrium [under capitalism]. But for a movement whose very existence depends on prompt action at any favorable moment and on the independent thought and action of its supporters, centralism could but be a curse."[19]

The form of organization that would, in the opinion of mass anarchists, simultaneously enable effective coordination between large groups of people and the free initiative of its members was the federation. What such federations were supposed to look like can be understood by examining in detail Malatesta's various descriptions of anarchist organizational structures, especially those he made during a series of debates with antiorganizationalist anarchists in the 1890s.[20] These organizational principles were later implemented by the specific anarchist organization Malatesta was a member of during the early 1920s, the Italian Anarchist Union.[21] It should nonetheless be kept in mind that these are Malatesta's proposals, and, despite being influential, do not reflect what all mass anarchists thought or how all mass anarchist organizations actually operated.

Malatesta advocated the formation of an organization that united individuals under a common program, which specified the goals of the group and the means they proposed to achieve them. The purpose of such an organization was to enable individuals to pursue their shared goals by educating one another, engaging in joint activity, and coordinating action over a large-scale. In so doing, an organization would develop a collective strength to change society that was not only impossible for an individual to develop in isolation, but was also greater than the sum of the individual strengths that composed it.

Such a formal organization must, given the unity of means and ends, be structured in a manner that prefigures an anarchist society. Whereas authoritarian organizations rest on a division between some who command and others who obey, anarchist organizations are free associations of equals that are formed in order to achieve a common goal. There should be no substantial difference between how anarchists organize before and after the social revolution. They need, "today for the purposes of propaganda and struggle, tomorrow in order to meet all of the needs of social life, organizations built upon the will and in the interest of all their members."[22] Anarchist formal organizations, therefore, have to be founded on "the principle of autonomy of individuals within groups, and of groups within federations" such that "nobody has the right to impose their will on anyone else, and nobody is forced to follow decisions that they have not accepted."[23] Within such a federalist organization, each group and individual member would be free to federate with whomever they desired, and to leave any federation whenever they wanted. This freedom of association included the freedom of the federation, or groups within the federation, to choose to disassociate from individuals who violated its common program, such as by campaigning for a politician or supporting an imperialist war.[24]

Decisions within the local groups that compose the federation would be made by a general assembly, in which each member had a vote and an equal say in collective decisions. Although Malatesta held that anarchists should aim for a situation in which everybody agreed on a decision, he understood that this would often not happen, and there would be a division between a majority of people in favor of one position and a minority opposed to it. In such situations, where it was impractical or impossible to pass multiple resolutions reflecting each faction's distinct viewpoint, it was expected that the minority would voluntarily defer to the majority, so that a decision was made and the organization would continue to function. If the minority disagreed strongly with the majority, and felt that this was an issue of supreme importance, then they were free to voluntarily dissociate and leave the organization.

Large-scale coordination would be achieved through the organization of congresses, which were attended by delegates that each section's general assembly had elected. According to Malatesta,

> congresses of an anarchist organization . . . do not lay down the law; they do not impose their own resolutions on others. They serve to maintain and increase personal relationships among the most active comrades, to coordinate and encourage programmatic studies on the ways and means of taking action, to acquaint all on the situation in the various regions and the action most urgently needed in each; to formulate the various opinions current among the anarchists and draw up some kind of statistics from them—and their decisions are not obligatory rules but suggestions, recommendations, proposals to be submitted to all involved, and do not become binding and enforceable except on those who accept them, and for as long as they accept them.[25]

In order to ensure that the delegates within the federation did not develop into a ruling minority who imposed decisions on the wider membership, Malatesta proposed a number of limits to their power. First, the delegate would be mandated to complete specific tasks by the group who elected them, such as being a treasurer or voting as instructed at a congress, rather than being granted decision-making power, which would remain in the hands of the general assembly who had elected the delegate. Second, the delegate would serve for fixed terms and the position would be rotated regularly, so that as many people as possible could learn to perform these tasks and take initiative. Third, the delegate could be instantly recalled and replaced by those who had elected them, if they did not approve of what the delegate had done.[26]

A more concrete understanding of what federations built on anarchist principles actually looked like can be seen by examining the Spanish anarcho-syndicalist trade union the CNT, which was founded in 1910, and had a membership of over 700,000 workers by 1919. Despite suffering multiple waves of state repression and being illegal for several years of its existence, the CNT was able to survive and maintain itself over time. By May 1936, the CNT was composed of 982 union sections with a total membership of 550,595 workers.[27] Its organizational structure is shown below in *figure 1*. The CNT was initially composed of craft unions that belonged both to a federation of every union in their specific or similar crafts, and a federation composed of all the other unions, irrespective of craft, in their local area. This formally changed at a national level in 1919, when delegates at the CNT's national congress voted to form "single unions" that united all workers in a specific industry, regardless of their profession, within the same union. These single unions were, in turn, broken down into individual trade sections that would deal with any issues specific to their craft.[28]

Decisions in the single unions were made by a general assembly composed of the entire membership. This general assembly elected a shop steward, who was granted the power to call for work stoppages when the membership instructed them to do so, and an administrative committee. The administrative committee of the single union was, according to the activist manual issued by the CNT during the Spanish revolution of 1936, composed of a general secretary, treasurer, accountant, first secretary, second secretary, third secretary, librarian, propaganda delegate, and federal delegate(s). All the different trade sections within the single union had to be represented within the administrative committee. Who performed what role was decided upon by the elected members of the administrative committee themselves. The exceptions to this were the general secretary, treasurer, and federal delegate who were specifically chosen by the general assembly of the single union.[29]

The single unions in a particular area combined to form a local federation. The local federations then combined to form a regional federation and the regional federations together formed the national federation.[30] The local, regional, and national federations were all self-managed by their own respective administrative committees. In order to prevent the rise of a bureaucracy within the CNT, the only paid delegates within the trade union were the general secretary of the national federation and the secretaries of the regional federations. Every other delegate was expected to earn a living working in a trade.[31] The administrative committees of the local, regional, and national federations lacked the ability to impose decisions on shop stewards, who were only subject to the instructions of their single union. The local, regional, and national administrative committees were, on paper, supposed to focus their activities exclusively on coordinating actions between various single unions, correspondence, collecting statistics, and prisoner support. During periods of state repression, they ended up taking on greater responsibilities because the close links between the single unions and the CNT's main delegates were broken down.[32]

The committees of the regional federations were elected each year at the regional congresses, that were attended by mandated delegates from the local federations. In certain unusual situations, the members of the regional committees were expected to consult local trade unions and federations by means of either a referendum or correspondence. A regional committee could be replaced if the majority of local federations within the regional federation called for an extraordinary congress to take place, at which new delegates would be elected. The committee of the national federation was, in contrast, a role that was delegated to one of the regional committees on a temporary basis by the national federation's congress, which was attended by mandated delegates from every single union in the country. Between national congresses, decisions in the CNT that involved multiple single unions were made at plenums. A local federation's plenum was composed of the federal delegates from each single union's administrative committee, who were mandated on how to vote at the plenum by those who had elected them. These local federal delegates then elected and mandated a delegate to represent the area at a regional plenum of local committees that, in turn, sent mandated delegates to a national plenum of regional committees.[33]

A more detailed description of how the CNT was organized is made by the brickmaker José Peirats, who was a member of the CNT from 1922 onward, and was elected as the organization's general secretary in 1947. In the CNT,

> The unions constitute autonomous units, linked to the ensemble of the Confederation only by the accords of a general nature adopted at national congresses, whether regular or extraordinary. Apart from this commitment, the unions, right up to their technical sections, are free to reach any decision which is not detrimental to the organization as a whole... it is the unions which decide and directly regulate the guidelines of the Confederation. At all times, the basis for any local, regional, or national decision is the general assembly of the union, where every member has the right to attend, raise and discuss issues, and vote on proposals. Resolutions are adopted by majority vote attenuated by proportional representation. Extraordinary congresses are held on the suggestion of the assembled unions. Even the agenda is devised by the assemblies where the items on the agenda are debated and delegates appointed as the executors of their collective will. This federalist procedure, operating from the bottom up, constitutes a precaution against any possible authoritarian degeneration in the representative committees.[34]

FIGURE 1: THE STRUCTURE OF THE CNT

Based on diagram in Ackelsberg, *Free Women of Spain*, 230, and the accounts cited above.

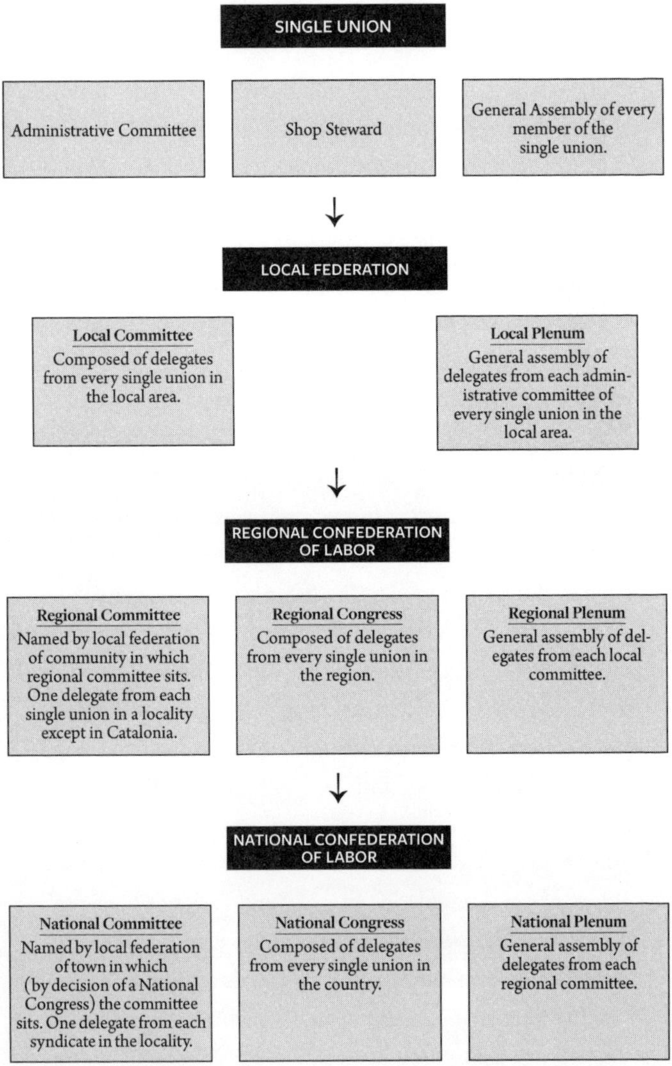

SINGLE UNION

Administrative Committee

Shop Steward

General Assembly of every member of the single union.

LOCAL FEDERATION

Local Committee
Composed of delegates from every single union in the local area.

Local Plenum
General assembly of delegates from each administrative committee of every single union in the local area.

REGIONAL CONFEDERATION OF LABOR

Regional Committee
Named by local federation of community in which regional committee sits. One delegate from each single union in a locality except in Catalonia.

Regional Congress
Composed of delegates from every single union in the region.

Regional Plenum
General assembly of delegates from each local committee.

NATIONAL CONFEDERATION OF LABOR

National Committee
Named by local federation of town in which (by decision of a National Congress) the committee sits. One delegate from each syndicate in the locality.

National Congress
Composed of delegates from every single union in the country.

National Plenum
General assembly of delegates from each regional committee.

The CNT's system of majority voting was explained in more detail within the organization's constitution, which was printed on the trade union's membership card. It declared that "Anarcho-syndicalism and anarchism recognize the validity of majority decisions. The militant has a right to his own point of view and to defend it, but he is obliged to comply with majority decisions, even when they are against his own feelings... We recognize the sovereignty of the individual, but we accept and agree to carry out the collective mandate taken by majority decision. Without this there is no organization."[35]

Members of the CNT did, nonetheless, disagree about whether or not this system of majority voting, in which decisions were binding on all members, should be applied to much smaller specific anarchist organizations. The Iberian Anarchist Federation (FAI) was a specific anarchist organization composed of small affinity groups. The FAI initially made most of their decisions via unanimous agreement and rarely used voting. In 1934, the Z and Nervio affinity groups pushed for the FAI to adopt binding agreements established through majority vote. The Afinidad affinity group, which included Peirats, agreed with the necessity of such a system within the CNT, but opposed it being implemented within small specific anarchist organizations or affinity groups. After a confrontational FAI meeting Afinidad left the organization in protest.[36]

The extent to which anarchists within the CNT valued its federalist system of organization can be seen in the actions of the twelve to fifteen thousand former members of the Durruti Column, who had fled to France after the defeat of the Spanish revolution in 1939, and were imprisoned in the Vernet d'Ariège concentration camp. Despite the abysmal conditions of the camp—lack of adequate housing, food shortages, disease, and very cold weather—the anarchists established a mirror image of the CNT. Every anarchist belonged to a general assembly within their hut, which elected a hut committee to represent them. These hut committees then federated

together and elected sector committees, which in turn voted for a
camp committee. The camp committee then sent demands from the
general assemblies to the French authorities running the concentration camp. In so doing, they practiced what little anarchism they
could within the direst of circumstances.[37]

Mass anarchists advocated and built large-scale federations,
but these were not the only kind of organizations they valued. They
understood that different forms of organization were appropriate
for different tasks and, to this end, also advocated the formation of
affinity groups that were either permanent or formed for specific
actions, and dissolved once the action was complete.[38] The CNT
itself contained numerous affinity groups that performed a wide
variety of tasks, ranging from publishing texts, organizing debates
and lectures, engaging in prisoner support, protecting prominent
anarchist militants, robbing banks, and assassinating class enemies.[39]

Reform not Reformism

Mass anarchists and insurrectionist anarchists agreed that fundamental social change can only be achieved by mass movements.
What separated the two is that mass anarchists believed that, given
their immediate social and historical context, the most realistic and
effective means to develop mass movements was through the long
and patient work of struggling for immediate reforms in the present,
rather than isolated individuals or small anarchist groups engaging
in propaganda of the deed in order to inspire a series of popular
uprisings. Mass anarchists used a variety of different terms to refer
to modifications to existing dominant structures and social relations, such as "gains," "improvements," or "reforms."

This position was originally advocated by anarchists in the
First International. In 1869 Bakunin argued that a significant number of workers could develop revolutionary socialist consciousness

"through [the] the collective action and practice" of *the organization and the federation of resistance funds* [strike funds]" and the "real struggle to reduce hours of work and increase pay."[40] An anarchist pamphlet published in 1872 claimed that the International "must gradually change the economic situation of the working class . . . improve working conditions, curtail, diminish and eliminate the privileges of capital, make these every day more dependent and precarious, until capital surrenders and disappears. . . . This can be achieved by *resistance*, with the legal and open weapon of the *strike*."[41]

This view was repeated four decades later by the CNT's paper *Solidaridad Obrera*, which claimed in January 1917 that radical trade union movements, such as the CNT, were simultaneously committed to achieving the "reformism" of "the reduction of the working day, the increase in wages, etc." and the "revolutionism" of "the emancipation of the proletariat through the abolition of capital and of the wage earner."[42] Fourteen years later, the CNT declared in its 1931 Madrid Congress resolutions that, although they were "openly at war with the state," and aimed "to educate the people to understand the need to unite with us to secure our complete emancipation by means of the social revolution," they also had "the ineluctable duty of indicating to the people a schedule of minimum demands that they should press by building up their own revolutionary strength."[43]

In order to understand why mass anarchists advocated this strategy, it is important to first outline their critique of insurrectionist anarchism. According to Malatesta, insurrectionists mistakenly viewed "present society as an indivisible block susceptible to no alteration beyond a radical transformation, and thus regarded as useless any attempt at improvements and concerned themselves solely with *making revolution* . . . which was then not made and remained a distant promise."[44] Propaganda of the deed had been conceived as the means by which anarchists would spark a revolutionary upsurge, but the two main versions of it—small armed bands launching insurrections and individual acts of violence (assassinations or bombings)—had consistently failed to pave the way for mass uprisings, let alone achieve the social revolution. This was despite the fact that insurrectionist anarchists had engaged in numerous revolts, assassinations, and bombings between the 1870s and 1890s.

It was argued that these tactics actively encouraged anarchists to isolate themselves from the majority of the working classes in order to avoid state repression, surveillance, and infiltration. Anarchists, thus, were unable to influence or inspire the working classes in the way that they had intended and hoped for. In 1889, twelve years after the Benevento affair, Malatesta wrote that small armed groups of anarchists failed to inspire revolts because inadequate preparation among and contact with the populace led to the group being "scattered and defeated before the people even get to learn what it is that the band wanted!"[45] Under these circumstances, the local populace were unable to join the band, and could merely look on impassively.

Malatesta expanded upon this argument in 1894, when he concluded that a "great spontaneous insurrection" would most likely not launch the social revolution, because "plots and conspiracies can only embrace a very limited number of individuals and are usually impotent to start a movement among the people of sufficient importance to give a chance of victory. Isolated movements, more or less spontaneous, are almost always stifled in blood before they have had time to acquire importance and become general."[46] A few years later in 1897, Malatesta insisted that uprisings "*cannot be improvised*" and that "a revolution without resources, without an agreed-upon plan, without weapons, without men" would be doomed to failure.[47] Anarchists attempting to launch insurrections while they were such a small minority had only resulted in a cycle of "six months of quiet activity, followed by a few microscopic uprisings—or more often, mere threats of uprisings—then arrests, flights abroad, interruption of propaganda, disintegration of the organization. . . . Just to start the whole thing all over again two or three years further down the line."[48] Given this, Malatesta concluded in 1899 that, in order for insurrections to be successful, anarchists must, "rather than face periodical and pointless slaughter . . . lay preparations appropriate for the force we are going to have to confront" and federate in order to accumulate "the strength required to steer the next popular uprising to victory."[49]

The tactics of assassination and bombings, in contrast, contributed toward the anarchist movement suffering an extreme amount of state repression, without achieving any substantial social change worth that price. Such tactics had been conceived of as acts of propaganda, but were instead a key factor in why a significant number of workers became less likely to listen to anarchists and adopt their ideas. They instead came to stereotype anarchists negatively as dangerous individuals, mindlessly spreading chaos and destruction.[50] The French anarchist Fernand Pelloutier remarked in 1895 that "I know many workers who are disenchanted with parliamentary socialism but who hesitate to support libertarian socialism because, in their view, anarchism simply implies the individualistic use of the bomb."[51] After McKinley's assassination in 1901, the Yiddish-speaking anarchist Yanovsky wrote, "the benefits that such an attempt can bring to the propaganda of our ideas are very questionable, the damage however is certain and sure."[52]

Even Most, who had been a fervent advocate of anarchist assassinations and bomb plots during the 1880s, ended up changing his mind.[53] He wrote in 1892 that "there is no greater error than to believe that we as anarchists need only to commit any deed, no matter when, where, and against whom. To have a propagandist effect, every deed needs to be popular. . . . If that is not the case, or if it actually meets with disapproval from the very part of the population it is intended to inspire, anarchism makes itself unpopular and hated. Instead of winning new adherents, many will withdraw."[54]

Shortly afterward, Most responded to Berkman's unexpected assassination attempt against the American capitalist Frick by publicly opposing the act. He argued that "in a country where we are so weakly represented and so little understood . . . we cannot afford the luxury of assassinations. . . . In countries like America, where we still need solid ground to stand on, we must limit ourselves to literary and verbal agitation."[55]

Insurrectionist anarchists had above all been wrong to assume that the revolution was imminent, and that the working classes would rise up in reaction to the violent actions of a few. As early as 1885, the Spanish anarchist Serrano had insisted that "individual actions—even if they employ thousands upon thousands of kilos of dynamite—will not succeed in any region, nor will they succeed in destroying the bourgeoisie or in bringing about the Social Revolution."[56] Over a decade later, in an 1897 interview, Malatesta said that "in the early days of the anarchist movement . . . there was the illusion that the revolution was just around the corner; and, as a result, any organizational work that required a long and patient endeavor was neglected."[57] He recalled in 1928 that "we put our hopes in general discontent, and because the misery that afflicted the masses was so insufferable, we believed it was enough to give an example, launching with arms in hand the cry of 'down with the masters,' in order for the working masses to fling themselves against the bourgeoisie and take possession of the land, the factories, and all that they produced with their toil and that had been stolen from them."[58]

In a 1902 letter to Max Nettlau, Kropotkin noted that the wave of propaganda of the deed was motivated by the belief "that all it took to trigger the revolution was a few heroic feats" and, when this failed to happen, several younger anarchists came to realize that "a revolution cannot be *provoked* by ten or a hundred" and that it was a delusion to imagine "that a sharp push by a few might successfully spark revolution."[59] A revolution, he said, could only be produced by "the slow work of organization and preparatory propaganda among the working masses."[60] This was, of course, not a new insight for mass anarchists, including Kropotkin. In his 1899 autobiography, he claimed that, in the late 1870s, he and other members of the Jura Federation understood that to abolish class society a period of "tedious propaganda and a long succession of struggles, of individual and collective revolts against the now prevailing forms of property, of individual self-sacrifice, of partial attempts at reconstruction and partial revolutions would have to be lived through."[61]

The strategy of engaging in individual acts of violence above all rested on a false view of social change. Social change is not just a matter of attacking the existing order until it collapses. The transformation of society requires the transformation of the working classes' capacities, drives, and consciousness in an anarchist direction such that they learn to self-organize horizontally and undertake a revolution. Killing a monarch or blowing up a building might temporarily scare the ruling classes or inspire a small number of workers, but it will not lead to fundamental social change. A new monarch will be crowned and the building will be repaired. Society will carry on as normal, because the general population will have merely observed the actions of an isolated individual and not have themselves engaged in forms of practice that transform them as people. In the aftermath of any anarchist attack, a typical worker could continue to behave as before, and thereby reproduce the dominant structures of class society.

"An edifice built upon centuries of history," Kropotkin remarked in 1891, "cannot be destroyed by a few kilos of explosives."[62] Malatesta made the same point in 1894: "one thing is certain, namely, that with a number of bombs and a number of blows of the knife, a society like bourgeois society cannot be overthrown, being based, as it is, on an enormous mass of private interests and prejudices, and sustained, more than it is by the force of arms, by the inertia of the masses and their habits of submission."[63]

The mass anarchist alternative to propaganda of the deed, as understood by insurrectionists, was not inaction and relying solely on print media and speaking tours to spread anarchism until the day of revolution. Malatesta's program of 1899 rejected this explicitly, because anarchists "would soon exhaust our field of action; that is, we would have converted all those who in the existing environment are susceptible to understand and accept our ideas."[64] Mass anarchists, in other words, held that, since what people think or are open to thinking is a product of their social environment, it follows that focusing on spreading ideas alone will not lead to fundamental social change. Under present conditions, which reproduce class society, only a small number of people will ever learn about and become anarchists through the written or spoken word.[65]

Anarchists therefore had to cause a "gradual transformation of the environment. Progress must advance contemporaneously and along parallel lines between man and their environment" until an increasingly large number of workers were in a position to learn about and adopt anarchism.[66] This view was repeated by Malatesta in 1922. He argued that, since "the will of humanity . . . is mostly determined by the social environment," it follows that anarchists must "work to change social conditions in such a way as to produce a change of will in the desired direction" and thereby cause "a recip- rocal interaction between the will and the surrounding conditions," such that changed people acted and changed social structures that, in turn, changed more people, and so on.[67]

Mass anarchists held that the most effective means for causing this gradual transformation in social structures, and the people who produced and reproduced them, was by organizing and participat- ing in working-class social movements that struggled for immediate reforms in the present. In 1892, Kropotkin said that anarchists should "permeate the great labor movement which is so rapidly grow- ing in Europe and America" in order to "bring our ideas into that movement, to spread them . . . among those masses which hold in their hands the future issue of the revolution."[68] In 1894, Malatesta argued that anarchists should win the working classes "over to our ideas by actively taking part in their struggles" and participating in "working-men's associations, strikes, collective revolt."[69] Three years later, he insisted that the success of anarchism required "long-term, constant, day-to-day work . . . done in conjunction with resistance societies, cooperatives, and educational circles, of gradually marshaling, organizing, and educating all the fighting forces of the proletariat."[70]

Malatesta, in addition to this, referred to specific reforms that were worth struggling for. In 1899, he argued that,

> we must always push them [workers] to demand greater
> things; but meanwhile we must encourage and assist them
> in the battles they want to fight, providing that they are in
> the right direction, which is to say, that they tend to facili-
> tate future gains and are fought in such a way that workers
> become used to thinking of their masters and governments as
> enemies, and to desiring to achieve what they want by them-
> selves. Many workers wish to not work over 8 hours. . . . The
> reform is among those that tend to actually improve the status
> of workers and facilitate future gains; and we, when we cannot
> convince them to demand more, we must support them in
> such a modest claim.[71]

Organizing to win reforms through direct action was considered valuable for three main reasons. First, and most obviously,
achieving reforms improved the lives of workers and put them in
a position where they had more time, energy, and motivation to
emancipate themselves fully. Malatesta wrote in 1897 that anarchists are "interested in people's circumstances being improved to
the greatest possible extent, starting today," both because of the

"immediate impact of reduced suffering" and "because when one is better nourished, has greater freedom, and is better educated, one has a greater determination and more strength to fully emancipate oneself."[72]

This line of reasoning persuaded Goldman to support the struggle for the eight-hour day and abandon her previous view, which she had learned from Most, that it was a pointless reform that distracted workers from launching a social revolution. She changed her mind after a worker at one of her talks against the eight-hour day explained that it would improve the lives of workers, many of whom would not live long enough to see a revolution, and would give them more time to read and enjoy life.[73] Rocker, in comparison, came to reject the idea that reforms should be opposed after he visited extremely poor areas of London. During these visits, he realized that "those who have been born into misery and never knew a better state are rarely able to resist and revolt. . . . It is contrary to all the experience of history and of psychology; people who are not prepared to fight for the betterment of their living conditions are not likely to fight for social emancipation."[74]

Second, participating in daily struggles for immediate reforms, such as strikes, provided the means to organize and make contact with not only committed socialists, who seek each other out, but also the large number of workers who are yet to become revolutionaries. This was especially important because, regardless of what anarchists did, state socialists would participate in working-class social movements and funnel them toward parliamentary politics. If this happened, given the arguments previously explained in chapter 5, social movements would be transformed from potential threats to ruling class power into maintainers of the status quo. As a result, it was essential that anarchists join struggles for immediate reforms in order to promote direct action and ensure that social movements remained, or became, forces outside of and against the state.[75]

Third, collectively struggling for reforms by means of direct action within prefigurative organizations is a form of practice that can positively transform workers. Whether or not a social movement wins great victories, the process of engaging in class struggle is valuable in and of itself. It enables workers to develop new skills, hopes, desires, and ways of thinking, such as learning how to organize a strike, or realizing that the police exist to violently defend the interests of the rich and powerful. As Guillaume wrote in 1914, "you think that the starting point is the revolutionary ideal and that the workers' struggle against the bosses only comes afterwards, as a consequence of the adoption of the 'ideal'; I think on the contrary ... that the starting point is the struggle and the ideal comes after, that it takes form in the workers' minds as the incidents of the class war give birth to it and cause it to develop."[76]

This theory was advocated for many decades by mass anarchists involved in the trade union movement. Baginski argued in 1909 that "the proletariat learns from its daily battles that it is always thrown back on itself, on its own strength and solidarity. Whenever it accomplishes small improvements of its situation, it does so as a consequence of direct intervention and struggle. Its condition is a function of the strength of its unity, its revolutionary insights, initiative, and solidarity; for exploiters concede only what is wrested from them through *the development of proletarian power*."[77] The practice of struggling for reforms through direct action was valued because it transformed workers—who are typically treated as objects acted upon or represented by others—into self-acting agents who fight for their own emancipation, and develop their collective power to transform society.[78] Given this, "no one disputes the utility and necessity of wrestling as much as possible for higher pay and shorter hours; but that should be considered in the light of merely preparatory exercises, as training for the final event, the Social Revolution and the overthrow of wage-slavery."[79]

These same ideas were expressed by Rocker through the language of pedagogy in 1938. He claimed that "the strike is for the workers not only a means for the defense of immediate economic interests, it is also a continuous schooling for their powers of resistance, showing them every day that every last right has to be won by unceasing struggle against the existing system."[80] As a result, "the economic alliance of the producers" is both "a weapon for the enforcement of better living conditions" and "a practical school, a university of experience, from which they draw instruction and enlightenment in richest measure."[81] The experience of class struggle transformed how workers thought about themselves and the world in which they lived. By reflecting on these life experiences, workers "developed . . . new needs and the urge for different fields of intellectual life."[82] The practice of engaging in class struggle was transformative not only at the individual level; it also altered the social relations between workers. Through their experience of cooperating with one another, such as going on strike in support of other striking workers, they developed a sense of solidarity among themselves, which Rocker defined as a "feeling of mutual helpfulness."[83] Developing this sense of solidarity was essential because, without it, they would never learn to act as a united class and thereby transform society in their shared class interests.

Although mass anarchists advocated struggling for immediate reforms, they were not reformists in the sense of people who view reforms as a political endpoint, or who hold that capitalism and the state could eventually be abolished through gradual reform. In September 1897, Malatesta wrote that "the reforms, both economic and political, that can be obtained under certain institutions, are limited by the very nature of those institutions, and sooner or later, depending on the degree of popular consciousness and the more or less blind resistance from the ruling classes, a point of irreconcilability is reached and the very existence of these institutions needs to be called into question."[84]

A month later, in an interview with a state socialist, Malatesta explained that anarchists were not "a reformist party" because "in our view, reforms, if and where they can be won, should be only a first step on the way to revolution; this is why we want the people to win them for themselves and feel that reforms are a result of their vigor, so that their determination to demand ever more may develop."[85] This was a restatement of a claim Malatesta had previously made in his 1890 article, "Matters Revolutionary":

> We must immerse ourselves in the life of the people as fully as we can, encourage and egg on all stirrings that carry a seed of material or moral revolt and get the people used to handling their affairs for themselves and relying on only their own resources; but without ever losing sight of the fact that revolution, by means of the expropriation and taking of property into common ownership, plus the demolition of authority, represents the only salvation for the proletariat and for Mankind, in which case a thing is good or bad depending on whether it brings forward or postpones, eases or creates difficulties for that revolution.
>
> As we see it, it is a matter of avoiding two reefs: on the one hand, the indifference toward everyday life and struggles that distance us from the people, making us unfathomable outsiders to them—and, on the other, letting ourselves be consumed by those struggles, affording them greater importance than they possess and eventually forgetting about the revolution.[86]

Mass anarchists, in other words, saw the struggle for reforms as the means to bring increasingly large numbers of workers together under a common aim, due to their shared interest in improving their lives in the here and now. In struggling for these reforms, workers would not only change social relations, such as reducing the length of the working day, but also change themselves due to the experience of participating in prefigurative organizations and engaging in direct action against the ruling classes. The consequence of this would be that a significant number of workers would, over varying lengths of time, go from only aiming at small improvements within existing society to being revolutionaries, who were organized and united as a class within federations and who had developed the initiative to act for themselves. This process would repeat, until the conflict between the working classes and the ruling classes escalated to the point of an armed insurrection being launched by the social movements that had been developed during previous struggles for reforms. To quote Malatesta's 1899 anarchist program, "one always comes back to insurrection, for if the government does not give way, the people will end by rebelling; and if the government does give way, then people gain confidence in themselves and make ever-increasing demands, until such time as the incompatibility between freedom and authority becomes clear and the violent struggle is engaged."[87]

Mass anarchists understood, alongside anarchists in general, that evolutionary change does not necessarily lead to progress or an anarchist revolution. They were careful about which reforms they supported, who they worked with, and the means they proposed to achieve these reforms. In 1897, Kropotkin insisted that anarchists "have to cling to our principles while working with others" and therefore must "never allow ourselves to be chosen as or turn into exploiters, bosses, leaders," "never have any truck with the building of some pyramidal organization, be it economic, governmental or educational-religious (even be it a revolutionary one)," and "never have any hand in conjuring up man's governance of his fellow man in the realm of production and distribution, political organization, leadership, revolutionary organization, etc."[88]

For mass anarchists, it was essential, in the words of Malatesta, to fight *as* anarchists, to "remain anarchists and act like anarchists before, during and after the revolution."[89] To participate within working-class social movements as committed anarchists was primarily for them to persuade other workers to act in an anarchistic manner, such as taking direct action against the ruling classes, making decisions within general assemblies, or coordinating action over a large area via federations. According to Malatesta, anarchists have to "take advantage of all the means, all the possibilities and the opportunities that the present environment allows us to act on our fellow men" and thereby incite the working class "to make demands, and impose itself and take for itself all the improvements and freedoms that it desires as and when it reaches the state of wanting them, and the power to demand them."[90]

Malatesta explained in his 1897 interview that "as a rule, we always support reforms that, more than the others, highlight the conflict between property-owners and proletarians, rulers and ruled, and therefore are apt to foster a conscious feeling of rebellion that will explode into the definitive, final revolution."[91] He rejected "false reforms" that "tend to distract the masses from the struggle against authority and capitalism" and instead "serve to paralyze their actions and make them hope that something can be attained through the kindness of the exploiters and governments."[92] One reform that mass anarchists consistently opposed was universal suffrage within existing capitalist states. In 1873, Bakunin argued against struggling to achieve the vote, because it would legitimize the state by giving it the "false appearance of popular government" and thereby provide the economic ruling classes "with a stronger and more reliable guarantee of their peaceful and intensive exploitation of the people's labor."[93] This opposition to struggling for universal suffrage included women's suffrage, which Goldman argued against in 1910, on the grounds that it would not further the emancipation of women.[94]

Mass anarchists also rejected methods of winning reforms that consolidated the dominant structures of class society, rather than building the revolutionary strength of the working classes. In Malatesta's words, anarchists "should never recognize the [existing] institutions. We shall carry out all possible reforms in the spirit in which an army advances ever forward by snatching the enemy-occupied territory in its path."[95] This led mass anarchists to argue that reforms should be won by imposing external pressure onto the ruling classes through direct action, rather than by campaigning for new legislation. For example, in 1875, Schwitzguébel wrote that "instead of begging the State for a law compelling employers to make them work only so many hours, the trade associations [*sociétés de métiers*] *directly impose* this reform on the employers [*patrons*]; in this way, instead of a legal text which remains a dead letter, a real economic change is effected *by the direct initiative of the workers*."[96] Or, as Malatesta told a court while on trial in April 1898, "there cannot be reforms on the part of a government, unless the people demand and impose them."[97]

The extent to which some mass anarchists were in favor of winning reforms through extremely radical means can be seen in the history of the CNT. In 1931, brick workers used a diversity of tactics to successfully end a system in which they worked for capitalists via exploitative contractors. They not only went on strike but also formed armed groups that would both hunt down scabs escorted by the police, and commit arson attacks against several brickworks. Bakery workers went further and, without even going on strike, forced capitalists to give in to their demands for the abolition of night work and changing the start of the working day to 5 a.m. This was achieved by bombing a number of bakeries. Those capitalists who refused to recognize the deal and punished organizers were subject to an escalation of resistance. This began with boycotts that, after they proved unsuccessful, were followed up with more militant activity, such as more bombings. On one occasion, Peirats and a comrade visited a capitalist armed with pistols in order to make him change his mind.[98]

It is clear that mass anarchists within the CNT did not reject the use of guns and bombs to achieve reform. They also used them in self-defense against the violence of the ruling classes. From 1914 onward, gunmen hired by capitalists and the state attempted to assassinate a significant number of anarchist trade unionists. In Catalonia, between 1920 and 1923, 104 anarchists were killed—including the former general secretary of the Catalan Regional Federation, Salvador Seguí—and thirty-three were wounded. The militant wing of the CNT responded to these violent attacks by organizing armed affinity groups to identify, locate, and kill those responsible.[99] This included the assassination of the Spanish Prime Minister Eduardo Dato on March 8, 1921, by members of an action group in the metal industry.[100] These kinds of assassinations had previously been viewed by insurrectionist anarchists in the 1880s and 1890s as one of the means that anarchists could use to develop a mass movement. Mass anarchists who supported assassinations, in contrast, appear to have viewed them as a means to defend already existing mass movements that had been developed through the struggle for immediate reforms.

Armed self-defense by anarchist militants continued over the following years. In July 1931, the CNT's builders' union responded to a police raid on their offices with gunfire. This led to a four-hour siege, during which the building was surrounded by hundreds of policemen, assault guards, and soldiers. Six workers were killed and dozens were wounded on both sides.[101] Violence was also used by some mass anarchists to acquire funds for the revolution. From 1933 to 1935, militants within the CNT responded to the trade union's dire financial problems by launching armed robberies against banks, which on several occasions involved shoot-outs with the police and fleeing the scene of the crime in stolen cars. Despite the financial gains these armed expropriations bought to the union, a significant section of the CNT opposed them, including Peirats.[102]

Another disagreement among mass anarchists concerned when social movements should shift from focusing on immediate reforms to attempting to spark the social revolution via armed insurrection. During the 1920s and 1930s, there was a long-lasting dispute within the CNT between moderate and radical syndicalist anarchists. The moderates sought to build up the trade union's strength gradually through workplace organizing, while the radicals, who belonged to CNT's defense committees and to armed affinity groups like Nosotros, thought that the social revolution was near and that the time for reform had passed. This led the radical faction to engage in what they termed "revolutionary gymnastics," which referred to the strategy of dedicated anarchist militants launching insurrections that would be repressed and thereby inspire an increasing number of workers to rise up. In practice, the series of armed uprisings they organized in January 1932, January 1933, and December 1933 were all unsuccessful and defeated quickly, due to a combination of lack of popular support, insufficient weaponry, and the state being prepared to repress them.[103]

Militant Minority

Mass anarchists believed that it was necessary to participate in social movements as a militant minority in order to ensure that struggles for reforms did not collapse into reformism and, instead, developed a revolutionary mass movement that could launch a large-scale armed insurrection. This meant spreading anarchist ideas, acting as key and effective organizers, encouraging or inspiring workers to take direct action, and ensuring that formal organizations or informal groups were horizontally structured and made decisions in a manner that prefigured an anarchist society. In 1931, Malatesta wrote that "anarchy can only come about gradually, as the masses become able to conceive it and desire it; but will never come to pass unless driven forward by a more or less consciously anarchist minority operating in such a way as to create the appropriate climate."[104]

The notion of a militant minority within working-class social movements was expressed by mass anarchists in a number of different ways. An 1892 article published in *La Révolte* claimed that, although the revolution would "be made by the pressure of the masses . . . these masses themselves are looking for people to take the initiative, they are looking for men and women who can better formulate their thoughts, who will be able to win over the hesitant and carry with them the timid."[105] This required "active minorities," who were "avant-gardist" and embodied "individual initiative, put at the service of the collectivity."[106] Malatesta referred to anarchists as a "conscious minority" and "vanguard."[107] Berkman thought that anarchists were "the most advanced and revolutionary element."[108] In Spain, the anarchist militants of the CNT were known among other workers as "the ones with ideas."[109]

Such language did not mean that anarchists viewed themselves as separate from the working classes or the workers' movement. Anarchism was a social movement whose members were overwhelmingly drawn from the working classes. As Fabbri noted, it "is *de facto* a teaching whose followers are almost exclusively proletarians: bourgeois, petit bourgeois, so-called intellectuals or professional people, etc. are very few and far between and wield no predominate influence."[110] In referring to themselves as a militant minority, anarchists were only expressing the view that they had the most advanced revolutionary ideas within the working classes and, by virtue of this, had a key role to play in the collective struggle for human emancipation.

The main task of anarchists as a militant segment of the working classes was to bring about a transformation in the consciousness of other workers such that they came to adopt anarchist ideas, overthrow capitalism and the state, and build an anarchist society. For Dunois, "our task as anarchists, the most advanced, the boldest and the most uninhibited sector of the militant proletariat, is to stay constantly by its side, to fight the same battles amongst its ranks . . . to provide this enormous moving mass that is the modern proletariat . . . with a goal and the means of action" and so act as the "educators, stimulators and guides of the working masses."[111] This point was repeatedly made by Malatesta. In 1897, he wrote that anarchists should "cultivate in the proletariat a consciousness of the class antagonism and the need for collective struggle, and a yearning to . . . [establish] equality, justice, and freedom for everyone."[112] During his trial in April 1898, Malatesta told the court that anarchists "want the complete transformation of society, which must spring from the will of the masses, once they become conscious. It is precisely toward the formation of that consciousness that we are working, through the press, the talks and organization."[113]

How anarchists acted as a militant minority varied according to the context. In 1891, it took the form of anarchists in Rome launching a preplanned riot by attacking the police at a May Day demonstration. This attack was triggered by the anarchist Galileo Palla giving his comrades a signal to begin when he ended his speech by declaring, "Long live the revolution!" and then jumped off the speaker's platform into the crowd. This riot, which the anarchist militant minority initiated, lasted for several hours after it spread quickly to the rest of the crowd and other districts of Rome. So sudden was the riot that both contemporary observers and modern historians have mistaken it for a purely spontaneous affair and failed to realize that it was the outcome of conscious anarchist activity. Six years later in 1897, Italian anarchists in Ancona, including Malatesta, acted as a militant minority in a different manner by actively supporting the unionization of dock workers, bakers, barbers, and shoemakers.[114]

The Yiddish-speaking anarchist Yanovsky acted as a militant minority during the early 1890s in London when he opposed a trade unionist called Lewis Lyons, who sought to organize master tailors, who were employers, alongside wage laborers. Yanovsky combated this attempt to unite groups with opposed class interests by denouncing Lyons's plans in articles he wrote for the *Arbeter Fraint* and by speaking at every public meeting that was held on the question, regardless of which side in the dispute organized it. In this way, Yanovsky was able to defeat Lyons and force him to leave the Jewish labor movement.[115] Yanovsky was not unique in this respect. Jewish anarchists living in London, alongside Rocker, played a key role in organizing trade unions and strikes. According to Rocker, "all the Jewish trade unions in the East End, without exception, were started by the initiative of the Jewish anarchists."[116]

In 1912, this activity culminated in Jewish tailors launching a general strike to abolish sweatshops in the East End. The strike, which mobilized 13,000 workers in two days, was launched in solidarity with striking tailors in the West End, whose strike had initially been undermined by strike-breaking work within the East End sweatshops. Rocker acted as a militant minority by attending all the meetings of the strike committee, acting as Chairman of the Finance Committee, editing the daily *Arbeter Fraint*, and addressing three or four strike meetings a day. After three weeks on strike, the workers employed in men's tailoring emerged victorious having won shorter hours; an end to piecework; better sanitary conditions; and the employment of union labor only. The strike continued within the women's garment industry, where Jewish workers were overwhelmingly employed, until the capitalists gave in. In so doing they had, according to Rocker, ended the sweatshop system.[117]

The majority of anarchist militants who played key roles as organizers were not famous authors like Malatesta or Kropotkin, but self-taught workers whose names rarely appear in surviving primary sources. In the Spanish village of Casas Viejas, a trade union was formed by workers in 1914. One of the main organizers of the local union was a poor charcoal burner named José Olmo García, who provided other workers with anarchist literature, gave fiery speeches on anarchist ideas, and made persuasive points at group meetings.[118] Anarchist attempts to organize or participate in mass movements as a militant minority were of course not always successful. To focus on England, Italian anarchists living in London failed on several occasions to organize restaurant workers into a long-lasting trade union due, in part, to the temporary and seasonal nature of the work.[119] In September 1908, English anarchists in Leeds participated in a movement of unemployed people that began positively, from an anarchist perspective, by engaging in direct action but ended up being taken over by politicians, despite anarchist attempts to push it in a radical direction.[120]

Although mass anarchists viewed themselves as a militant minority who sought to influence the consciousness of other workers, they explicitly rejected authoritarian forms of vanguardism due to their commitment to the self-emancipation of the working classes. This rejection took four main forms. First, mass anarchists sought only to influence other members of the working classes through persuasion and engaging in actions that provided an example to others. For Malatesta, while "authoritarians see the mass of the people as raw material to be manipulated into whatever mold they please through the wielding of power by decree, the gun and the handcuff," anarchists "need the consent of the people and must therefore persuade by propaganda and by example."[121] The Russian anarchist Voline similarly wrote that, since revolutionary success can only be achieved by *the broad popular masses....* Our role in this realization will be limited to that of a ferment, an element providing assistance, advice, and an example."[122] Such influence was entirely consistent with the goal of anarchism since, according to Malatesta, an anarchist society is one in which nobody is "in a position to oblige others to submit to their will or to exercise their influence other than through the power of reason and by example."[123]

Second, mass anarchists encouraged other workers to act for themselves and self-organize. In 1894, Malatesta claimed that "it is necessary that the people be conscious of their rights and their strength; it is necessary that they be ready to fight and ready to take the conduct of their affairs into their own hands. It must be the constant preoccupation of the revolutionists, the point toward which all their activity must aim, to bring about this state of mind among the masses."[124] In a 1929 letter to Makhno, he wrote, "what matters most is that the people, men and women lose the sheeplike instincts and habits that thousands of years of slavery have instilled in them, and learn to think and act freely. And it is to this great work of moral liberation that the anarchists must specially dedicate themselves."[125]

Third, influential mass anarchist authors, rejected the view that they were superior to others and instead sought to treat nonanarchist workers as their equals. In 1890, Kropotkin wrote that anarchists who label others as unintelligent if they do not immediately embrace anarchism "forget that they were not anarchists from birth," and that it took an extended period of transformation for them to unlearn the prejudices they had been socialized into by class society.[126] Five years later, in 1895, he argued that, although anarchist militants had "an obligation to do everything possible to spread the anarchist idea among the working masses," they should not view themselves as "better than the 'ignorant masses' just because we are anarchists and they are not yet."[127] As Malatesta argued in 1894, anarchists should not "refuse to associate with working men who are not already perfect Anarchists" since "it is absolutely necessary to associate with them in order to make them becomes Anarchists."[128] Anarchists had to, in short, "take the people as they are and . . . move forward with them."[129] This coincided with the view that anarchists had to not only teach anarchist ideas to other workers, but also themselves learn from the various collective struggles that were organized by workers independently of anarchists.[130]

Fourth, mass anarchists opposed the seizure of state power in the name of the working classes because, as was explained in chapter 5, it would lead to the death of the revolution, and the establishment of a new system of minority rule in which the majority of workers were oppressed and exploited. The social revolution could only be achieved if workers decided to reorganize society themselves through their own organs of self-management. All mass anarchists could do to facilitate this process was to act as a militant minority in the same manner that they had done prior to the revolution: spreading anarchist ideas and engaging in actions that implemented the anarchist program and thereby served as an example to others. For Kropotkin, anarchists should not "let themselves be hoisted into power" during a revolution, but should instead "remain on the streets, in their own districts, with the people—as propagandists and organizers . . . joining in with the people as they looked to their food and their livelihoods and the city's defenses; living alongside the poor, getting impassioned about *their* everyday issues, their interests, and rebuilding, in the sections, the life of society with them."[131]

Mass anarchists continued to advocate this position in the aftermath of the 1917 Russian revolution. In 1922, Goldman opposed "the political power of the Party, organized and centralized in the state," in favor of "the industrial power of the masses, expressed through their libertarian associations."[132] Given this aim, the role of anarchists was "to guide the released energies of the people toward the reorganization of life on a libertarian foundation."[133] Two years later, Malatesta explained that "we cannot make the revolution exclusively 'ours' because we are a small minority. . . . [W]e must therefore content ourselves with a revolution that is as much 'ours' as possible, favoring and taking part, both morally and materially, in every movement directed toward justice and liberty and, when the insurrection has triumphed, ensure that the pace of the revolution is maintained, advancing toward ever greater freedom and justice."[134] If anarchists were successful in this, their position as a militant minority would fade away during the course of, or in the aftermath of, the social revolution itself, as more and more workers came to adopt and implement anarchist ideas themselves.[135]

According to Kropotkin and Malatesta, one of the main ways that anarchists should act as a militant minority during a revolution was by establishing autonomous regions, which refused to recognize the authority of any revolutionary government that was formed. In 1891, Kropotkin wrote that, during a revolution, anarchists would not "be able to avert . . . attempts at revolutionary government," but could instead only "conjure up from within the people itself a force that is mighty in its actions and in the constructive revolutionary tasks that it is to carry out, ignoring the authorities, no matter what name they may go under, growing exponentially by virtue of its revolutionary enterprise, its revolutionary vigor and its achievements in terms of tearing down and reorganizing."[136] This self-organized, federated force would undermine any attempts at revolutionary government because

> a people that will itself have organized the consumption of wealth and the reproduction of such assets in the interest of society as a whole will no longer be governable. A people that will itself be the armed strength of the country and which will have afforded armed citizens the requisite cohesion and concerted action, will no longer be susceptible to being ordered around. A people that will itself have organized railways, its navy, its schools is not going to be susceptible to being administered anymore. And finally, a people that will have shown itself capable of organizing arbitration to settle minor disputes will be one where every single individual will deem it his duty to stop the bully misusing the weakling, without waiting for providential intervention by the town sergeant, and will have no use for warders, judges or jailors.[137]

In the 1920 edition of Malatesta's anarchist program, which was based on the previous 1899 version and adopted by the Italian Anarchist Union, he recommended that anarchists "push the people" to expropriate the ruling classes, establish workplace and community assemblies that collectively own and control the means of production, and refuse "to nominate or recognize any government."[138] If the wider working classes choose not to do so, then anarchists "must—in the name of the right we have to be free even if others wish to remain slaves and because of the force of example—put into effect as many of our ideas as we can, refuse to recognize the new government and keep alive resistance and seek that those localities where our ideas are received with sympathy should constitute themselves into anarchist communities, rejecting all governmental interference and establishing free agreements with other communities which want to live their own lives."[139]

In 1925, Malatesta clarified that this included, if necessary, engaging in armed self-defense against the violence of the new state:

> If, despite our efforts, new forms of power were to arise that seek to obstruct the people's initiative and impose their own will, we must have no part in them, never give them any recognition. We must endeavor to ensure that the people refuse them the means of governing—refuse them, that is, the soldiers and the revenue; see to it that those powers remain weak… until the day comes when we can crush them once and for all. Anyway, we must lay claim to and demand, with force if needs be, our full autonomy, and the right and the means to organize ourselves as we see fit and to put our own methods into practice.[140]

CHAPTER 8

The History of Syndicalist Anarchism

Syndicalist anarchism advocated the formation of federally structured trade unions that united the working classes into a collective force, were independent of political parties, and engaged in direct action against the ruling classes. This was to be achieved either by forming whole new revolutionary trade unions, or by participating within existing reformist trade unions and transforming them from within. Historically, anarchist authors used a variety of different terms to refer to trade unions, such as *societies of resistance against capital, resistance societies, workers' associations,* or simply the *labor movement*.[1] The term *syndicalism* is itself derived from the French word for trade union—*syndicat*—and the phrase *syndicalisme révolutionnaire,* meaning trade unionism that is revolutionary.[2] For the sake of simplicity, I shall be using the English term trade union, rather than such historical terms.

Syndicalist anarchism was a form of mass anarchism, and so argued that anarchists should struggle for immediate reforms via direct action, especially strikes, sabotage, and boycotts. These collective struggles for reforms would, over time, develop an organized mass trade union movement with the necessary radical capacities, drives, and consciousness for abolishing capitalism and the state, in favor of an anarchist society. The social revolution would unfold through an insurrectionary general strike, during which the working classes would stop work, occupy their workplaces, expropriate the means of production from the ruling classes, and smash the state. In the course of the social revolution, the federally structured trade unions would evolve, from organizations engaged in economic resistance against the ruling classes into organizations that self-managed the economy, either in part or whole.[3]

Although all syndicalist anarchists generally agreed on the above strategy, they disagreed with one another on two main questions. These were:

1.   Should trade unions be politically neutral, or should they be explicitly committed to achieving an anarchist society through anarchist means?

2.   Are trade unions sufficient in and of themselves to achieve an anarchist society, or do they need to be assisted by a specific anarchist organization?

Three main forms of syndicalist anarchism emerged in response to these two questions: revolutionary syndicalism, syndicalism-plus, and anarcho-syndicalism.[4] In this chapter, I will establish what these positions meant, and why anarchists came to advocate them. This will be achieved through a detailed overview of the history of syndicalist anarchism, from its prehistory in the First International, to the formation of anarcho-syndicalism as an international movement in the early twentieth century. With this context in place, I will explain the main strategies that were generally advocated by syndicalist anarchists in chapter 9.

The Prehistory of Syndicalism

The strategy of revolutionary trade unionism, which would come to be known as syndicalism, was first advocated during debates within the First International and Saint-Imier International. At the September 1868 Brussels Congress of the First International, the Belgian delegate and typesetter César De Paepe advocated the formation of *resistance societies* that organized strikes to win immediate improvements and revolt against the ruling classes. In order to do so, they had to be "federated with one another—not only at the level of a trade or country, but across different countries and trades."[5] In the long term they would aim to achieve "the abolition of the wages system" through "the absorption of capital by labor."[6] The Brussels section of the International supported resistance societies "not only from regard to the necessities of the present, but also the future social order . . . we see in these trade unions the embryos of the great workers' companies which will one day replace the capitalist companies" and "embrace whole industries."[7] In February 1869, De Paepe expanded upon this point by arguing that "the International already offers the model of the society to come and that its various institutions, with the required modifications, will form the future social order. . . the society of resistance is destined to organize labor in the future. . . . Nothing will be more easy, when the moment comes, than to transform the societies of resistance into cooperative workshops, when the workers have agreed to demand the liquidation of the present society."[8]

Several months later, the Swiss Courtelary District section of the First International held a general assembly on August 29, 1869, in which a report on strike funds was approved. The report had been written by the engraver Adhémar Schwitzguébel, who would go on to become the corresponding secretary of the anarchist Jura Federation's Federal Committee.[9] The report advocated the formation of an international federation of trade unions, with a shared strike fund, on the grounds that they were an effective means to collectively resist the domination of capitalists and win higher wages. At the same time, they were viewed as having "the great advantage of preparing the general organization of the proletariat, of accustoming workers to identify their interests, to practice solidarity and to act in common for the interests of all. In short, they are the basis for the coming organization of society, since workers' associations will have to do no more than take over the running of industrial and agricultural enterprises."[10]

The strategy of revolutionary trade unionism continued to be articulated within the First International at its Basel Congress, held between September 5 and 12, 1869, and attended by, among others, Bakunin and Guillaume. During the morning session of September 11, the delegate Jean-Louis Pindy, who would go onto participate in the Paris Commune and become an anarchist, presented a report that was subsequently passed as a resolution of the congress.[11] Pindy, a cabinetmaker and the delegate of the Paris Construction Workers' Trade Union, proposed that all workers should establish strike funds, organize local trade unions, and then link these local trade unions together at national and international levels. In so doing, workers would create an organizational structure that enabled the exchange of information and coordinated strike action both within a country and between countries. The goal of these trade unions would be to engage in strikes until capitalism had been abolished and replaced by the federation of free producers. As capitalism was abolished, the trade unions would take over the organization of production, and be converted from organs of class struggle into organs of economic self-management. The federation of workers at the level of the town would form "the commune of the future" just as the federation of workers at the national and international level would form "the workers' representation of the future" under which "politics" would be replaced by "the associated councils of the various trades and a committee of their respective delegates" administrating and regulating "work relations."[12] The formation of national and international federations of trade unions was, therefore, not only necessary in order to engage in effective class struggle. It was also an essential component of establishing the social structures through which workers could organize a global socialist economy that "no longer recognizing frontiers, establishes a vast allocation of labor from one end of the world to the other."[13]

The same idea was advocated by the French bookbinder, collectivist, and trade union organizer Eugène Varlin, who later played a key role in the Paris Commune and was murdered by the French state in May 1871. He argued that working-class social movements "must actively work to prepare the organizational elements of the future society in order to make the work of social transformation that is imposed on the Revolution easier and more certain."[14] He was convinced that trade unions were one of the main forms of working-class self-organization that could do so: "trade societies (resistance, solidarity, union) deserve our encouragement and sympathy, for they are the natural elements of the social construction of the future; it is they who can easily become producer associations; it is they who will be able to operate social tools and organize production."[15]

One of the main proponents of revolutionary trade unionism in the First International was Bakunin. In August 1869, he argued that, prior to the social revolution, the main task of the First International should be to "give an essentially *economic character* to workers' agitation in every land; setting as its goal the reduction of working hours and higher wages" through "*the organization of the mass of workers* and *the creation of resistance* [strike] funds."[16] In so doing, the First International would, Bakunin predicted, grow into a mass movement that unified and organized millions of workers across Europe, if not the entire world, into trade unions with "the capacity to replace the political world of the state, and the departing bourgeois."[17] In a revolutionary situation, the First International would, due to its extensive experience of collective struggle, be "capable of taking things in hand and capable of giving them a sense of direction that will be really salutary for the people."[18] This included trade unions being converted from organs of class struggle into organs of economic self-management. In 1871 Bakunin declared that "the organization of the sections of skilled workers, their federations within the International Association, and their representation through the chambers of labor . . . sow the living seed of a new social order which shall replace the bourgeois world. They create not only the ideas but also the very facts of the future."[19]

The strategy of revolutionary trade unionism was also embraced by the sections of the First International that would go onto form the anarchist movement. On April 4, 1870, what would become the Jura Federation passed a resolution at the La Chaux-de-Fonds Congress. It recommended to all sections of the First International that they "direct all their activity toward the federative constitution of labor organizations, the sole means of assuring the success of the social revolution. This federation is the true representation of labor, which absolutely must take place outside of the political governments."[20] An almost identical resolution was passed by the Spanish section of the First International at its founding congress in 1870, attended by ninety delegates representing 40,000 members.[21]

The first congress of the Saint-Imier International in 1872 declared that trade unions "increase the sense of fraternity and community of interests" among the proletariat, and "give some experience in collective living and prepare for the supreme struggle."[22] Given this, "our broad intent is to build solidarity and organization. We regard strikes as a precious means of struggle, but we have no illusions about their economic result. We accept them as a consequence of the antagonism between labor and capital; they have as a necessary consequence that workers should become more and more alive to the abyss that exists between the proletariat and bourgeoisie and that workers' organizations should be strengthened, and, through ordinary economic struggles, the proletariat should be prepared for the great and final revolutionary struggle."[23]

The resolutions of the 1877 Verviers Congress expanded upon this point: "Congress, while it recognizes the importance of trades' organizations and recommends their formation on an international basis, declares that trades' organizations that have as their goal only the improvement of workers' situations, either through the reduction of working hours, or by the organization of wage levels, will never accomplish the emancipation of the proletariat, and that trade's organizations should adopt as their principal goal the abolition of the proletariat" through the forceful expropriation of the ruling classes.[24]

After the collapse of the Saint-Imier International, this strategy continued to be endorsed by a number of prominent anarchists. In 1884, Malatesta advocated "organizing the laboring masses into trades associations based on the principle of resistance and of attacking the bosses."[25] Three years earlier, Kropotkin wrote that anarchists should organize workers to wage war against capitalist exploitation "relentlessly, day by day, by the strike, by agitation, *by every revolutionary means*" in order to build "a formidable MACHINE OF STRUGGLE AGAINST CAPITAL," that united workers from every city, village, and trade into one union.[26] This process of class struggle would, at the same time, lead to an increasingly large number of workers becoming aware of their distinct class interests, developing a hatred of their oppressors, and acquiring the belief that capitalism must be overthrown.

For Kropotkin, the primary contemporary example of this strategy in action were Spanish anarchists who "remain within the working class, they struggle with it, for it" and "bring the contribution of their energy to the workers' organization and work to build up a force that will crush capital, come the day of the revolution: the revolutionary trades associations."[27] In so doing, they were not only furthering the cause of working-class self-emancipation, but were also being "faithful to the anarchist traditions of the International."[28] The Spanish anarchists to which Kropotkin was referring had founded the Workers' Federation of the Spanish Region, on September 24, 1881. The organization, which grew out

of the Spanish section of the First International (FRE), was a federation of trade unions that by the end of 1882 was composed of 218
federations, 663 sections, and 57,934 members. Its main paper, *La
Revista Social*, had 20,000 subscribers.[29]

Spanish anarchists were not the only anarchists to actively
participate within the trade union movement during the 1880s.
Anarchists in Chicago, including the future Haymarket martyrs
Albert Parsons and August Spies, attempted to build revolutionary trade unions and joined the struggle for the eight-hour day as
a means to spread anarchist ideas.[30] In Turin and Piedmont, Italian
anarchists played a key role within trade unions as organizers, delegates or editors of newspapers. This included Galleani, who had yet
to adopt his later rejection of trade unions and formal organizations
but was already beginning to move in this direction by 1889.[31] The
extent to which anarchists participated in trade union movements
during the late nineteenth century only becomes fully apparent
when one looks beyond the United States and Europe. Between
1870 and 1900 anarchists were instrumental in the creation of trade
unions and the organization of strikes in, at least, Argentina, Brazil,
Cuba, Mexico, Peru, and Uruguay.[32]

The Emergence of Revolutionary Syndicalism

Within Europe, the strategy of revolutionary trade unionism came
to be endorsed by an increasingly large number of anarchists in
response to the London dockland strike of 1889, during which a
strike by casual laborers grew over two weeks into a mass mobilization of 130,000 workers that shut down the entire dock and
disrupted supply chains such that factories in multiple industries
were forced to close. The strike, which ended with workers winning a wage increase, was reported on by Kropotkin, Malatesta, and
Pouget in several anarchist papers.[33] In response to these events,

Malatesta critiqued anarchists who had opposed participating in the trade union movement, and thereby enabled it to be taken over by moderates and parliamentary socialists. He argued that anarchists should instead "get back among the people ... let us organize as many strikes as we can; let us see to it that the strike becomes a contagion and that, once one erupts, it spreads to ten or a hundred different trades in ten or a hundred towns."[34]

In parallel to these developments, revolutionary syndicalism as a self-organized working-class movement began to emerge in France, with the creation of the first *bourse du travail* in 1887, three years after trade unions had been legalized in the country. The bourses du travail were initially labor exchanges where workers could find employment, but over the next decade morphed into working-class cultural, educational, and mutual aid centers, and then eventually trade unions that collected strike funds and organized strikes. In 1892, the delegates of ten bourses, including Fernand Pelloutier, met at Saint-Etienne and formed a national federation. A few years later, in 1895, Pelloutier, who had since become an anarchist after moving to Paris in 1893, was appointed general secretary of the Federation of Bourses du Travail.[35]

It was within this context that a significant number of French speaking anarchists came to publicly advocate anarchist participation within the trade union movement. This included Kropotkin, who wrote several articles for *La Révolte* between 1890 and 1891, that advocated revolutionary trade unionism.[36] A few years later, in October 1894, Pouget argued in *Le Père Peinard* that trade unions provided anarchists with an excellent space in which to act and make contact with the wider working class that existed beyond anarchist affinity groups and subcultures.[37] A year later in 1895, Pelloutier wrote an article called "Anarchism and the Workers' Union" for *Les Temps Nouveaux*. In it, he called on fellow anarchists to join the trade union movement en masse, and thereby spread their ideas among the working classes and instill in them the idea

that they should self-manage their own affairs. Previous and ongoing anarchist participation within the trade union movement had,
according to Pelloutier, already been successful in teaching workers
"the true meaning of anarchism" and expanding their notion of what
a trade union could be and become.[38]

Pouget and Pelloutier's call for anarchist participation within
the trade union movement was even echoed by some anarchist
groups who had previously been opposed to revolutionary trade
unionism, due to their commitment to the iron law of wages. By
1899, *Le Libertaire* had begun to change its attitude and published
an article by Luis Grandidier that claimed anarchists should "leave
this ivory tower in which we are suffocating" and "enter the trade
unions."[39] The ideas of French syndicalism also influenced anarchists from other countries. In 1900, Goldman visited France as
a delegate for the international anarchist congress in Paris, which
ended up being banned by the police and occurring in secret.
During her visit, she became an advocate of syndicalism after seeing it in action as a social movement, and hearing so many positive
things about Pelloutier. In 1913, she claimed that "on my return to
America I immediately began to propagate Syndicalist ideas, especially Direct Action and the General Strike."[40]

By the time of Pelloutier's premature death in 1901 at the age of
thirty-three, the National Federation of Bourses du Travail was composed of sixty-five bourses to which 782 dues-paying local unions
were affiliated. A year later in 1902, the federation merged with the
General Confederation of Labor (CGT) to form a new CGT. This
resulted in the emergence of revolutionary syndicalism as a mass
movement.[41] The CGT had, according to its own congress reports,
a membership of 100,000 workers at its refounding in 1902. Over
the next decade, it rapidly grew to 300,000 members by 1906, and
600,000 by 1912. Of these 600,000 members, an estimated 400,000
paid their dues. The scale of the CGT can only be understood relative to its historical context. In 1912, an estimated 1,027,000 workers

belonged to a trade union in France. The CGT therefore contained, if you limit the figure to dues-paying members, almost half of the unionized workers in France.[42]

The CGT was not itself a majority anarchist organization and contained several different factions. This included, but was not limited to, reformist syndicalists; anarchists who also identified as revolutionary syndicalists; anarchists who did not identify as revolutionary syndicalists; and revolutionary syndicalists who did not view themselves as anarchists. Nevertheless, anarchists did exert a significant influence on the organization in the early years of its existence.[43] In 1901, the anarchists Georges Yvetot and Paul Delesalle were elected as the general secretary and vice secretary of the National Federation of Bourses du Travail. That same year Pouget, who had been the editor of the CGT's paper *La Voix du peuple* since its creation in 1900, was elected as the vice secretary of the CGT. Pouget would remain in this position until late 1908, when he was briefly imprisoned for his involvement in the CGT's campaign for the eight-hour day and subsequently, after his release on October 31, ceased to be active within the organization. Delesalle, likewise, resigned from his position as vice secretary of the National Federation of Bourses du Travail at the CGT's 1908 congress of Marseilles, and instead focused his energies on running a second-hand bookshop and publishing radical literature. By 1914, despite anarchist influence within the CGT waning, roughly 100,000 members of the CGT supported anarchist positions at congresses through their elected delegates.[44]

The ideas of revolutionary syndicalism were formally crystalized by the CGT at its October 1906 congress, where it adopted the Charter of Amiens with 830 votes in favor and only eight opposed. The Charter, which was drafted in a restaurant by Victor Griffuelhes, Louis Niel, André Morizet, Pouget, and Delesalle, emerged out of a compromise between the revolutionary and reformist factions within the CGT.[45] It declared that the CGT sought to unite "all

workers conscious of the struggle to be conducted for the disappear-
ance of the system of wage-earning and management" regardless of
"their political schooling" in order to win immediate improvements,
and eventually overthrow capitalism via expropriation and the general strike.[46] It affirmed

> the complete liberty of members to participate, outside the
> union, in whatsoever forms of struggle conform to their polit-
> ical or philosophical views, and limits itself to requesting, in
> reciprocity, that they should not introduce into the unions
> opinions held outside it. As for the organization, Congress
> resolves, that since economic action must be conducted
> directly against employers for syndicalism to achieve its max-
> imum effect, the organization of the confederation, insofar as
> they are unions should not concern themselves with parties
> and sects, which, outside and alongside, may pursue social
> transformation in complete freedom.[47]

The charter's advocacy of political neutrality was worded in
such a manner that revolutionaries and reformists could interpret
the text in contradictory ways. For revolutionaries, the charter only
committed the CGT to independence from political parties and
so parliamentarism. Reformists, in comparison, interpreted the
charter as entailing a much stricter commitment to independence
from all forms of politics, including anarchism. This had the effect
that, when the CGT engaged in propaganda campaigns against militarism and patriotism, reformists viewed this as contradicting its
commitment to political neutrality.[48] This disagreement over the
meaning of political neutrality went alongside multiple attempts by
some reformist factions within the CGT to establish a formal alliance or tie between the trade union and socialist parties.[49]

Anarchists who were revolutionary syndicalists advocated
political neutrality because they believed that the function of a

trade union was to unite workers on the basis of their shared class interests, rather than on the basis of the specific school of political thought they subscribed to. The trade union, to quote Pouget, "groups together those who work against those who live by human exploitation: it brings together interests and not opinions."[50] He held that the CGT should be open to all workers, whatever their political or religious beliefs, including those amenable to the state. In theory, workers would join the trade union "imbued with the teachings of some (philosophical, political, religious, etc.) school of thought or another" and, through their experiences of engaging in direct action, "have their rough edges knocked off until they are left only with the principles to which they all subscribe: the yearning for improvement and comprehensive emancipation."[51]

This perspective on trade unions was articulated by the anarchist and revolutionary syndicalist Pierre Monatte on August 28 at the 1907 International Anarchist Congress in Amsterdam. According to Monatte,

> instead of opinion-based syndicalism, which gave rise to anarchist trade-unions in, for example, Russia and to Christian and social-democratic trade unions in Belgium and Germany, anarchists must provide the option of French-style syndicalism, a neutral—or more precisely, independent—form of syndicalism. Just as there is only one [working] class, so there should be only one single workers' organization, one single syndicate, for each trade and in each town. Only on this condition can the class struggle—no longer facing the obstacle of arguments between the various schools of schools of thought and rival sects on every point—develop to its fullest extent and have the greatest possible effect.[52]

From this, it followed that revolutionary syndicalism was sufficient unto itself. By this, he meant that revolutionary syndicalist trade unions could, by themselves, abolish class society. They could: (a) unite workers as a class; (b) organize direct action that enabled workers to develop radical capacities, drives, and consciousness; (c) launch the social revolution through a general strike; and (d) provide the organizational framework through which workers would take over and self-manage the economy. For Monatte to say that "syndicalism is sufficient unto itself" was merely to say "that the now-mature working class finally intends to be sufficient unto itself and not to entrust its emancipation to anyone other than itself."[53] This position was shared by Pouget who argued in 1908 that "the trade union is . . . sufficient for all purposes" including "the expropriation of capital and the reorganization of society."[54]

Anarchists who advocated revolutionary syndicalism held that syndicalism was sufficient unto itself because trade unions could independently develop a large organized working-class social movement with the necessary radical traits to launch a social revolution and establish an anarchist society. They thought that, in order to achieve this, trade unions had to be politically neutral toward different left-wing factions, including political parties, and therefore not have an explicitly anarchist program. This was because they believed that the goal of a trade union was to unite as many workers as possible on the basis of their shared class interests, rather than because of their shared ideological commitment to, for example, anarchism or Marxism. Anarchists who were revolutionary syndicalists did write critiques of political parties and parliamentarism, but they did not think that such positions should be the official position of the trade union. The trade union only had to be independent of political parties, rather than being explicitly opposed to them.

The CGT was the first self-described revolutionary syndicalist trade union, but it was not the only one. After the CGT's merger with the National Federation of Bourses du Travail in 1902, numerous trade unions around the world either came to adopt syndicalist programs, or were founded as syndicalist organizations.

This occurred due to the combined activity of anarchist syndicalists and syndicalists who did not identify as anarchists, acting as a militant minority during a global wave of working-class revolt against the ruling classes. In Europe and the United States, at least seven syndicalist trade unions emerged between 1905 and 1912: the Irish Transport and General Workers' Union, Dutch National Secretariat of Labor (NAS), American IWW, Central Organization of Swedish Workers (SAC), Spanish National Confederation of Labor (CNT), Italian Syndicalist Union (USI), and Free Association of German Trade Unions (FVdG), which would develop into the Free Workers' Union of Germany (FAUD). In England the Industrial Syndicalist Education League (ISEL) was founded in order to spread syndicalism within existing reformist trade unions.[55]

Anarchists in Latin America were actively involved in the formation of various syndicalist trade unions, including the Argentine Regional Workers' Federation (FORA) in 1904, Uruguayan Regional Workers' Federation (FORU) in 1905, and Brazilian Workers' Confederation (COB) in 1906. This was followed by the creation of the Peruvian Regional Workers' Federation (FORP) and Bolivian International Workers' Federation in 1912. Anarchists in Cuba organized trade unions and strikes throughout the early 1900s, and this culminated in the founding of the Workers Federation of Havana in 1922, and then the Cuban National Confederation of Labor in 1925. Branches of the IWW were established around the world, including Canada, Mexico, Chile, South Africa, Australia, and New Zealand. A series of trade unions were also founded by anarchists in Asia, including China's first modern trade unions in 1917 and the All-Japan Libertarian Federation of Labor Unions (Zenkoku Rôdô Kumiai Jiyû Rengôkai) in 1926.[56]

The fact that multiple trade unions in Europe, North America, and Latin America embraced syndicalism shortly after the appearance of the CGT can make it appear that they were established simply due to revolutionaries hearing of and deciding to copy the

French example. This narrative ignores the fact that they were created after an extended period of anarchists, and other socialists,
actively participating within trade union movements. In the United
States, for example, Italian anarchists helped organize strikes and
founded local trade unions during the 1890s and early 1900s. After
the founding of the IWW in 1905, which anarchists participated in,
these anarchist-led trade unions decided to affiliate with the IWW
and form sections, such as the IWW Silk Workers' Union Local 152.
Italian anarchists within the IWW then continued to act as a militant minority and push the class struggle forward. This included
Local 152, which was the main organizing force behind the IWW's
1913 strike among silkworkers in Paterson, New Jersey. This is not to
say that the Italian anarchists were not influenced by French syndicalism at all. Italian anarchist papers, including *La Questione Sociale*,
published translations of French syndicalist texts prior to the founding of the IWW. The actions of Italian anarchists cannot, however,
be entirely reduced to this influence.[57]

This point only becomes more apparent when examining the
history of syndicalism in Latin America. In Argentina, anarchists
organized trade unions and strikes from 1887 onward. This included
Spanish and Italian immigrants who had previous experiences of
participating in anarchist-led trade unions, such as Errico Malatesta,
Pietro Gori, Antonio Pellicer Paraire, Gregorio Inglán Lafarga, and
José Prat. The participation of anarchists and state socialists in the
labor movement led to the founding of the Argentine Workers'
Federation (FOA) in 1901. After a series of conflicts between
anarchist and state socialist workers within the trade union, the
anarchist wing emerged as the majority, and the state socialists left
the organization in June 1902. That year, the FOA organized a series
of strikes that, in November, escalated into the first general strike in
Argentina's history. In 1904, the FOA was renamed the FORA. The
FORA then explicitly committed itself to anarchist communism in
1905. In Latin America it was the FORA, rather than just the French

CGT, which served as a key source of inspiration for how to organize a revolutionary trade union.[58]

In addition, French syndicalist theory repeated ideas that had previously been articulated and implemented by anarchists in multiple countries over several decades. In Spain, where anarchists had organized within trade unions since the 1870s, the anarchist journal *Natura* responded to the translation of a pamphlet on syndicalism by Pouget in 1904 by claiming it covered topics "well known here" and showed that "the spirit of free syndicalism, common in Spain, is making strides in France."[59] Anselmo Lorenzo, who translated pamphlets by Pouget and Yvetot, held that the French syndicalists had "returned to us, amplified, corrected and perfectly systematized, ideas with which the Spanish anarchists inspired the French."[60]

The Spanish anarchists were not unique in this respect. During this period, many anarchists looked upon the theory and practice of revolutionary syndicalism as a direct continuation of collectivism within the First International. Pouget himself wrote that the CGT emanated from and was the "historical continuation" of "the International Working Men's Association" and "the federalists or autonomists" within it who opposed the conquest of state power.[61] In 1907, Malatesta remarked, during his speech at the International Anarchist Congress in Amsterdam, that what some syndicalists considered to be a new path had already been "established and followed within the international" by "the first anarchists."[62] That same year, Kropotkin wrote in the preface to a pamphlet on syndicalism by the Georgian anarchist Georgi Gogeliia that "the current opinions of the French syndicalists are organically linked with the early ideas formed by the left wing of the International."[63] The connection between revolutionary syndicalism and anarchism was, in addition to this, understood by at least some Marxists at the time. In 1909, Karl Kautsky, who was one of the most influential Marxists within the Social Democratic Party of Germany, wrote that "syndicalism" was "the latest variety of anarchism" and that "the syndicalism of the

Romance countries" was committed to "anti-parliamentarism" due to its "anarchistic origin."[64]

Despite the connection between the politics of revolutionary syndicalism and the collectivists of the First International, a growing number of syndicalist anarchists came to believe that the revolutionary syndicalism of the CGT was not sufficient to achieve a social revolution that would abolish class society and build an anarchist society. These critics came to embrace either syndicalism-plus or anarcho-syndicalism. Anarchists who advocated syndicalism-plus agreed with revolutionary syndicalists that trade unions should be politically neutral but explicitly rejected the idea that syndicalism was sufficient unto itself. They held that anarchists had to both actively participate within the trade union movement and at the same time maintain an independent existence by organizing outside trade unions within specific anarchist organizations. For proponents of syndicalism-plus, these specific anarchist organizations were essential for spreading anarchist values, theory, and practices among the working classes both in and outside of trade unions. They argued, in short, that revolutionaries should create a syndicalist trade union plus a specific anarchist organization. The details of this position will be discussed in chapter 10 as part of my overview of organizational dualism.

Anarcho-syndicalists, unlike proponents of revolutionary syndicalism and syndicalism-plus, believed that trade unions should not be politically neutral, and had to instead be explicitly committed to achieving an anarchist society through anarchist means. This typically took the form of trade unions advocating an anarchist society as their end goal, and opposing state socialist strategies and political parties within the union's constitution, declaration of principles, or congress resolutions. Some anarcho-syndicalists argued that specific anarchist organizations should be formed in parallel with anarcho-syndicalist trade unions, while others opposed it.

Anarcho-Syndicalism

The phrase "anarcho-syndicalist," like many left-wing terms, began life as an insult. The earliest known usage of the term occurred in 1907, when some French state socialists used it as a pejorative against revolutionary syndicalists who advocated the independence of trade unions from political parties.[65] During this same period, anarchists in Argentina and Russia, who do not appear to have been aware of one another's ideas, came to argue that trade unions should be committed to an explicitly anarchist program. This position was not initially referred to as "anarcho-syndicalism." On August 26, 1905, the FORA explicitly committed itself to an anarchist program at its fifth congress, which was attended by delegates representing ninety-eight trade unions. It was agreed that "the Fifth Congress of the Regional Workers' Federation of Argentina consistent with the philosophical principles that have provided the *raison d'être* of the organization of workers' federations declares: We advise and recommend to all our followers the broadest possible study and propaganda with the aim of instilling in workers the economic and philosophical principles of anarchist-communism. This education, not content with achieving the eight-hour day, will bring total emancipation and, consequently, the social evolution we pursue."[66]

Independently, anarchists in Russia also came to advocate the same approach. A notable example is the South Russian Group of Syndicalist Anarchists, whose membership included factory workers, sailors, dockworkers, bakers, and tailors. Yakob Isaevich Kirillovsky, who was the group's main theorist and wrote under the pen name Daniil Novomirsky, advocated what would later be called anarcho-syndicalism in his 1907 book *The Programme of Syndicalist Anarchism*.[67] He argued that anarchists should participate in the revolutionary trade union movement in order to "make that movement anarchist," advocating the formation of "anarchist revolutionary syndicates which are bent on bringing syndicalist anarchism to pass."[68] It is not a coincidence that, in August 1907, the revolutionary syndicalist and anarchist Monatte contrasted the politically "neutral" trade unions he advocated with "anarchist trade-unions in, for example, Russia."[69]

Anarcho-syndicalism continued to be advocated by anarchists a decade later in the Russian revolution. On June 4, 1917, the Petrograd Union of Anarcho-Syndicalist Propaganda adopted a founding declaration of principles that proclaimed that the social revolution had to be "anti-statist in its method of struggle, Syndicalist in its economic content and federalist in its political tasks," with "the Anarcho-Communist ideal" as its goal.[70] The meaning of Russian "anarcho-syndicalism" can also be seen in *The Organizational Platform of the General Union of Anarchists* (1926), which was written by Russian and Ukrainian anarchists who had fled to Germany and then France in order to escape being killed or imprisoned by the Bolshevik government. The *Platform* carefully distinguishes between "revolutionary syndicalism," which exists "solely as a trades movement of the toilers possessed of no specific social and political theory," and "Anarcho-syndicalism," which advocates "the creation of anarchist-type unions."[71]

The term "anarcho-syndicalist" did not immediately catch on and spread outside the Russian anarchist movement. Alexander Schapiro, who had been active within the anarcho-syndicalist movement during the Russian revolution, claimed years later that "when the Russian anarchists nearly a half a century ago pioneered the hoisting of the anarcho-syndicalist colors, the word was rather coldly received by the anarchist movement."[72] Anarchists instead continued to refer to their ideas as revolutionary syndicalism, while advocating what Russian anarchists called anarcho-syndicalism.

This can be seen in the resolutions of the 1913 International Syndicalist Congress in London, which was organized in order to establish a revolutionary alternative to the state socialist Second

International and the reformist International Secretariat of National Trade Union Centers (ISNTUC). It was attended by delegates representing the major syndicalist trade unions in Europe, including the FVdG, USI, NAS, SAC, ISEL, and the Catalonian Regional Confederation of the CNT. Only a few French trade union sections affiliated with the CGT attended. This was because the CGT supported participating in the much larger ISNTUC in order to radicalize it from within. The congress was not a strictly European affair, and was also attended by delegates representing the COB, the explicitly anarchist FORA, the politically neutral Regional Workers' Confederation of Argentina, and the Havana Union of Café Employees. According to Schapiro, the thirty-three delegates of the London Congress represented in total roughly sixty local, regional, and national trade unions that had a collective membership of 250,000 members.[73]

Despite the congress featuring a great deal of personal animosity and conflict between certain delegates, it nonetheless succeeded in passing a declaration of principles and establishing an International Syndicalist Information Bureau based in Amsterdam. The declaration of principles broke with the CGT's Charter of Amiens and its commitment to political neutrality by endorsing a number of anarchist positions, including the abolition of the state and an opposition to state socialist strategies. It claimed that

this Congress, recognizing that the working class of every country suffers from capitalist slavery and State oppression, declares for the class struggle and international solidarity, and for the organization of the workers into autonomous industrial Unions on a basis of free association. Strives for the immediate uplifting of the material and intellectual interests of the working class, and for the overthrow of the capitalist system and the State. . . . Recognizes that, internationally, Trade Unions will only succeed when they cease to be divided

by political and religious differences; declares that their fight
is an economic fight, meaning thereby that they do not intend
to reach their aim by trusting their cause to governing bodies or their members, but by using Direct Action, by workers
themselves relying on the strength of their economic organizations. . . . Congress appeals to the workers of all countries
to organize into autonomous industrial unions, and to unite
themselves on the basis of international solidarity, in order
finally to obtain their emancipation from capitalism and
the State.[74]

From 1919 onward, multiple syndicalist trade unions moved in
an increasingly anarcho-syndicalist direction. The idea that it was
necessary to commit trade unions to an explicitly anarchist program
largely gained popularity in reaction to a wider international context. The politically neutral CGT had, in contrast to the majority
of the anarchist movement, recently abandoned its commitment to
working-class internationalism and collaborated with the French
state in World War I. Around the same time, a one-party Bolshevik
dictatorship was established during the 1917 Russian revolution,
which proceeded to dismantle organs of workers' control and violently repress other forms of socialism—including anarchism—in
order to maintain a system of minority rule. This created a situation
in which many anarchists felt compelled to ensure that trade unions
were opposed to state socialist strategies, and were not taken over
by Bolshevik supporters.[75]

   Although the CNT had been founded in 1910, it was not originally committed to an explicitly anarchist program. This began to
change in late 1918, when the National Conference of Anarchist
Groups called on anarchists in Spain to actively participate in the
CNT and take on positions of responsibility within the trade union,
such as delegates within committees.[76] The CNT passed a resolution at its December 1919 Second Congress, held at the La Comedia

Theater in Madrid, that declared that the CNT was "a staunch advocate of the principles of the First International as upheld by Bakunin."[77] A number of key delegates, including the organization's national committee, went further and signed a declaration of principles that was unanimously approved by the congress:

> Bearing in mind that the tendency most strongly manifested in the bosom of workers' organizations in every country is the one aiming at the complete and absolute moral, economic and political liberation of mankind, and considering that this goal cannot be attained until such time as the land, means of production and exchange have been socialized and the overweening power of the state has vanished, the undersigned delegates suggest that, in accordance with the essential postulates of the First International, it declares the desired end of the CNT to be anarchist communism.[78]

That same month, the FVdG transformed itself into the FAUD at its Twelfth Congress, attended by 109 delegates representing over 110,000 members. As part of this transformation, the FAUD asked Rocker, recently released from the British internment camp where he had been imprisoned for opposing World War I, to write a new declaration of principles for the organization. Rocker's speech on the principles of syndicalism, which was passed by the congress with minor changes, contained what would become the defining features of anarcho-syndicalism.[79] Although Rocker presented himself as just describing what syndicalists believe, he was in fact articulating a specific understanding of syndicalism that was not shared by everybody who used the label.

According to Rocker the aim of syndicalism is the creation of "free, i.e. stateless, communism, which finds its expression in the motto 'from each according to his ability, to each according to his needs!'"[80] He not only claimed that syndicalists should aim for an anarchist society, but also that they should use anarchist means to get there. He described syndicalists as advocates of revolutionary trade unionism, direct action, and the simultaneous abolition of capitalism and the state. This went alongside a rejection of trying to build socialism through parliamentarism, the conquest of state power, and the nationalization of the economy. These anarchist strategies were explicitly grounded by Rocker in the unity of means and ends. He wrote, "syndicalists are firmly grounded in direct action and support all endeavors and struggles of the people that do not conflict with their goals – the abolition of economic monopolies and of the tyranny of the state."[81]

The final shift toward the theory of anarcho-syndicalism as an idea, but not yet as a label, occurred with the formation of the International Workingmen's Association (IWMA), at an illegal congress held in Berlin between December 25, 1922, and January 2, 1923. The congress was attended by over thirty delegates representing an estimated 1.5 to 2 million workers within various trade unions around the world. This included the FAUD, SAC, FORA-V, USI, and NAS as well as the Mexican General Confederation of Workers (CGT-M), Norwegian Syndicalist Federation (NSF), Dutch National Secretariat of Labor (NAS) and Danish Syndicalist Propaganda Association. The delegates representing the CNT were arrested in Paris while traveling to Berlin, and so were unable to attend. The Portuguese General Confederation of Labor (CGT-P) sent a written endorsement. The delegates representing the Chilean Industrial Workers of the World (IWW-C) and FORU arrived too late to participate in the congress.[82]

The congress adopted a declaration of ten principles of "revolutionary syndicalism," which had been agreed upon at a previous conference in June and were written by Rocker. The principles, which Rocker had based on his earlier speech in 1919 at the founding congress of the FAUD, committed the IWMA to an anarcho-syndicalist program in all but name.[83] This occurred as part of syndicalist anarchists formally breaking with the Red International of Labor Unions (RILU), which was affiliated with the Bolshevik-led Communist Third International, after the congresses of the RILU and Comintern declared themselves in favor of core state-socialist tenets that syndicalist anarchists could not subscribe to. Those tenets included parliamentarism, the seizure of state power by a Communist Party, joining reformist unions, centralization, and the subordination of trade unions to Communist parties.[84]

The IWMA's declaration of principles were, unlike those of the RILU and Comintern, explicitly in favor of the anarchist goal of "free communism" and the establishment of "economic communes and administrative organs run by the workers in the fields and factories, forming a system of free councils without subordination to any authority or political party."[85] This goal was to be achieved through anarchist means: the activity of workers themselves, direct action, the general strike, and freely federated, bottom-up organizational structures. The state socialist strategies of parliamentary activity and conquering political power were explicitly rejected because "no form of statism, even the so-called 'Dictatorship of the Proletariat,' can ever be an instrument for human liberation . . . on the contrary, it will always be the creator of new monopolies and new privileges."[86] The "defense of the revolution" would "be the task of the masses themselves and their economic organizations, and not of a particular military body, or any other organization, outside of the economic associations."[87]

After its founding congress, a total of thirty trade unions affiliated with the IWMA. Of these, fifteen were from Europe, fourteen were from Latin America, and one was from Asia. Within Europe, this included the FAUD, USI, SAC, NSF, CNT, and CGT-P. They were joined by the Dutch Syndicalist Federation (NSV), which split from the NAS in 1923, and the French Revolutionary Syndicalist General Confederation of Labor (CGTSR), which split from the United General Confederation of Labor in 1926. Other European sections included the Russian Anarcho-Syndicalist Minority; Bulgarian Federation of Autonomous Unions; Polish Trade Union Opposition, Romanian anarcho-syndicalist propaganda organization; and anarcho-syndicalist groups in Austria, Denmark, Belgium, and Switzerland. In Latin America, the FORA-V, CGT-M, IWW-C, and FORU affiliated in 1923–4. This was followed by the affiliation of the Regional Workers' Federation of Paraguay (FORP), and various workers' federations in Brazil, including those based in Rio de Janeiro, Rio Grande do Sul, and São Paulo.[88] Several propaganda groups or local unions in Bolivia, Colombia, Peru, Ecuador, Guatemala, Cuba, Costa Rica, and El Salvador also affiliated. The American IWW did not affiliate with the IWMA, despite multiple requests to do so, and the support of various sections, including the Marine Transport Workers Industrial Union.[89]

The one trade union in Asia that affiliated with the IWMA was the All-Japan Libertarian Federation of Labor Unions. It had, according to Rocker, "entered into formal alliance with the IWMA" and "held connections with the Bureau of the IWMA in Berlin."[90] The IWMA also maintained contact with anarchist groups in China and India. The founding December 1922 Berlin congress of the IWMA had itself been attended by a group of Indian revolutionaries, including M.P.T. Acharya. Having been persuaded of the truth of anarchism, they set up a committee to send anarcho-syndicalist literature into India. The British empire responded by banning the importation of IWMA literature into the country.[91]

It was only after the founding of the IWMA that anarchists within Europe began to call themselves anarcho-syndicalists on a significant scale. This shift in language can be seen in the fact that, in 1925, Malatesta felt the need to critique what he called "Anarcho-Syndicalists" within the periodical *Pensiero e Volontà*.[92] In September 1927, Fabbri distinguished between "a labor organization open to all workers, and thereby having no particular ideological program" and "the anarcho-syndicalists in Germany and Russia" who advocate a "labor organization which has an anarchist program, tactics and ideology."[93] A year later, the French anarchist Sébastien Faure wrote a text advocating a synthesis of the different forms of anarchism, and included "anarcho-syndicalism" as one of the three main "anarchist currents."[94] Valeriano Orobón Fernández, who worked within the secretariat of the IWMA from 1926 to 1931, wrote a letter to Ángel Pestaña on August 9, 1930, claiming:

> The evolution of politics following the war has spelt the end of the syndical neutrality of the Amiens Charter. In the whole world there is not a syndicalist organization existing today that does not practice politics, either directly or as an appendage of a political party. The CNT brought itself up to date with this international trend, adopting at the congress at La Comedia [Madrid 1919] an ideological platform, and, at the Zaragoza conference, a political platform. The CNT is therefore a complete organization. Whereas pure syndicalism is not "sufficient in itself," anarcho-syndicalism clearly is.[95]

It is important to note that this shift in language did not occur everywhere at once. In France, the CGTSR was founded in 1926 after a series of splits within the CGT. Its founding declaration of principles, the Lyon Charter, explicitly committed the trade union to opposition to political parties. Despite this, members of the organization referred to themselves as "revolutionary syndicalists" or "federalist anti-statist revolutionary syndicalists," rather than "anarcho-syndicalist," until 1937.[96] That year, Pierre Besnard, who was the secretary of the CGTSR, publicly used the term "anarcho-syndicalist" for the first time to describe the ideology of the trade union he belonged to.[97] During his speech, he stated that "Anarcho-Syndicalism is an organizational and organized movement. It draws its doctrine from Anarchism and its organizational format from Revolutionary Syndicalism."[98]

The view that anarcho-syndicalism was the synthesis of anarchist theory with revolutionary syndicalist modes of organization was repeated and popularized by Rocker in his 1938 book *Anarcho-Syndicalism: Theory and Practice*, but with one major difference. Unlike Besnard, Rocker did not specify that he was describing what it is for an organization or movement to be anarcho-syndicalist. He instead wrote as if he was describing anarcho-syndicalism as a set of ideas such that an anarcho-syndicalist is anyone who advocates both anarchist theory and syndicalist organizational structures, rather than the position that trade unions should have a syndicalist organizational structure and be committed to an anarchist program.[99] This had the effect that the distinction between anarcho-syndicalism and revolutionary syndicalism was blurred, because if anarcho-syndicalism is an ideology based on the combination of anarchist theory with revolutionary syndicalist forms of organization, then anarchists who were revolutionary syndicalists, such as Pouget, could now be viewed as anarcho-syndicalists. Doing so would be a mistake, due to the important debates and differences between revolutionary syndicalist anarchists, who advocated politically neutral trade unions, and anarcho-syndicalists, who advocated explicitly anarchist trade unions.

Rocker not only blurred the distinction between anarcho-syndicalism and revolutionary syndicalism. He wrote that "Anarcho-Syndicalism had maintained its hold upon organized labor [within Spain] from the days of the First International" and in so doing anachronistically imposed anarcho-syndicalism as a category onto the prehistory of syndicalism before the term and idea had been formed.[100] Rocker's 1946 essay, "Anarchism and Anarcho-Syndicalism," which is an abridged and slightly revised version of *Anarcho-Syndicalism: Theory and Practice*, only made things more unclear for future generations. He repeated his previous claim that anarcho-syndicalism is a synthesis of anarchist theory and syndicalist modes of organization, but then goes on to equate the two by writing that "Revolutionary Syndicalism . . . was later called, Anarcho-Syndicalism."[101]

Rocker's claim was technically correct in the sense that the organizations he belonged to, the FAUD and the IWMA, did initially call themselves revolutionary syndicalists while advocating anarcho-syndicalism as an idea and then, as language evolved, switched to calling themselves anarcho-syndicalists. This can be seen in the fact that Rocker himself referred to "syndicalism" in his declaration of principles adopted at the founding of the FAUD in 1919 and "revolutionary syndicalism" in his declaration of principles adopted at the founding of the IWMA in 1922. By 1938, his language had shifted. He now referred to the trade unions that formed the IWMA, including the FAUD, as the representatives of "MODERN Anarcho-Syndicalism."[102] Unfortunately, twenty-first-century readers of Rocker have often been unaware of these historical details and have misunderstood both the origins and nature of anarchosyndicalism, and how it differed from the revolutionary syndicalism of politically neutral trade unions like the CGT. It should also be noted that sections of the IWMA continued to have members who did not identify as anarchists or anarcho-syndicalists.

CHAPTER 9

The Theory and Practice of Syndicalist Anarchism

All forms of syndicalist anarchism argued that workers should form federally structured trade unions that engaged in direct action and were independent of political parties. It was believed that, in order to achieve working-class self-emancipation, these syndicalist trade unions had to pursue the *double aim* of winning immediate improvements in the present, and overthrowing capitalism and the state via a social revolution in the long term. These unions also had a *dual function*. Under present conditions, they performed the function of engaging in class struggle against the ruling classes. During the social revolution, they would expropriate the means of production from the ruling classes and take over the organization of the economy in part or whole. In so doing, they would acquire the new function of being the organs through which the self-management of production and distribution occurred. This social revolution could be initiated by workers launching an insurrectionary general strike.

The Double Aim of Syndicalist Anarchist Unions

Syndicalist anarchists held that trade union activity should have two main goals. These were: (a) defending and advancing the interests of the working classes within existing society and (b) preparing for

279

and ultimately carrying out a social revolution that abolishes capitalism and the state in favor of an anarchist society.[1] For Pouget, "trade union endeavor has a double aim: with tireless persistence, it must pursue betterment of the working class's current conditions. But, without letting themselves become obsessed with this passing concern, the workers should take care to make possible and imminent the essential act of comprehensive emancipation: the expropriation of capital."[2]

Syndicalist anarchism, therefore, like mass anarchism in general, sought to win immediate reforms in the interests of the working classes—such as shorter working hours, better pay, and improved conditions—force the ruling classes to actually implement previously won reforms, and protect these previously won reforms from encroachment by the ruling classes. Crucially, syndicalist anarchists held that reforms had to be achieved, enforced, and protected through the direct action of the working classes. Even reforms that involved changes to the law had to be achieved "through outside pressure brought to bear upon the authorities and not by trying to return specially mandated deputies to Parliament."[3]

This strategy generally, but not always, involved a rejection of the iron law of wages, which held that under capitalism real wages would always tend toward the amount required to secure the subsistence of the worker due to either population growth decreasing the value of labor, or higher wages being neutralized by increased costs of living. Pouget labeled it as "illusory" and "false," because it was empirically untrue, and ignored the fact that increased living costs were themselves a product of class struggle, such as those between landlords and tenants.[4] Malatesta argued against the iron law of wages on the grounds that between the minimum limit of a worker being paid enough to survive and the maximum limit of a capitalist earning some profit, "wages, hours and other conditions of employment are the result of the struggle between bosses and workers" and so could be changed through collective action.[5]

Pouget and Malatesta's position was not shared by all syndicalist anarchists. Pelloutier, for example, opposed partial strikes; he subscribed to the iron law of wages while still being a syndicalist, because he advocated revolutionary trade unionism as the means to overthrow class society.[6] Others held that, although any increase in wages would be canceled out by increases in the cost of living, partial strikes were nonetheless important and should be encouraged due to their transformative effect on workers. A 1900 article by Delesalle's for *Les Temps Nouveaux* argued that, while any increase in wages would only be temporary due to the iron law, a strike would still promote "a state of rebellion," develop class consciousness, and "could be the spark that heralds the revolution."[7]

The main forms of direct action that syndicalist anarchists advocated to achieve reforms were strikes, boycotts, and sabotage. By sabotage, syndicalist anarchists meant "workers putting every possible obstacle in the way of the ordinary modes of work."[8] This included such tactics as working slowly, strictly following legislation or contracts in order to reduce productivity and, at its most militant, damaging machinery or infrastructure so that strike breakers could not continue production.

This strategy of struggling for reforms through militant tactics was put into practice on multiple occasions by syndicalist trade unions. In 1904 the CGT agreed at its congress in Bourges to campaign for the eight-hour day, which workers had unsuccessfully been petitioning for since 1889. Instead of begging the state to grant this reform, the CGT, following Pouget's suggestion, decided that they should try to force the ruling classes to give in to their demands by engaging in direct action: workers were to either cease work after eight hours, or go on strike until their demands were met. The CGT selected May 1, 1906, as the day of action and proceeded to prepare for the coming struggle over the next two years. This included holding union meetings and distributing posters with revolutionary messages in order to persuade workers to participate in the movement. How much energy was devoted by the CGT to this campaign can be seen in the fact that during December 1905 alone ten famous syndicalist militants organized conferences in eighty cities.

The French state unsurprisingly responded to the campaign with repression. On the eve of the strike, key delegates, including Griffuelhes, Pouget, Alphonse Merrheim (secretary of the Federation of Metalworkers), and Gaston Lévy (the CGT treasurer), were arrested and jailed for a few days, after the minister of the interior, Georges Clemenceau, claimed to have discovered a nonexistent plot by syndicalists, anarchists, monarchists, and right-wing Catholics to overthrow the Republic. Clemenceau, in addition to this, moved 60,000 soldiers into Paris. Despite this state violence, the strike went ahead and on May 1, 1906, the CGT publicly demanded that the French state reduce the legal working day to eight hours. The next day, the CGT launched a national general strike. The general strike was composed of 295 separate strikes at 12,585 businesses, which demanded a reduction to the workday. A total of roughly 200,000 workers participated in this direct action. Some of the strikes lasted over a hundred days. Only 10,177 workers out of 202,507 succeeded in forcing a capitalist to grant them any reduction to the workday. Despite this, the general strike was not a total defeat. On July 13, 1906, France's political ruling class responded to the pressure from below by passing a law granting workers a mandatory day off work once per week. Although the CGT continued to campaign for the eight-hour day over the following years, it was not granted to the French working classes until April 1919—as part of the French government's successful attempt to prevent anything like the ongoing Russian revolution from happening in France.[9]

The CGT was not unique in attempting to wrestle reforms from the ruling classes through direct action. In February 1919, the

CNT's Catalan Regional Confederation (CRT) organized a strike at the Barcelona offices of the Anglo-American electricity company Ebro Power and Irrigation. This action was launched by the CNT, in response to the company firing workers for attempting to form a union.[10] When the company refused to give in to the workers' demands for higher wages and the reinstatement of all the workers who had been fired, the CNT escalated the struggle and organized a strike at the company's electricity generating plant. This resulted in Barcelona being plunged into darkness, and trams being stranded in the street unable to move. The strike soon grew to include most of the city's gas, water, and electricity workers when, on February 26, they voted to strike in retaliation to the Spanish state sending in the military to restore the power supply. They were subsequently joined by solidarity strikes outside of Barcelona, in Sabadell, Vilafranca, and Badalona.

On March 8, the Spanish state responded to the growing strike movement by militarizing the gas, water, and electricity workers who were army reservists subject to military law. The workers were then given the choice between breaking the strike by returning to work or being confined to the barracks as punishment. This state violence did not dampen the strike, which expanded to include tram workers and carters who transported essential supplies such as coal. They, like the gas, water, and electricity workers before them, were soon militarized as well. Almost none of these militarized workers betrayed their class interests by returning to work and, in response, the Spanish state imprisoned 800 of them in the fortress of Montjuïc, in Barcelona. These workers were supported in their struggle by the printers' union, which refused to publish any of the Spanish state's proclamations calling up workers for military service or articles in the press opposed to the strike. This even included an announcement by the managers of Ebro Power and Irrigation that declared that workers who did not return to their job by March 6 would be fired. Workers who wanted to learn about the strike could instead read the CNT's daily *Solidaridad Obrera*, which published articles informing readers of the latest news.

Throughout the strike, the CNT sought to win its demands by mobilizing large groups of workers in order to impose unbearable pressure on the company and the state via direct action. This included workers implementing syndicalist tactics by sabotaging the transformers and power cables used by the company to try and restore power to the city, and thereby break the strike. By early March, the CNT's strike committee were, as a result of this working-class militancy, in a position where they could negotiate with the ruling classes. They successfully forced Ebro Power and Irrigation to increase wages, pay workers' wages for the period they had been on strike, recognize the union, grant an eight-hour day, and reinstate workers who had lost their jobs due to participation in the strike. The CNT not only issued demands to the economic ruling class, but also demanded that the Spanish state release all prisoners who had been arrested for engaging in class struggle. If the state did not do so in seventy-two hours, the CNT threatened to relaunch the strike.

In response to the general strike, the Spanish prime minster, Álvaro de Figueroa, attempted to soothe the working classes by decreeing the eight-hour day in the construction industry on March 11, which was later expanded to include all industries on April 3. The CNT had previously agreed to struggle for the eight-hour day at its founding 1910 congress. They achieved this goal in nine years through direct action alone.[11] Despite this great victory, the CNT decided to launch another general strike on March 24 (the resolution was passed by one vote) in response to the electricity, gas, and water companies not allowing all the strikers to return to work immediately, and the Spanish state refusing to free a number of workers imprisoned in Montjuïc—including the CNT's general secretary Manuel Buenacasa. This time, the Spanish state was ready, and retaliated swiftly to the general strike by imposing martial law, closing all CNT union headquarters, arresting key anarchist militants, and censoring the press. Following this wave of state repression, the CNT was forced to call for a return to work on April 7, 1919.

Both the CGT's campaign for the eight-hour day and the CNT's strike against Ebro Power and Irrigation illustrate the general tendency for syndicalist trade unions to focus on struggling for reforms through organizing workers at the point of production. In response to this tendency, there were multiple attempts in both theory and practice to expand the scope of syndicalist action from the workplace to the wider community. The Spanish syndicalist anarchist Joan Peiró argued that the CNT had focused too much on strikes in workplaces, and should establish district committees that organized collective action around any issue facing the working classes, thereby fostering direct action on a mass scale.[12] This same conclusion was reached in a January 1931 article for the CNT's *Solidaridad Obrera*. It claimed that syndicalists had focused too much on mitigating "the exploitation of the producers," and in so doing had "almost entirely forgotten to combat exploitation in the field of consumption," such as landlords charging extortionate rent.[13] Organizing against these other forms of exploitation was not only important in and of itself, but also provided an opportunity to radicalize people who might be indifferent to labor struggles, or even oppose union demands when they suffer the negative consequences of prolonged industrial action.

Such community-based direct action was organized by the CNT itself during the Barcelona rent strike of July 1931.[14] The strike grew out of previous rent strikes that had been independently organized by workers in October 1930. This movement then gained the support of the Economic Defense Commission, which had been created by the CNT's Construction Workers' Union on April 12, 1931, in order to study the living expenses of workers and examine ways they could be reduced. The Construction Union's concern with these topics stemmed from the fact that 12,000 of its 30,000 membership were unemployed. On May 1, the commission presented its first demand to a large CNT meeting: a 40 percent reduction in rent. This demand, alongside proposals for combating unemployment and high food prices, was then announced to the wider public through a series of articles in *Solidaridad Obrera* that appeared over May 12, 13, and 15. At the end of June and the beginning of July, the commission held a series of meetings in working-class areas of Barcelona and nearby towns, where workers, a significant number of whom were women, were informed of the campaign and heard speeches attacking landlords as thieves.

These meetings were followed by a mass rally on July 5, where the following three demands were agreed upon: (a) that the extra month's rent demanded by landlords from new tenants as security should be taken as normal rent such that new tenants had to pay no more during the month of July; (b) that rent should be reduced by 40 percent; and (c) that unemployed people should not have to pay any rent. If landlords refused to reduce the rent, workers would respond by announcing that they were going on rent strike as part of a wider movement, and pay nothing.

The rent strike rapidly grew after its launch and expanded from 45,000 workers in July to over 100,000 in August. The ruling classes responded in late July by banning public meetings of the Economic Defense Commission and evicting workers with the assistance of the police. The tenants organized protests to prevent evictions, reoccupying houses after the eviction had taken place, moving evicted workers to the homes of other CNT members, and marching on the homes of landlords in order to warn them not to reevict tenants. One eviction in early October was prevented by a crowd of pregnant women and children, whom the police officer in charge decided not to attack. Other women protesting evictions were less fortunate, such as those who were charged by eighty police officers on October 21. The rent strike was eventually defeated between November and December, as a result of the state arresting any worker who resisted evictions or returned to their home after eviction. Despite this, it did succeed in bringing many workers into the anarchist movement, and thereby laid the foundation for future mobilizations. The rent strike even continued in some areas, such as in the La Torrassa neighborhood; rent strikers at the end of 1932 attacked the police, seized some of their weapons and attempted to burn down the local office of the chamber of urban property, which was the main landlord association in Barcelona, and had actively encouraged repression of the rent strike.

One of the main driving forces behind attempts to expand the scope of syndicalist action beyond the workplace were women within trade unions struggling simultaneously against both class and gender oppression. This can be seen in the FAUD's Syndicalist Women's Union (SFB), which was created by and for women in 1920. One of the cofounders of the group was the Ukrainian Jewish anarchist Milly Witkop-Rocker, whose romantic partner was Rudolf Rocker. In 1922 Witkop-Rocker argued in her pamphlet *What Does the Syndicalist Women's Union Want?* that "the organization of women on the basis of anarcho-syndicalism is as necessary as the organization of male workers on the same basis. . . . Wherever there is a syndicalist organization, an attempt must be made to create one of women, so that the sections of the syndicalist women's federation will cover the whole country like a net."[15] The main goal of the syndicalist women's federation was to persuade women to participate in the union, especially those who were full-time housewives not employed as wage laborers, and to develop their consciousness such that they became anarchists. To this end Witkop-Rocker advocated the formation of women's-only groups that organized a range of activities. This included mutual aid, artistic pursuits, cooking, and educational clubs equipped with libraries, "where the comrades can meet anytime to read or to speak on important issues, and where they can bring their children, if necessary."[16] This would have the consequence that women, who were often isolated from one another within their respective homes, would be brought closer together, establish bonds of solidarity with one another, and, through their participation in the union, develop a spirit of independence and personal initiative that they did not have before due to their patriarchal socialization. It was important to organize housewives not only to further the emancipation of women, but also because they could support strikes by boycotting a particular company.

Witkop-Rocker realized that, in order for women to be able to participate effectively in the workers' movement, they first had to be emancipated from the crushing toil of housework, giving birth to large numbers of children, and looking after said children. One of the main ways the FAUD and the SFB attempted to contribute toward this emancipation was by organizing around what would today be called reproductive justice. They not only demanded the abolition of laws that criminalized advocating contraception and prohibited abortion, but also held meetings on the "childbearing strike," educated women about birth control, distributed contraceptives, and either performed illegal abortions or put women in contact with physicians who would. Syndicalist anarchists in Germany did this through participating in, and often becoming prominent members of, public organizations that were neither explicitly anarchist nor syndicalist. This included such organizations as the Reich Association of Birth Control and Sexual Hygiene and the Working Committee of the Free Sexual Reformers Association. A few syndicalist anarchists paid heavily for their actions. For example, the FAUD member Albrecht was sentenced to three years of imprisonment in 1930 because she performed more than a hundred abortions for the local chapter of the League for the Protection of Mothers and Sexual Hygiene.[17]

Syndicalist anarchists were clearly committed in both theory and practice to achieving, enforcing, and protecting reforms through direct action within both the workplace and the wider community. In line with mass anarchist theory, they did not view the struggle for reforms as an end in and of itself. For Pouget, winning reforms, "far from constituting a goal, can only be considered as a means of stepping up demands and wresting further improvements from capitalism."[18] Goldman similarly believed that, although syndicalist anarchism struggles for "immediate gains" and "wrests from the enemy what it can force him to yield," it ultimately "aims at, and concentrates its energies upon, the complete overthrow of the wage system."[19]

Instead of viewing reform and revolution as inherently opposed to one another, syndicalist anarchists viewed struggling for reforms as an evolutionary moment within a process of social change that would eventually culminate in a revolutionary moment. This was because organizing to win immediate improvements under capitalism was the concrete means to generate a mass social movement that was capable of, and driven to, launch a social revolution. Pouget argued that, in order to create an anarchist society, "preparatory work must have drawn together within existing society those elements whose role it will be to make it happen" through "day to day struggles against the current master of production" that undermined the legitimacy and power of capitalists and gradually escalated and intensified to the point where the working classes had developed sufficient "strength and consciousness" to forcefully expropriate the capitalist class.[20] For Pouget, "whenever one analyzes the methods and value of trade union action, the fine distinction between 'reformist' and 'revolutionary' evaporates," because, when syndicalist trade unions struggle for either, they use the same method: the direct action of the working classes.[21] Reforms like wage increases are "a reduction in capitalist privileges" and a form of "partial expropriation."[22] They are, therefore, a step toward and component of the social transformation that the social revolution will fully bring about.

The Dual Function of Syndicalist Anarchist Unions

Syndicalist anarchists were, like anarchists in general, committed to the unity of means and ends. The application of this theory led them to conclude that, in order to successfully overthrow capitalism and the state, trade unions had to be structured in a manner that prefigured the kinds of large-scale organizations that would exist after the social revolution. As the Russian anarchist Gregori Maximoff wrote in 1927, trade unions "must be built on principles which will serve in the future, i.e. on liberty—the autonomy of individuals and organizations—and on equality."[23] In order to instantiate these values, trade unions had to be organized through a system of federalism that practiced, to quote Rocker, "free combination from below upward, putting the right of self-determination of every member above everything else and recognizing only the organic agreement of all on the basis of like interests and common convictions."[24]

Syndicalist anarchists thought that, in constructing and expanding trade unions that prefigured the future anarchist society, they were literally, in the famous words of the preamble to the 1908 IWW constitution, "forming the structure of the new society within the shell of the old."[25] They held that the trade union had, in addition to its double aim, a dual function. Under capitalism, it performed the function of bringing the working classes together in order to resist the power of the ruling classes through their own direct action. During the social revolution, the trade union would take on a new function by forcefully expropriating the means of production from the ruling classes and establishing federations of workers' assemblies organized by trade and geographic region. This would be achieved by converting the federations and local sections of the trade union from organizations of economic resistance into organizations of economic administration that self-managed the emerging anarchist economy.[26]

The idea that trade unions should perform the dual function of resisting dominant institutions in the present, and taking
over and organizing the economy in the future, was not invented
by syndicalist anarchists during the 1890s and 1900s. It was, as I
showed in chapter 8, first advocated during debates within the
First International. It continued to be advocated by anarchists
years after the congresses of the First International. In 1887, Lucy
Parsons, who would later attend the founding convention of the
IWW in 1905, claimed that trade unions built under capitalism were
the "embryonic groups of the ideal anarchistic society."[27] In 1927,
Maximoff wrote that "the revolutionary trade union, in the view of
the Anarchists, are not only organs of the struggle against the contemporary structure; they are also the cells of the future society."[28]

Although syndicalist anarchists thought that trade unions
should be the organization through which workers took control
of and reorganized the economy, they were not generally committed to the view that trade unions should be the only organs of
self-management during and after the social revolution. In 1909, in
their fictional account of a successful syndicalist revolution Pouget
and Émile Pataud claimed that, in addition to trade unions, village
assemblies in the countryside, and community assemblies in urban
areas at the level of street, district, and city would be formed. These
community assemblies could be attended by anyone, regardless
of their occupation, and so brought people together as "inhabi-
tants, and not as producers."[29] Meetings "concerned themselves
with measures of hygiene and health . . . [and] took part in the
administration of the City. They undertook the work of the moral
administration of house property, now proclaimed collective property, and, as a matter of course, placed at the free disposition of all."[30]
This view was shared by Besnard, who explained in his address
to the IWMA in 1937, that "this notion does not at all imply that
anarcho-syndicalism—which is, remember, against the State and
federalist—means and aims to be *everything* and that *nothing else*

should exist alongside it."[31] It instead aims for self-management in every sphere of life, rather than just the workplace, and as a result, advocates a federation of regional, national, and international communes in parallel to the federation of trade unions.[32]

The CNT also advocated communes alongside trade unions. The Spanish syndicalist anarchist Isaac Puente argued in his pamphlet *Libertarian Communism* in 1932 that "life in the future will be organized" through two currently existing institutions: "the free union," which unites workers on the basis of their labor, and "the free municipality," which "is the assembly of the workers in a very small locality, village or hamlet" united on the basis of their location.[33] These ideas went onto inspire the CNT's 1936 Zaragoza Congress resolutions. They proposed that during the social revolution workers should establish both federations of producers' associations, which would self-manage the workplace, and "libertarian communes" in each locality, which would organize such things as housing, education, and the "beautification of the settlement" and federate together to form the "Confederation of Autonomous Libertarian Communes."[34]

It is also a mistake to view syndicalist trade unions themselves as being purely workplace organizations. The district committees of the CNT were located in union centers within working-class neighborhoods. They were social spaces that established bonds of mutual support between workers from different workplaces, migrants new to the area, and unemployed workers. In so doing, they spread anarchist theory and practice to workers in varied circumstances, on the basis of their shared belonging to a local community. The ability of the CNT to mobilize large groups of workers during waves of direct action was not based exclusively on union sections in specific workplaces or industries. It also stemmed from the influence that anarchist militants had in face-to-face conversations with their neighbors, friends, and family in homes, cafés, and the streets. Nor did workers in the CNT limit themselves to workplace organizing.

They also organized tenants unions and, despite patriarchal opposition from within the union, women's groups such as Mujeres
Libres. This went alongside the construction of numerous forms of
associational life, including affinity groups, schools, neighborhood
educational and cultural centers called ateneos, theater clubs, hiking clubs, and more. In 1932, youth groups that had emerged from
ateneos in Granada, Madrid, Barcelona, and Valencia formed the
Iberian Federation of Libertarian Youth. The CNT's construction
of prefigurative organizations therefore occurred both within the
workplace and the community.[35]

Syndicalist anarchists, like anarchists in general, advocated
prefigurative organizations because it was only through participating in such organizations that the working classes would develop
the radical capacities, drives, and consciousness necessary both
for struggling effectively against existing dominant institutions
and producing and reproducing the future anarchist society. It was
thought that workers would learn how to self-manage the economy
through their experience of self-managing a trade union, which,
like the economy of the future, was structured in a horizontal and
federalist manner, made decisions within general assemblies in
which everyone had a vote, and coordinated action on a large scale
through a system of delegates. Rocker thought that trade unions
should function as both "the fighting organization of the workers
against the employers" and "the school for the intellectual training
of the workers to make them acquainted with the technical management of production and economic life in general so that when
a revolutionary situation arises they will be capable of taking the
socio-economic organism into their own hands and remaking it
according to Socialist principles."[36]

Syndicalist anarchists thought it was very important to provide
such technical education to the working classes, because of their
commitment to grounding their revolutionary strategy in an understanding of what the world was really like. In Baginski's words,

the economic power to rule and lead production does not fall in the workers' laps (in quiet submission to the fate of economic development) without their active engagement; no, they must gain it themselves by fighting with endurance and strength. Workers dream themselves too easily into the idea that one day the "social revolution" will descend to earth like a supernatural godhead in order to heal all wounds and dry all tears in one swoop. Oh no! The sun, which as it set today looked down on shackled slaves, will not as it rises tomorrow behold free people. Workers must educate themselves through their own strength to become thinking and acting people. They have to educate and prepare themselves for the great profession of administration and leadership in production.[37]

Syndicalist anarchists faced two major problems when trying to implement this theory. First, in order for individual workers to be transformed through their participation within the trade union, they had to be members of the trade union for an extended period of time. A significant number of workers would often join trade unions due to their immediate economic interests, such as a strike, but would leave them once the situation ended. This was especially the case for temporary workers who lacked a permanent employer. As a result of this and other factors, such as workers deciding to join larger reformist trade unions, syndicalist trade unions had a high membership turnover. The SAC, for example, was founded in 1910 and by 1935 had 36,000 members. During this twenty-five year period, a total of 250,000 workers had at one time been registered members of the trade union.[38] Even if workers did remain within the trade union over an extended period of time, it did not follow from this that they would actively participate within it and thereby be transformed. In the Spanish village of Casas Viejas, three hundred workers joined the local union of the CNT in 1932, but only a minority of them were committed anarchist militants. A significant number joined the trade union because it was necessary to find a job, and they did not subsequently absorb anarchist ideas.[39]

Second, syndicalist trade unions, like anarchists in general, experienced a huge amount of state repression. The CNT was founded in 1910, only to be made illegal and have its headquarters shut down in September 1911. This occurred as part of the Spanish state's violent repression of a wave of strikes and antiwar protests, which anarchist workers had encouraged and participated in. The CNT began to reorganize itself from June 1912 onward, when all the militants who had been arrested the previous September were released. The CNT's paper, *Solidaridad Obrera*, reappeared in May 1913, and members of the CNT were able to elect the regional committee of the recently legalized CRT in July. By August, the CRT was once again made illegal after it attempted to organize a general strike in support of textile workers. The CRT re-emerged as a public organization from August 1914 onwards only to be briefly banned again in 1920.[40]

In 1924 the CNT was made illegal for a fourth time due to its resistance to the Primo de Rivera dictatorship, which had been established in September 1923. The new regime required that trade unions provide the state with a complete list of their activities and membership, including the positions members held in the trade union and their home addresses. The CNT refused, and different segments of the movement disagreed with one another over whether or not the organization should go underground or try to operate as publicly as possible. On May 28, the Spanish state forced the decision when it responded to the assassination of the executioner of Barcelona, Rogelio Pérez Vicario, by making the trade union illegal, banning *Solidaridad Obrera*, and arresting leading militants. The CNT was only made legal again in 1930 with the collapse of the Primo de Rivera dictatorship, but nonetheless continued to experience significant state repression both under the quasi-dictatorship of Berenguer and the Spanish Republic, which was inaugurated in April 1931.[41]

The General Strike

One of the main tactics that syndicalist anarchists advocated and engaged in were general strikes in which a significant number of workers went on strike at once. Rocker viewed the general strike as "the most powerful weapon which the workers have at their command" because it "brings the whole economic system to a standstill and shakes it to its foundations."[42] He proposed that the working classes use the general strike in order to achieve both reforms, such as compelling capitalists to grant workers the eight-hour day, and the revolutionary goal of abolishing capitalism and the state in favor of an anarchist society.[43] This same perspective can be seen in Delesalle's 1906 distinction between four different kinds of general strike: (a) a general strike by individual unions; (b) a general strike across all industries on a specific day; (c) a general strike across all industries that places the working class in "a state of open war with capitalist society"; and (d) a general strike that is a revolution.[44]

Syndicalist anarchists were neither the first nor the only group to advocate the general strike as a strategy through which the working classes could transform society in a positive direction.[45] In October 1833, an assembly of Glasgow workers associated with the Owenite movement passed a resolution that declared that rather than launching an insurrection to achieve social change, workers should simply fold their arms and abstain from work. This mass stoppage of work would, according to their optimistic prediction, have the consequence that "capital is destroyed, the revenue fails, the system of government falls into confusion, and every link in the chain which binds society together is broken in a moment by this inert conspiracy of the poor against the rich."[46]

The idea of the general strike continued to be advocated during the First International. At the Brussels Congress of September 1868, a resolution was passed that stated that, if a war broke out, then workers would stop it through the "legal practical means" of ceasing

all work.⁴⁷ Several months later Bakunin argued in "Organization
and the General Strike," which was published in *Égalité* on April 3,
1869, that the recent wave of strikes in Europe indicated that "the
struggle of labor against capital is growing ever stronger . . . and that
we are advancing at a great pace toward Social Revolution. . . . As
strikes spread and as neighbors learn about them the general strike
comes ever closer. These days, with the idea of liberation so current
amongst the proletariat, a general strike can result only in a great
cataclysm, giving society a new skin."⁴⁸

The Belgian Federation of the Saint-Imier International, which
included both anarchists and collectivists who were not anarchists,
endorsed the general strike as a revolutionary strategy during their
congress of August 1873 held in Antwerp. Guillaume responded
to this in May, writing that "the general strike, if it was realizable,
would certainly be the most powerful lever of a social revolution.
Just imagine the effect of the immense labor machine being stopped
on a fixed day in all countries at once. . . . In a word, the whole people descending into the street, and saying to their masters: 'I will
only start work again after having accomplished the transformation
of property which must put the instruments of labor into the hands
of the workers.'"⁴⁹

He was nonetheless unsure if "the International Federation of
trade unions . . . will ever be strong enough, solid enough, universal
enough to be able to carry out a general strike."⁵⁰ The general strike
continued to be discussed and debated during the September 1873
Geneva Congress of the Saint-Imier International. The Belgian delegates unsurprisingly argued that the general strike was "a means
of bringing a movement onto the street and leading the workers to
the barricades."⁵¹ Guillaume similarly insisted that the general strike,
as understood by the International, was the social revolution and
that revolutionaries should focus on bringing it about. Although
Guillaume had previously described a general strike as occurring
on a fixed day, he now asked: "Should the ideal of the general strike

... be that it has to break out everywhere at an appointed day and hour? Can the day and hour of the revolution be fixed in this way? No! ... The revolution has to be contagious."[52]

After the collapse of the Saint-Imier International in 1878, the idea of the general strike was frequently discussed by French trade unionists during the emergence of revolutionary syndicalism as a social movement. In 1887, at the Montluçon Congress of the National Federation of Trade Unions (FNS), two anarchist workers, Berger and Combomreil, responded to the French state socialist Jules Guesde's proposal that capitalism should be abolished through the seizure of state power. They advocated the general strike as an alternative method for achieving social change. A year later, the FNS passed a resolution at its congress from October 28–November 4 in Le Bouscat which stated that "the general strike, i.e., the complete cessation of labor, or the revolution, may be used by the workers for their emancipation."[53]

During the 1880s and 1890s, many French trade unionists conceived of the general strike in a manner that differed significantly from how syndicalist anarchists would later theorize it in the early twentieth century. Aristide Briand cowrote a text with Pelloutier in 1892, while Pelloutier was still a member of the Marxist led French Workers' Party and had yet to become an anarchist. It was not published in full, but, in it, they depict the general strike as a "peaceful and legal" affair in which workers saved up enough money and provisions to last fifteen days without work and, on an agreed date, stayed at home. It was imagined that, in the absence of the working classes' labor, capitalism would quickly cease to function and be abolished "smoothly, without the spilling of blood, solely by the combination of rest."[54]

Syndicalist anarchists, in comparison to many earlier advocates of the general strike, were not naive and understood that a society-wide strike that encompassed all branches of production was extremely unlikely to occur, especially at the beginning of the strike. Nacht, for example, wrote in 1905 (under the pen name Arnold Roller) that a general strike in which the entire international working classes simultaneously laid down their tools and overthrew capitalism was a beautiful idea that will nonetheless "always be a dream."[55] Given this, syndicalist anarchists aimed to achieve the more feasible goal of organizing a general strike that began in key industries the economy could not function without, such as coal, gas, railway, and shipping. From this starting point, the general strike would, in theory, spread to the wider economy as workers in more and more industries either decided to join the strike in solidarity with its aims and as a response to state repression toward the strike, or were forced to cease work entirely due to the strike's disruption of key infrastructure and raw materials not being transported to factories. This would in turn create a situation in which the large number of workers who were not organized within trade unions, or who were apolitical, were forced by the unfolding wave of events to take sides, participate in the general strike and thereby become radicalized.[56]

Unlike the previously mentioned proponents of the general strike, syndicalist anarchists did not view it as a form of passive resistance in which the working classes simply ceased work, folded their arms, and waited for dominant structures to collapse. In the advent of a revolutionary situation, they proposed that workers should use the general strike as a platform from which to launch the forceful expropriation of the means of production, land, and the necessities of life from the ruling classes and establish federations of workplace and community assemblies. During her speech at the 1905 founding convention of the IWW, Lucy Parsons proposed that socialism could be achieved via a "general strike," in which workers occupied their workplaces in order to "take possession of the necessary property of production."[57] That same year, Nacht wrote that a successful general strike "accomplishes expropriation and communalizes the means of production."[58] Pouget and Pataud imagined in

1909 a fictional revolutionary general strike in which "the Unions in each industry, in each profession, took possession of the factories and workshops" and reorganized production on a communist basis by means of free agreement between federations.[59] Besnard argued in 1930 that a revolutionary general strike was distinguished from normal strikes on the grounds that workers would not only cease work, but also "*occupy* the place of production, *get rid* of the boss, *expropriate* him, and *get ready* to get production moving again, but in the interests of the revolution."[60]

Syndicalist anarchists tried to clearly differentiate their active militant conception of the general strike from previous passive conceptions. For Nacht, writing in 1905, the term "social general strike" should be used to refer to a general strike that involves the expropriation of the ruling classes and the establishment of an anarchist society, in order to clearly differentiate it from general strikes for reforms, such as higher wages or universal suffrage.[61] In 1907, the International Anarchist Congress in Amsterdam passed a series of resolutions on syndicalism that varyingly referred to "the revolutionary General strike" and "the General Strike with Expropriation."[62] Decades later, in 1930, Besnard referred to "the expropriatory general strike, with violence," which would be "*insurrectional*."[63]

Some syndicalist anarchists equated the general strike with the social revolution, while others were careful to distinguish between the two. Nacht claimed that since a "social general strike" would involve the expropriation of the means of production and the establishment of an anarchist society, it followed that "the General Strike is not only the introduction of the revolution but is the social revolution itself."[64] Malatesta, in comparison, held in 1907 that "the general strike has always struck me as an excellent means to set off the social revolution."[65] Malatesta's conceptualization was shared by at least some syndicalist trade unions. At the founding 1910 congress of the CNT, a report on the general strike was approved and later read aloud again at the CNT's 1911 congress. The report proposed that "the general strike, the withdrawal of labor by all the workers at any given moment, entails such a great disturbance in the ordinary course of today's society of exploited and exploiters that it will unavoidably have to cause an explosion, a clash, between the antagonistic forces that are now fighting for survival."[66] The IWMA's 1922 declaration of principles described "the social general strike . . . as the prelude to the social revolution."[67]

Syndicalist anarchists did not think that all it took to initiate a revolutionary general strike was a trade union boldly proclaiming it on a fixed date whenever they fancied.[68] They believed, instead, that it would develop out of smaller strikes for immediate improvements. In Pouget and Pataud's 1909 novel *How We Shall Bring About the Revolution*, they describe a period of escalating class conflict prior to the launching of the general strike: "strikes followed strikes; lockouts were replied to by boycotts; sabotage was employed with ruinous intensity."[69] Under such conditions the antagonism between workers and capitalists developed to the point that workers came to consider themselves to be in a continuous war against the ruling classes. Through their experience of collective struggle within trade unions, they developed radical capacities, drives, and consciousness such that "the working class became more warlike. They took possession of the streets, and familiarized themselves with the tactics of resistance. They learned how to stand their ground before bodies of police, and how to deal with the troops marched against them."[70]

In this fictional account, the class conflict then exploded into a revolutionary situation, after a violent skirmish between striking construction workers and the police and army culminated in a massacre, during which the military shot at and launched a cavalry charge against the demonstrators. In response, syndicalist trade unions seized their opportunity and called for a general strike in solidarity with the victims of state violence, a strike they claimed would continue until the state had prosecuted the soldiers.[71] This general strike against a specific act of state violence morphed over time into a revolutionary movement against capitalism and the state due to a combination of: (a) syndicalist trade unions spreading anarchist ideas among participants of the general strike, publicly calling for the social revolution and preparing for the social revolution by seizing weapons and organizing workers' militias; (b) the working classes being compelled to expropriate and distribute goods in order to meet people's needs, especially for food; and (c) the working classes responding to increasingly extreme state violence against the general strike by overthrowing the ruling classes.[72]

The manner in which syndicalist anarchists described the general strike can sometimes give the false impression that they thought a general strike could overthrow class society without the need for armed conflict and the violent destruction of the state. Such an interpretation ignores what the vast majority of syndicalist anarchists wrote. Pouget and Pataud's fictional general strike included workers assaulting government buildings, such as police stations and parliament, in order to achieve "the dissolution of the bourgeois State" by "disorganizing . . . dismantling and thoroughly disabling it."[73] The IWMA's 1922 declaration of principles claimed that "the decisive struggle between the capitalism of today and free communism of tomorrow will not be without conflict," and, as a result, they recognized the need for "violence as a means of defense against the violent methods of the ruling classes during the struggle for the possession of the factories and the fields by the revolutionary people."[74] At the 1910 founding congress of the CNT, it was agreed that, given the violence of the state, "it would be impossible for a peaceful general strike to last very long"; workers would have to engage in "violent" protests against the forces of state repression and thereby defeat "the tyrants."[75] This position was expanded upon in resolutions of the CNT's 1936 Zaragoza Congress that proposed that the defense of the revolution should be achieved by "the people armed."[76]

Some syndicalist anarchists did argue that a revolutionary general strike would provide a more effective means of defeating the police and military than the previous strategy of launching insurrections that established barricades. Nacht claimed in 1905 that the widening of streets since the French Revolution of 1789 and the uprisings of 1848 meant that "the heroic times of the battle on the barricades have gone by."[77] In the aftermath of World War I, Berkman wrote in 1929 that workers at a barricade would not be able to defeat a trained military supported by artillery, tanks, bombers, and poison gas. Such an idea of revolution was "obsolete," and had to be replaced by one that focused on the true power of the working classes: their ability to withdraw labor.[78] Rocker similarly wrote that the general strike was a replacement for "the barricades of the political uprising."[79]

Rocker, Nacht, Pouget, and Pataud all hoped that a general strike would occur over such a large area and involve so many workers that the military would be forced, by the sheer scale of the revolt, to scatter their troops into smaller units that could then be more easily defeated in combat or persuaded to join the workers in revolt.[80] The idea that a significant number of troops would mutiny and refuse to obey their orders to crush the general strike was not purely wishful thinking and had some basis in experience. In 1871, the Paris Commune was created after army soldiers, who had been sent to seize cannons from the national guard in the district of Montmartre, disobeyed multiple orders to fire on workers and guardsmen defending the cannons and, instead, fraternized with the people, a significant number of whom were women. Several years later, in 1907, a detachment of troops decided to mutiny on their way to suppress a CGT picket line.[81] During Spain's tragic week of 1909, a general strike against army reservists being called up to fight in Morocco mutated into an armed insurrection, in which, the working classes attacked the police specifically, while persuading some local soldiers to not fire on them. The insurrection was soon defeated when soldiers from outside Barcelona were called in and the barricades that workers had assembled were destroyed by artillery.[82]

Even if Rocker, Nacht, Pouget, and Pataud were overly optimistic about the effectiveness of a general strike in diminishing the power of the military and police, they nonetheless did all advocate an armed uprising as part of the general strike, and thought that workers would have to defend themselves from the violence of the police and army. Pouget and Pataud's account of how this would happen was, by far, the most eccentric. In their novel, they depicted the forces of reaction, including the invading armies of foreign states, being easily defeated by a variety of science-fiction weapons. This included electromagnetic waves that caused far away enemy ammunition to explode and aerial torpedoes dropped from remote-controlled planes.[83] These weapons were so ridiculous for the time that it is unclear if the authors seriously advocated them, or merely intended to entertain the reader. Kropotkin nonetheless asserted in his preface to the 1913 English edition of Pouget and Pataud's book that the authors had significantly underestimated the violent resistance that the social revolution would face and have to overcome.[84]

Although syndicalist anarchists generally attempted to produce a realistic conception of the general strike, they consistently faced two key problems when trying to implement it. First, syndicalist trade unions in Europe and the United States were unable to organize or initiate genuine national general strikes across multiple key industries by themselves, due to them having either small memberships or large memberships concentrated in specific parts of a country or industries. Given this, in order to launch national general strikes they had to rely on support from reformist trade unions, which failed to materialize on a number of occasions. In Spain, the CNT, whose membership was largest in Catalonia, organized a short general strike in December 1916 with the General

Union of Workers (UGT), which was affiliated with the Spanish Socialist Workers' Party (PSOE). This was followed by a general strike in August 1917, for which the leadership of the PSOE-UGT seriously failed to prepare, and which was only launched after they were forced into action by the UGT's largest union independently calling for a general strike. A few years later, the UGT refused to support a general strike in 1920. When Primo de Rivera established himself as dictator of Spain in September 1923, the CNT responded by calling for a general strike, while the UGT not only did not support the general strike but collaborated with the regime.[85]

Second, general strikes organized by anarchists were militarily crushed on numerous occasions. A long list of examples can be found in the history of Spanish anarchism. To give one, on February 16, 1902, a general strike in Barcelona—which spread to nearby industrial towns—was launched in solidarity with the striking Metalworkers' Federation, who had been on strike for two months. The general strike only lasted a week and was defeated following the declaration of martial law, the deployment of the military, the closure of union headquarters, and the arrest of several hundred organizers.[86] Spanish syndicalist anarchists were themselves aware of this problem. The CNT's report on the general strike, which was approved at the founding 1910 congress, claimed that "experience has taught us that" when the general strike is "localized at one point and the workers of the rest of the nation remain completely passive, the forces of public order, at the service of the bourgeoisie, will concentrate on that location, and it will be relatively easy for the government to crush the revolt."[87]

This is not to say that general strikes were always unsuccessful. Swiss anarchists participated in a 1907 general strike against local chocolate companies, including Nestlé, after a worker was unfairly fired. The general strike, which lasted from March 25 to 29, spread to Montreux, Lausanne, and Geneva in response to gendarmes firing on and wounding ten workers. It resulted in the rehiring of the worker, recognition of the trade union, and various material improvements.[88] Even when general strikes were militarily crushed or failed to achieve their immediate objectives, they could still bring about social change. This includes the previously mentioned 1906 CGT general strike that won the weekend and the 1919 CNT general strike that won the eight-hour day. On other occasions general strikes were, even if defeated, important acts of working-class resistance against domination and exploitation by the ruling classes. It is, from an anarchist perspective, better to rebel against oppression and lose than to not rebel at all, especially since workers do not know going into a struggle whether or not they will emerge victorious.

CHAPTER 10

Organizational Dualism:
From Bakunin to the Platform

A significant number of mass anarchists thought that federations of trade unions or community groups were insufficient to bring about the social revolution. They held that anarchists must, in addition to this, form specific anarchist organizations that would exist alongside mass organizations. These specific anarchist organizations were advocated as the means to unite committed revolutionaries in order to develop correct theory and strategy, coordinate their actions both among themselves and within broader mass organizations or movements, and push the revolutionary struggle forward through persuasion and engaging in actions that provided an example to others. This theory has come to be known as organizational dualism. In the past, specific anarchist organizations were often called an anarchist union. This language was not confusing to historical anarchists because they mostly spoke languages other than English and so distinguished between syndicates and the anarchist union, rather than trade unions and the anarchist union.

During the course of anarchism's history, numerous specific anarchist organizations were founded. For example, in January 1891, Italian anarchists formed the Anarchist Socialist Revolutionary Party, at a congress in Capolago, Switzerland. In the following months, anarchist groups from across Italy formed regional federations committed to the Capolago program. This growth in formal organization was cut short by the combination of state repression following May Day demonstrations, and significant push back from antiorganizationalist anarchists. By the end of the year, the Anarchist Socialist Revolutionary Party had, for all intents and purposes, vanished.[1] Later attempts by Italian anarchists to form a national federation committed to a common program culminated in the establishment of the Italian Anarchist-Communist Union in 1919, which changed its name to the Italian Anarchist Union in 1920. The Italian Anarchist Union, which participated as a key force in the USI and the factory occupation movement of the Bienno Rosso, spread its ideas via the paper *Umanità Nova*. At its peak in the early 1920s, the paper sold 50,000 copies a day, and was in some areas the most widely read paper among workers.[2]

Given the enormous scale of the history of organizational dualism, I shall focus on only three main aspects of its theoretical development. These are: (a) Bakunin's advocacy of organizational dualism between 1868 and 1872; (b) various proposals made between the 1890s and 1930s on what the relationship between anarchism and syndicalism (or trade unions in general) should be; and (c) debates between proponents of platformist and synthesist specific anarchist organizations that occurred from 1926 onward.

Bakunin and the Alliance

The strategy of organizational dualism was first advocated by Bakunin. During the late 1860s and early 1870s, he argued that anarchists should simultaneously organize and participate within mass public organizations that had a broad program, such as trade unions, and also form small secret organizations committed to a narrow anarchist program. This theorizing occurred, in parallel, to Bakunin's actual attempts to form secret revolutionary organizations. The history of these attempts is extremely complex, but a condensed version follows.

During his 1864–67 stay in Italy, Bakunin tried to transform the loose network of revolutionaries he knew into an organization that adhered to a specific program.[3] In late 1864, Bakunin, who had recently moved from London to Florence, founded his first proper revolutionary organization: the Brotherhood. Although the Brotherhood certainly existed, and had a membership of at least thirty individuals from largely republican circles, it did not last long and soon faded away after Bakunin moved to Sorrento, near Naples, at the end of May 1865. Bakunin, who was becoming increasingly socialist and shifting closer to his mature anarchist politics, then moved to Naples in October, and met a number of republican revolutionaries. Sometime between late 1865 and early 1866, Bakunin persuaded these individuals to join a new secret revolutionary socialist organization called the International Brotherhood, which was the spiritual successor to the previous Brotherhood based in Florence.[4]

Bakunin subsequently cofounded two distinct but overlapping organizations: the public International Alliance and the secret Alliance in October 1868. The public International Alliance applied to join the First International and, after its application was rejected, converted itself into a Geneva section of the First International in July 1869. The Geneva public Alliance decided to disband in August 1871, in the aftermath of various splits and conflicts within the Romance Federation of the First International, and took this decision without consulting Bakunin. The original secret Alliance disbanded soon after its founding, due to personal conflicts between its members. It continued to exist only as an informal social network composed of a few individuals who were mainly from Spain, Italy, and Switzerland and members of Bakunin's inner circle. At around the same time, a distinct secret organization called the Alianza de la Democracia Socialista was founded in Spain, to coordinate the activity of key militants and promote the growth of the Spanish section of the First International. The Alianza decided to dissolve itself in April 1872 and continued to adhere to this decision, despite Bakunin writing a letter attempting to persuade them to do otherwise. A few months later, Bakunin cofounded a new secret society, called the Alliance of Social Revolutionaries in September 1872, after Bakunin had been expelled from the First International by the Hague Congress.[5]

An early example of Bakunin's strategy of organizational dualism can be found in his 1866 *Programme of the Brotherhood*. He proposed that *"the dedicated revolutionaries of every land"* should gather *"at once into both public and private association* with the twofold object of broadening the revolutionary front and at the same time paving the way for simultaneous concerted action in all countries in which action proves initially possible, through secret agreement among the wisest revolutionaries of those countries."[6] The central task of these revolutionaries was to fuse, or in other words, organize, "the elements of social revolution" that "are already widespread in practically all countries of Europe" into "an effective force."[7] In the autumn of 1868, Bakunin wrote in the draft program of the secret Alliance that the organization had been founded in order to help "prepare, organize and hasten" the social revolution by pursuing the immediate "dual objective" of (a) spreading revolutionary consciousness through "journals, pamphlets and books" and "founding public associations" and (b) recruiting "intelligent, energetic, discreet men of good will who are sympathetic to our ideas, both in Europe and as far as possible in America, in order to form an invisible network of dedicated revolutionaries, strengthened by the fact of alliance."[8]

The same idea was expressed by Bakunin in the March 27, 1872, letter he wrote to an Italian named Celso Ceretti, who admired the republican revolutionary Garibaldi. In it, Bakunin advocated a "secret alliance" composed of "nuclei intimately bound together with similar nuclei presently being organized, or that will be organized, in other regions of Italy and abroad."[9] This organization had "a double mission: at first they will form the inspiring and vivifying soul . . . of the International Workingmen's Association in Italy and elsewhere, and later they will occupy themselves with questions *that will be impossible to discuss publicly.* They will form the necessary bridge between the propaganda of socialist theories and revolutionary practice."[10]

Bakunin did not propose the formation of a secret revolutionary organization because he had a hidden authoritarian agenda. He was motivated by the deeply practical view that a secret revolutionary organization was necessary in order to avoid state repression. In a April 1872 letter to members of the Spanish Alianza, he argued that the organization could not be public, because, if it were, it would be persecuted and crushed.[11] This concern with secrecy is especially understandable given that Bakunin himself had been imprisoned in 1849 by the state of Saxony for having fought in an insurrection launched by the people of Dresden. He was subsequently handed from one state to another, imprisoned by Saxony, then by Austria, which kept him chained to a cell wall for a year, and then finally Russia from May 1851 onward. Both Saxony and Austria sentenced Bakunin to death, only to alter his sentence at the last minute after a secret agreement was made to transfer him ultimately to Russia. He remained imprisoned in Russia's Peter and Paul Fortress, where all his teeth fell out due to scurvy, until the Tsar permanently banished him to Siberia in 1857.[12]

Bakunin thought that the mass public organization—the First International—and the small secret anarchist organization—the Alliance—had distinct but complementary roles in the revolutionary process. The role of the mass public organization was to unite as many workers as possible within an organization that prefigured the future society and to engage in large-scale direct action against the ruling classes. The role of the small, secret, specific anarchist organization was, in comparison, to enable dedicated revolutionaries to coordinate their activity effectively and participate in the collective struggles of the working classes. In so doing, anarchists would spread their ideas and help organize and coordinate the uprisings of the working classes into a force capable of abolishing capitalism and the state in favor of an anarchist society. Bakunin explained his views on this topic in a private letter he wrote to the Alianza member Charles Alerini between May 3 and 6, 1872. According to Bakunin,

> The Alliance and the International, although they both seek the same final goals, follow, at one and the same time, different paths. One has a mission to bring together the labor masses—millions of workers—[reaching] across differences of trades or lands, across the frontier of every state into one single compact and immense body. The other, the Alliance, has a mission to give a really revolutionary direction to these masses. The programs of the one and the other, without in any way being opposed, are different, in keeping with the extent of the development of each. That of the International, if it is taken seriously, contains in germ—but only in germ—the whole program of the Alliance. The program of the Alliance is the elaboration of the program of the International.[13]

Bakunin thought that the mass public organization and the specific anarchist organization should have distinct programs due to their different roles. The First International's role was to unite workers from around the world into federations of trade unions that engaged in the struggle for immediate improvements via direct action, and thereby laid the foundation from which the social revolution could arise. Given this, it should have a broad program inclusive to as many workers as possible and be based on their shared class interests to achieve better living conditions, emancipation, and international solidarity in the class struggle.[14] Were the First International to adopt a narrow program, it would fail in its mission, and merely create "a very small association, a sect, but not an armed camp for the proletariat of the entire world [set] against the exploiting and dominant classes."[15] The Alliance, in contrast, had to have an explicitly revolutionary program that advocated the simultaneous abolition of capitalism and the state. This included a commitment to atheism, which Bakunin held should not be part of the First International's program, because that would exclude the millions of workers who believe in God.[16]

This view was repeated almost word for word by Bakunin in his April 1872 letter to the members of the Spanish Alianza. This went alongside the clarification that Bakunin rejected the position that all socialist consciousness had to be brought to workers in the mass public organization by the secret organization of revolutionaries. Bakunin instead maintained that workers would develop their own radical ideas, due to both the influence of revolutionaries and their own experiences of class struggle. He thought that in an International with a broad program "it will happen that, more and more educated by the struggle and by the free propaganda of different ideas, directed by their own instinct and increasingly raised to revolutionary consciousness by practice itself and the inevitable consequences of the universal solidarity of the struggle of labor against capital, the masses will elaborate, slowly, it is true, but infallibly, their own thoughts, theories that will emerge from bottom to top."[17]

Although Bakunin thought that a small secret society of dedicated revolutionaries would play an important role in the process of workers becoming organized and adopting socialist ideas, he remained committed to the self-emancipation of the working classes. In his resignation letter to the Jura Federation in 1873, he reminded them that the "organization of the forces of the proletariat . . . should be the work of the proletariat itself."[18] A number of modern authors have argued against such an interpretation of Bakunin on the grounds that these public declarations are contradicted by his private programs and letters in which, they allege, he argued for a fundamentally authoritarian and un-anarchist strategy. According to these critics, Bakunin preached anarchism in public while privately advocating the organization of a hierarchical secret society that would seize power and establish an unaccountable top-down dictatorship that ruled society from the shadows. The two main sources cited to support this interpretation are Bakunin's April 1, 1870, letter to Albert Richard and his June 2, 1870, letter to Sergei Nechaev.[19] These interpretations misrepresent what Bakunin proposed within his letters and take certain quotes out of context.

His letter to Richard did advocate ideas that can sound authoritarian and incompatible with anarchist strategy, such as his endorsement of a "collective, invisible dictatorship."[20] In order to refute ominous authoritarian readings of Bakunin, it is necessary to establish in detail exactly what Bakunin meant by an "invisible dictatorship" by placing this phrase within the full context of the letter. First, Bakunin repeated both the standard anarchist critique of state socialism and the standard anarchist conception of a social revolution. He rejected centralization, minority rule, and a revolutionary state modeled on the French Revolution, in which decisions for an entire country are made by a single committee, on the grounds that they were a means that would never lead to a free socialist society. The revolution, he said, should instead be achieved through the formation of a federation of workers' associations that would expropriate the means of production, liquidate the state, establish workers militias, and coordinate production and distribution through a system of delegates.[21] Bakunin's letter is, in this respect, entirely consistent with his statements elsewhere.

Second, the reason Bakunin referred to an "invisible dictatorship" is that he is attempting to persuade Richard to abandon state socialist strategies. Richard was a French member of the Alliance who never fully endorsed its anarchist program, and would go on to write a pamphlet arguing for the reinstatement of Napoleon III as

Emperor. Bakunin wrote, "you remain more than ever a supporter of centralization and the revolutionary State. Whereas I am more opposed to it than ever, and see no salvation except in revolutionary anarchy, guided on all issues by an invisible collective power—the only dictatorship I accept."[22] As a result the only occasions when Bakunin uses the phrase in the letter is when he is contrasting the "invisible dictatorship" he supports with the "overt dictatorship" that Richard wrongly advocates.[23] Bakunin's use of language for rhetorical purposes is similar to how Marx used the phrase "dictatorship of the proletariat," instead of "rule of the proletariat," when he was in dialogue with followers of Blanqui due to their support for revolutionary dictatorships.[24]

Third, at no point does Bakunin claim that the "invisible dictatorship" will make decisions and impose them on the working classes. He instead held that it would only act to influence or guide the working classes. He declared that, during a revolution,

> supporters of overt dictatorship, advocate the muting of passions, and speak for order, trust and submission to the established revolutionary powers—in this way they reconstitute the state. We, on the other hand, must foment, awaken and unleash all the passions, we must produce anarchy and, like invisible pilots in the thick of the popular tempest, we must steer it not by any open power but by the collective dictatorship of all the allies—a dictatorship without insignia, titles or official rights, and all the stronger for having none of the paraphernalia of power.[25]

This view is repeated later in the letter when Bakunin wrote that only the "invisible collective force . . . can preserve and guide the revolution."[26] In advocating an "invisible collective force," Bakunin was not endorsing a clandestine organization that guides workers by violently forcing them to behave in a particular manner. Bakunin is instead repeating language from Proudhon, who defined *collective force* as when the combined and organized action of individuals results in a group that possesses collective capacities to change the world that are greater than the sum of the capacities of each individual member.[27]

Bakunin made similar points in his later letter to Nechaev, who was a Russian acquaintance of Bakunin committed to the formation of an authoritarian top-down secret society that engaged in any means, including assassinating members of the ruling classes and launching coups, to trigger a revolution. As in the previous letter, sections of it can be quoted out of context in order to give the false impression that Bakunin was a hidden authoritarian, such as his advocacy of "*the collective dictatorship* of a secret organization."[28] Such an interpretation should be rejected once again. Bakunin argued, in line with anarchist theory, that any revolution based on the seizure of state power by a ruling minority would result in new forms of oppression and exploitation, rather than emancipation. He thought that any attempt to abolish class society that "is at all artificial, and deals in secret plots, sudden assaults, surprises and blows, is bound to wreck itself against the State, which can only be conquered and broken by a spontaneous popular socialist revolution. And therefore the sole object of a secret society must be not to create an artificial force outside the people, but to arouse, unite and organize spontaneous popular forces; in this way the only possible, the only effective army of the revolution is not outside the people, but consists of the people themselves."[29]

During this period, the word "spontaneous" was generally used by anarchists to refer to when workers acted voluntarily of their own volition, rather than being forced to do something. Such spontaneous action was compatible with workers being influenced to act in a particular manner by the words and deeds of those around them. The role of the secret organization of committed revolutionaries was, therefore, to encourage and support a process of working-class self-emancipation. Bakunin wrote that if the working classes are the "revolutionary army," then the secret organization would be the "general headquarters of this army, and the organizer not of its own, but of the people's forces, as a link between the people's instincts and revolutionary thought."[30]

This would be achieved by forming a series of secret small groups that were dispersed throughout a country and united under a common program. During a revolutionary situation, they would formulate a set of ideas that were "the very essence of popular instincts, desires and demands," spread them "among a crowd of people who would be struggling without any purpose or plan," and thereby "create round themselves a circle of people who are more or less devoted to the same idea, and who are naturally subject to their influence."[31] They would then collectively participate within ongoing popular movements in order to "lead the people toward the most complete realization of the social-economic ideal and the organization of the fullest popular freedom. This is what I call *the collective dictatorship* of a secret organization."[32]

Just as in his letter to Richard, Bakunin introduced this phrase in order to contrast the methods by which anarchists will "influence the people" with the "publicly declared dictatorship" that he opposed.[33] Bakunin's so-called dictatorship would not give orders to workers who were subject to their authority and forced to obey by the threat of corporal punishment or court-martial. He explicitly wrote that,

> It does not impose any new resolutions, regulations or ways of living on the people, and only unleashes their will and gives a wider opportunity for their self-determination and their social-economic organizations, which should be created by them alone from the bottom upwards, and not from the top downwards. The organization must be sincerely impregnated with the idea that it is the servant and helper of the

people, and by no means their ruler, and also not in any circumstances, not even on the pretext of the people's welfare,
should it ever be their master.[34]

The secret organization instead "influences the people exclusively through the natural, personal influence of its members,
who have not the slightest power, are scattered in an unseen web
throughout the regions, districts and communes, and, in agreement
with each other, try, in whatever place they may be, to direct the
spontaneous revolutionary movement of the people toward the
plan that has been discussed beforehand and firmly determined."[35]
Its only methods to direct and influence mass social movements
were persuasion and acting as organizers. It would, Bakunin
believed, "carry out a broadly based popular propaganda, a propaganda that would *really* penetrate to the people, and by the power of
this propaganda and also by *organization among the people themselves*
join together separate popular forces into a mighty strength capable
of demolishing the State."[36]

Critics of Bakunin have not only misrepresented what Bakunin
meant by an invisible or collective dictatorship but also failed to
mention that, in several other sources, he makes exactly the same
proposals as in his letters to Richard and Nechaev without using
any dictatorial language. This is extremely important, because the
only two instances in which Bakunin advocates a dictatorship as
an anarchist are in two letters he wrote as attempts to persuade
authoritarian revolutionaries to adopt anarchist strategy. Outside
this context, Bakunin does not use this language, and so it appears
most likely that he only adopted the language as a rhetorical device,
and not as an expression of his hidden authoritarian agenda.

In the 1868 program of the International Brotherhood, Bakunin
wrote that a social revolution must be created by workers themselves through their own organs of self-management. Within such
a revolution, "*the unity of revolutionary thought and action must find*

an agent in the thick of the popular anarchy which will constitute the very life and all the energy of the revolution. That agent must be *the secret universal association of international brothers*" which is "a kind of revolutionary general staff" that spreads ideas and organizes workers in order to act as the "intermediaries between the revolutionary idea and popular instinct."[37] This text is almost identical to passages from Bakunin's letters to Albert and Nechaev but, at no point, does he refer to any invisible dictatorship. Indeed, he explicitly writes that "this organization rules out any idea of dictatorship and custodial control" since "supreme control must always belong to the people."[38]

The same opposition to dictatorship appears elsewhere. In September 1869 *La Liberté* published Bakunin's article, "A Few Words to My Young Brothers in Russia." In the article, he insisted that formally educated young people in Russia should "go among the people" and "learn amid these masses whose hands are hardened by labor how you should serve the people's cause. And remember well, brothers, that the cultured youth should be neither master nor protector nor benefactor nor dictator to the people, only the midwife of their spontaneous emancipation, the uniter and organizer of their efforts and their strength."[39]

Two years later, he wrote in "The Paris Commune and the Idea of the State" that during a social revolution,

> All that individuals can do is elaborate, clarify and propagate the ideas that correspond to the popular feeling and, beyond this, to contribute by their ceaseless efforts to the revolutionary organization of the natural power of the masses, but nothing beyond that. And everything else should not and could not take place except by the action of the people themselves. Otherwise one would end with political dictatorship, that is to say, the reconstruction of the State . . . and one would arrive by a devious but logical path at the

re-establishment of the political, social and economic slavery
of the popular masses.[40]

Bakunin described the Alliance in his April 1872 letter to members of the Spanish Alianza as

> Fundamentally a militant organization whose purpose is the
> organization of the power of the masses for the destruction
> of all states and all of the religious, political, judicial, social,
> and economic institutions currently existing, for the absolute
> emancipation of the subjugated and exploited laborers of the
> whole world. The purpose of our organization is to push
> the masses to make a clean sweep, so that agricultural and
> industrial populations can reorganize and federate themselves
> according to the principles of justice, equality, freedom and
> solidarity, from the bottom up, spontaneously, freely, apart
> from any official tutelage, whether of the reactionary or even
> the so-called revolutionary kind.[41]

The evidence clearly shows that Bakunin was not a hidden
authoritarian who preached anarchism in public, and top-down
minority rule by a secret society in private. His public and private
statements were entirely consistent with one another, and with his
anarchist commitment to the self-emancipation of the working
classes. Bakunin held, in short, that the success of a social revolution required a specific anarchist organization of dedicated militants
who organized secretly to avoid state repression and were united
under a common theoretical and strategic program. The main goal
of this organization was to participate in popular social movements
in order to spread anarchist ideas, and help organize and coordinate
the uprisings of the working classes into a force capable of abolishing capitalism and the state and building an anarchist society.

In two letters, Bakunin referred to this as an invisible or

collective dictatorship, but in so doing all he actually meant was that a specific anarchist organization would influence the wider working classes through persuasion and acting as key organizers and militants within the ongoing class struggle. In his mind, this would occur in parallel with, and as a complement to, workers transforming themselves through their own experiences of revolutionary practice within mass public organizations that were committed to broad programs. During an evolutionary period, this included such organizations as trade unions. Once a revolution had been launched, increasingly large numbers of workers would continue this process of self-transformation and self-organization within federations of producers' and consumers' associations, and federations of workers' militias. The role of the specific anarchist organization was to prevent the emergence of any new system of minority rule and to promote forms of organization and decision-making that enabled worker self-management.

Bakunin attempted to implement this theory by participating in the broad public First International via a secret informal social network known as the Alliance. This secret network was never in a position where it could influence the working classes during a social revolution, and failed to live up to the great role that Bakunin had given it. Despite these limitations, its importance should not be underestimated. It was arguably the first specific anarchist organization in history, and its members played a key role in formulating the theory and practice of the anarchist movement. From the intellectual and practical foundation that Bakunin and the Alliance built, the future history of specific anarchist organizations would emerge.

Syndicalism and Specific Anarchist Organizations

After the collapse of the Saint-Imier International in 1878, mass anarchists continued to advocate the strategy of simultaneously forming mass organizations and small specific anarchist organizations. In the buildup to the 1881 International Social Revolutionary Congress in London, Kropotkin proposed in letters to Malatesta, Cafiero, Schwitzguébel and an unnamed Belgian comrade, that anarchists should form "two organizations; one open, vast, and functioning openly; the other secret intended for action."[42] The secret organization was to be composed of dedicated anarchist militants who were experienced and action oriented. The public organization was, in comparison, to be a trade union that grouped workers "under the flag of the Strikers' International."[43] The trade union was advocated both because it was the sole means through which "the forces of labor, the masses, can be successfully grouped together" and because it would "provide forces, money and a place for secret groups" to operate.[44] This secret organization would be a direct continuation of the Intimité Internationale, a secret association of anarchists within the Saint-Imier International that he had joined in 1877 and that, when he was writing, still existed.[45]

In the years after 1881, Kropotkin remained an advocate of organizational dualism. Nettlau described him as advocating *"the penetration of the masses and their stimulation by libertarian militants, in much the same way as the Alliance acted within the International."*[46] To support this view, Nettlau cited a 1914 letter where Kropotkin argued that "the syndicate is absolutely necessary. It is the only form of workers' association which allows the direct struggle against capital to be carried on without a plunge into parliamentarism. But, evidently, it does not achieve this goal automatically, since in Germany, in France and in England, we have the examples of syndicates linked to the parliamentary struggle . . . There is need of the other element which Malatesta speaks of *and which Bakunin always professed,*" namely a specific anarchist organization.[47]

What element Malatesta spoke of can be established by examining the articles he wrote during the 1890s. In 1894, Malatesta argued that anarchists "should organize among ourselves, among folk who are perfectly persuaded and perfectly in agreement; and, around us, in broad, open associations, we should organize as many of the workers as we can, accepting them for what they are and striving to nudge them into whatever progress we can."[48] This view was repeated in 1897, when he wrote that anarchists should "set up as many groups of convinced and agreeable comrades as possible," and also "join the labor movement with fervor, helping already existing workers' organizations and striving to promote new ones."[49] In 1899, he continued to argue for the "organization of us anarchists and the anarchist organization of the masses."[50]

Malatesta held, in line with Bakunin, that the mass organization should not have a distinctly anarchist program. In June 1897, he argued that "the workers' organizations . . . gather the exploited for the economic struggle against the masters" on the basis of "the interests shared by all workers . . . regardless of persuasion" and so must "be separate and distinct from the organizations of the various parties," including specific anarchist organizations.[51] Several months later in November, he distinguished between "the workers' movement—which should be whatever it can be and vary with the varying degree of development attained by the proletarians . . . and the anarchist party, which should be made up of men subscribing to the same ideas and bound by common purposes."[52] Malatesta came to adopt this position in response to the lessons of the International in Italy. The Italian section "was never anything other than the anarchist socialist party," and so "was weak as an organization for economic resistance" because "it was unable to make headway among the masses who were frightened by its overly advanced program . . . and it was weak as an anarchist party because many of its members were workers who had little grasp of anarchy and socialism and, having been drawn by the hope of immediate revolution, melted away every time an insurrectional attempt, or the hope of it, failed."[53]

After the birth of revolutionary syndicalism as a doctrine between the late 1890s and the early 1900s, Malatesta's advocacy of organizational dualism was articulated in response to the ideas of the CGT and other revolutionary syndicalist trade unions. Malatesta's critique of the theory of revolutionary syndicalism is sometimes misrepresented as a rejection of revolutionary trade unionism in and of itself. Such a perspective ignores the fact that during his debate with the revolutionary syndicalist and CGT member Monatte at the 1907 International Anarchist Congress in Amsterdam, Malatesta argued that he was a supporter of the labor movement and advocated anarchists entering trade unions to spread anarchist ideas among workers. As a result, he described himself as "a syndicalist, in the sense of being a supporter of the syndicates," who advocated "syndicates that are open to all workers without distinction of opinions, absolutely neutral syndicates," rather than "anarchist syndicates."[54] What Malatesta rejected was revolutionary syndicalism as "a doctrine" in the sense of the position that trade unionism is "*sufficient unto itself*" and "a necessary and sufficient means for social revolution."[55]

Over the following decades, Malatesta repeatedly argued that revolutionary syndicalism was wrong, because trade unions are a necessary but insufficient means to revolution. In 1927, he insisted that,

> Today the major force for social transformation is the labor movement (union movement). . . . The anarchists must recognize the usefulness and importance of the union movement; they must support its development and make it one of the levers in their action, doing all they can to ensure that, by cooperation with other forces for progress, it will open the way to a social revolution. . . . But it would be a great and fatal mistake to believe, as many do, that the labor movement can

and should, of its own volition, and by its very nature, lead to such a revolution.[56]

Malatesta thought that trade unionism was insufficient to achieve a social revolution, because he believed that trade union activity was constituted by forms of practice that, over time, had a tendency to transform them into reformist institutions concerned with reproducing themselves within capitalism, rather than abolishing class society. As he explained in 1907, "Labor movements, which always commence as movements of protest and revolt, and are animated at the beginning by a broad spirit of progress and human fraternity, tend very soon to degenerate; and in proportion as they acquire strength, they become egoistic, conservative, occupied exclusively with interests immediate and restricted, and develop within themselves a bureaucracy which, as in all such cases, has no other object than to strengthen and aggrandize itself."[57]

Trade unions must, if they are to fulfill their purpose, be open to any worker who wants to win immediate improvements from the economic ruling classes. The consequence of this is that trade unions will be forced by circumstances to "moderate their aspirations, first so that they should not frighten away those they wish to have with them, and next because, in proportion as numbers increase, those with ideas who have initiated the movement remain buried in a majority that is only occupied with the petty interests of the moment."[58] In addition, given their function of winning immediate improvements for their membership, trade unions will have to operate not too far outside the law, interact with the political and economic ruling classes, and concern themselves primarily with the interests of workers who belong to the trade union, rather than workers who their membership competes with in the labor market. These factors would, in turn, lead trade unions that gain a large membership to "assure, in accord with rather than against the masters, a privileged situation for themselves, and so create difficulties of entrance for new members, and for the admission of apprentices in the factories; a tendency to amass large funds that afterwards they are afraid of compromising; to seek the favor of public powers; to be absorbed, above all, in co-operation and mutual benefit schemes; and to become at last conservative elements in society."[59]

For Malatesta, this tendency of trade unions to develop into reformist institutions that balanced the interests of capital and labor was confirmed by such examples as the American Federation of Labor in the United States. It "does not carry on a struggle against the bosses except in the sense that two businessmen struggle when they are discussing the details of a contract. The real struggle is conducted against the newcomers, the foreigners, or natives who seek to be allowed to work in any industrial job" such that "skilled workers look down on manual workers; whites despise and oppress blacks; the 'real Americans' consider Chinese, Italians, and other foreign workers as inferiors. If a revolution were to come in the United States, the strong and wealthy Unions would inevitably be against the Movement, because they would be worried about their investments and the privileged position they have assured for themselves."[60] Kropotkin shared Malatesta's concerns. In 1919, he complained that in England, after the collapse of the First International, "the daily struggle of local unions against the exploiters took the place of more distant ends . . . the majority of the active members of the workers' unions, occupied day after day with the organization of these unions and their strikes, lost sight of the final end of the workers' organization—social revolution."[61]

The history of the CGT can itself be used to illustrate Malatesta's argument against revolutionary syndicalism. In 1919, a major and potentially revolutionary strike wave spread across France. It mobilized 1,150,718 workers in 2,026 strikes. One of the major strikes in this wave of revolt began on June 2, when 170,750 metalworkers in Paris and its suburbs, who belonged to thirteen local unions, went on strike for a forty-four-hour workweek and higher wages. This strike was independently organized by the rank and file as a reaction to the secretaries of the CGT's Federation of Metalworkers signing an agreement with capitalists that granted a forty-eight-hour workweek. In so doing, the Federation had undercut ongoing negotiations between the capitalists and the Parisian local unions concerning a forty-four-hour workweek.

A significant number of workers who took part in the strike, which expanded to include other regions of France, attempted to transform it into a revolutionary movement against capitalism itself and to achieve political objectives, such as an end to French military intervention against the Russian revolution and amnesty for political and military prisoners. They called for a general strike and the establishment of a new Paris Commune. The strike ended on June 28, before any of this could occur, because the union secretaries decided to achieve a purely economic settlement with the capitalists and government, which won increased wages and reaffirmed the previous agreement of a forty-eight-hour workweek. Despite thinking of themselves as genuine radicals committed to the ideas of revolutionary syndicalism, the secretaries decided to not support political or revolutionary demands or enlist the wider support of the CGT as a whole. Given their social position as trade union bureaucrats, they acted to balance the interests of capital and labor and focused exclusively on reformist rather than revolutionary goals.[62]

Anarcho-syndicalists argued that revolutionaries should respond to the problem of trade unions becoming increasingly reformist over time by explicitly committing them to achieving an anarchist society through anarchist means. In 1925, Malatesta rejected this position and argued against those who aspired to merge the labor and anarchist movements by giving unions an explicitly anarchist program. He noted that the purpose of a trade union is to unite as many workers as possible in order to win immediate reforms, such as higher wages and improved working conditions, and thereby act as "a means of education and a field for propaganda" until workers "are in a position to make the social revolution."[63] Yet, since the majority of workers are not anarchists, any trade union that allowed only committed anarchists to join it would "be the very same thing as an anarchist group and would remain unable either to obtain better conditions or to bring about the revolution."[64] His claim that anarcho-syndicalist trade unions would end up being specific anarchist organizations that called themselves trade unions was certainly applicable to some groups. The French CGTSR, for example, had only six thousand members in 1936, hardly the size necessary to be an organ of genuinely large-scale class struggle.[65]

On the other hand, if an anarcho-syndicalist trade union allowed any worker into it and thereby performed its function as an organ of large-scale class struggle then, as it grew in size, it would come to be an organization in which the majority of members were not anarchists and its anarchist program would exist only on paper as "an empty formula to which nobody pays any more attention."[66] Malatesta concluded that any "fusion" of anarchism and the trade union movement would result "either in rendering the union powerless to attain its specific aim, or in attenuating, falsifying and extinguishing the spirit of Anarchism."[67]

Given this, Malatesta rejected the strategy of committing existing trade unions to an anarchist program or splitting off from large, moderate trade unions to form much smaller anarchist ones. He instead argued that anarchists should participate within the largest trade unions as a militant minority in order to be able to influence the largest number of workers and counteract the tendency of trade unions to become reformist. In Malatesta's specific context during 1920s Italy, this was the syndicalist USI and the General Confederation of Labor, which had close ties with the Italian Socialist Party. His position, though, could apply just as well to less radical trade unions.[68]

According to Malatesta, the "revolutionary spirit must be introduced, developed, and maintained by the constant actions of revolutionaries who work from within their ranks as well as from outside, but it cannot be the normal, natural definition of the Trade Unions' function."[69] Anarchists who participate in the trade union movement should, "strive to make them as much as possible instruments of combat in view of the Social Revolution. They should work to develop in the Syndicates all that which can augment its educative influence and its combativeness—the propaganda of ideas, the forcible strike, the spirit of proselytism, the distrust and hatred of the authorities and of the politicians, the practice of solidarity toward individuals and groups in conflict with the masters. They should combat all that which tends to render them egotistic, pacific, conservative," which included amassing large amounts of money and "the appointment of bureaucratic officials, paid and permanent."[70]

Although Malatesta advocated anarchist participation within the trade union movement, he insisted that anarchism should not subsume itself into it, but instead maintain an independent existence within specific anarchist organizations. He argued that anarchists should work within the trade union movement for "anarchistic purposes as individuals, groups and federations of groups" and "always keep in contact with the Anarchists and remember that the labor organizations do not constitute the end but only one of the various means, no matter how important it may be, of preparing the advent of anarchy."[71] There is, he said, "an impelling need for a specifically anarchist organization which, both from within and outside the unions, struggle for the achievement of anarchism and seek to sterilize all the germs of degeneration and reaction."[72] In other words, Malatesta advocated syndicalism (in the broad sense of revolutionary trade unionism) plus a specific anarchist organization.

He was not alone. In 1888, Spanish anarchists formed the Anarchist Organization of the Spanish Region in order to provide

the Federation of Resistance Against Capital, a federation of politically neutral trade unions, with a revolutionary orientation.[73]
Decades later in 1907, an anonymous member of the anarchist
movement in Bohemia reported: "We are syndicalists. But syndicalism for us is only a means of action and not an end. We view
it as a means of anarchist propaganda. It is thanks to syndicalism
that we have been able to put down firm roots among the textile
workers and miners in northern Bohemia, whose trade unions are
under our direct influence. Most of these unions are flanked by an
anarchist group made up of the best educated and most conscious
workers. Our revolutionary miners are preparing the struggle for an
eight-hour day."[74]

Some, but not all, anarcho-syndicalists advocated the formation of both mass syndicalist trade unions committed to an
anarchist program, which were open to all workers, and smaller specific anarchist organizations, which were composed exclusively of
dedicated militants. Focusing on Spain, the former general secretary
of the CNT's Catalan Regional Federation, Salvador Seguí, gave
a speech on anarchism and syndicalism in 1920. He claimed that
although anarchists should participate in trade unions in order to
"watch over their development and to provide them with direction"
such that they "become more libertarian," this "does not by any
means imply that the existing anarchist groups must be dissolved.
Not at all. The more influence they exercise, the more Anarchism
and anarchists there will be."[75] Ultimately, as Seguí pointed out, it
was the influence of anarchist groups that led to the CNT adopting
anarchist communism as its goal in 1919.

Several years later in 1927, the FAI was founded during the
CNT's period of illegality—between 1924 and 1930—under the
Primo de Rivera dictatorship. Its founding was initiated by the
Portuguese Anarchist Union, the Federation of Spanish-Speaking
Anarchist Groups in France, and the Federation of Anarchist
Groups in Spain.[76] The strategic motivations for a new specific

anarchist organization can be seen in the manifesto issued by the Anarchist Liaison Committee of Catalonia, which had been set up to organize the founding of the FAI. They described themselves as workers who were active CNT militants and supporters of the doctrine of the IWMA. It was asserted that "it is not enough to be active inside the union. . . . Outside of the unions, absolutely independently, we disseminate our theories, form our groups, organize rallies, publish anarchist reading material, and sow the seed of anarchism in every direction."[77] This activity in anarchist groups was essential in order to ensure that anarchists both instigated and inspired the coming social revolution such that it was not defeated, as had recently happened in Russia, by the establishment of a new minority political ruling class. Anarchists had to "organize ourselves in anarchist groupings in order to impregnate the anarchist revolution" and "propel it as far forward as we may."[78]

This commitment to an anarcho-syndicalist version of organizational dualism was repeated at the founding meeting of the FAI in July 1927. The minutes claim that the labor organization itself should struggle not only for day-to-day improvements, but also, for universal human emancipation and anarchism. At the same time, an "anarchist organization of groups should be established alongside it, with the two organizations working together for the anarchist movement."[79] It was proposed that the CNT and the FAI should "hold joint plenums and local, district, and regional meetings" and "form general federations of the full anarchist movement" with "general councils composed of representatives of the unions and the groups. The general councils will name Commissions of Education, Propaganda, Agitation, and other areas of equal concern for both organizations."[80] By organizing joint councils, the FAI and CNT would establish a *trabazón* with one another, which can be translated into English as an "organic link." This trabazón was subsequently implemented at the CNT's national conference in January 1928, where delegates from the FAI and CNT agreed to form a National Committee of Revolutionary Action and a National Prisoners' Aid Committee composed of members of both organizations.[81]

The strategy of anarcho-syndicalism plus a specific anarchist organization was also advocated by anarchists outside of Spain. The French anarcho-syndicalist Besnard argued during his speech at the IWMA congress of 1937 that "anarcho-communist groups," which were distinct from the trade union, should "go *prospecting* among the laboring masses," "seek out recruits and temper militants" and "carry out active propaganda and intensive pioneering work with an eye to winning the greatest possible number of workers hitherto deceived and gulled by all the political parties, without exception, over to their side and thus to the anarcho-syndicalist trade unions."[82]

The relationship between mass organizations and specific anarchist organizations was not the only topic that anarchists debated. They also argued with one another about how specific anarchist organizations should be structured and what role they should play in the class struggle.

Platformism and Synthesism

In 1918, the Confederation of Anarchist Organizations (Nabat) was founded in Ukraine. It was viewed by Voline, who was one of its members, as a specific anarchist organization that would embrace anarchist communists, anarcho-syndicalists, and individualist anarchists and thereby achieve what he termed a "united anarchism."[83] The Nabat's first congress on November 18 described its primary duty as "organizing all of the life forces of anarchism; uniting the various strands of anarchism; bringing together through a common endeavor all anarchists seriously desirous of playing an active part in the social revolution."[84] This aspiration never became a reality due to the anarcho-syndicalists deciding not to join. In response, the Nabat choose not to send a delegate to the third All-Russian Conference of Anarcho-Syndicalists.[85]

In November 1920, the militants of the Nabat, including Voline, were arrested by the Bolshevik secret police and imprisoned in Moscow. After an extensive campaign for the release of anarchist prisoners, which included imprisoned anarchists going on hunger strike, the Bolshevik government released a number of anarchists on the condition that they leave the country immediately. Among them was Voline, who left for Berlin in January 1922. That year, the anarchists who had fled to Berlin in order to escape Bolshevik state repression formed the Group of Russian Anarchists Abroad. Between June 1923 and May 1924, this group published the anarchist journal *Anarkhichesky Vestnik* (Anarchist Herald) as part of a collaboration with the New York Union of Russian Toilers. The journal, edited by Voline and Peter Arshinov, published articles advocating the formation of specific anarchist organizations that united anarchists from different tendencies in order to combine the best ideas from anarchist communism, anarcho-syndicalism, and individualist anarchism.[86]

This position came to be known as the *anarchist synthesis* and was expounded not only by Voline but also by the French anarchist Sébastien Faure. In his 1928 article *The Anarchist Synthesis*, Faure utilized an analogy with chemistry to argue that anarchist communism, anarcho-syndicalism, and individualist anarchism were "three elements" that should be mixed together and synthesized through a process of ongoing experimentation. This would reveal which "dosage" of each element was most appropriate for a given context such that the "formula" would vary "locally, regionally, nationally or internationally."[87] The organizational basis for this synthesis in France was the recently formed Association of Anarchist Federalists (AFA), which was described by Faure as "an entirely new regrouping of anarchist forces" that would unite all committed anarchists "without distinction of tendency" in order to "give more cohesion, influence and effectiveness to our dear propaganda" and enable anarchists "to work together rather than against one another, to live in peace rather than make war."[88]

In Faure's *Anarchist Encyclopedia*, published in 1934, Voline repeated this view when he defined the anarchist synthesis as "a tendency currently emerging within the libertarian movement seeking to reconcile and then 'synthesize' the different currents of thought that divide this movement into several more or less hostile fractions."[89] Voline, in other words, sought not only to unite different anarchists in the same organization but also to combine the different ideas of anarchist tendencies together. This was motivated by two main positions. First, although anarchism's fragmentation into distinct subtypes had initially led to beneficial developments in anarchist theory and practice, it had in the long run ceased to be useful and resulted in unnecessary conflict between anarchists who each viewed their "parcel" as "the sole truth and bitterly fought against the partisans of the other currents."[90] In so doing, they ignored the important ideas that other anarchist tendencies had to offer and the fact that anarchism could be improved by fusing each separate element together into an organic whole. Second, any specific anarchist organization composed of different kinds of anarchist that did not establish a synthesis of their different ideas would only be "a 'mechanical' assemblage" in which "each holds on to his intransigent position," resulting in "not a synthesis, but chaos."[91]

In parallel with the emergence of Voline and Faure's anarchist synthesis, a distinct and opposed tendency developed that came to be known as *platformism*. In June 1926, members of the Group of Russian Anarchists Abroad, which had relocated to Paris in 1925, issued *The Organizational Platform of the General Union of Anarchists (Draft)* through their new journal *Dielo Truda* (The Cause of Labor). The *Platform* emerged out of discussions within the Group of Russian Anarchists Abroad, whose members included

Nestor Makhno, Peter Arshinov, and Ida Mett, about how a specific anarchist organization should be structured and operate in order to overcome the perceived disorganization and ineffectiveness that the anarchist movement had fallen into. In so doing, they hoped to ensure that the anarchist movement would not be defeated, as it had been in Russia, during the next revolution.[92]

The Dielo Truda group, in line with organizational dualism in general, advocated the formation of mass organizations that brought the working classes together on the basis of production and consumption, such as trade unions, workers' councils, or cooperatives, and a specific anarchist organization that united the most revolutionary and militant workers under an anarchist-communist program.[93] The function of such a specific anarchist organization, which they called *the general union of anarchists*, was to prepare the working classes for a social revolution, awaken and nurture class consciousness, spread anarchist ideas, coordinate action, and participate effectively in collective struggles. In so doing, it would ensure that anarchism became "the guiding light," "spearhead," or "driving force" of the social revolution when it occurred, such that there was an *"anarchist theoretical direction of events."*[94]

By this, the Dielo Truda group did not mean that the general union of anarchists should seize power, establish themselves as a political ruling class, and impose their ideas from the top down in the name of the working classes whom they claimed to represent. Rather, they sought only "to assist the masses to choose the genuine path of social revolution and socialist construction" and establish the "genuine self-governance of the masses," which would be "the practical first step along the road to the realization of libertarian communism."[95] This goal was to be achieved by participating within mass movements, such as trade unions, in order to spread anarchist ideas within them and steer the movement in an anarchist direction.

The *Platform* differed from other forms of organizational dualism in its conception of how the specific anarchist organization should be structured. The Dielo Truda group held that specific anarchist organizations should, in order to effectively influence the working classes, adhere to a narrow ideological and tactical program that would act as a guide for achieving their shared goals via an agreed-upon route. This position emerged from their experiences of the Russian revolution. Arshinov argued in his 1925 article "Our Organizational Problem" that the anarchist movement in Russia had been outmaneuvered by other revolutionary tendencies because it had adopted "positions that were, yes, correct, but too general, acting all at once in a diffuse way, in multiple tiny groups, often at odds on many points of tactics."[96] In order to prevent this from happening again, specific anarchist organizations should be committed to ideological and tactical unity such that every member agrees on a specific route to achieve concrete objectives. Doing so ensures that the organization's limited resources are deployed in the same direction and prevents different segments of the organization from engaging in tactics that do not complement and support one another, such as one group advocating participation in trade unions while another tried to persuade workers not to join them.[97]

The Dielo Truda group therefore rejected Voline and Faure's theory of the anarchist synthesis. They thought it made little sense to advocate the synthesis of anarchist communism, anarcho-syndicalism, and individualist anarchism. It was already the case that anarcho-syndicalists advocated communism as a goal and most anarchist communists advocated participation in trade unions. Nor was there any need to incorporate the insights of individualist anarchism. Individualists rejected the need for collectively organized class struggle, and anarcho-syndicalism and anarchist communism were already based on a commitment to the freedom of the individual. In addition, it was impractical to attempt to synthesize the different anarchist tendencies into a single organization, because its members would continue to have fundamentally incompatible views on theory and practice. The organization would

inevitably disintegrate when these disagreements arose to prominence during collective struggles.[98]

The authors of the *Platform* believed that the common ideological and tactical program of the specific anarchist organization
should be implemented through each individual member engaging
in revolutionary self-discipline, and enacting the decisions that had
been collectively agreed upon.[99] They wrote that "the federalist type
of anarchist organization, while acknowledging every member of
the organization's right to independence, to freedom of opinion,
initiative and individual liberty, charges each member with specific
organizational duties, insisting that these be rigorously performed,
and that decisions jointly made be put into effect."[100] This included
a commitment to seeing decisions made by majority vote at congresses as binding on every group within the organization. The
authors of the *Platform*, in parallel with this, rejected the "unaccountable individualism" of some anarchist groups in favor of a
system of *"collective responsibility"* whereby the general union of
anarchists "will be answerable for the revolutionary and political
activity of each of its members" and "each member will be answerable for the revolutionary and political activity of the Union as
a whole."[101]

Most controversially of all, the Dielo Truda group proposed the
formation of an executive committee that would achieve coordination and coherence between different sections of the general union
of anarchists. They advocated an *"Executive Committee"* tasked with
the "implementation of decisions made by the Union, which the
latter have entrusted to it; theoretical and organizational oversight
of the activity of isolated organizations, in keeping with the Union's
theoretical options and overall tactical line; scrutiny of the general
state of the movement; maintenance of working and organizational ties between all of the organizations of the Union, as well
as with outside organizations."[102] The authors of the Platform were
aware that the executive committee could potentially take on a life

of its own and subordinate or oppress the membership. In order to prevent this from happening, they proposed that "the rights, responsibilities and practical tasks of the Executive Committee will be prescribed by the Congress of the General Union."[103]

The *Platform* aroused a great deal of debate within the European anarchist movement. These responses tended to be based on misunderstanding or misrepresenting its ideas due, in part, to a poor French translation produced by Voline, and the ambiguous language within the *Platform* itself, such as references to collective responsibility, an executive committee, and anarchists providing theoretical direction.[104] In 1927, a different group of Russian anarchists, which included Mollie Steimer, Senya Fleshin, and Voline, released a critique of the *Platform*. They interpreted the *Platform* as advocating the formation of a centralized party ruled from the top-down, by an executive committee that was merely a central committee under a different name. This centralized party would, in turn, act as leader and director of both the anarchist movement and working-class movements in general, rather than offering only ideological assistance to other workers as equals in the class struggle. As a result, they concluded that the Dielo Truda group had abandoned anarchist principles in favor of authoritarian Bolshevik ones.[105] This negative evaluation of the *Platform* was shared by Berkman and Goldman.[106]

A more politely written response was issued by Malatesta in October 1927. Malatesta, like Steimer, Fleshin, and Voline, viewed the *Platform* as rejecting the anarchist commitment to free initiative and free agreement in favor of a Bolshevik-inspired authoritarian system of organization. The *Platform's* advocacy of collective responsibility, binding congress resolutions made by majority vote, and an executive committee was interpreted by Malatesta as being a proposal for an organization in which decisions are made by elected representatives. If these representatives make binding decisions through simple majority voting then, when there are more than two factions at a meeting, the decision will be made by a numerical

minority of representatives elected by a minority of the organization.[107] He argued that,

> if the Union is responsible for what each member does, how
> can it leave to its individual members and to the various groups
> the freedom to apply the common program in the way they
> think best? How can one be responsible for an action if one
> does not have the means to prevent it? Therefore, the Union
> and in its name the Executive Committee, would need to
> monitor the action of the individual members and order them
> what to do and what not to do; and since disapproval after
> the event cannot put right a previously accepted responsibil-
> ity, no-one would be able to do anything at all before having
> obtained the go-ahead, the permission of the committee.[108]

As a result, Malatesta concluded that the Dielo Truda group
had proposed means that would, "far from helping to bring about
the victory of anarchist communism . . . only falsify the anarchist
spirit and lead to consequences that go against their intentions."[109]

In response to these critiques the authors of the *Platform* issued
a number of texts clarifying their position. First, they were not in
favor of subordinating the working class to the top-down rule of
an anarchist organization. They explicitly wrote that "the action of
steering revolutionary elements and the revolutionary movement of
the masses in terms of ideas should not be and cannot ever be considered as an aspiration on the part of anarchists that they should
take the construction of the new society into their own hands. That
construction cannot be carried out except by the whole of laboring
society, for that task devolves upon it alone, and any attempt to strip
it of that right must be deemed anti-anarchist."[110]

Given this, anarchists "will never agree to wield power, even for
a single instant, nor impose their decisions on the masses by force. In
this connection their methods are: propaganda, force of argument,

and spoken and written persuasion."[111] The *Platform's* references to anarchists providing direction to the working classes only meant that they would influence other workers and persuade them to adopt anarchist ideas in just the same manner that famous anarchist theorists such as Bakunin, Kropotkin, Reclus, and Malatesta had already done. The *Platform* merely held that in order for this ideological direction to become a "permanent factor" it was necessary to form "an organization possessed of a common ideology . . . whose membership engage in ideologically coordinated activity, without being side-tracked or dispersed as has been the case hitherto."[112] This organization would then participate in, for example, the trade union movement "as *the carriers of a certain theory, a prescribed work plan*" in order to "*disseminate* within the unions its ideas regarding the revolutionary tactics of the working class and on various events."[113]

In summary, although the revolution can only be made by the working classes themselves, it is also the case that "the revolutionary mass is forever nurturing in its bosom a minority of initiators, who precipitate and direct events" and "in a true social revolution the supporters of worker anarchism alone will account for that minority."[114] Once the working classes "have defeated capitalist society, a new era in their history will be ushered in, an era when all social and political functions are transferred to the hands of workers and peasants who will set about the creation of the new life. At that point the anarchist organizations and, with them, the General Union, will lose all their significance and they should, in our view, gradually melt away into the productive organizations of the workers and peasants," rather than subjecting workers to their rule.[115]

Second, in advocating an executive committee within the specific anarchist organization they were not proposing the formation of "a Party Central Committee . . . that issues orders, makes laws and commands."[116] The authors of the *Platform* not only thought that an executive committee was consistent with anarchism, but that "such an organ exists in many anarchist and anarchist-syndicalist organizations."[117] What the *Platform* called an "Executive Committee" had no coercive powers. It was merely "a body *performing functions of a general nature in the Union*" that would not restrict the activity of groups within the organization and instead only "steer their activity" by providing "ideological or organizational assistance," such as advising a group on the current "tactical or organizational line adopted by the Union on a variety of matters."[118]

If a group within the specific anarchist organization decided to adopt its own tactical approach then one of three outcomes would occur: the minority would agree to follow the majority position within the organization because it is not an issue of supreme importance; the minority and majority position would coexist if feasible; or, the minority would leave the organization to form their own group. Crucially, which of these outcomes transpired "will be resolved, not by the Executive Committee which, let us repeat, is to be merely an executive organ of the Union, but by the entire Union as a body: by a Union Conference or Congress."[119]

Third, the idea of collective responsibility did not entail the view that the members of the organization would have to follow the orders of an executive committee. Arshinov explained in his response to Malatesta that the members of the organization would be united under a common program that they all supported and which, in so far as they were members, was binding upon them. Given this,

> the practical activity of a member of the organization is naturally in complete harmony with the overall activity, and conversely the activity of the organization as a whole could not be at odds with the conscience and activity of each member, assuming he has accepted the program fundamental to this organization. It is this which characterizes the principle of collective responsibility: the Union as a body is answerable for the activity of each member, in the knowledge that he could only

carry out his political and revolutionary work in the political
spirit of the Union. Likewise, each member is fully answerable
for the Union as a whole, since its activity could not be at odds
with what has been determined by the whole membership.[120]

From Arshinov's response, it is clear that Malatesta's critique
was based on a misunderstanding of what the authors of the
Platform meant by collective responsibility. Malatesta himself realized that this was potentially the case. He wrote in a December 1929
letter to Makhno that,

> I accept and support the view that anyone who associates
> and cooperates with others for a common purpose must feel
> the need to coordinate his actions with those of his fellow
> members and do nothing that harms the work of others and,
> thus, the common cause; and respect the agreements that
> have been made—except when wishing sincerely to leave the
> association. . . . I maintain that those who do not feel and do
> not practice that duty should be thrown out of the associa-
> tion. Perhaps, speaking of collective responsibility, you mean
> precisely that accord and solidarity that must exist among the
> members of an association. And if that is so, your expression
> amounts, in my view, to an incorrect use of language, but basi-
> cally it would only be an unimportant question of wording
> and agreement would soon be reached.[121]

Malatesta further clarified his views on the topic in a July 1930 letter he wrote to a platformist group, based in the Montmartre district of
Paris. Although he continued to reject the phrase "collective responsibility" in favor of "moral responsibility," he wrote "I find myself
more or less in agreement with their way of conceiving the anarchist
organization (being very far from the authoritarian spirit which the
'Platform' seemed to reveal) and I confirm my belief that behind the

linguistic differences really lie identical positions."[122] Malatesta was, nonetheless, not a platformist since he thought that specific anarchist organizations should have a slightly broader program, and rejected the position that congress resolutions passed by majority vote should be binding on every group within a specific anarchist organization, rather than only those groups who voted in favor of them.

The immediate practical effect of the Platform appears to have been somewhat limited. The Dielo Truda group organized a number of discussion meetings on the *Platform* that were attended by militants from around the world, including France, Italy, Spain, Bulgaria, Poland, and China. This culminated in an attempt to form an Anarchist International at a meeting held in a Parisian cinema on March 20, 1927.[123] During the meeting, Makhno proposed a five-point program to be discussed: "(1) recognition of the class struggle as the most important factor of the anarchist system; (2) recognition of anarcho-communism as the basis of the movement; (3) recognition of syndicalism as one of the principal methods of anarcho-communist struggle; (4) the necessity of a 'General Union of Anarchists' based on ideological and tactical unity and collective responsibility; (5) the necessity of a positive program to realize the social revolution."[124]

These five points were then pedantically rephrased by the attending delegates in a manner that changed their language but not their ultimate meaning. The wording agreed upon was:

1.   recognition of the struggle of all oppressed and exploited against state and capitalist authority as the most important factor of the anarchist system;

2.   recognition of anarcho-communism as the basis of the movement;

3.   recognition of the labor and union struggle as one of the most important means of anarchist revolutionary action;

4.   necessity in each country of as general as possible
        a Union of Anarchists who have the same goals and
        tactics, as well as collective responsibility;
5.   necessity of a positive program of action for the anar-
        chists in the social revolution.[125]

Before the delegates could move on to discuss these points,
the French police broke into the meeting and arrested everybody
in attendance. The commission elected to form the Anarchist
International, whose members were Makhno (Ukrainian), Ranko
(Polish), and Chen (Chinese), issued a letter on April 1 that
declared the existence of an International Libertarian Communist
Federation and, for reasons that are unclear, expressed the original five-point program for discussion that had been formulated by
Makhno, rather than the version that delegates had revised. This
contributed toward delegates from other anarchist groups, includ-
ing the Italian anarchists who were members of the Italian Anarchist
Union, deciding to disassociate from the project.[126] Fabbri, Camillo
Berneri, and Ugo Fedeli explained in their letter that the members
of the Pensiero e Volontà group had decided not to join because,

> there exists among you a spirit which is quite distant from
> that which underlies our way of conceiving an international
> anarchist organization, that is one which is open to the great-
> est number of individuals, groups and federations who agree
> with the principles of struggle organized in an anarchist way
> against capitalism and the State, on a permanent national
> and international basis, but all this without any ideological
> or tactical exclusivism and without any formalism that could
> impede the autonomy or freedom of the individuals in the
> groups or of the groups themselves in the various national
> and international unions.[127]

The first specific, anarchist organization to express support for platformism was the Federation of Anarcho-Communist Groups of the United States and Canada, which was composed of workers from the Russian empire and financially supported the publication of *Dielo Truda*.[128] The federation declared in January 1927 that "the Conference agrees with the Organizational Platform" and views its ideas as "timely and desirable."[129] Other Russian anarchists living in North America rejected the ideas of the Platform, and formed the Federation of Russian Workers' Organizations of the United States and Canada in 1927. After several years of dialogue and negotiations, the two rival federations united into a single federation in July 1939.[130]

The second specific anarchist organization to adopt platform-ism was the French Anarchist Communist Union. At its autumn 1927 congress in Paris, a majority of delegates voted to rename the organization the Revolutionary Anarchist Communist Union. This was accompanied by a number of dramatic changes to how the organization functioned. The results of majority votes were now binding on all individual members; positions adopted at annual congresses could not be subject to criticisms within the pages of the Union's official paper, *Le Libertaire*, except during a three-month period immediately prior to the next congress; membership was only possible via a group, meaning isolated individuals could no longer join; and being a member involved paying a subscription fee and receiving a membership card. The 1927 congress resulted in a split within the organization. Proponents of synthesist anarchism left to form the previously mentioned AFA. These changes to the Anarchist Union did not last long. The platformist position was soon defeated at the 1930 Paris Congress where, despite a speech by Makhno, the synthesist delegates won the vote by fourteen to seven, regained control of the organization, and abandoned the above pol-icies. In response, the platformists left and formed the Libertarian Communist Federation in 1934, only to rejoin the Anarchist Union two years later in 1936.[131]

Despite the various negative interpretations of the Platform, its commitments were not a break with anarchism. They were instead one of many ways in which anarchists sought to build upon and update the kind of specific anarchist organization that Bakunin had advocated, decades previously. This remains true even though other anarchists thought their proposals were misguided. Although proponents of organizational dualism disagreed about how specific anarchist organizations should be structured and make decisions, they nonetheless agreed on the need to unite committed revolutionaries under a common program in order to develop correct theory and strategy, coordinate their actions both among themselves and within broader mass organizations or movements, and to push the revolutionary struggle forward through persuasion and engagement in actions that provided an example to others.

CHAPTER 11

Conclusion

Between 1868 and 1939, anarchists living in Europe and the United States developed a political theory that guided their attempts to bring about fundamental social change. This theory can be summarized as follows. Anarchists were antistate socialists who advocated the achievement of freedom, equality, and solidarity. For anarchists, these values were interdependent, such that the realization of one of them can only occur through the realization of all three at once. Although all anarchists advocated freedom, they disagreed with one another about how to define it. Some anarchists defined freedom as nondomination such that a person is free if and only if they are not subordinate to someone who wields the arbitrary power to impose their will on them. Other anarchists defined freedom as the real possibility to do and/or be a broad range of things such that a person becomes more free as their opportunities expand. One of the main reasons why anarchists valued freedom is that it is a prerequisite for people fully developing themselves and realizing their human potential. Irrespective of how they defined freedom, anarchists agreed that humans can, given the kind of animals we are, only be free in and through society.

In order for this to occur, society has to be structured in an egalitarian manner. There must be no hierarchical divisions between rulers who issue commands and make decisions and subordinates

347

who obey and lack decision-making power. Organizations should instead be structured horizontally, such that each member is neither a master nor a subject. They are instead an associate who has an equal say in collective decisions, and so, codetermine the voluntary organization with every other member. Such equality of self-determination must go alongside equality of opportunity. Each individual should have access to the external conditions that are necessary for self-development, and having the real possibility to do and/or be a broad range of things, such as food, health care, and education. The reproduction of such a society requires solidarity, in the sense of individuals and groups cooperating with one another in pursuit of common goals and people, in their personal lives, forming reciprocal caring relationships, such as by being a loving parent, good friend, or supportive teacher.

Anarchists argued that capitalism and the state, alongside all structures of domination and exploitation,[1] should be abolished in favor of a stateless classless society without authority, in which everyone is free, equal, and bonded together through relations of solidarity. They called this society *anarchy*. The abolition of capitalism and the state was primarily justified on the grounds that they are violent hierarchical pyramids in which decision-making flows from the top to the bottom. The majority of the population are workers who lack real decision-making power over the nature of their life, workplace, community, or society as a whole. They are instead subject to the power of an economic ruling class—capitalists, landowners, bankers, etc.—and a political ruling class—monarchs, politicians, heads of the police, generals, etc. The economic ruling class derive their power from the private ownership of land, raw materials, and the means of production. Workers own personal possessions but not private property and so, in order to survive, must sell their labor to capitalists and landowners in exchange for a wage. The political ruling class sit at the top of the centralized, hierarchical state and possess the authority to make laws and issue commands at a societal level that others must obey, due to the threat or exercise of institutionalized force, such as the police, prisons, and courts. All states, regardless of whether they are a monarchy, dictatorship, or parliamentary democracy, exercise institutionalized violence in order to enforce and maintain the domination and exploitation of workers, and thereby perpetuate the power and privilege of both the economic and political ruling classes.

The creation of anarchy requires the abolition of capitalism and the state but the ruling classes will never give up their power voluntarily and instead violently defend it. They must be overthrown. The majority of anarchist theory was concerned with how to do this. Anarchists argued that the goal of universal human emancipation could only be achieved through the formation of working-class social movements that engage in class struggle against the political and economic ruling classes and, ultimately, launch a social revolution.

Anarchists envisioned the social revolution as a lengthy process of simultaneous destruction and construction. Workers would destroy the old world by launching an armed insurrection that violently smashed the state and forcefully expropriated the ruling classes. This victory would be achieved by workers' militias, who would also defend the social revolution from counterattack. Workers would build the new world by creating an anarchist society, which is the totality of social structures from which anarchy could later emerge. During and immediately after the social revolution, anarchists aimed to establish: (a) the collective ownership of land, raw materials, and the means of production; (b) the self-management of social life, including production and distribution, through workplace and community assemblies in which collective decisions are made via either unanimous agreement, majority vote, or a combination of the two; (c) the abolition of money and markets in favor of a system of decentralized planning; and (d) the reorganization of production, such that people engage in a combination of mental and physical labor, unsatisfying labor is either removed, automated, or shared among producers, and the length of the working day is significantly reduced.

In order to achieve this goal, anarchists had to overcome the fact that capitalism and the state are self-reproducing. Society is constituted by a process of human beings with particular consciousness engaging in practice: deploying their capacities to satisfy a psychological drive. In so doing, they simultaneously change both the world and themselves. The interplay between practice producing social relations and practice being performed through social relations results in the formation of relatively stable and enduring social structures. These social structures simultaneously enable and constrain practice, such that individuals engage in practices that develop historically specific capacities, drives, and consciousness. The consequence of this is that as people engage in practice, they also create and re-create themselves as the kinds of people who reproduce the social structure itself.

Abolishing capitalism and the state, creating an anarchist society, and the day-to-day reproduction of an anarchist society requires the bulk of the population to have developed a vast array of different capacities, drives, and consciousness, such as the capacity to make decisions through general assemblies, the drive to not oppress others, and the consciousness that capitalism and the state make people unfree. The dominant structures of class society are constituted by forms of practice that develop people fit mainly for reproducing capitalism and the state, rather than abolishing them. Class society systematically fails to produce the kinds of people that both an anarchist revolution and an anarchist society need. Such individuals, of course, would be produced by a properly functioning anarchist society, but this fact does not help anarchists presently living under class society. Anarchists therefore face a paradox: in order to transform society they need transformed people. In order to have transformed people, they need a new society.

The anarchist solution to this problem was revolutionary

practice. Humans are not solely the product of their circumstances. They can also chose to engage in actions that simultaneously develop new capacities, drives, and consciousness; modify existing social structures; and construct whole new social structures. This is not to say that any form of revolutionary practice could lead to an anarchist society. Anarchists argued that working-class social movements should only use means that were in conformity with the ends of creating anarchy. They, in short, advocated the unity of means and ends: the means that revolutionaries propose for achieving social change have to be constituted by forms of practice that develop people into the kinds of individuals who are capable of, and are driven to: (a) overthrow capitalism and the state, and, (b) construct and reproduce the end goal of an anarchist society. If social movements select means that fail to do this then they would, regardless of people's good intentions, never achieve the ends of anarchism.

The anarchist commitment to the unity of means and ends shaped both what strategies they advocated and which ones they rejected. Anarchists thought that the social revolution would emerge out of an extended evolutionary period, during which change was slow, gradual, and partial. In order for this evolutionary period to culminate in a revolution, working-class social movements have to spread their ideas and form social networks through print media, talks, and recreational activities; construct organizations that prefigure the future anarchist society; and engage in class struggle via direct action. Anarchists advocated these means not only because they were effective and won results, but also because of the forms of practice that constituted them. Through engaging in direct action with prefigurative organizations, workers simultaneously change the world and themselves. A group of workers might form a tenant union, organize a rent strike against their landlord, and make collective decisions about the rent strike within a general assembly. In so doing, they change social relations—rent decreases and workers gain more power over their landlord—and change people—workers develop the capacity to organize a rent strike and make decisions within a general assembly, acquire an increased sense of solidarity with one another, and realize that housing should be free.

During the course of the strike, these workers not only change social relations and themselves, but also construct a new social structure that did not exist before—a tenant union. Long-term participation in this tenant union would, in turn, cause workers to develop their capacities, drives, and consciousness further. This makes the organization of new actions possible, such as a larger rent strike that mobilizes workers in an entire city. These kinds of actions could continue and multiply over time, as increasingly large numbers of workers engage in the process of simultaneously transforming social relations and themselves. This would eventually culminate in a shift from workers only modifying the dominant structures of class society, to workers abolishing them and replacing them with new ones. Through the struggle against capitalism and the state, workers could develop into people ready to emancipate themselves and achieve anarchist goals.

Anarchism emerged in parallel with, and in opposition to, various forms of state socialism that aimed to achieve a stateless classless society through the conquest of state power. Anarchists replied that the means of conquering state power could never achieve the ends of universal human emancipation. Socialist parties that engaged in parliamentarism within the existing bourgeois state would, over time, abandon their revolutionary program and become mere reform movements that defended the status quo and only aimed at the improvement of conditions within the cage of capitalism and the state. If a socialist party succeeded in conquering state power, whether by elections or force, the result would not be a society in which workers themselves self-managed social life. They would instead create a new form of minority class rule, in which the working classes were dominated and exploited by the party leadership that actually wielded state power. The minority of rulers would be transformed by the exercise of state power and become tyrants who were primarily concerned with expanding and reproducing their power and furthering their specific interests in opposition to, and in conflict with, the interests of the working classes whose name they ruled in. They would never give up their power voluntarily, and would violently repress any working-class social movements who resisted them. The state would never wither away. It had to be intentionally and violently destroyed.

Although anarchists in general shared these basic strategic commitments, the movement was divided between two main strategic schools of thought: insurrectionist anarchism and mass anarchism. Insurrectionist anarchists opposed formal organization and advocated the formation of small affinity groups, that were linked together via informal social networks and periodicals. They rejected the struggle for immediate reforms, and argued that anarchists should immediately engage in an escalating series of assassinations, bombings, and armed insurrections against the ruling classes and their institutions. The goal of these attacks was to spread anarchist ideas and inspire other workers to rise up. This would result in a chain reaction of revolt, as an increasingly large number of workers launched insurrections, formed a mass movement, and initiated the social revolution.

Mass anarchists, in contrast, advocated the formation of both affinity groups and large-scale formal federations of autonomous groups, which coordinated large-scale action through regular congresses attended by instantly recallable mandated delegates. They argued that anarchists could generate a mass movement that was driven to, and capable of, launching an armed insurrection that abolished class society through the struggle for immediate reforms in the present. In order for this struggle to build toward revolution, rather than collapse into reformism, it had to be achieved by engaging in direct action within prefigurative organizations. Anarchists would facilitate this process by acting as a militant minority within social movements in order to influence other workers to adopt anarchist ideas and implement anarchist strategy.

The main form of mass anarchism was syndicalist anarchism, which argued that trade unions were the primary social movement under capitalism that could fulfill anarchist goals. This was because trade unions could pursue the double aim of struggling for immediate reforms and attempting to launch a social revolution via an insurrectionary general strike. In so doing, they would perform a dual function. They could act as organs of resistance that struggle against dominant institutions in the present and then, during the social revolution, take over the organization of the economy (in part or whole) and transform into organs of self-management. Syndicalist anarchists disagreed about whether or not trade unions should be politically neutral, or formally committed to achieving an anarchist society through anarchist means.

A significant number of mass anarchists thought that trade unions were a necessary but insufficient means to achieve revolution. These proponents of organizational dualism argued that anarchists should simultaneously form mass organizations open to all workers and, in addition, smaller specific anarchist organizations composed exclusively of anarchist militants. These specific anarchist organizations were the means to unite committed revolutionaries in order to develop correct theory and strategy, coordinate their actions both among themselves and within larger and broader mass organizations or movements, and push the revolutionary struggle forward through persuasion and engaging in actions that provided an example to other workers. Proponents of organizational dualism nonetheless disagreed about how to do this, and argued with one another about a variety of topics, including how broad or narrow a specific anarchist organization's program should be, and whether or not congress resolutions should be binding on every section of an organization, or only those who voted in favor of them. These disagreements led to the formation of distinct tendencies, such as synthesists and platformists.

Numerous anarchist women, and some men who supported them, realized that the achievement of anarchy required the organization of women-only groups in order to struggle against class and gender oppression simultaneously. These groups aimed to combat sexism and promote women's liberation within both the anarchist movement, and wider society. In so doing, they would enable women to unlearn their patriarchal socialization and fully participate in the class struggle as equals to male workers. These women-only groups were either mass organizations that were open to all women workers, informal anarchist affinity groups, or formal organizations of dedicated anarchist militants. Some organizations were women's sections of syndicalist trade unions, while others were independent.

This book has been concerned with what historical anarchists thought. It was not written as a mere exercise in digging up curious individuals from the past or compiling historical facts for their own sake. I want to help modern workers develop their own ideas about how to change the world, and I thought I could do this by summarizing the theory and actions of the main antiauthoritarian wing of the historical workers' movement. This project is only partially complete since, for the purposes of this book, I narrowly focused on anarchists living in Europe and the United States. To properly understand the history of anarchism one must also examine the ideas and actions of anarchists who lived in Latin America, Asia, Oceania, and Africa.

Modern anarchists should read not only Bakunin, Malatesta, Kropotkin, and Goldman but also authors like Ricardo Flores Magón, M. P. T. Acharya, He-Yin Zhen, Liu Shipei, Itō Noe, Kōtoku Shūsui, and Hatta Shūzō. These anarchists should not be treated as tokens, who are only referenced when responding to false accusations that anarchism was historically an exclusively white or

European social movement. Their ideas must instead be treated as being of equal importance, such that their views are fully incorporated into our understanding of what anarchism is. Nor should they be viewed as separate from the anarchist movement in Europe and the United States. All these authors read and were influenced by European anarchists. Several of them, such as Magón, Acharya, and Kōtoku, lived in Europe or the United States for parts of their life. The different anarchist movements around the world were so interconnected with one another, through transnational networks and migration flows, that the complete history of anarchism can only be written as a global history.

Modern anarchists should not merely repeat the ideas of dead anarchists. The fact that a dead anarchist wrote it does not make it true. We must make arguments grounded in evidence for why anarchist positions are correct, rather than merely quoting dead anarchists as if their words were scripture. We must learn not only from their successes, but also from their failures, inadequacies, and inconsistencies. Most importantly of all, we have to develop our own ideas in response to our specific situations and problems, such as climate breakdown and ecological collapse; the resurgence of fascism; modern border systems; the gig economy; and transphobia. This is itself in line with what historical anarchist authors themselves wrote. They consistently reiterated the point that anarchist theory and practice had to develop in response to specific concrete situations and that people in the future would, and should, develop ideas that they were not in a position to even conceive. In order to do so, we need to draw upon not only distinctly anarchist theory, but also the best ideas that have been developed by various social movements of the oppressed and exploited over the past 150 years. This includes, but is not limited to, feminism, queer theory, the disability rights movement, Marxism, the Black radical tradition, Indigenous critiques of settler-colonialism, and the Zapatista Army of National Liberation.

This work has already begun. During the 1970s, participants in the woman's liberation and Black power movements came into contact with anarchist ideas and, independently of one another, developed anarcha-feminism and Black anarchism as distinct tendencies. Anarcha-feminists argue that the personal is political and analyze the manner in which women are oppressed by men in daily life, such as women being expected to do the majority of chores, men talking over women at meetings, or women being subject to emotional and physical abuse, sexual harassment, and sexual violence. In response to patriarchy within the anarchist movement, anarcha-feminists have advocated the formation of women's only groups and insisted that prefiguration requires transforming interpersonal dynamics and interactions, rather than only organizational structures and methods of collective decision-making. This has included arguing that anarchists must develop effective responses to intimate partner violence within social movements.[2]

Proponents of Black anarchism argue that Black people have been excluded from the benefits of citizenship and subject to specific forms of white supremacist state violence. This has resulted in numerous examples of Black people self-organizing independently of the state in order to survive. Emancipation cannot be achieved through the incorporation of Black people into white supremacist states, or the creation of new Black states. They reject authoritarian modes of organization and suggest that the centralization and hierarchy of the Black Panther Party played an important role in its demise and failure to achieve fundamental social change. Black liberation can only be achieved through the formation of horizontal social movements that bring all workers of color together in order to engage in direct action and self-direct their struggle, rather than be subordinate to the leadership of white radicals.[3]

Both anarcha-feminism and Black anarchism are part of a more general tendency within modern anarchism that draws upon Black feminism to emphasize the manner in which all structures of oppression form an interlocking web in which each component is defined in terms of its relationship to every other component. Different structures of oppression interact with, shape, and support one another to such an extent that they mutually constitute one another. The relations between structures of oppression are part of what each structure is. A Black working-class lesbian, for example, does not experience patriarchal + racist + homophobic + economic + state oppression, whereby each form of oppression is separate and independent. She instead experiences the product of these five structures interacting with one another to create life experiences that cannot be reduced to a single primary oppressive structure or the sum total of multiple oppressive structures. Society is not a Venn diagram where Black men experience racism, women experience sexism, and Black women experience both. Black women experience not only racism and sexism but also forms of oppression that are unique to them as Black women and are not shared by Black men or white women. This is because the interconnections between structures of oppression, such as racism and patriarchy, create outcomes that are greater than the sum of their parts.[4]

The abolition of capitalism and the state will not, by itself, lead to the abolition of patriarchy, racism, queerphobia, ableism, and so on. Even if we accept the premise that these structures of oppression arose, or at least massively expanded, due to the development of class society in general or capitalism in particular, it is still the case that these social structures have become self-reproducing and will not automatically disappear due to the establishment of socialism. They will instead continue to exist, but be mediated through new economic and political relations. The creation of stateless socialism would, for example, end elements of patriarchy that require the existence of capitalism and the state, such as sexist corporate advertising and anti-abortion laws, but other aspects of patriarchy would continue to exist, like people of all genders being socialized into patriarchal gender roles, or men sexually harassing women in public. This would result in the fusion of patriarchal and socialist relations, such as, possibly, collective decisions being made in general assemblies where men treat women as their intellectual inferiors. We cannot focus exclusively on class and wait until after the revolution—which may never come or be defeated—to address other issues. We must instead struggle against all forms of oppression simultaneously. The self-emancipation of the working classes can only be achieved through intersectional class struggle.

Although historical anarchist theory needs to be updated, it should not be abandoned or discarded. It contains numerous insights that can guide us in the modern world. The oppression we witness on a daily basis is not an inevitable nor an unchangeable aspect of human life. It is instead the product of hierarchical social structures that divide humanity into masters and subjects. These social structures are made by human beings and so can be unmade and replaced with new and better ways of living together. Authoritarians imagine that emancipation can be achieved if good people with the correct ideas take control of the reins of power. Anarchists realize that this has never happened, and will never happen. Regardless of people's good intentions, or the stories they tell themselves, they will be corrupted by their position at a top of a hierarchy and become primarily concerned with exercising and expanding their power over others in order to serve their own interests. If human beings are not inherently good, then no person is good enough to be a ruler.

Cold war propaganda taught us that our only choice is between really existing capitalism or really existing state socialism. We are asked to pick between rule by a minority of elected politicians who serve the interests of capital, or rule by a one-party dictatorship led by a supreme leader; the impersonal domination of market forces, or the top-down bureaucracy of state central planning; the prison industrial complex, or the gulag; surveillance and repression by the FBI, or the NKVD. The history of socialism reveals that a large segment of the workers' movement developed a third way: anarchist socialism and the establishment of federations of workplace and community assemblies that enable people to self-manage their own lives. This is not to say that creating anarchist socialism will be easy. The history of the workers' movement shows how hard it is to change the world. Any struggle for emancipation will face the overwhelming violence of the ruling classes, and we must prepare ourselves for this. The modern state is better armed and has developed superior forms of surveillance, crowd-control, and counterinsurgency than its historical predecessors.

When reading about the history of social movements it is easy to focus on large-scale acts of revolt that can appear to have come out of nowhere. This book has itself mentioned numerous strikes, riots, insurrections, and revolutions. Learning about these events is an important part of labor history, but to focus exclusively on them leads to a distorted view of the past and how social change happens. Members of historical socialist movements did not spend the majority of their time participating in huge actions that rapidly transformed society and the future course of history. The bulk of their lives as revolutionaries were spent doing much more mundane activities. They produced, distributed, and read radical literature; organized and attended picnics; performed in a theater club; watched a public debate; discussed politics with friends, family, and colleagues; attended an endless series of meetings for their affinity group or trade union; wrote and received a vast amount of letters; and so on.

These small, mundane activities can appear to be of little importance when viewed in isolation. Yet when they were repeated day after day, week after week, month after month, and year after year by groups of people, they took on greater significance. These small activities produced and reproduced the social relations, capacities, drives, and consciousness that were the foundation of social movements. Without these seemingly insignificant acts, repeated over and over again, the large exciting moments of rebellion and revolution never would have occurred in most instances or would have occurred on a much smaller scale.

Unfortunately, time is not on our side. Capitalism's insatiable drive for profit and economic growth is destroying the environment. The climate crisis is not merely coming, it has already begun. Things are only going to get worse. Billionaires and politicians are not going to save us. We have to save ourselves. The actions we take now determine the future we and future generations face. Our only choice is collective struggle. We have to generate a social force that can dismantle the fossil fuels industry and, in so doing, achieve survival pending revolution. In response to these dire circumstances, a large number of people have put their hopes in the election of socialist politicians into parliaments and congresses. Historical anarchist theory informs us why this strategy is mistaken: even if socialists manage to win an election, which frequently does not happen, they will be compelled by the threat of capital flight and their institutionalized role as managers of the capitalist economy to implement policies that serve the interests of the very corporations driving climate change forward. Socialist politicians will not transform the state. The state will transform them. We have to instead develop the power of workers to engage in direct action outside of and against the state, disrupt the smooth functioning of the economy, and, in so doing, impose external pressure onto the ruling classes to give into our demands.

Even if the specifics of historical insurrectionist anarchism, mass anarchism, syndicalist anarchism, and organizational dualism are deemed to be no longer appropriate strategies within modern society, the core insight of historical anarchist strategy would remain—anarchist ends can only be achieved through anarchist means. Our task remains that of anarchists in the nineteenth and early twentieth centuries: to develop forms of practice that can simultaneously resist, and ultimately overthrow, the ruling classes

and render us fit to establish a society with neither masters nor subjects. Tomorrow can only grow out of today and the march toward
anarchy begins now.

Notes

Introduction

1. Benedict Anderson, *The Age of Globalization: Anarchists and the Anti-Colonial Imagination* (London: Verso 2013), 54.
2. Eric Hobsbawm, *Revolutionaries* (London: Phoenix, 1994), 61.
3. David Berry and Constance Bantman, eds., *New Perspectives on Anarchism, Labour and Syndicalism: The Individual, the National and the Transnational* (Newcastle, UK: Cambridge Scholars Publishing, 2010); Constance Bantman and Bert Altena, eds., *Reassessing the Transnational Turn: Scales of Analysis in Anarchist and Syndicalist Studies* (Oakland, CA: PM Press, 2017); Steven Hirsch and Lucien van der Walt, eds., *Anarchism and Syndicalism in the Colonial and Postcolonial World, 1870–1940: The Praxis of National Liberation, Internationalism, and Social Revolution* (Leiden: Brill, 2010).
4. De Cleyre was initially an individualist anarchist and mutualist but came to reject this position during the 1890s. Between 1897 and 1900, she came to identify as an anarchist without adjectives who was agnostic about the nature of the future society, while advocating the same strategies as anarchist collectivists and anarchist communists. I shall only be including texts by her from this later period. See "Vision of an Alternative Society" in chapter 3 for a discussion of this view and the supporting references.
5. Federico Ferretti, *Anarchy and Geography: Reclus and Kropotkin in the UK* (London: Routledge, 2019), 61–62; Kenyon Zimmer, "Archiving the American Anarchist Press: Reflections on Format, Accessibility, and Language," *American Periodicals: A Journal of History & Criticism* 29, no. 1 (2019): 10–11.
6. Michael Beaney, "Analytic Philosophy and History of Philosophy: The Development of the Idea of Rational Reconstruction," in *The Historical Turn*

in Analytic Philosophy, ed. Erich H. Reck (London: Palgrave Macmillan, 2013), 253.

7. Quentin Skinner, "Meaning and Understanding in the History of Ideas," in *Visions of Politics*, vol. 1, *Regarding Method* (Cambridge: Cambridge University Press, 2002), 82–87; Skinner, "Interpretation and the Understanding of Speech Acts," in *Visions*, 110–14; Skinner, *The Foundations of Modern Political Thought*, vol. 1, *The Renaissance* (Cambridge: Cambridge University Press, 1978), x–xiv; Ellen Meiksins Wood, *Citizens to Lords: A Social History of Western Political Thought from Antiquity to the Middle Ages* (London: Verso, 2011), 7–16.

8. Tom Goyens, *Beer and Revolution: The German Anarchist Movement in New York City, 1880–1914* (Urbana: University of Illinois Press, 2007), 34–51, 168–82.

9. Errico Malatesta, *Towards Anarchy: Malatesta in America, 1899–1900*, ed. Davide Turcato (Chico, CA: AK Press, 2019), 65.

10. For discussions of women's participation in historical anarchist movements see David Berry, *A History of the French Anarchist Movement: 1917 to 1945* (Oakland, CA: AK Press, 2009), 313–17; Jennifer Guglielmo, *Living the Revolution: Italian Women's Resistance and Radicalism in New York City, 1880–1945* (Chapel Hill: University of North Carolina Press, 2010), 139–75; Martha Ackelsberg, *Free Women of Spain: Anarchism and the Struggle for the Emancipation of Women* (Oakland, CA: AK Press, 2005); Goyens, *Beer and Revolution*, 155–8; Kenyon Zimmer, *Immigrants Against the State: Yiddish and Italian Anarchism in America* (Urbana: University of Illinois Press, 2015), 43–47, 66–70; Ferretti, *Anarchy and Geography*, 91–111.

11. Lydia H. Liu, Rebecca E. Karl, and Dorothy Ko, eds., *The Birth of Chinese Feminism: Essential Texts in Transnational Theory* (New York: Columbia University Press, 2013); Zimmer, *Immigrants*, 21, 44.

12. Ackelsberg, *Free Women*, 93–95.

Chapter 1: Defining Anarchism

1. For example Peter Marshall, *Demanding the Impossible: A History of Anarchism* (London: Harper Perennial, 2008), 3; David Miller, *Anarchism* (London: J.M. Dent and Sons, 1984), 2–3; George Woodcock, *Anarchism: A History of Libertarian Ideas and Movements*, 2nd ed. (Harmondsworth: Penguin Books, 1986), 17–18.

2. Friedrich Nietzsche, *On the Genealogy of Morality* (Cambridge: Cambridge University Press, 2006), 53. For discussions of Nietzsche's views on definitions, see Lawrence J. Hatab, *Nietzsche's 'On the Genealogy of Morality': An Introduction* (Cambridge: Cambridge University Press, 2008), 97–99; Raymond Geuss, *History and Illusion in Politics* (Cambridge: Cambridge University Press, 2001), 6–8, 69–72; *Morality, Culture and History: Essays on German Philosophy* (Cambridge: Cambridge University Press, 1999), 9–14.

3.   Marshall, *Demanding the Impossible*, xiii–xiv, 3–5, 96–99; John A. Rapp, *Daoism and Anarchism: Critiques of State Autonomy in Ancient and Modern China* (London: Continuum Books, 2012), 3–5; Robert Graham, *We Do Not Fear Anarchy, We Invoke It: The First International and the Origins of the Anarchist Movement* (Oakland, CA: AK Press, 2015), 2–3.

4.   Marie Fleming, *The Anarchist Way to Socialism: Élisée Reclus and Nineteenth-Century European Anarchism* (London: Croom Helm Ltd, 1979), 15–23; Steven Hirsch and Lucien van der Walt, eds., *Anarchism and Syndicalism in the Colonial and Postcolonial World, 1870–1940: The Praxis of National Liberation, Internationalism, and Social Revolution* (Leiden: Brill, 2010), xxxvi–lv; Lucien van der Walt, "Anarchism and Marxism," in *Brill's Companion to Anarchist Philosophy*, ed. Nathan Jun (Leiden: Brill Academic Publishers, 2017), 510–15.

5.   Peter Kropotkin, *Modern Science and Anarchy*, ed. Iain McKay (Chico, CA: AK Press, 2018), 84, 136. On other occasions, Kropotkin appears to adopt a historicist perspective and defines anarchism as a historically specific form of antistate socialism. For an overview of this topic, see Zoe Baker, *Kropotkin's Definition of Anarchism* (forthcoming).

6.   Rudolf Rocker, *Anarcho-Syndicalism: Theory and Practice* (Oakland, CA: AK Press, 2004), 9, 3.

7.   Charlotte Wilson, *Anarchist Essays*, ed. Nicolas Walter (London: Freedom Press, 2000), 28, 19. See also, 78.

8.   Errico Malatesta, *The Anarchist Revolution: Polemical Articles, 1924–1931*, ed. Vernon Richards (London: Freedom Press, 1995), 52.

9.   Errico Malatesta, *Life and Ideas: The Anarchist Writings of Errico Malatesta*, ed. Vernon Richards (Oakland, CA: PM Press, 2015), 13.

10.   Ba Jin, "Anarchism and the Question of Practice," in *Anarchism: A Documentary History of Libertarian Ideas*, vol. 1, *From Anarchy to Anarchism (300 CE to 1939)*, ed. Robert Graham (Montréal: Black Rose Books, 2005), 362.

11.   Kubo Yuzuru, "On Class Struggle and the Daily Struggle," in Graham, ed., *Anarchism*, vol. 1, 380.

12.   Rapp, *Daoism and Anarchism*, 37–40, 227–29.

13.   Gerrard Winstanley, *"The Law of Freedom" and other Writings*, ed. Christopher Hill (Cambridge: Cambridge University Press, 1983), 77–95.

14.   Élisée Reclus, *Anarchy, Geography, Modernity: Selected Writings of Élisée Reclus*, ed. John Clark and Camille Martin (Oakland, CA: PM Press, 2013), 120, 127.

15.   Christopher Boehm, *Hierarchy in the Forest: The Evolution of Egalitarian Behavior* (Cambridge, MA: Harvard University Press, 2001), 10–12; James C. Scott, *The Art of Not Being Governed: An Anarchist History of Upland Southeast Asia* (New Haven: Yale University Press, 2009).

16.   Boehm, *Hierarchy in the Forest*, 43–88, 101–24. This point was previously made, but with less empirical evidence, by Pierre Clastres, *Society Against the State: Essays in Political Anthropology* (New York: Zone Books, 1989), 7–47, 189–218; Clastres, *Archeology of Violence* (New York: Semiotext(e), 1994), 87–92.

17.   Robert L. Kelly, *The Lifeways of Hunter-Gatherers: The Foraging Spectrum*, 2nd ed. (Cambridge: Cambridge University Press, 2013), 4–7, 15–18, 241–48. There is limited knowledge of what gender relations were like prior to the emergence of writing due to the nature of archaeological evidence. See Marcia-Anne Dobres, "Digging Up Gender in the Earliest Human Societies," in *A Companion to Gender History*, ed. Teresa A. Meade and Merry E. Wiesner-Hanks (Malden, MA: Blackwell Publishing, 2004), 211–26.

18.   David Graeber and David Wengrow, *The Dawn of Everything: A New History of Humanity* (London: Allen Lane, 2021), 106–15.

19.   Alan B. Spitzer, *The Revolutionary Theories of Louis Auguste Blanqui* (New York: Columbia University Press, 1957), 173n37; Karl Marx and Friedrich Engels, "Manifesto of the Communist Party," in Karl Marx, *Later Political Writings*, ed. Terrell Carver (Cambridge: Cambridge University Press, 1996), 20; Vladimir Lenin, *Selected Works* (Moscow: Progress Publishers, 1977), 320, 335; Joseph Stalin, *Works*, vol. 1, *1901–1907* (Moscow: Foreign Languages Publishing House, 1954), 336–37.

20.   For a summary of the language Winstanley used to refer to himself and his companions, see John Gurney, *Gerrard Winstanley: The Digger's Life and Legacy* (London: Pluto Press, 2013), 59–64.

21.   Woodcock, *Anarchism*, 12, 41. Some historical anarchists were themselves aware of its usage during the French Revolution. See Peter Kropotkin, *The Great French Revolution* (Montréal: Black Rose Books, 1989), 346–47, 350–60.

22.   Pierre-Joseph Proudhon, *What is Property?* (Cambridge: Cambridge University Press, 1994), 205, 209, 216. See also Pierre-Joseph Proudhon, *Property Is Theft: A Pierre-Joseph Proudhon Anthology*, ed. Iain McKay (Oakland, CA: AK Press, 2011), 205, 254, 480, 711. For an overview of Proudhon's life and ideas see Steven K. Vincent, *Pierre-Joseph Proudhon and the Rise of French Republican Socialism* (Oxford: Oxford University Press, 1984); George Woodcock, *Pierre-Joseph Proudhon: A Biography* (Montréal: Black Rose Books, 1987).

23.   Proudhon, *Property is Theft*, 61, 609–10, 742, 766.

24.   Proudhon, *Property is Theft*, 254–55, 291–92, 348, 615–16, 718, 725.

25.   For the history of the term, see Shawn P. Wilbur, "Mutualism," in *The Palgrave Handbook of Anarchism*, ed. Carl Levy and Matthew S. Adams (London: Palgrave Macmillan, 2019), 213–24; Vincent, *Proudhon*, 162–64.

26.   Proudhon, *What is Property*, 65–66, 73, 86, 94, 214–16. For a summary of Proudhon's vision of a postcapitalist society, see Iain McKay, "Introduction," in Proudhon, *Property is Theft*, 28–35.

27.   Proudhon, *Property is Theft*, 164, 281–93; McKay, "Introduction," in Proudhon, *Property is Theft*, 23–28; Vincent, *Proudhon*, 142–51, 170–74. For the wider context and how Proudhon's ideas developed during this period, see Edward Castleton, "The Many Revolutions of Pierre-Joseph Proudhon," in *The 1848 Revolutions and European Political Thought* ed. Douglas Moggach and Gareth Stedman Jones (Cambridge: Cambridge University Press, 2018), 39–69.

28. David Berry, *A History of the French Anarchist Movement: 1917 to 1945* (Oakland, CA: AK Press, 2009), 16–17; Julian P.W. Archer, *The First International in France, 1864–1872: Its Origins, Theories, and Impact* (Lanham, MD: University Press of America, 1997), 41–47, 66–75; James J. Martin, *Men Against the State: The Expositors of Individualist Anarchism in America, 1827–1908* (Colorado Springs: Ralph Myles Publisher, 1970), 103–66; Bernard H. Moss, *The Origins of the French Labor Movement: The Socialism of Skilled Workers* (Berkeley: University of California Press, 1980), 31–52.

29. Josiah Warren, *The Practical Anarchist: Writings of Josiah Warren*, ed. Crispin Sartwell (New York: Fordham University Press, 2011); Martin, *Men Against the State*, 1–102.

30. Anselme Bellegarrigue, "Anarchy, A Journal of Order," trans. Paul Sharkey, Anarchist Library website, http://www.theanarchistlibrary.org/library/anselme-bellegarrigue-the-world-s-first-anarchist-manifesto.

31. Élisée Reclus, "The Development of Liberty in the World," trans. Shawn P. Wilbur, Libertarian Labyrinth website, September 2, 2016, https://www.libertarian-labyrinth.org/anarchist-beginnings/elisee-reclus-the-development-of-liberty-in-the-world-c-1850.

32. Max Nettlau, *A Short History of Anarchism*, ed. Heiner M. Becker (London: Freedom Press, 1996), 74–76; Shawn P. Wilbur, "Joseph Déjacque and the First Emergence of Anarchism," in *Contr'un 5: Our Lost Continent* (2016).

33. Joseph Déjacque, *Down with the Bosses and Other Writings, 1859–1861* (Gresham, OR: Corvus Editions, 2013), 11–17, 40–41; Joseph Déjacque, "On the Human Being, Male and Female," trans. Jonathan Mayo Crane, Libertarian Labyrinth website, April 4, 2011, https://www.libertarian-labyrinth.org/from-the-archives/joseph-dejacque-the-human-being-i.

34. Déjacque, *Down with the Bosses*, 20–21, 42–44.

35. Déjacque, "The Revolutionary Question," trans. Shawn P. Wilbur, Libertarian Labyrinth website, May 13, 2012, https://www.libertarian-labyrinth.org/working-translations/joseph-dejacque-the-revolutionary-question.

36. Déjacque, "The Revolutionary Question."

37. Déjacque, "The Revolutionary Question."

38. Arthur Lehning, *From Buonarroti to Bakunin: Studies in International Socialism* (Leiden: E. J. Brill, 1970), 150–210.

39. Archer, *First International in France*, 100–101, 126–28, 168–72; Edward Castleton, "The Origins of 'Collectivism': Pierre-Joseph Proudhon's Contested Legacy and the Debate About Property in the International Workingmen's Association and the League of Peace and Freedom," *Global Intellectual History* 2, no. 2 (2017): 169–95.

40. For a general overview of how this happened, see Graham, *We Do Not Fear Anarchy*. For greater detail, see Archer, *First International in France*; Moss, *Origins of the French Labor Movement*, 52–82.

41. Berry, *French Anarchist Movement*, 19; Fleming, *Anarchist Way*, 119, 126; Graham, *We Do Not Fear Anarchy*, 225, 262.

42. Paul Avrich and Karen Avrich, *Sasha and Emma: The Anarchist Odyssey of Alexander Berkman and Emma Goldman* (Cambridge, MA: Harvard University Press, 2012), 44–47; Nettlau, *Short History*, 144–45, 161–62, 184–85.

43. Wolfgang Eckhardt, *The First Socialist Schism: Bakunin vs. Marx in the International Working Men's Association* (Oakland, CA: PM Press, 2016), 53–55, 104–9, 159–64, 166; Nunzio Pernicone, *Italian Anarchism, 1864–1892* (Princeton: Princeton University Press, 1993), 57–59; T.R. Ravindranathan, *Bakunin and the Italians* (Kingston and Montréal: McGill-Queen's University Press, 1988), 176–78.

44. For a condensed summary of the conflict within the International see Graham, *We Do Not Fear Anarchy*, 167–92. For a detailed examination, see Eckhardt, *First Socialist Schism*.

45. René Berthier, *Social Democracy and Anarchism in the International Workers' Association, 1864–1877* (London: Anarres Editions, 2015), 73–75; Graham, *We Do Not Fear Anarchy*, 187–92, 199; Eckhardt, *First Socialist Schism*, 283–352, 357–68, 383–97.

46. Berthier, *Social Democracy and Anarchism*, 77–81; Eckhardt, *First Socialist Schism*, 354–7.

47. "Resolutions of the Saint-Imier Congress of the International Workers' Association, 15–16 September, 1872," in Appendix to Berthier, *Social Democracy and Anarchism*, 179–83.

48. Luigi Fabbri, "Anarchy and 'Scientific' Communism," in *Bloodstained: One Hundred Years of Leninist Counterrevolution*, ed. Friends of Aron Baron (Chico, CA: AK Press, 2017), 18.

49. Errico Malatesta, *Towards Anarchy: Malatesta in America, 1899–1900*, ed. Davide Turcato (Chico, CA: AK Press, 2019), 150. In the original, Malatesta gives the incorrect date of 1867 for the founding of the Alliance. I have corrected this in order to avoid confusing the reader. In the nineteenth century, the word *party* was often used in a broad sense to refer to a social movement or a group of people who shared the same principles. For Malatesta's definition, see Malatesta, *Towards Anarchy*, 65.

50. Maurizio Antonioli, ed. *The International Anarchist Congress Amsterdam (1907)* (Edmonton, AB: Black Cat Press 2009), 122.

51. Quoted in Davide Turcato, *Making Sense of Anarchism: Errico Malatesta's Experiments with Revolution, 1889–1900* (Basingstoke, UK: Palgrave Macmillan, 2012), 18.

52. Berthier, *Social Democracy and Anarchism*, 80–81, 104–129; Caroline Cahm, *Kropotkin and the Rise of Revolutionary Anarchism, 1872–1886* (Cambridge: Cambridge University Press, 1989), 29–34; Graham, *We Do Not Fear Anarchy*, 197–220.

53. "Resolutions of the Saint-Imier Congress of the International Workers' Association," 181.

54. Berthier, *Social Democracy and Anarchism*, 130–40; Graham, *We Do Not Fear Anarchy*, 225–27. For more information about the anarchist sections in Argentina, Mexico, Uruguay, and Egypt see Ángel J. Cappelletti, *Anarchism in Latin America* (Chico, CA: AK Press, 2017), 47–50, 115–18, 351–55; Graham, *We Do Not Fear Anarchy*, 252–54; Ilham Khuri-Makdisi, *The Eastern Mediterranean and the Making of Global Radicalism, 1860–1914* (Berkeley: University of California Press, 2010), 114–15.

55. Berthier, *Social Democracy and Anarchism*, 153; Moss, *The Origins of the French Labor Movement*, 79; A.W. Zurbrugg, *Anarchist Perspectives in Peace and War, 1900–1918* (London: Anarres Editions, 2018), 6n*.

56. "Resolutions of the Congresses of Verviers, 5 to 8 September 1877, and Ghent, 9 to 14 September 1877," in Appendix to Berthier, *Social Democracy and Anarchism*, 188–91.

57. "Resolutions of the Congresses of Verviers," 189.

58. "Resolutions of the Congresses of Verviers," 189.

59. Accounts of the anarchist-led sections of the International typically refer to named delegates representing various workers' associations, but do not specify the trade these anonymous workers were involved in. For detailed information on occupations in the Italian and Swiss movements, see Pernicone, *Italian Anarchism*, 76–80; Eckhardt, *First Socialism Schism*, 13–15.

60. The Group of Russian Anarchists Abroad, "The Organizational Platform of the General Union of Anarchists (Draft)," in Alexandre Skirda, *Facing the Enemy: A History of Anarchist Organization from Proudhon to May 1968* (Oakland CA: AK Press, 2002), 196.

61. Peter Kropotkin, *Words of a Rebel* (Montréal: Black Rose Books, 1992), 77. For a summary of the strategies proposed by mutualists in the First International see Archer, *First International in France*, 44–47, 79–82.

62. Peter Kropotkin, *Direct Struggle Against Capital: A Peter Kropotkin Anthology*, ed. Iain McKay (Oakland, CA: AK Press, 2014), 170.

63. Quoted in Eckhardt, *First Socialist Schism*, 453n47.

64. E. H. Carr, *Michael Bakunin* (London: The Macmillan Press, 1975), 307, 337.

65. Michael Bakunin, *Selected Writings*, ed. Arthur Lehning (London: Jonathan Cape, 1973), 191, 238.

66. Michael Bakunin, *Statism and Anarchy* (Cambridge: Cambridge University Press, 1990), ed. Marshall Shatz, 179, 133.

67. Bakunin, *Statism and Anarchy*, 135–36.

68. Marshall Shatz, "Introduction" in Bakunin, *Statism and Anarchy*, xxxv.

69. Bakunin, *Selected Writings*, 197–98.

70. Bakunin, *Statism and Anarchy*, 186.

71. Quoted in Eckhardt, *First Socialist Schism*, 375–76.

72. Quoted in Eckhardt, *First Socialist Schism*, 175. For the 1867 English edition of the rules of the First International, see Karl Marx and Friedrich Engels, *Collected Works*, vol. 20 (London: Lawrence and Wishart, 1985), 441–46.

73. Karl Marx and Friedrich Engels, *Collected Works*, vol. 22 (London: Lawrence and Wishart, 1986), 429.

74. Peter Kropotkin, *Memoirs of a Revolutionist* (Montréal: Black Rose Books, 1989), 260.

75. Malatesta, *Towards Anarchy*, 11.

76. Malatesta, *Towards Anarchy*, 43n36, 150.

77. Quoted in Eckhardt, *First Socialist Schism*, 375. For other examples, see 180, 218–19, 252, 272, 278, 290, 334, 357, 362–63, 376–77, 387–88; Pernicone, *Italian Anarchism*, 72–73.

78. Fleming, *Anarchist Way*, 126.

79. Quoted in Eckhardt, *First Socialist Schism*, 376.

80. For a summary of these congresses, see Archer, *First International in France*, 119–29, 166–75.

81. Castleton, "The Origins of 'Collectivism,'" 169.

82. I have assembled this quote from extracts in Eckhardt, *First Socialist Schism*, 376 and Marianne Enckell, "Bakunin and the Jura Federation," in *Arise Ye Wretched of the Earth: The First International in Global Perspective*, ed. Fabrice Bensimon, Quentin Deluermoz, and Jeanne Moisand (Leiden: Brill, 2018), 363n26.

83. Malatesta, *The Method of Freedom: An Errico Malatesta Reader*, ed. Davide Turcato (Oakland, CA: AK Press 2014), 11.

84. Cahm, *Kropotkin*, 38.

85. Quoted in Graham, *We Do Not Fear Anarchy*, 225.

86. Tom Goyens, *Beer and Revolution: The German Anarchist Movement in New York City, 1880–1914* (Urbana: University of Illinois Press, 2007), 11–13, 71–5, 80–83, 96–97.

87. Lehning, *From Buonarroti to Bakunin*, 16–17.

88. Woodcock, *Anarchism*, 233.

89. Kropotkin, *Direct Struggle*, 170.

90. Quoted in Berthier, *Anarchism and Social Democracy*, 109.

91. James Guillaume, "On the Abolition of the State," in *Workers Unite! The International 150 Years Later*, ed. Marcello Musto (New York: Bloomsbury Academic, 2014), 192.

92. For example, Karl Marx and Friedrich Engels, *Collected Works*, vol. 43 (London: Lawrence and Wishart, 1988), 437, 479–80, 494.

93. Quoted in Georges Haupt, *Aspects of International Socialism, 1871–1914* (Cambridge: Cambridge University Press, 1986), 4.

94. Michael Bakunin, *Selected Texts, 1868–1875*, ed. A. W. Zurbrugg (London: Merlin Books, 2016), 247–48.

95. Karl Marx and Friedrich Engels, *Collected Works*, vol. 23 (London: Lawrence and Wishart, 1988), 102, 450, 466, 468.

96. Karl Marx and Friedrich Engels, *Collected Works*, vol. 44 (London: Lawrence and Wishart, 1989), 255.

97. Karl Marx and Friedrich Engels, *Collected Works*, vol. 44, 306. In 1886, Engels claimed, in comparison to his previous statement, that what Bakunin labeled anarchism was a blend of Proudhon and Max Stirner. See Karl Marx and Friedrich Engels, *Collected Works*, vol. 26 (London: Lawrence and Wishart, 1990), 382.

98. This topic is made confusing by the fact that, during the 1850s, Proudhon's ideas and terminology underwent a complicated process of development. By the 1860s, he called for the abolition of government in favor of a federated society while claiming that the state in the sense of the "power of collectivity" would be a part of a free society and lack "authority." See Shawn P. Wilbur, "Pierre-Joseph Proudhon: Self-Government and the Citizen-State," Libertarian Labyrinth website, June 5, 2013, https://www.libertarian-labyrinth.org/contrun/pierre-joseph-proudhon-self-government-and-the-citizen-state-2.

99. Castleton, "The Origins of 'Collectivism,'" 184; Martin A. Miller, *Kropotkin* (Chicago: University of Chicago Press, 1976), 279n30. For Proudhon and Bakunin's friendship see Woodcock, *Proudhon*, 87–89, 266; Carr, *Bakunin*, 130–31.

100. Errico Malatesta, *A Long and Patient Work: The Anarchist Socialism of L'Agitazione, 1897–1898*, ed. Davide Turcato (Chico, CA: AK Press, 2016), 296.

101. Bakunin, *Selected Texts*, 105–6.

102. Bakunin was also critical of mutualists within the First International who viewed themselves, and not the collectivists, as the true successors of Proudhon. In April 1869, he wrote a letter to Guillaume in which he referred to Tolain and Chemallé, who were leading members of the French section of the First International, as "Proudhon-ians of the second and bad sort" who "want individual property" and to "debate and parade along with the bourgeoisie." See Bakunin, *Selected Texts*, 38.

103. Bakunin, *Statism and Anarchy*, 142.

104. Quoted in James Joll, *The Anarchists* (London: Methuen, 1969), 108. I have corrected Joll's translation such that the German word anarchische is translated as anarchic, rather than anarchist.

105. Bakunin, *Statism and Anarchy*, 200–202; Michael Bakunin, *The Basic Bakunin: Writings 1869–1871*, ed. and trans. Robert M. Cutler (Buffalo, NY: Prometheus Books, 1985), 151–54. This shift in strategy from advocating gradual change via co-ops in the 1840s to violent revolution in the 1870s was part of a wider process of development within French socialism. It included individuals who held similar views to anarchists but did not use the label, such as Eugène Varlin. See Moss, *The Origins of the French Labor Movement*, 4–6, 31–102.

106. Benjamin Tucker, *Instead of a Book, by a Man Too Busy to Write One: A Fragmentary Exposition of Philosophical Anarchism*, 2nd ed. (New York: Benj. R. Tucker, Publisher, 1897), ix, 14.

107. For a summary of this history, see Nettlau, *Short History*, 30–42; Rudolf Rocker, *Pioneers of American Freedom: Origin of Liberal and Radical Thought*

in America (Los Angeles: Rocker Publications Committee, 1949), 145–54. For individualist anarchism in Britain, see Peter Ryley, *Making Another World Possible: Anarchism, Anti-Capitalism and Ecology in Late Nineteenth- and Early Twentieth-Century Britain* (New York: Bloomsbury Academic, 2013), 87–111.

108.   Benjamin Tucker, *Instead of a Book*, 390. See also, 15–16, 111–12, 383–404.

109.   John Henry Mackay, *The Anarchists: A Picture of Civilization at the Close of the Nineteenth Century* (Benj. R. Tucker, Publisher, 1891), ix. For Mackay's fictional debate between an individualist anarchist and anarchist communist, see, 116–50.

110.   Quoted in Ryley, *Making Another World*, 108.

111.   Quoted in Fleming, *Anarchist Way*, 153.

112.   Kropotkin, *Direct Struggle*, 203. See also Peter Kropotkin, *Modern Science and Anarchy*, ed. Iain McKay (Chico, CA: AK Press, 2018), 139, 173.

113.   Kropotkin, *Direct Struggle*, 169, 171–72; Rocker, *Anarcho-Syndicalism*, 6, 9.

114.   Dyer D. Lum, "On Anarchy," in *Anarchism: Its Philosophy and Scientific Basis*, ed. Albert Parsons (Honolulu: University Press of the Pacific, 2003), 149–58; Dyer D. Lum, *Philosophy of Trade Unions* (New York: American Federation of Labor, 1892); Dyer D. Lum, "Why I Am a Social Revolutionist," *Twentieth Century* 5, no. 18 (October 1890). See also, Paul Avrich, *An American Anarchist: The Life of Voltairine de Cleyre* (Chico, CA: AK Press, 2018), 56–66.

115.   Goyens, *Beer and Revolution*, 214.

116.   Max Nettlau, "Anarchism: Communist or Individualist? Both," in *Anarchy: An Anthology of Emma Goldman's Mother Earth*, ed. Peter Glassgold (New York: Counterpoint, 2000), 79–83.

117.   Sébastien Faure, "The Anarchist Synthesis: The Three Great Anarchist Currents," trans. Shawn P. Wilbur. Libertarian Labyrinth website, August 3, 2017, https://www.libertarian-labyrinth.org/anarchist-beginnings/sebastien-faure-the-anarchist-synthesis-1828; Voline, "Synthesis (anarchist)," in *The Anarchist Encyclopedia Abridged*, ed. Mitchell Abidor (Chico, CA: AK Press, 2019), 197–205.

118.   Pernicone, *Italian Anarchism*, 239–41, 270–72; Pietro Di Paola, *The Knights Errant of Anarchy: London and the Italian Anarchist Diaspora, 1880–1917* (Chico, CA: AK Press, 2017), 63–78; Malatesta, *Patient Work*, 357, 415–7. For an overview of different strains of individualist anarchism in Milan, see Fausto Buttà, *Living Like Nomads: The Milanese Anarchist Movement Before Fascism* (New Castle, UK: Cambridge Scholars Publishing, 2015), 66–91.

119.   Malatesta, *Patient Work*, 80.

120.   Rocker, *Pioneers of American Freedom*, 152–53; Kropotkin, *Direct Struggle*, 169; Laurence S. Stepelevitch, "The Revival of Max Stirner," *Journal of the History of Ideas* 35, no. 2 (1974): 324; Buttà, *Living Like Nomads*, 75–6. For a summary of Stirner's life see David Leopold, "A Solitary Life," in *Max Stirner*, ed. Saul Newman (Basingstoke, UK: Palgrave Macmillan, 2011), 21–41.

121.   Mackay, *The Anarchists*, ix. Stirner also influenced a few anarchist

communists, but the majority rejected his ideas. For a review of Stirner's book by a syndicalist anarchist, see Max Baginski, "Stirner: 'The Ego and His Own,'" *Mother Earth* 2, no. 3 (1907), 142–51. Bakunin briefly mentions Stirner on at least one occasion but does not claim that he was an anarchist or influenced anarchism. See Bakunin, *Statism and Anarchy*, 141–42.

122. Malatesta, *Patient Work*, 77.
123. Malatesta, *Method of Freedom*, 199. See also *Towards Anarchy*, 151.
124. Malatesta, *Life and Ideas*, 23.
125. Malatesta, *Life and Ideas*, 24.

Chapter 2: Theoretical Framework

1. For previous reconstructions of the theory of practice, see Laurence Cox and Alf Gunvald Nilsen, *We Make Our Own History: Marxism and Social Movements in the Twilight of Neoliberalism* (London: Pluto Press, 2014), 21–59; Paul Raekstad and Sofa Saio Gradin, *Prefigurative Politics: Building Tomorrow Today* (Cambridge: Polity Press, 2020), 40–59.
2. Michael Bakunin, *The Political Philosophy of Bakunin: Scientific Anarchism*, ed. G.P. Maximoff (New York: The Free Press of Glencoe, 1964), 57, 60–68; Peter Kropotkin, *Modern Science and Anarchy*, ed. Iain McKay (Chico, CA: AK Press, 2018), 89–92, 100–101, 125; Peter Kropotkin, *Ethics: Origin and Development* (London: George G. Harrap & Co, 1924), 1, 3–4; Lucy Parsons, *Freedom, Equality and Solidarity: Writings and Speeches, 1878–1937*, ed. Gale Ahrens (Chicago: Charles H. Kerr, 2004), 137; Errico Malatesta, *The Method of Freedom: An Errico Malatesta Reader*, ed. Davide Turcato (Oakland, CA: AK Press 2014), 38, 132. For examples of Christian anarchists who rejected materialism, see Peter Ryley, *Making Another World Possible: Anarchism, Anti-Capitalism and Ecology in Late Nineteenth- and Early Twentieth-Century Britain* (New York: Bloomsbury Academic, 2013), 135–47.
3. Bakunin, *Political Philosophy*, 54.
4. Carlo Cafiero, *Revolution* (Edmonton, AB: Black Cat Press, 2012), 3. See also Peter Kropotkin, *Direct Struggle Against Capital: A Peter Kropotkin Anthology*, ed. Iain McKay (Oakland, CA: AK Press, 2014), 163; Peter Kropotkin, *Fugitive Writings*, ed. George Woodcock (Montréal: Black Rose Books, 1993), 100–104; Ricardo Mella, *Anarchist Socialism in Early Twentieth-Century Spain: A Ricardo Mella Anthology*, ed. Stephen Luis Vilaseca (London: Palgrave Macmillan, 2020), 3–4.
5. Malatesta, *Method of Freedom*, 39. See also Bakunin, *Political Philosophy*, 57, 69, 83–91; Kropotkin, *Modern Science*, 125.
6. Bakunin, *Political Philosophy*, 54.
7. Michael Bakunin, *Selected Writings*, ed. Arthur Lehning (London: Jonathan Cape, 1973), 155.

8. Élisée Reclus, *Anarchy, Geography, Modernity: Selected Writings of Élisée Reclus*, ed. John Clark and Camille Martin (Oakland, CA: PM Press, 2013), 232, 217.

9. Peter Kropotkin, *The Great French Revolution* (Montréal: Black Rose Books, 1989), xxx.

10. Bakunin, *Selected Writings*, 162. See also Bakunin, *Political Philosophy*, 76.

11. Rudolf Rocker, *Nationalism and Culture* (Los Angeles: Rocker Publications Committee, 1937), 25, 26.

12. Bakunin, *Political Philosophy*, 85–86, 92–93, 100; Malatesta, *Method of Freedom*, 19, 121–22, 446–47, 456; Reclus, *Anarchy*, 184; Mella, *Anarchist Socialism*, 6, 21.

13. Rocker, *Nationalism and Culture*, 24.

14. Bakunin, *Political Philosophy*, 67.

15. Bakunin, *Political Philosophy*, 84–85, 92–94, 100–101, 108.

16. Quoted in John Clark, "An Introduction to Reclus' Social Thought" in Reclus, *Anarchy*, 3.

17. Cafiero, *Revolution*, 3.

18. Bakunin, *Political Philosophy*, 155.

19. Bakunin, *Political Philosophy*, 155.

20. Peter Kropotkin, *Mutual Aid: A Factor of Evolution* (Mineola, NY: Dover Publications, 2006), 228.

21. Peter Kropotkin, "Proposed Communist Settlement: A New Colony for Tyneside or Wearside," *The Newcastle Daily Chronicle*, February 20, 1895.

22. Kropotkin, "Proposed Communist Settlement." See also Kropotkin, *Fugitive Writings*, 77–78.

23. Emma Goldman, *Red Emma Speaks: An Emma Goldman Reader*, ed. Alix Kates Shulman, 3rd ed. (Atlantic Highlands, NJ: Humanities Press, 1996), 438. See also, 73.

24. Malatesta, *Method of Freedom*, 402. See also Bakunin, *Political Philosophy*, 149–50, 153–54, 330–31; Kropotkin, *Fugitive Writings*, 105.

25. Rocker, *Nationalism and Culture*, 27.

26. Cafiero, *Revolution*, 5–8; Malatesta, *Method of Freedom*, 121.

27. Errico Malatesta, *Life and Ideas: The Anarchist Writings of Errico Malatesta*, ed. Vernon Richards (Oakland, CA: PM Press, 2015), 65–6.

28. Malatesta, *Life and Ideas*, 65, 68.

29. Kropotkin, *Ethics*, 22. See also Charlotte Wilson, *Anarchist Essays*, ed. Nicolas Walter (London: Freedom Press, 2000), 38–39.

30. This interpretation of capacities and drives is based on Paul Raekstad and Sofa Saio Gradin, *Prefigurative Politics*, 41–9; Paul Raekstad, *Karl Marx's Realist Critique of Capitalism: Freedom, Alienation, and Socialism* (London: Palgrave Macmillan, 2022), 23–41.

31. For examples see Bakunin, *Political Philosophy*, 86–88, 93–95; Mella, *Anarchist Socialism*, 21, 26, 85; Peter Kropotkin, *The Conquest of Bread* (Oakland, CA: AK Press, 2007), 137–8, 206; *Direct Struggle*, 651–52.

32. Malatesta, *Method of Freedom*, 122.

33. Alexander Berkman, *What is Anarchism?* (Oakland, CA: AK Press, 2003), 175.

34. Kropotkin, *Direct Struggle*, 645.

35. Bakunin, *Political Philosophy*, 86.

36. Bakunin, *Political Philosophy*, 88.

37. Malatesta, *Life and Ideas*, 65.

38. Bakunin, *Political Philosophy*, 159, 164, 167–68.

39. Bakunin, *Selected Writings*, 121; Michael Bakunin, *The Basic Bakunin: Writings 1869–1871*, ed. and trans. Robert M. Cutler (Buffalo, NY: Prometheus Books, 1985), 174, 188–91; Cafiero, *Revolution*, 5–34; Errico Malatesta, *Towards Anarchy: Malatesta in America, 1899–1900*, ed. Davide Turcato (Chico, CA: AK Press, 2019), 44. Kropotkin had a more complicated model but the basic point remains the same. See Kropotkin, *Mutual Aid*, 62–247; Kropotkin, *Ethics*, 17–18; Kropotkin, *Modern Science*, 276–77.

40. Kropotkin, *Direct Struggle*, 609–10; Reclus, *Anarchy*, 150, 153; Federico Ferretti, *Anarchy and Geography: Reclus and Kropotkin in the UK* (London: Routledge, 2019), 125.

41. Bakunin, *Political Philosophy*, 229, 231; Kropotkin, *Mutual Aid*, 64, 68–69; Reclus, *Anarchy*, 213–18.

42. For an overview of how this view of history developed, see Ronald L. Meek, *Smith, Marx, and After: Ten Essays in the Development of Economic Thought* (Dordrecht, NL: Springer, 1977), 18–32; Christopher J. Berry, *The Social Theory of the Scottish Enlightenment* (Edinburgh: Edinburgh University Press, 1997), 91–115; Adam Kuper, *The Reinvention of Primitive Society: Transformations of a Myth* (London: Routledge, 2005), 3–81.

43. Luigi Galleani, *The End of Anarchism?* (London: Elephant Editions, 2012), 43.

44. Galleani, *End of Anarchism*, 45. See also Cafiero, *Revolution*, 4; Malatesta, *Method of Freedom*, 122, 456; Kropotkin, *Direct Struggle*, 163, 598; *Conquest of Bread*, 137–9.

45. Galleani, *End of Anarchism*, 44–45.

46. Bakunin, *Political Philosophy*, 158.

47. Kropotkin, *Fugitive Writings*, 119–20.

48. Malatesta, *Method of Freedom*, 132–33. See also Reclus, *Anarchy*, 208.

49. Bakunin, *Political Philosophy*, 95.

50. Berkman, *Anarchism*, 99.

51. Rocker, *Nationalism and Culture*, 27.

52. Malatesta, *Towards Anarchy*, 48.

53. Malatesta, *Method of Freedom*, 110. See also Kropotkin, *Modern Science*, 272; Mella, *Anarchist Socialism*, 66–68.

54. Malatesta, *Method of Freedom*, 19.

55. Malatesta, *Method of Freedom*, 23.

56. Malatesta, *Method of Freedom*, 24, 39. For Malatesta's later rejection of this position see Errico Malatesta, *The Anarchist Revolution: Polemical Articles,*

1924–1931, ed. Vernon Richards (London: Freedom Press, 1995), 45–57; *Method of Freedom*, 363–73, 445–48.

57.   Albert Parsons, *Anarchism: Its Philosophy and Scientific Basis* (Honolulu: University Press of the Pacific, 2003), 97.

58.   Albert Parsons, *Anarchism*, 22–48.

59.   Rudolf Rocker, *The London Years* (Nottingham, UK: Five Leaves, 2005), 58.

60.   Errico Malatesta, *A Long and Patient Work: The Anarchist Socialism of L'Agitazione, 1897–1898*, ed. Davide Turcato (Chico, CA: AK Press, 2016), 302.

61.   Malatesta, *Life and Ideas*, 198–99.

62.   Nunzio Pernicone, *Italian Anarchism, 1864–1892* (Princeton: Princeton University Press, 1993), 135; Carlo Cafiero, *Compendium of Capital*, trans. Paul M. Perrone (London: The Anarchist Communist Group, 2020).

63.   Bakunin, *Selected Writings*, 256.

64.   Bakunin, *Selected Writings*, 256. See also Bakunin, *Political Philosophy*, 64–65; Bakunin, *Statism and Anarchy*, 142. It is important to note that Bakunin is critiquing a strawman, since Marx held that the economy and other aspects of society mutually determined one another. In later editions of *Capital*, which appeared just before Bakunin wrote his October 1872 critique, Marx added a footnote that clarified that during certain historical periods aspects of the superstructure could play a chief causal role, such as politics in ancient Athens and Rome or religion in the Middle Ages. The economy was nonetheless primary since it enabled politics or religion to play a chief part, such as by producing the food necessary for survival. See Karl Marx, *Capital, A Critique of Political Economy*, vol. 1 (London: Penguin Books, 1990), 175–76n35.

65.   Rocker, *Nationalism and Culture*, 23–41; Kropotkin, *Modern Science*, 125–28, 183–84, 197–99.

66.   Goldman, *Red Emma*, 181.

67.   Rocker, *Nationalism and Culture*, 28.

68.   Kropotkin, *Modern Science*, 367. See also 212–15; *Mutual Aid* 188–89, 219–41.

69.   This language is borrowed from Cox and Nilsen, *We Make Our Own History*, 42–44, 53.

70.   Kropotkin, *Direct Struggle*, 611.

71.   Malatesta, *Towards Anarchy*, 44.

Chapter 3: Values, Critique, and Vision

1.   Michael Bakunin, *Selected Writings*, ed. Arthur Lehning (London: Jonathan Cape, 1973), 148–49; Nestor Makhno, *The Struggle Against the State and Other Essays*, ed. Alexandre Skirda (San Francisco: AK Press, 1996), 70.

2. Lucy Parsons, *Freedom, Equality and Solidarity: Writings and Speeches, 1878–1937*, ed. Gale Ahrens (Chicago: Charles H. Kerr, 2004), 38.

3. Anarchism shares this emphasis on nondomination with republicanism. See Kinna and Alex Prichard, "Anarchism and Non-domination," *Journal of Political Ideologies* 24, no. 3 (2019): 221–40.

4. Michael Bakunin, *The Basic Bakunin: Writings 1869–1871*, ed. and trans. Robert M. Cutler (Buffalo, NY: Prometheus Books, 1985), 121.

5. Bakunin, *Basic Bakunin*, 124.

6. Bakunin, *Basic Bakunin*, 46. See also Bakunin, *Selected Writings*, 64, 148.

7. Bakunin, *Selected Writings*, 191. Bakunin labels restrictions on freedom as domination on multiple occasions. See ibid., 136, 150, 167, 192, 212, 254.

8. Charlotte Wilson, *Anarchist Essays*, ed. Nicolas Walter (London: Freedom Press, 2000), 54.

9. Wilson, *Anarchist Essays*, 54, 58–59.

10. Luigi Galleani, *The End of Anarchism?* (London: Elephant Editions, 2012), 50. See also, 61, 62–63. 68.

11. Errico Malatesta, *The Method of Freedom: An Errico Malatesta Reader*, ed. Davide Turcato (Oakland, CA: AK Press 2014), 40, 446. See also Errico Malatesta, *A Long and Patient Work: The Anarchist Socialism of L'Agitazione, 1897–1898*, ed. Davide Turcato (Chico, CA: AK Press, 2016), 249, 366; Errico Malatesta, *Life and Ideas: The Anarchist Writings of Errico Malatesta*, ed. Vernon Richards (Oakland, CA: PM Press, 2015), 38.

12. Malatesta, *Life and Ideas*, 41.

13. Errico Malatesta, *Towards Anarchy: Malatesta in America, 1899–1900*, ed. Davide Turcato (Chico, CA: AK Press, 2019), 56.

14. Alexander Berkman, "A Decade of Bolshevism," in *Bloodstained: One Hundred Years of Leninist Counterrevolution*, ed. Friends of Aron Baron (Chico, CA: AK Press, 2017), 119.

15. Alexander Berkman, *What is Anarchism?* (Oakland, CA: AK Press, 2003), 13.

16. Emma Goldman, *Red Emma Speaks: An Emma Goldman Reader*, ed. Alix Kates Shulman, 3rd ed. (Atlantic Highlands, NJ: Humanities Press, 1996), 121.

17. Rudolf Rocker, *Anarcho-Syndicalism: Theory and Practice* (Oakland, CA: AK Press, 2004), 16.

18. Goldman, *Red Emma*, 438. See also Peter Kropotkin, *Fugitive Writings*, ed. George Woodcock (Montréal: Black Rose Books, 1993), 119; Peter Kropotkin, *Direct Struggle Against Capital: A Peter Kropotkin Anthology*, ed. Iain McKay (Oakland, CA: AK Press, 2014), 164; Makhno, *Struggle*, 62.

19. Goldman, *Red Emma*, 72–73.

20. Wilson, *Anarchist Essays*, 27.

21. Michael Bakunin, *Bakunin on Anarchism*, ed. Sam Dolgoff (Montréal: Black Rose Books, 1980), 236.

22. Bakunin, *Selected Writings*, 147.

23. Bakunin, *Selected Writings*, 197.
24. Kropotkin, *Direct Struggle*, 202–3. This exact same language was used by Mella. See Ricardo Mella, *Anarchist Socialism in Early Twentieth-Century Spain: A Ricardo Mella Anthology*, ed. Stephen Luis Vilaseca (London: Palgrave Macmillan, 2020), 117–18.
25. Malatesta, *Life and Ideas*, 40.
26. Berkman, *Anarchism*, 156.
27. Malatesta, *Towards Anarchy*, 149. See also, 141.
28. Malatesta, *Towards Anarchy*, 73, 93–94, 130, 133.
29. Malatesta, *Life and Ideas*, 78.
30. Bakunin, *Selected Writings*, 153.
31. Bakunin, *Selected Writings*, 76–77.
32. Errico Malatesta, *At the Café: Conversations on Anarchism* (London: Freedom Press, 2005), 57; *Towards Anarchy*, 56.
33. Berkman, *Anarchism*, 165.
34. The following interpretation of solidarity differs from but is indebted to the discussion of Bakunin's and Kropotkin's understanding of solidarity in John Nightingale, "The Concept of Solidarity in Anarchist Thought" (PhD diss., Loughborough University, 2015), 34–108.
35. Peter Kropotkin, *Modern Science and Anarchy*, ed. Iain McKay (Chico, CA: AK Press, 2018), 478.
36. Malatesta, *Café*, 57.
37. Malatesta, *Life and Ideas*, 68.
38. Malatesta, *Method of Freedom*, 124.
39. Élisée Reclus, "An Anarchist on Anarchy," in Albert Parsons, *Anarchism: Its Philosophy and Scientific Basis* (Honolulu: University Press of the Pacific, 2003), 144.
40. Malatesta, *Method of Freedom*, 415. See also Malatesta, *Patient Work*, 400; Kropotkin, *Fugitive Writings*, 74; Reclus, "An Anarchist on Anarchy," 147.
41. Berkman, *Anarchism*, 7–8; Peter Kropotkin, *The Conquest of Bread* (Oakland, CA: AK Press, 2007), 58–60, 100–101.
42. Malatesta, *Method of Freedom*, 38–39.
43. Malatesta, *Method of Freedom*, 63. See also Kropotkin, *Direct Struggle*, 109–10.
44. Michael Bakunin, *Statism and Anarchy* (Cambridge: Cambridge University Press, 1990), ed. Marshall Shatz, 7.
45. Bakunin, *Statism and Anarchy*, 51.
46. The Group of Russian Anarchists Abroad, "The Organizational Platform of the General Union of Anarchists (Draft)," in Alexandre Skirda, *Facing the Enemy: A History of Anarchist Organization from Proudhon to May 1968* (Oakland CA: AK Press, 2002), 195.
47. The Group of Russian Anarchists Abroad, "Organizational Platform," 199.
48. Berkman, *Anarchism*, 4.
49. Berkman, *Anarchism*, 190.

50. Berkman, *Anarchism*, 125, 181, 211, 218, 229, 7. The exact same class analysis features in Rocker, *Anarcho-Syndicalism*, 19–26, 47–48, 66, 72.

51. The historian Bernard Moss has argued that the term "artisan" is misleading, due to it conflating "independent artisans, master artisans and skilled wage earners" into one social group. See Bernard H. Moss, *The Origins of the French Labor Movement: The Socialism of Skilled Workers* (Berkeley: University of California Press, 1980), 13. To avoid this misunderstanding, I have added the qualification that the artisans anarchists referred to did not exploit the labor of others.

52. Malatesta, *Method of Freedom*, 493.

53. Berkman, *Anarchism*, 11–12; Malatesta, *Café*, 45.

54. Malatesta, *Café*, 32.

55. Goldman, *Red Emma*, 50.

56. Rocker, *Anarcho-Syndicalism*, 25; Max Baginski, *What Does Syndicalism Want? Living, Not Dead Unions* (London: Kate Sharpley Library, 2015), 10.

57. Wilson, *Anarchist Essays*, 63.

58. Goldman, *Red Emma*, 67.

59. Goldman, *Red Emma*, 50.

60. Malatesta, *Method of Freedom*, 49.

61. Malatesta, *Method of Freedom*, 49–50, 149, 151–53; Berkman, *Anarchism*, 25–38; Kropotkin, *Fugitive Writings*, 79.

62. Anarchists did not all use the same terminology. Malatesta argued in 1891 that anarchists should use the term "government," instead of "the state." To avoid confusion, I shall consistently refer to the state. See Malatesta, *Method of Freedom*, 111–12.

63. Bakunin, *Statism and Anarchy*, 9, 26. In 1871, two years before the publication of *Statism and Anarchy*, Bakunin had dated the "foundation of modern States" to the seventeenth and eighteenth centuries. Kropotkin dated the rise of the modern state to the sixteenth century. See Bakunin, *Basic Bakunin*, 137; Kropotkin, *Modern Science*, 183, 234, 252.

64. Bakunin, *Statism and Anarchy*, 13.

65. Kropotkin, *Modern Science*, 184.

66. Kropotkin, *Modern Science*, 183–84.

67. Kropotkin, *Modern Science*, 299, 317–19.

68. Malatesta, *Method of Freedom*, 118.

69. Élisée Reclus, *Anarchy, Geography, Modernity: Selected Writings of Élisée Reclus*, ed. John Clark and Camille Martin (Oakland, CA: PM Press, 2013), 147. See also Bakunin, *Basic Bakunin*, 140; Rocker, *Anarcho-Syndicalism*, 11–15.

70. Malatesta, *Café*, 45.

71. Kropotkin, *Modern Science*, 306. See also, 313–17, 234 and, for anarchist critiques of the police and prisons, 499–508; Berkman, *Anarchism*, 42–59; Goldman, *Red Emma*, 332–46; Voltairine de Cleyre, *The Voltairine de Cleyre Reader* ed. A. J. Brigati (Oakland, CA: AK Press, 2004), 151–72.

72. Michael Bakunin, *The Political Philosophy of Bakunin: Scientific Anarchism*, ed. G.P. Maximoff (New York: The Free Press of Glencoe, 1964), 210–11; *Bakunin on Anarchism*, 317–20; Makhno, *Struggle*, 56.

73. Kropotkin, *Modern Science*, 234.

74. Kropotkin, *Modern Science*, 226–27. Kropotkin claims that the state is necessarily centralized and hierarchical multiple times in this text and others. See ibid., 199, 275, 310; Kropotkin, *Direct Struggle*, 566.

75. Malatesta, *Method of Freedom*, 113. See also, 136.

76. Malatesta, *Patient Work*, 212–13. See also Malatesta, *Towards Anarchy*, 29, 44.

77. Quoted in Zurbrugg, "Introduction," in Michael Bakunin, *Selected Texts, 1868–1875*, ed. A. W. Zurbrugg (London: Merlin Books, 2016), 15.

78. Bakunin, *Statism and Anarchy*, 24.

79. Peter Kropotkin, *Words of a Rebel* (Montréal: Black Rose Books, 1992), 25, 27; Malatesta, *Method of Freedom*, 115, 118.

80. Bakunin, *Selected Texts*, 63.

81. Galleani, *End of Anarchism*, 42, 50, 61; Errico Malatesta, *The Anarchist Revolution: Polemical Articles, 1924–1931*, ed. Vernon Richards (London: Freedom Press, 1995), 73–79.

82. Malatesta, *Anarchist Revolution*, 78.

83. Malatesta, *Anarchist Revolution*, 77. See also Bakunin, *Statism and Anarchy*, 13, 23.

84. Wilson, *Anarchist Essays*, 50. This idea was later repeated almost word for word by Goldman. See Goldman, *Red Emma*, 64.

85. Kropotkin, *Direct Struggle*, 197–98.

86. Berkman, *Anarchism*, 189–90, 203, 207; Lucy Parsons, *Writings and Speeches*, 70; Rudolf Rocker, *Nationalism and Culture* (Los Angeles: Rocker Publications Committee, 1937), 298–339; Kenyon Zimmer, *Immigrants Against the State: Yiddish and Italian Anarchism in America* (Urbana: University of Illinois Press, 2015), 71–72, 182, 188; Federico Ferretti, *Anarchy and Geography: Reclus and Kropotkin in the UK* (London: Routledge, 2019), 120–143.

87. Bakunin, *Selected Writings*, 174; *Bakunin on Anarchism*, 396–7; Goldman, *Red Emma*, 175–189; Emma Goldman, *Anarchy and the Sex Question: Essays on Women and Emancipation, 1896–1926*, ed. Shawn P. Wilbur (Oakland, CA: PM Press, 2016); Lucy Parsons, *Writings and Speeches*, 79, 92–93.

88. Terence Kissack, *Free Comrades: Anarchism and Homosexuality in the United States, 1895–1917* (Oakland, CA: AK Press, 2008); Ferretti, *Anarchy and Geography*, 169–180.

89. Bakunin, *Selected Writings*, 111–135; Goldman, *Red Emma*, 150–57.

90. Goldman, *Red Emma*, 131–49; Paul Avrich, *The Modern School Movement: Anarchism and Education in the United States* (Oakland, CA: AK Press, 2006), 6–18.

91. Reclus, *Anarchy*, 136–7, 156–62, 233; Ferretti, *Anarchy and Geography*, 160–1; Kropotkin, *Fugitive Writings*, 136. For a discussion of vegetarianism in the

Spanish anarchist movement see Jerome R. Mintz, *The Anarchists of Casas Viejas* (Bloomington: Indiana University Press, 2004), 87–8, 161–2.

92. Zoe Baker, "Bakunin was a Racist," Anarchopac.com, October 31, 2021, https://theanarchistlibrary.org/library/zoe-baker-bakunin-was-a-racist.

93. Martha Ackelsberg, *Free Women of Spain: Anarchism and the Struggle for the Emancipation of Women* (Oakland, CA: AK Press, 2005), 115–8; A.W. Zurbrugg, *Anarchist Perspectives in Peace and War, 1900–1918* (London: Anarres Editions, 2018), 34–5. See also endnote 10 in the introduction.

94. Emma Goldman, *Living My Life*, vol. 2 (New York: Dover Publications, 1970), 555.

95. Malatesta, *Patient Work*, 150, 151.

96. Malatesta, *Method of Freedom*, 299. For other definitions of anarchy, see Reclus, *Anarchy*, 120–21; Berkman, *Anarchism*, 144; Kropotkin, *Modern Science*, 133–34; Carlo Cafiero, *Revolution* (Edmonton, AB: Black Cat Press, 2012), 40; Galleani, *End of Anarchism*, 26, 58; Lucy Parsons, *Writings and Speeches*, 38.

97. Bakunin, *Selected Writings*, 99. See also Rocker, *Anarcho-Syndicalism*, 15–16.

98. Malatesta, *Method of Freedom*, 140

99. Malatesta, *Method of Freedom*, 141.

100. Malatesta, *Method of Freedom*, 142.

101. Malatesta, *Method of Freedom*, 128.

102. Malatesta, *Method of Freedom*, 302. See also Malatesta, *Patient Work*, 304. The same point is made by Mella, *Anarchist Socialism*, 1–9, 27.

103. Gregori P. Maximoff, *Program of Anarcho-Syndicalism* (n.p., Guillotine Press, 2015). For other examples, see James Guillaume, "Ideas on Social Organization," in *No Gods, No Masters: An Anthology of Anarchism*, ed. Daniel Guérin (Oakland, CA: AK Press, 2005), 247–67; Kropotkin, *Conquest of Bread*; Diego Abad de Santillán, *After the Revolution: Economic Reconstruction in Spain*, trans. Louis Frank (New York: Greenberg, 1937).

104. Cafiero, *Revolution*, 41.

105. Cafiero, *Revolution*, 49

106. Malatesta, *Method of Freedom*, 299.

107. Malatesta, *Method of Freedom*, 300.

108. Malatesta, *Method of Freedom*, 302.

109. Malatesta, *Method of Freedom*, 301, 302.

110. Malatesta, *Method of Freedom*, 300.

111. Berkman, *Anarchism*, 231.

112. Maximoff, *Program of Anarcho-Syndicalism*, 47.

113. Cafiero, *Revolution*, 49–62; Berkman, *Anarchism*, 156–68, 215–30.

114. This system of decision-making is often referred to as direct democracy without the state by modern anarchists. This language was largely not used by historical anarchists because they used the word "democracy" to refer to systems of government that were incompatible with anarchism, such as

bourgeois parliamentary representative democracy or Ancient Athens. For an overview of this topic, see Baker, "Anarchism and Democracy," Anarcho-pac.com, April 15, 2022, https://anarchopac.com/2022/04/15/anarchism -and-democracy.

115. Kropotkin, *Modern Science*, 133.

116. Malatesta, *Towards Anarchy*, 148–49; Kropotkin, *Direct Struggle*, 614. For a few different proposals on how an anarchist society could respond to people who engaged in acts of violent oppression, see Guillaume, "Ideas on Social Organization," 260–61; Malatesta, *Café*, 130–35; Maximoff, *Program of Anarcho-Syndicalism*, 46–48.

117. Anarchist authors used a variety of different terms when referring to assemblies, such as associations of production and consumption, labor councils, popular assemblies, communal assemblies, and communes. To avoid confusion I have chosen to use the language of workplace, community, and general assemblies.

118. Errico Malatesta, *Between Peasants: A Dialogue on Anarchy* (Johannesburg: Zabalaza Books, n.d.), 30. See also Malatesta, *Patient Work*, 17–19, 390–91; *Towards Anarchy*, 74; *Method of Freedom*, 488.

119. Malatesta, *Method of Freedom*, 488; Wilson, *Anarchist Essays*, 67, 69–70.

120. Malatesta, *Method of Freedom*, 136.

121. Malatesta, *Between Peasants*, 28–29.

122. Bakunin, *Selected Writings*, 170.

123. Malatesta, *Method of Freedom*, 128.

124. Galleani, *End of Anarchism*, 105, 58, 73–75.

125. The following account is based on Bakunin, *Selected Writings*, 170–71, 179, 206; Guillaume, "Ideas on Social Organization," 253, 264–66; Rocker, *Anarcho-Syndicalism*, 60–63; Kropotkin, *Direct Struggle*, 105, 188; Malatesta, *Method of Freedom*, 60–65.

126. Anarchists throughout Latin America referred to national federations as the regional federations of a country in the world—for example, the Argentine Regional Workers' Federation (FORA), rather than the Argentine National Workers' Federation. See Ángel J. Cappelletti, *Anarchism in Latin America* (Chico, CA: AK Press, 2017), 5–6, 63.

127. Compare Malatesta, *Method of Freedom*, 489–90 and Peter Arshinov, "The Old and New in Anarchism: Reply to Comrade Malatesta (May 1928)," in Alexandre Skirda, *Facing the Enemy*, 240–41.

128. Kropotkin, *Rebel*, 133.

129. Kropotkin, *Rebel*, 133. See also Kropotkin, *Direct Struggle*, 475.

130. Malatesta, *Between Peasants*, 30.

131. Kropotkin, *Direct Struggle*, 163.

132. Kropotkin, *Modern Science*, 134.

133. Peter Kropotkin, *Memoirs of a Revolutionist* (Montréal: Black Rose Books, 1989), 376.

134. Kropotkin, *Modern Science*, 163. See also Rocker, *Anarcho-Syndicalism*, 46–51.

135. Bakunin, *Selected Writings*, 90; Malatesta, *Method of Freedom*, 9, 46, 96; "Resolutions of the Saint-Imier Congress of the International Workers' Association," in Appendix to René Berthier, *Social Democracy and Anarchism in the International Workers' Association, 1864–1877* (London: Anarres Editions, 2015), 183.

136. Bakunin, *Selected Writings*, 108. See also, 78.

137. Guillaume quoted in Bakunin, *Bakunin on Anarchism*, 158–59; Kropotkin, *Direct Struggle*, 170–71, 186–87; The Jura Federation, "Minutes of the Jura Federation Congress (1880)" in *No Gods, No Masters*, 283.

138. Quoted in Caroline Cahm, *Kropotkin and the Rise of Revolutionary Anarchism, 1872–1886* (Cambridge: Cambridge University Press, 1989), 59.

139. Guillaume, "Ideas on Social Organization," 251, 255–57. A similar proposal about labor vouchers was made by Kropotkin in 1873 before he became an anarchist communist. In 1879, he proposed "Anarchist communism" as the long-term goal and "collectivism as a transitory form of property." By 1880, he had abandoned this view and only advocated anarchist communism. See Kropotkin, *Fugitive Writings*, 29–30, 34–35; Cahm, *Kropotkin*, 48–58.

140. Malatesta, *Method of Freedom*, 11–12, 46–48, 95–99; Cafiero, *Revolution*, 49–62. Berkman, *Anarchism*, 215–19; Kropotkin, *Conquest of Bread*, 74–78; 102–106. For the history of anarchist communism, see Cahm, *Kropotkin*, 36–67; Davide Turcato, "Anarchist Communism," in *The Palgrave Handbook of Anarchism*, ed. Carl Levy and Matthew S. Adams (London: Palgrave Macmillan, 2019), 237–47.

141. George Richard Esenwein, *Anarchist Ideology and the Working-Class Movement in Spain, 1868–1898* (Berkeley: University of California Press, 1989), 98–116; Temma Kaplan, *Anarchists of Andalusia, 1868–1903* (Princeton: Princeton University Press, 1977), 139–142.

142. Mella, *Anarchist Socialism*, 9–17, 60–62; Esenwein, *Anarchist Ideology*, 134–54. Similar views were advocated by Malatesta in 1889. See Malatesta, *Method of Freedom*, 95–99.

143. Paul Avrich, *An American Anarchist: The Life of Voltairine de Cleyre* (Chico, CA: AK Press, 2018), 46–47, 58, 107–120, 144–46; de Cleyre, *Reader*, 9.

144. Avrich, *An American Anarchist*, 147–49; Voltairine de Cleyre, *Exquisite Rebel: The Essays of Voltairine de Cleyre—Feminist, Anarchist, Genius* (State University of New York, 2005), ed. Sharon Presley and Crispin Sartwell, 105; de Cleyre, *Reader*, 31–32, 60, 107–8, 173–74; de Cleyre, "A Suggestion and Explanation" in *Free Society* 6, no. 29 (June 3, 1900): 1. In 1908, *Mother Earth* published a lecture by de Cleyre titled "Why I am an Anarchist." During the lecture, she advocates a moneyless society based on distribution according to need. It is unclear when this was written. *Mother Earth* claimed that the lecture was delivered in Hammond, Indiana but I have been unable to find a date for this talk. De Cleyre had previously given a

talk with the exact same title during her 1897 visit to England. She could have given the same talk multiple times or given different talks with the same title. As a result, it is unclear if she advocated a moneyless society based on distribution according to need before or after adopting anarchism without adjectives. See Avrich, *An American Anarchist*, 120; de Cleyre, *Exquisite Rebel*, 51–65.

145. Kropotkin, *Rebel*, 201–4.

146. Kropotkin, *Modern Science*, 131–32.

147. Kropotkin, *Modern Science*, 130–31.

148. Kropotkin, *Rebel*, 203.

149. Rocker, *Anarcho-Syndicalism*, 15–16; Galleani, *End of Anarchism*, 109.

150. Malatesta, *Towards Anarchy*, 48. This problem has since been articulated by a number of modern socialist theorists drawing upon Marxism. See Al Campbell and Mehmet Ufuk Tutan, "Human Development and Socialist Institutional Transformation: Continual Incremental Changes and Radical Breaks," *Studies in Political Economy* 82, no. 1 (2008): 153–70; Sam Gindin, "Socialism 'With Sober Senses': Developing Workers' Capacities," *The Socialist Register* 34 (1998): 75–99.

151. Malatesta, *Towards Anarchy*, 48.

152. Malatesta, *Towards Anarchy*, 49.

153. Malatesta, *Method of Freedom*, 450.

154. De Cleyre, *Reader*, 37.

155. Mella, *Anarchist Socialism*, 81–82.

156. Malatesta, *Towards Anarchy*, 49. This same idea was expressed by Marx. See Karl Marx, *Selected Writings*, ed. David McLellan, 2nd ed. (Oxford: Oxford University Press, 2000), 172; Marx and Engels, *Collected Works*, vol. 5 (London: Lawrence and Wishart, 1976), 214.

Chapter 4: Anarchist Strategy

1. Michael Bakunin, *Selected Texts, 1868–1875*, ed. A. W. Zurbrugg (London: Merlin Books, 2016), 77.

2. Peter Kropotkin, *Words of a Rebel* (Montréal: Black Rose Books, 1992), 204. See also, 219.

3. Quoted in Davide Turcato, *Making Sense of Anarchism: Errico Malatesta's Experiments with Revolution, 1889–1900* (Basingstoke, UK: Palgrave Macmillan, 2012), 55.

4. Quoted in Turcato, *Making Sense*, 55.

5. Errico Malatesta, *The Anarchist Revolution: Polemical Articles, 1924–1931*, ed. Vernon Richards (London: Freedom Press, 1995), 52.

6. Quoted in Ruth Kinna, *Kropotkin: Reviewing the Classical Anarchist Tradition* (Edinburgh: Edinburgh University Press, 2016), 132.

7. Emma Goldman, *Red Emma Speaks: An Emma Goldman Reader*, ed. Alix Kates Shulman, 3rd ed. (Atlantic Highlands, NJ: Humanities Press, 1996), 74.

8. Errico Malatesta, *The Method of Freedom: An Errico Malatesta Reader*, ed. Davide Turcato (Oakland, CA: AK Press 2014), 449–50.

9. James Guillaume, "Ideas on Social Organization," in *No Gods, No Masters: An Anthology of Anarchism*, ed. Daniel Guérin (Oakland, CA: AK Press, 2005), 247.

10. For example Charles Tilly, *European Revolutions, 1492–1992* (Oxford: Blackwell, 1993), 5.

11. Alexander Berkman, *What is Anarchism?* (Oakland, CA: AK Press, 2003), 180, 176.

12. Peter Kropotkin, *Modern Science and Anarchy*, ed. Iain McKay (Chico, CA: AK Press, 2018), 275.

13. Charlotte Wilson, *Anarchist Essays*, ed. Nicolas Walter (London: Freedom Press, 2000), 53.

14. Goldman, *Red Emma*, 220–21

15. Peter Kropotkin, *The Conquest of Bread* (Oakland, CA: AK Press, 2007), 156–57. For other examples see Errico Malatesta, *Towards Anarchy: Malatesta in America, 1899–1900*, ed. Davide Turcato (Chico, CA: AK Press, 2019), 197–99; Errico Malatesta, *At the Café: Conversations on Anarchism* (London: Freedom Press, 2005), 88–96. It should be kept in mind that, despite the ideas and actions of antipatriarchal anarchists within the movement, many anarchist men were sexists.

16. Michael Bakunin, *Statism and Anarchy* (Cambridge: Cambridge University Press, 1990), ed. Marshall Shatz, 133, 171; Mark Leier, *Bakunin: The Creative Passion—A Biography* (New York: Seven Stories Press, 2009), 345n6. It should be kept in mind that on other occasions anarchists used the term "spontaneous" in a different sense to refer to actions that occurred impulsively, suddenly or without planning. For example, in 1924, Malatesta complained about some anarchists who wrongly believed that "human events," including revolutions, "happen automatically, *naturally*, without preparation, without organization, without preconceived plans." See Malatesta, *Method of Freedom*, 461.

17. Karl Marx and Friedrich Engels, *Collected Works*, vol. 20 (London: Lawrence and Wishart, 1985), 14.

18. Errico Malatesta, *Life and Ideas: The Anarchist Writings of Errico Malatesta*, ed. Vernon Richards (Oakland, CA: PM Press, 2015), 83. For other examples of anarchists repeating the words of the preamble, see Bakunin, *Selected Texts*, 234; Peter Kropotkin, *Direct Struggle Against Capital: A Peter Kropotkin Anthology*, ed. Iain McKay (Oakland, CA: AK Press, 2014), 537.

19. Berkman, *Anarchism*, 174.

20. Malatesta, *Life and Ideas*, 45. See also Errico Malatesta, *A Long and Patient*

Work: The Anarchist Socialism of L'Agitazione, 1897–1898, ed. Davide Turcato (Chico, CA: AK Press, 2016), 241. There were a few anarchists who were pacifists committed to strict nonviolent resistance, but they were in the minority. See Bart de Ligt, *The Conquest of Violence: An Essay on War and Revolution* (London: Pluto Press, 1989).

21. Malatesta, *Method of Freedom*, 53, 55, 59.
22. Malatesta, *Method of Freedom*, 156–57.
23. Malatesta, *Method of Freedom*, 157.
24. Quoted in George Woodcock and Ivan Avakumović, *Peter Kropotkin: From Prince to Rebel* (Montréal: Black Rose Books, 1990), 160.
25. Kropotkin, *Direct Struggle*, 305.
26. Kropotkin, *Direct Struggle*, 470, 477.
27. Kropotkin, *Modern Science and Anarchy*, 169. See also, 275, 277.
28. Kropotkin, *Direct* Struggle, 207. For other examples, see, 145.
29. Quoted in Caroline Cahm, *Kropotkin and the Rise of Revolutionary Anarchism, 1872–1886* (Cambridge: Cambridge University Press, 1989), 104.
30. Woodcock and Avakumović, *From Prince to Rebel*, 365–66.
31. For example Bakunin, *Statism and Anarchy*, 171; Carlo Cafiero, *Revolution* (Edmonton, AB: Black Cat Press, 2012), 24–25, 36–37, 47; Nestor Makhno, *The Struggle Against the State and Other Essays*, ed. Alexandre Skirda (San Francisco: AK Press, 1996), 86–7; Luigi Galleani, *The End of Anarchism?* (London: Elephant Editions, 2012), 76–77.
32. Quoted in Albert Parsons, *Anarchism: Its Philosophy and Scientific Basis* (Honolulu: University Press of the Pacific, 2003), 83, 82, 78.
33. Rocker, "The Soviet System or the Dictatorship of the Proletariat," in *Bloodstained: One Hundred Years of Leninist Counterrevolution*, ed. Friends of Aron Baron (Chico, CA: AK Press, 2017), 56.
34. Rocker, "The Soviet System or the Dictatorship of the Proletariat," 56.
35. Andrew R. Carlson, *Anarchism in Germany*, vol. 1, *The Early Movement* (Metuchen, NJ: The Scarecrow Press, 1972), 253–55.
36. Malatesta, *Method of Freedom*, 201–4.
37. Malatesta, *Method of Freedom*, 203. See also Malatesta, *Anarchist Revolution*, 62–65.
38. Kropotkin, *Direct Struggle*, 563–64.
39. Quoted in Paul Avrich, *The Haymarket Tragedy* (Princeton: Princeton University Press, 1984), 67.
40. Bakunin, *Statism and Anarchy*, 28. Bakunin made a similar remark in 1842 prior to becoming an anarchist. See Michael Bakunin, *Selected Writings*, ed. Arthur Lehning (London: Jonathan Cape, 1973), 58. For examples of this idea being repeated by later anarchists, see Berkman, *The Blast* (Oakland, CA: AK Press, 2005), 10; Kropotkin, *Rebel*, 222; Kropotkin, *Direct Struggle*, 579.
41. Berkman, *Anarchism*, 183–84. See also Malatesta, *Life and Ideas*, 145–46.

42. Kropotkin, *Conquest of Bread*, 67–68.

43. Peter Kropotkin, *Memoirs of a Revolutionist* (Montréal: Black Rose Books, 1989), 270–71.

44. Goldman, *Red Emma*, 400.

45. Kropotkin, *Rebel*, 72. See also Kropotkin, *Direct Struggle*, 322, 535, 553.

46. Luigi Fabbri, "Anarchy and 'Scientific' Communism," in *Bloodstained: One Hundred Years of Leninist Counterrevolution*, ed. Friends of Aron Baron (Chico, CA: AK Press, 2017), 28.

47. Nabat, "Proceedings of Nabat," in *No Gods, No Masters*, 487.

48. The following account of social revolution can be seen in Berkman, *Anarchism*, 177–236; Kropotkin, *Rebel*, 99–103; Malatesta, *Café*, 122–25.

49. Anarchists typically claimed that only means of production and land that was used by a capitalist or landowner to profit off the labor of others would be expropriated. See Kropotkin, *Rebel*, 214; Kropotkin, *Conquest of Bread*, 89. For how the expropriation of food, clothing, and housing was envisioned, see ibid., 70–71, 103–4, 121–22, 127.

50. Bakunin, *Selected Writings*, 170–71.

51. Bakunin, *Selected Writings*, 179. For his participation in 1848 and the 1849 insurrection, see E. H. Carr, *Michael Bakunin* (London: The Macmillan Press, 1975), 149–62, 189–94.

52. Malatesta, *Life and Ideas*, 157.

53. Berkman, *Anarchism*, 232. See also Malatesta, *Patient Work*, 85; Makhno, *Struggle*, 57–58, 89; Gregori P. Maximoff, *Program of Anarcho-Syndicalism* (n.p., Guillotine Press, 2015), 43–46.

54. Quoted in José Peirats, *The CNT in the Spanish Revolution*, vol. 1, ed. Chris Ealham (Oakland, CA: PM Press, 2011), 109.

55. Quoted in José Peirats, *The CNT in the Spanish Revolution*, vol. 1, 110.

56. The complex history of anarchist military participation in the Russian and Spanish civil wars goes beyond the scope of this book. For overviews, see Peter Arshinov, *History of the Makhnovist Movement, 1918–1921* (London: Freedom Press, 2005); Makhno, *Struggle*, 6–23; Agustín Guillamón, *Ready for Revolution: The CNT Defense Committees in Barcelona, 1933–1938* (Oakland, CA: AK Press, 2014).

57. Kropotkin, *Direct Struggle*, 542–4, 551–5; Kropotkin, *Modern Science*, 191–5; Kropotkin, *Rebel*, 101–2, 186–89, 203. Malatesta also pointed out that anarchists would be but one faction within the revolution. See Malatesta, *Method of Freedom*, 472.

58. Kropotkin, *Rebel*, 218. The fear that a social revolution could be crippled by food shortages was shared by Malatesta. See Malatesta, *Method of Freedom*, 428–9.

59. Kropotkin, *Rebel*, 207, 218–20; Kropotkin, *Conquest of Bread*, 95–97; Kropotkin, *Direct Struggle*, 588.

60. Guillaume, "Ideas on Social Organization," 266.

61.   Guillaume, "Ideas on Social Organization," 266. See also Kropotkin, *Rebel*, 37–38.

62.   Kropotkin, *Conquest of Bread*.

63.   Berkman, *Anarchism*, 228.

64.   Bakunin, *Selected Texts*, 34, 43.

65.   Bakunin, *Selected Texts*, 43.

66.   Rudolf Rocker, *Anarcho-Syndicalism: Theory and Practice* (Oakland, CA: AK Press, 2004), 71.

67.   Malatesta, *Café*, 137. See also Kenyon Zimmer, *Immigrants Against the State: Yiddish and Italian Anarchism in America* (Urbana: University of Illinois Press, 2015), 111.

68.   Malatesta, *Towards Anarchy*, 153.

69.   Zimmer, *Immigrants*, 182–88.

70.   Quoted in Zimmer, *Immigrants*, 182.

71.   Peter Cole, David Struthers, and Kenyon Zimmer, ed., *Wobblies of the World: A Global History of the IWW* (London: Pluto Press, 2017), 4–7, 29–43; Zimmer, *Immigrants*, 101–10.

72.   Kropotkin, *Direct Struggle*, 138–41; Malatesta, *Towards Anarchy*, 221–37; Zimmer, *Immigrants*, 120–24; Federico Ferretti, *Anarchy and Geography: Reclus and Kropotkin in the UK* (London: Routledge, 2019), 104–15, 120–43.

73.   Maximoff, *Program of Anarcho-Syndicalism*, 43.

74.   "International Anarchist Manifesto Against War (1915)," in *Anarchism: A Documentary History of Libertarian Ideas*, vol. 1, *From Anarchy to Anarchism (300 CE to 1939)*, ed. Robert Graham (Montréal: Black Rose Books, 2005), 290. See also Malatesta, *Method of Freedom*, 379–87.

75.   Kinna, *Kropotkin*, 177–83; Matthew S. Adams and Ruth Kinna, eds. *Anarchism, 1914–18: Internationalism, Anti-Militarism and War* (Manchester: Manchester University Press, 2017); A. W. Zurbrugg, *Anarchist Perspectives in Peace and War, 1900–1918* (London: Anarres Editions, 2018), 157–81.

76.   Marie Fleming, *The Anarchist Way to Socialism: Élisée Reclus and Nineteenth-Century European Anarchism* (London: Croom Helm Ltd, 1979), 77, 157–58; Kropotkin, *Memoirs*, 412; Kropotkin, *Modern Science*, 95, 97; Kropotkin, *Direct Struggle*, 195–96, 342; Malatesta, *Towards Anarchy*, 55.

77.   Bakunin, *Selected Writings*, 172.

78.   Élisée Reclus, *Anarchy, Geography, Modernity: Selected Writings of Élisée Reclus*, ed. John Clark and Camille Martin (Oakland, CA: PM Press, 2013), 138.

79.   Émile Pouget, "The Party of Labour," Libcom website, November 19, 2010, https://libcom.org/article/party-labour-emile-pouget.

80.   Pouget, "The Party of Labour."

81.   Bakunin, *Selected Texts*, 251–52. Bakunin used similar imagery in a letter to Nechaev. See Bakunin, *Selected Writings*, 183.

82.   Guillaume, "Ideas on Social Organization," 247. This dam metaphor can also be found in Malatesta, *Anarchist Revolutions*, 81.

83. Berkman, *Anarchism*, 179.

84. This idea has been falsely attributed to Kropotkin. Malatesta, for example, makes this claim in his 1931 article "Peter Kropotkin: Recollections and Criticisms by One of His Old Friends." See Malatesta, *Method of Freedom*, 516–20. For a critique of fatalistic readings of Kropotkin, see Matthew S. Adams, *Kropotkin, Read, and the Intellectual History of British Anarchism: Between Reason and Romanticism* (Basingstoke, UK: Palgrave MacMillan, 2015) 106–11.

85. Reclus, *Anarchy*, 139.

86. Malatesta, *Café*, 105.

87. Mella, "Evolution and Revolution," Biblioteca Anarquista website, https://es.theanarchistlibrary.org/library/ricardo-mella-evolucion-y-revolucion. See also Ricardo Mella, *Anarchist Socialism in Early Twentieth-Century Spain: A Ricardo Mella Anthology*, ed. Stephen Luis Vilaseca (London: Palgrave Macmillan, 2020), 87–92, 227.

88. Malatesta, *Café*, 105.

89. James Yeoman, *Print Culture and the Formation of the Anarchist Movement in Spain, 1890–1915* (New York: Routledge, 2020), 40–44, 248–49; George Richard Esenwein, *Anarchist Ideology and the Working-Class Movement in Spain, 1868–1898* (Berkeley: University of California Press, 1989), 127; Chris Ealham, *Living Anarchism: José Peirats and the Spanish Anarcho-Syndicalist Movement* (Oakland, CA: AK Press, 2015), 72–74.

90. Jerome R. Mintz, *The Anarchists of Casas Viejas* (Bloomington: Indiana University Press, 2004), 80, 120n3; Yeoman, *Print Culture*, 46.

91. Yeoman, *Print Culture*, 16–19, 43–50, 146–47.

92. Pietro Di Paola, *The Knights Errant of Anarchy: London and the Italian Anarchist Diaspora, 1880–1917* (Chico, CA: AK Press, 2017), 1–2; Paul Avrich, *Sacco and Vanzetti: The Anarchist Background* (Princeton: Princeton University Press, 1991), 47.

93. Yeoman, *Print Culture*, 147–48.

94. Lucy Parsons, *Freedom, Equality and Solidarity: Writings and Speeches, 1878–1937*, ed. Gale Ahrens (Chicago: Charles H. Kerr, 2004), 31.

95. Malatesta, *Towards Anarchy*, 46.

96. Kropotkin, *Memoirs*, 390–91.

97. For examples of anarchist counterculture see Avrich, *Haymarket*, 131–49; Di Paola, *Knights Errant*, 169–83; Tom Goyens, *Beer and Revolution: The German Anarchist Movement in New York City, 1880–1914* (Urbana: University of Illinois Press, 2007), 34–51, 168–82; Andrew Douglas Hoyt, "And They Called Them 'Galleanisti': The Rise of the *Cronca Sovversiva* and the Formation of America's Most Infamous Anarchist Faction (1895–1912)," (PhD diss., University of Minnesota, 2018), 76–125; Esenwein, *Anarchist Ideology*, 124–31; Angel Smith, *Anarchism, Revolution and Reaction: Catalan Labor and the Crisis of the Spanish State, 1989–1923* (New York: Berghahn Books, 2007), 155–62, 259–62; Zimmer, *Immigrants*, 24–26, 35–37, 62–66.

98. Martha Ackelsberg, *Free Women of Spain: Anarchism and the Struggle for the Emancipation of Women* (Oakland, CA: AK Press, 2005), 84–88; Ealham, *Living Anarchism*, 50–55; Chris Ealham: *Anarchism and the City: Revolution and Counter-Revolution in Barcelona, 1898–1937* (Oakland, CA: AK Press, 2010), 45–47; Danny Evans, *Revolution and the State: Anarchism in the Spanish Civil War, 1936–1939* (Chico, CA: AK Press, 2020), 23.

99. Kropotkin, *Direct Struggle*, 303.

100. Malatesta, *Towards Anarchy*, 46.

101. Goldman, *Red Emma*, 401–2.

102. Goldman, *Red Emma*, 404.

103. Kropotkin, *Direct Struggle*, 306–7.

104. Bakunin, *Statism and Anarchy*, 179.

105. Quoted in A. W. Zurbrugg, "Introduction" in Bakunin, *Selected Texts*, 14.

106. Malatesta, *Method of Freedom*, 420, 426. See also Malatesta, *Towards Anarchy*, 46–47.

107. Luigi Fabbri, "Revolution and Dictatorship: On One Anarchist Who Has Forgotten his Principles," trans. Paul Sharkey, Kate Sharpley Library website, https://www.katesharpleylibrary.net/8932r8. See also Berkman, *Anarchism*, 136; Malatesta, *Method of Freedom*, 3, 143.

108. Malatesta, *Towards Anarchy*, 147, 148.

109. Malatesta, *Towards Anarchy*, 147.

110. Malatesta, *Towards Anarchy*, 147.

111. Kropotkin, *Direct Struggle*, 200.

112. For the first uses of these terms, see Carl Boggs, "Marxism, Prefigurative Communism and the Problem of Workers' Control," *Radical America* 11 (1977): 99–122; Wini Breines, "Community and Organization: The New Left and Michels' 'Iron Law,'" *Social Problems* 27, no. 4 (1980): 419–29. For a broad overview of this topic, see Paul Raekstad and Sofa Saio Gradin, *Prefigurative Politics: Building Tomorrow Today* (Cambridge: Polity Press, 2020).

113. Some anarchists rejected this idea. Nettlau argued that anarchist organizations built in the present should not be viewed as the embryo of the future society because we should not "permit the present to mortgage or lay its hands upon the future" and we "have no real knowledge of the nature of *the society of the future, which, like life itself, will have to remain 'without adjectives.'*" See Max Nettlau, *A Short History of Anarchism*, ed. Heiner M. Becker (London: Freedom Press, 1996), 196, 208, 282.

114. Bernard H. Moss, *The Origins of the French Labor Movement: The Socialism of Skilled Workers* (Berkeley: University of California Press, 1980), 32–41, 69.

115. César De Paepe, "The Present Institutions of the International in Relation to the Future," trans. Shawn P. Wilbur, Libertarian Labyrinth website, March 20, 2018, https://www.libertarian-labyrinth.org/working-translations/the -present-institutions-of-the-international-from-the-point-of-view-of-the -future-1869.

116. César De Paepe, "The Present Institutions of the International in Relation to the Future." For an overview of his life and ideas, see William Whitham, "César De Paepe and the Ideas of the First International," *Modern Intellectual History* 16, no. 3 (2019): 897–925.

117. Robert Graham, *We Do Not Fear Anarchy, We Invoke It: The First International and the Origins of the Anarchist Movement* (Oakland, CA: AK Press, 2015), 109; Wolfgang Eckhardt, *The First Socialist Schism: Bakunin vs. Marx in the International Working Men's Association* (Oakland, CA: PM Press, 2016), 9.

118. For the context of the "Sonvilier Circular," see Graham, *We Do Not Fear Anarchy*, 167–75; Eckhardt, *First Socialist Schism*, 85–120.

119. The Jura Federation, "The Sonvilier Circular," in *Libertarian Ideas*, vol. 1, 97–98. For Marx and Engels's response, in which they reject this position, see Karl Marx and Friedrich Engels, *Collected Works*, vol. 23 (London: Lawrence and Wishart, 1988), 64–70.

120. Bakunin, *Selected Texts*, 180–81. See also Michael Bakunin, *The Basic Bakunin: Writings 1869–1871*, ed. and trans. Robert M. Cutler (Buffalo, NY: Prometheus Books, 1985), 139.

121. Peter Kropotkin, *Fugitive Writings*, ed. George Woodcock (Montréal: Black Rose Books, 1993), 41.

122. Malatesta, *Patient Work*, 20.

123. Goldman, *Red Emma*, 397.

124. Mella, *Anarchist Socialism*, 91.

125. Isaac Puente, Libertarian Communism, (Johannesburg: Zabalaza Books, 2005), 10.

126. Bakunin, *Basic Bakunin*, 153; Malatesta, *Patient Work*, 358–60; Fleming, *Anarchist Way*, 129–30; Reclus, *Anarchy*, 152–55. For examples of anarchist cooperatives and intentional communities, see Andrew Cornell, *Unruly Equality: US Anarchism in the Twentieth Century* (Oakland, CA: University of California Press, 2016), 96–100, 129–33; John Quail, *The Slow Burning Fuse: The Lost History of British Anarchists* (London: Granada Publishing Limited, 1978), 224–31.

127. Paul Avrich, *The Modern School Movement: Anarchism and Education in the United States* (Oakland, CA: AK Press, 2006), 50–51, 261–64; Constance Bantman, *The French Anarchists in London, 1880–1914: Exile and Transnationalism in the First Globalisation* (Liverpool: Liverpool University Press, 2013), 90–91; Fausto Buttà, *Living Like Nomads: The Milanese Anarchist Movement Before Fascism* (Newcastle, UK: Cambridge Scholars Publishing, 2015), 120–29; Hoyt, "And They Called Them 'Galleanisti,'" 102–20; Yeoman, *Print Culture*, 151–62.

128. Ardouin et al., "Liberty Through Education: The Libertarian School," trans. Shawn P. Wilbur, Libertarian Labyrinth website, https://www.libertarian-labyrinth.org/working-translations/liberty-through-education-1898.

129. Francisco Ferrer, *Anarchist Education and the Modern School: A Francisco Ferrer Reader*, ed. Mark Bray and Robert H. Haworth (Oakland, CA: PM Press, 2019), 86. See also, 50–51.

130. Ferrer, *Anarchist Education*, 85–93. Anarchists disagreed on whether or not schools run by anarchists should teach anarchist ideas. See ibid., 188–206; Mella, *Anarchist Socialism*, 185–201.

131. Avrich, *Modern School*, 29–31.

132. Cornell, *Unruly Equality*, 159–60, 163, 208–9.

133. Wilson, *Anarchist Essays*, 43.

134. Malatesta, *Patient Work*, 140. See also Reclus, *Anarchy*, 188.

135. Quoted in Jennifer Guglielmo, *Living the Revolution: Italian Women's Resistance and Radicalism in New York City, 1880–1945* (Chapel Hill: University of North Carolina Press, 2010), 165.

136. Ackelsberg, *Free Women*, 46–52, 171–2; Goyens, *Beer and Revolution*, 155–58, 195–99; J. Mintz, *Casas Viejas*, 91–99; Zimmer, *Immigrants*, 44–46; Guglielmo, *Living the Revolution*, 154, 156, 171–72; Ginger Frost, "Love is Always Free: Anarchism, Free Unions and Utopianism in Edwardian England," *Anarchist Studies* 17, no. 1 (2009): 73–94.

137. Quoted in Ackelsberg, *Free Women*, 115.

138. Ackelsberg, *Free Women*, 77, 87–88, 103, 115–20, 123.

139. Guglielmo, *Living the Revolution*, 156, 159–60, 162–63.

140. Ackelsberg, *Free Women*, 21, 115, 120–37.

141. Quoted in Ackelsberg, *Free Women*, 148.

142. Ackelsberg, *Free Women*, 151–54.

143. Rocker, *Anarcho-Syndicalism*, 78.

144. Rocker, *Anarcho-Syndicalism*, 78.

145. For example Bakunin, *Selected Writings*, 203.

146. Wilson, *Anarchist Essays*, 58. See also, 53, 84; Malatesta, *Method of Freedom*, 105; Kropotkin, *Direct Struggle*, 298.

147. Vadim Damier, *Anarcho-Syndicalism in the Twentieth Century* (Edmonton, AB: Black Cat Press, 2009), 13–15, 23–24.

148. Émile Pouget, *Direct Action* (London: Kate Sharpley Library, 2003), 1.

149. Pouget, *Direct Action*, 3.

150. Goldman, *Red Emma*, 76–77. A few years later in her 1913 pamphlet *Syndicalism: Its Theory and Practice*, Goldman used the term "direct action" in its original narrow syndicalist sense. See ibid., 94.

151. Goldman, *Red Emma*, 202.

152. Voltairine de Cleyre, *The Voltairine de Cleyre Reader* ed. A. J. Brigati (Oakland, CA: AK Press, 2004), 48.

153. de Cleyre, *Reader*, 52–55.

154. John Merriman, *The Dynamite Club: How a Bombing in Fin-de-Siècle Paris Ignited the Age of Modern Terror* (New Haven: Yale University Press, 2016), 55.

155. Paul Avrich and Karen Avrich, *Sasha and Emma: The Anarchist Odyssey of*

Alexander Berkman and Emma Goldman (Cambridge, MA: Harvard University Press, 2012), 127–32; Emma Goldman, *Living My Life*, vol. 1 (New York: Dover Publications, 1970), 246–49, 257–8, 275–77.

156. Maurizio Antonioli, ed. *The International Anarchist Congress Amsterdam (1907)* (Edmonton, AB: Black Cat Press, 2009), 164.

157. Cornell, *Unruly Equality*, 71–74.

158. Abel Paz, *Durruti in the Spanish Revolution* (Oakland, CA: AK Press, 2006), 49–54.

159. Zimmer, *Immigrants*, 77–78; Antonio Senta, *Luigi Galleani: The Most Dangerous Anarchist in America* (Chico, CA: AK Press, 2019), 98–99, 106–11.

160. Antonioli, ed. *International Anarchist Congress*, 92.

161. Pouget, *Direct Action*, 5. See also Malatesta, *Life and Ideas*, 170–71.

162. Kropotkin, *Modern Science*, 189.

163. Pouget, *Direct Action*, 7.

164. Pouget, *Direct Action*, 20.

165. Galleani, *End of Anarchism*, 32.

166. Malatesta, *Method of Freedom*, 83.

167. Malatesta, *Method of Freedom*, 90.

168. Malatesta, *Method of Freedom*, 91.

169. This phrase continued to be used by Kropotkin over several decades. See Kropotkin, *Direct Struggle*, 140, 200, 348, 374; Peter Kropotkin, *The Great French Revolution* (Montréal: Black Rose Books, 1989), 18–19; Kropotkin, *Modern Science*, 190, 194.

170. Kropotkin, *Rebel*, 70–73.

171. Kropotkin, *Rebel*, 186.

172. Kropotkin, *Rebel*, 186.

173. Kropotkin, *Rebel*, 187.

174. Kropotkin, *Rebel*, 187–90.

175. Kropotkin, *Rebel*, 189.

176. Kropotkin, *Rebel*, 189–90.

177. Kropotkin, *Rebel*, 192–96.

178. Kropotkin, *Rebel*, 73–74.

179. Kropotkin, *Rebel*, 74.

180. Kropotkin, *Rebel*, 74.

181. Kropotkin, *Rebel*, 75.

182. Kropotkin, *Rebel*, 75.

Chapter 5: Anarchism and State Socialism

1. Gary P. Steenson, *After Marx, Before Lenin: Marxism and Socialist Working-Class Parties in Europe, 1884–1914* (Pittsburgh: University of Pittsburgh Press, 1991); Keven McDermott and Jeremy Agnew, *The Comintern: A*

History of International Communism from Lenin to Stalin (Basingstoke, UK: Macmillan, 1996), 1–27.

2.   For illustrative examples, see Alexander Berkman, *What is Anarchism?* (Oakland, CA: AK Press, 2003), 89–136; Emma Goldman, *Red Emma Speaks: An Emma Goldman Reader*, ed. Alix Kates Shulman, 3rd ed. (Atlantic Highlands, NJ: Humanities Press, 1996), 101–8, 383–420; Peter Kropotkin, *Direct Struggle Against Capital: A Peter Kropotkin Anthology*, ed. Iain McKay (Oakland, CA: AK Press, 2014), 371–82, 432; Errico Malatesta, *A Long and Patient Work: The Anarchist Socialism of L'Agitazione, 1897–1898*, ed. Davide Turcato (Chico, CA: AK Press, 2016), 24–27, 120–24; Rudolf Rocker, *Anarcho-Syndicalism: Theory and Practice* (Oakland, CA: AK Press, 2004), 11–12, 48–49; Rudolf Rocker, "Marx and Anarchism," Anarchist Library website, April 26, 2009. https://theanarchistlibrary.org/library/rudolf-rocker-marx-and-anarchism.

3.   For an overview of Marx and Engels's strategy, see Hal Draper, *Karl Marx's Theory of Revolution*, vol. 3, *The "Dictatorship of the Proletariat"* (New York: Monthly Review Press, 1986); Richard N. Hunt, *The Political Ideas of Marx and Engels*, vol. 1, *Marxism and Totalitarian Democracy, 1818–1850* (Pittsburgh: University of Pittsburgh Press, 1974); Hunt, *The Political Ideas of Marx and Engels*, vol. 2, *Classical Marxism, 1850–1895* (Pittsburgh: University of Pittsburgh Press, 1984).

4.   Peter Kropotkin, *Words of a Rebel* (Montréal: Black Rose Books, 1992), 91–92; Peter Kropotkin, *Modern Science and Anarchy*, ed. Iain McKay (Chico, CA: AK Press, 2018), 211, 220–21, 233.

5.   For an overview of these movements and their ideas, see Steenson, *After Marx, Before Lenin*. For important primary sources, see Karl Kautsky, *The Class Struggle (Erfurt Program)* (Chicago: Charles H. Kerr, 1910); Mike Taber, ed. *Under the Socialist Banner: Resolutions of the Second International 1889–1912* (Chicago: Haymarket Books, 2021).

6.   Edward Bernstein, *Evolutionary Socialism: A Criticism and Affirmation* (New York: B. W. Huebsch, 1909), x–xvi, 145–46, 163, 196–99, 216–19; Rosa Luxemburg, *Rosa Luxemburg Speaks*, ed. Mary-Alice Waters (New York: Pathfinder Press, 1970), 48–59, 76–83.

7.   Berkman, *Anarchism*, 91–93; Kropotkin, *Modern Science*, 193; Malatesta, *Patient Work*, 30–31.

8.   Kropotkin, *Direct Struggle*, 378–81; Malatesta, *Patient Work*, 64–71; Errico Malatesta, *Towards Anarchy: Malatesta in America, 1899–1900*, ed. Davide Turcato (Chico, CA: AK Press, 2019), 178–82.

9.   Malatesta, *Patient Work*, 30–31.

10.   Voltairine de Cleyre, *The Voltairine de Cleyre Reader* ed. A. J. Brigati (Oakland, CA: AK Press, 2004), 59.

11.   Malatesta, *Long and Patient*, 4.

12.   Malatesta, *Long and Patient*, 9.

13.   Malatesta, *Long and Patient*, 180–81.

14. De Cleyre, *Reader*, 59.

15. Rocker, *Anarcho-Syndicalism*, 54.

16. Malatesta, *Towards Anarchy*, 178. See also, 77; *Patient Work*, 10, 44.

17. Michael Bakunin, *Selected Texts, 1868–1875*, ed. A. W. Zurbrugg (London: Merlin Books, 2016), 54.

18. Élisée Reclus, *Anarchy, Geography, Modernity: Selected Writings of Élisée Reclus*, ed. John Clark and Camille Martin (Oakland, CA: PM Press, 2013), 147.

19. Kropotkin, *Modern Science*, 193.

20. Reclus, *Anarchy*, 122.

21. Reclus, *Anarchy*, 122.

22. Max Baginski, *What Does Syndicalism Want? Living, Not Dead Unions* (London: Kate Sharpley Library, 2015), 13.

23. Rocker, *Anarcho-Syndicalism*, 55.

24. Rocker, *Anarcho-Syndicalism*, 55.

25. For the programs of socialist parties in Austria, Germany, and Italy, see the appendix to Steenson, *After Marx, Before Lenin*, 285–307.

26. Berkman, *Anarchism*, 92–93, 99–102; Reclus, *Anarchy*, 145–7; Kropotkin, *Direct Struggle*, 338, 372–74; Malatesta, *Towards Anarchy*, 115.

27. Rocker, *Anarcho-Syndicalism*, 55.

28. Michael Bakunin, *Statism and Anarchy* (Cambridge: Cambridge University Press, 1990), ed. Marshall Shatz, 180; Luigi Galleani, *The End of Anarchism?* (London: Elephant Editions, 2012), 30.

29. René Berthier, *Social Democracy and Anarchism in the International Workers' Association, 1864–1877* (London: Anarres Editions, 2015), 48–9; Peter Kropotkin, *Memoirs of a Revolutionist* (Montréal: Black Rose Books, 1989), 259–60.

30. Bakunin, *Selected Texts*, 181.

31. Galleani, *End of Anarchism*, 29–30.

32. Berkman, *Anarchism*, 92.

33. Berkman, *Anarchism*, 92–93.

34. Quoted in Jeremy Jennings, *Syndicalism in France: A Study of Ideas* (Basingstoke, UK: Macmillan, 1990), 36. See also Malatesta, *Towards Anarchy*, 111–17. In response to Millerand's actions, the 2nd International passed resolutions at its 1900 and 1904 congresses that opposed the entry of socialist politicians into a bourgeois government's cabinet. See Taber, ed. *Under the Socialist Banner*, 77–78, 83–84.

35. Jennings, *Syndicalism in France*, 36; F. F. Ridley, *Revolutionary Syndicalism in France: The Direct Action of Its Time* (Cambridge: Cambridge University Press, 1970), 58–61; Robert G. Neville, "The Courrières Colliery Disaster, 1906," *Journal of Contemporary History* 13, no. 1 (1978): 33–52.

36. S. F. Kissin, *War and the Marxists: Socialist Theory and Practice in Capitalist Wars*, vol. 1, *1848–1918* (London: Routledge, 2019). For anarchist responses

to the war, see Matthew S. Adams and Ruth Kinna, eds. *Anarchism, 1914–18: Internationalism, Anti-Militarism and War* (Manchester: Manchester University Press, 2017); A. W. Zurbrugg, *Anarchist Perspectives in Peace and War, 1900–1918* (London: Anarres Editions, 2018), 157–81.

37. Berkman, *Anarchism*, 99.

38. Berkman, *Anarchism*, 99, 98.

39. Kropotkin, *Modern Science*, 310, 199, 227.

40. Michael Bakunin, *Selected Writings*, ed. Arthur Lehning (London: Jonathan Cape, 1973), 255. The same point is made in Malatesta, *Patient Work*, 388.

41. Rocker, *Anarcho-Syndicalism*, 14–15; Malatesta, *The Method of Freedom: An Errico Malatesta Reader*, ed. Davide Turcato (Oakland, CA: AK Press 2014), 130; Kropotkin, *Modern Science*, 273–75, 352.

42. Malatesta, *Method of Freedom*, 113.

43. Malatesta, *Method of Freedom*, 130. See also Bakunin, *Selected Writings*, 253, 265–66.

44. Bakunin, *Statism and Anarchy*, 178.

45. Malatesta, *Patient Work*, 27.

46. Kropotkin, *Modern Science*, 164, 352.

47. Malatesta, *Patient Work*, 120–21.

48. Council communists are an example of Marxists who advocated a dictatorship of the proletariat that was similar to, but not identical with, what anarchists advocated. For a discussion of the similarities between council communism and anarchism, see Saku Pinta, "Towards a Libertarian Communism: a Conceptual History of the Intersections Between Anarchisms and Marxisms" (PhD Diss., Loughborough University, 2013).

49. Malatesta, *Method of Freedom*, 392.

50. Malatesta, *Method of Freedom*, 392.

51. Malatesta, *Method of Freedom*, 392. There appears to be a typo in this edition, where Malatesta says that it will "defend the revolution for its external enemies." I choose to replace "for" with "against" based on the translation available in *No Gods, No Masters: An Anthology of Anarchism*, ed. Daniel Guérin (Oakland, CA: AK Press, 2005), 392.

52. Karl Marx and Friedrich Engels, *Collected Works*, vol. 24 (London: Lawrence and Wishart, 1989), 320–21; *Collected Works*, vol. 26, 269–72

53. Marx and Engels, *Collected Works*, vol. 24, 321.

54. Karl Marx and Friedrich Engels, *Collected Works*, vol. 26 (London: Lawrence and Wishart, 1990), 272. For Marx's vision of a stateless classless society, see Paul Raekstad, *Karl Marx's Realist Critique of Capitalism: Freedom, Alienation, and Socialism* (London: Palgrave Macmillan, 2022), 155–72.

55. Carlo Cafiero, *Revolution* (Edmonton, AB: Black Cat Press, 2012), 45.

56. Michael Bakunin, *Bakunin on Anarchism*, ed. Sam Dolgoff (Montréal: Black Rose Books, 1980), 145.

57. Malatesta, *Patient Work*, 124.

58. Bakunin, *Statism and Anarchy*, 52. See also Bakunin, *Selected Texts*, 63.

59. Malatesta, *Method of Freedom*, 147.

60. Berkman, *Anarchism*, 43. See also Bakunin, *Statism and Anarchy*, 136.

61. Malatesta, *Method of Freedom*, 115–16, 130–31, 289–90; Rocker, *Anarcho-Syndicalism*, 11–13.

62. Luigi Fabbri, "Anarchy and 'Scientific' Communism," in *Bloodstained: One Hundred Years of Leninist Counterrevolution*, ed. Friends of Aron Baron (Chico, CA: AK Press, 2017), 20.

63. Malatesta, *Patient Work*, 123.

64. Bakunin, *Statism and Anarchy*, 179.

65. Fabbri, "Anarchy and 'Scientific' Communism," 20.

66. Vladimir Lenin, *Selected Works* (Moscow: Progress Publishers, 1977), 635, 682–83, 685–86.

67. Bakunin, *Statism and Anarchy*, 181.

68. Kropotkin, *Modern Science*, 170.

69. Kropotkin, *Direct Struggle*, 165, 210, 288, 385–86,

70. Malatesta, *Patient Work*, 123–24.

71. Kropotkin, *Modern Science*, 274.

72. Fabbri, "Anarchy and 'Scientific' Communism," 29–30.

73. Bakunin, *Selected Texts*, 88–89.

74. Kropotkin, *Direct Struggle*, 130–31.

75. Kropotkin, *Modern Science*, 198.

76. Kropotkin, *Modern Science*, 191, 193.

77. Kropotkin, *Modern Science*, 306.

78. Kropotkin, *Modern Science*, 306.

79. For a brief overview of this very complex history from an anti-Leninist perspective, see: Maurice Brinton, "The Bolsheviks and Workers' Control 1917–1921: The State and Counter-Revolution," in *For Workers' Power: The Selected Writings of Maurice Brinton*, ed. David Goodway (Oakland, CA: AK Press, 2004), 293–378; Iain McKay, "The State and Revolution: Theory and Practice," in *Bloodstained*, 61–117.

80. Malatesta, *Method of Freedom*, 392.

81. Goldman, *Red Emma*, 388, 394. For details about Goldman and Berkman's deportation, see Paul Avrich and Karen Avrich, *Sasha and Emma: The Anarchist Odyssey of Alexander Berkman and Emma Goldman* (Cambridge, MA: Harvard University Press, 2012), 269–72, 291–302.

82. Goldman, *Red Emma*, 387.

83. Goldman, *Red Emma*, 389.

84. Goldman, *Red Emma*, 391.

85. Goldman, *Red Emma*, 404. For other anarchist critiques of the Bolsheviks, see Berkman, *Anarchism*, 103–36; Peter Arshinov, *History of the Makhnovist Movement, 1918–1921* (London: Freedom Press, 2005); Voline, *The Unknown Revolution, 1917–1921* (Oakland, CA: PM Press, 2019).

86. For example Hal Draper, *Karl Marx's Theory of Revolution*, vol. 4, *Critique of Other Socialisms* (New York: Monthly Review Press, 1990), 154; Paul Thomas, *Karl Marx and the Anarchists* (London: Routledge & Kegan Paul, 1980), 12, 16, 343–48; Vladimir Lenin, *Collected Works*, vol. 10, ed. Andrew Rothstein (Moscow: Progress Publishers, 1978), 71–73; George Plechanoff, *Anarchism and Socialism* (Chicago: Charles H. Kerr, 1912), 94–100.

87. Karl Marx and Friedrich Engels, *Collected Works*, vol. 43 (London: Lawrence and Wishart, 1988), 490–91.

88. Karl Marx and Friedrich Engels, *Collected Works*, vol. 23 (London: Lawrence and Wishart, 1988), 254–55.

89. Karl Marx and Friedrich Engels, *Collected Works*, vol. 44 (London: Lawrence and Wishart, 1989), 331.

90. Malatesta, *At the Café: Conversations on Anarchism* (London: Freedom Press, 2005), 155. See also Bakunin, *Statism and Anarchy*, 171.

91. Rudolf Rocker, *The London Years* (Nottingham, UK: Five Leaves, 2005), 28; *Anarcho-Syndicalism*, 73–78; Peter Kropotkin, *Rebel*, 39–43.

92. Bakunin, *Selected Texts*, 238.

93. Bakunin, *Selected Texts*, 226.

94. Bakunin, *Political Philosophy*, 313.

95. Quoted in Berthier, *Social Democracy and Anarchism*, 59.

96. Bakunin, *Selected Texts*, 22, 53, 225.

97. Michael Bakunin, *The Political Philosophy of Bakunin: Scientific Anarchism*, ed. G.P. Maximoff (New York: The Free Press of Glencoe, 1964), 313.

98. Quoted in Wolfgang Eckhardt, *The First Socialist Schism: Bakunin vs. Marx in the International Working Men's Association* (Oakland, CA: PM Press, 2016), 341.

99. Quoted in T.R. Ravindranathan, *Bakunin and the Italians* (Kingston and Montréal: McGill-Queen's University Press, 1988), 183.

100. Malatesta, *Patient Work*, 20–21.

101. Malatesta, *Towards Anarchy*, 53, 52.

102. Malatesta, *Towards Anarchy*, 53. See also Kropotkin, *Direct Struggle*, 310–11.

103. Malatesta, *Patient Work*, 167–68.

104. Quoted in Jerome R. Mintz, *The Anarchists of Casas Viejas* (Bloomington: Indiana University Press, 2004), 13.

105. Kropotkin, *Direct Struggle*, 535.

106. Kropotkin, *Modern Science*, 164. See also Kropotkin, *Rebel*, 144.

107. Kropotkin, *Modern Science*, 159.

108. Lucien van der Walt, "Anarchism and Marxism," in *Brill's Companion to Anarchist Philosophy*, ed. Nathan Jun (Leiden: Brill Academic Publishers, 2017), 515. This distinction was first proposed in Michael Schmidt and Lucien van der Walt, *Black Flame: The Revolutionary Class Politics of Anarchism and Syndicalism* (Oakland, CA: AK Press, 2009), 123–24. It should be noted that, since its publication, Schmidt was revealed to be a racist.

109.   Kenyon Zimmer, *Immigrants Against the State: Yiddish and Italian Anarchism in America* (Urbana: University of Illinois Press, 2015), 99.

Chapter 6: Insurrectionist Anarchism

1.   Prior to the creation of the anarchist movement in the 1870s, the strategy of insurrectionist anarchism was advocated by Déjacque in the 1850s. Since I do not know if his ideas on strategy had any influence on the movement in general or the key insurrectionist theorists, such as Cafiero, Most, or Galleani, I have decided to not discuss his ideas. See Joseph Déjacque, *Down with the Bosses and Other Writings, 1859–1861* (Gresham, OR: Corvus Editions, 2013), 40–42.

2.   Michael Schmidt and van der Walt, *Black Flame: The Revolutionary Class Politics of Anarchism and Syndicalism* (Oakland, CA: AK Press, 2009), 20, 123, 128–131.

3.   Luigi Galleani, *The End of Anarchism?* (London: Elephant Editions, 2012), 99.

4.   Galleani, *End of Anarchism*, 32.

5.   Carlo Cafiero, *Revolution* (Edmonton, AB: Black Cat Press, 2012), 47.

6.   David Stafford, *From Anarchism to Reformism: A Study of the Political Activities of Paul Brousse, 1870–90* (London: Weidenfeld and Nicolson, 1971), 104–5, 108–9.

7.   Tom Goyens, *Beer and Revolution: The German Anarchist Movement in New York City, 1880–1914* (Urbana: University of Illinois Press, 2007), 74, 102–9.

8.   Cafiero, *Revolution*, 41–42; Pietro Di Paola, *The Knights Errant of Anarchy: London and the Italian Anarchist Diaspora, 1880–1917* (Chico, CA: AK Press, 2017), 61–62; Antonio Senta, *Luigi Galleani: The Most Dangerous Anarchist in America* (Chico, CA: AK Press, 2019), 57, 91–93. For an example of an insurrectionist group, see Paul Avrich, *The Haymarket Tragedy* (Princeton: Princeton University Press, 1984), 150–56.

9.   Quoted in Kenyon Zimmer, *Immigrants Against the State: Yiddish and Italian Anarchism in America* (Urbana: University of Illinois Press, 2015), 59.

10.   Galleani, *End of Anarchism*, 61, See also, 58, 105.

11.   Galleani, *End of Anarchism*, 73.

12.   Galleani, *End of Anarchism*, 75.

13.   Quoted in George Richard Esenwein, *Anarchist Ideology and the Working-Class Movement in Spain, 1868–1898* (Berkeley: University of California Press, 1989), 114.

14.   Malatesta, *The Method of Freedom: An Errico Malatesta Reader*, ed. Davide Turcato (Oakland, CA: AK Press 2014), 102. See also Errico Malatesta, *Towards Anarchy: Malatesta in America, 1899–1900*, ed. Davide Turcato (Chico, CA: AK Press, 2019), 62; Maurizio Antonioli, ed. *The International Anarchist Congress Amsterdam (1907)* (Edmonton, AB: Black Cat Press 2009), 95–97.

15. Quoted in Nunzio Pernicone and Fraser M. Ottanelli, *Assassins against the Old Order: Italian Anarchist Violence in Fin de Siècle Europe* (Urbana: University of Illinois Press, 2018), 34.

16. Pernicone and Ottanelli, *Assassins against the Old Order*, 25–29.

17. Quoted in Nunzio Pernicone, *Italian Anarchism, 1864–1892* (Princeton: Princeton University Press, 1993), 169.

18. Pernicone and Ottanelli, *Assassins against the Old Order*, 30–33.

19. Quoted in Pernicone, *Italian Anarchism*, 216.

20. Davide Turcato, *Making Sense of Anarchism: Errico Malatesta's Experiments with Revolution, 1889–1900* (Basingstoke, UK: Palgrave Macmillan, 2012), 102.

21. David Berry, *A History of the French Anarchist Movement: 1917 to 1945* (Oakland, CA: AK Press, 2009), 19; Pernicone, *Italian Anarchism*, 191.

22. Quoted in Pernicone, *Italian Anarchism*, 216.

23. Galleani, *End of Anarchism*, 74.

24. Galleani, *End of Anarchism*, 74–75.

25. Galleani, *End of Anarchism*, 74.

26. Quoted in Senta, *Galleani*, 126.

27. Senta, *Galleani*, 126. Formal congresses were also rejected by Jean Grave. See Caroline Cahm, *Kropotkin and the Rise of Revolutionary Anarchism, 1872–1886* (Cambridge: Cambridge University Press, 1989), 65.

28. Andrew Douglas Hoyt, "And They Called Them 'Galleanisti': The Rise of the *Cronca Sovversiva* and the Formation of America's Most Infamous Anarchist Faction (1895–1912)," (PhD diss., University of Minnesota, 2018), 49–53; Chris Ealham: *Anarchism and the City: Revolution and Counter-Revolution in Barcelona, 1898–1937* (Oakland, CA: AK Press, 2010), 34–35; Agustín Guillamón, *Ready for Revolution: The CNT Defense Committees in Barcelona, 1933–1938* (Oakland, CA: AK Press, 2014), 29.

29. Quoted in Berry, *French Anarchist Movement*, 19.

30. Carlo Cafiero, "The Organisation of Armed Struggle," trans. Paul Sharkey, *The Cienfuegos Press Anarchist Review* 1, no. 3 (Autumn 1977): 101.

31. Quoted in Alexandre Skirda, *Facing the Enemy: A History of Anarchist Organization from Proudhon to May 1968* (Oakland CA: AK Press, 2002), 50.

32. Hoyt, "And They Called Them 'Galleanisti,'" 8–9, 24–27, 33–35, 294–96.

33. Zimmer, *Immigrants*, 60; Pernicone, "Introductory Essay" in Malatesta, *Towards Anarchy*, xxiii.

34. Quoted in Di Paola, *Knights Errant*, 52–53.

35. Galleani, *End of Anarchism*, 76–80; Senta, *Galleani*, 134–48; Zimmer, *Immigrants*, 28–29; Paul Avrich, *Sacco and Vanzetti: The Anarchist Background* (Princeton: Princeton University Press, 1991), 53, 61. Galleani did not adopt a rigid antisyndicalist perspective until around 1910 or 1911 and prior to this appears to have had a more positive view of trade unions. See Hoyt, "And They Called Them 'Galleanisti,'" 243–44; Senta, *Galleani*, 106–7, 158–59, 172–73, 191–92.

36. Galleani, *End of Anarchism*, 29–30.

37.   Galleani, *End of Anarchism*, 30.

38.   Galleani, *End of Anarchism*, 31.

39.   G. D. H. Cole, *A History of Socialist Thought*, vol. 2, *Marxism and Anarchism, 1850–1890* (London: Macmillan & Co, 1974), 80–1; Jeremy Wolf, "Iron Law of Wages," in *The Encyclopedia of Political Thought*, ed. Michael Gibbons (New York: Wiley-Blackwell, 2014), http://onlinelibrary.wiley.com/doi/10.1002/9781118474396.wbept0541/abstract.

40.   Galleani, *End of Anarchism*, 28, 79.

41.   Galleani, *End of Anarchism*, 29.

42.   Galleani, *End of Anarchism*, 96–97.

43.   Galleani, *End of Anarchism*, 29.

44.   Quoted in Berry, *French Anarchist Movement*, 21.

45.   For example, David C. Rapoport, "The Four Waves of Modern Terrorism," in *Attacking Terrorism: Elements of a Grand Strategy*, ed. Audrey Cronin and James Ludes (Washington, DC: Georgetown University Press, 2004), 50–52; Mary S. Barton, "The Global War on Anarchism: The United States and International Anarchist Terrorism, 1898–1904," *Diplomatic History* 39, no. 2 (2015): 306–8.

46.   Paul Avrich, *Anarchist Portraits* (Princeton: Princeton University Press, 1988), 243.

47.   There are some usages of the term "propaganda by the deed" by anarchist authors that cannot be neatly fit into these two main versions. Malatesta wrote an article in 1889 called "Propaganda by Deeds," in which he proposed that anarchists should, either as individuals or affinity groups, beat up tax collectors, push landowners down the stairs when they show up to collect rent, seize and distribute the harvest among peasants rather than allowing it to be taken to the landowner, kill the animals of landowners and distribute the meat to starving peasants, and provide landowners who evict people unable to pay rent "with a terrifying example of the vengeance of the oppressed." See Malatesta, *Method of Freedom*, 79–83.

48.   Avrich, *Anarchist Portraits*, 229–39; Julian P.W. Archer, *The First International in France, 1864–1872: Its Origins, Theories, and Impact* (Lanham, MD: University Press of America, 1997), 255–73; E. H. Carr, *Michael Bakunin* (London: The Macmillan Press, 1975), 394–96, 400–7; Guillaume, "Michael Bakunin: A Biographical Sketch," in Michael Bakunin, *Bakunin on Anarchism*, ed. Sam Dolgoff (Montréal: Black Rose Books, 1980), 40–42. Bakunin later claimed that the Lyon and Marseille insurrections failed because of a lack of effective organization. See Bakunin, *Basic Bakunin*, 65.

49.   John Merriman, *Massacre: The Life and Death of the Paris Commune of 1871* (New Haven: Yale University Press, 2014), 250–1. For anarchist estimates of the death count, see Errico Malatesta, *A Long and Patient Work: The Anarchist Socialism of L'Agitazione, 1897–1898*, ed. Davide Turcato (Chico, CA: AK Press, 2016), 305; Peter Kropotkin, *Direct Struggle Against Capital: A*

Peter Kropotkin Anthology, ed. Iain McKay (Oakland, CA: AK Press, 2014), 354, 406; Rudolf Rocker, *The London Years* (Nottingham, UK: Five Leaves, 2005), 22.

50. Esenwein, *Anarchist Ideology*, 45–50; Temma Kaplan, *Anarchists of Andalusia, 1868–1903* (Princeton: Princeton University Press, 1977), 101–10.

51. Bakunin, *Bakunin on Anarchism*, 195–96.

52. Michael Bakunin, *Selected Writings*, ed. Arthur Lehning (London: Jonathan Cape, 1973), 61.

53. Bakunin, *Selected Writings*, 62. See also Michael Bakunin, *Statism and Anarchy* (Cambridge: Cambridge University Press, 1990), ed. Marshall Shatz, 123.

54. Stafford, *From Anarchism to Reformism*, 35–40. For a short overview of Brousse's life, see Avrich, *Anarchist Portraits*, 240–46.

55. Quoted in Cahm, *Kropotkin*, 76–77.

56. Paul Brousse, "Propaganda by the Deed," in *Anarchism: A Documentary History of Libertarian Ideas*, vol. 1, *From Anarchy to Anarchism (300 CE to 1939)*, ed. Robert Graham (Montréal: Black Rose Books, 2005), 150.

57. Paul Brousse, "Propaganda by the Deed," 151.

58. Cahm, *Kropotkin*, 77–78.

59. Pernicone, *Italian Anarchism*, 35–36, 44, 64–70.

60. Bakunin, *Selected Writings*, 261. See also, 184–85.

61. Cafiero, *Revolution*, 63. The piece was never published in full during his lifetime because, in September 1881, the newspaper *La Révolution Sociale* suspended publication when its editor, the undercover police agent Égide Spilleux, fled with its funds and Cafiero was arrested. See ibid., xi.

62. Kropotkin, *Direct Struggle*, 111. Kropotkin had himself been radicalized by news of the Paris Commune. See Martin A. Miller, *Kropotkin* (Chicago: University of Chicago Press, 1976), 73–75.

63. Quoted in Cahm, *Kropotkin*, 102.

64. Kropotkin, *Direct Struggle*, 500. Kropotkin thought his idea of the spirit of revolt was distinct from Brousse's theory of propaganda by the deed. This disagreement appears to be largely semantic given that Kropotkin held, like Brousse, that ideas should be spread through actions and that these actions included insurrections which established communes. See Miller, *Kropotkin*, 260; Cahm, *Kropotkin*, 92, 102–105.

65. Kropotkin, *Direct Struggle*, 111. Kropotkin predicted that a revolution was near several times during this period. For other examples, see Peter Kropotkin, *Words of a Rebel* (Montréal: Black Rose Books, 1992), 32, 34–35, 205–6; Kropotkin, *Direct Struggle*, 119, 291, 542.

66. Gary P. Steenson, *After Marx, Before Lenin: Marxism and Socialist Working-Class Parties in Europe, 1884–1914* (Pittsburgh: University of Pittsburgh Press, 1991), 29–31.

67. Kropotkin, *Direct Struggle*, 545.

68. Quoted in Cahm, *Kropotkin*, 78.

69. Pernicone, *Italian Anarchism*, 82, 85–86; T.R. Ravindranathan, *Bakunin and the Italians* (Kingston and Montréal: McGill-Queen's University Press, 1988), 190, 194–95.

70. Pernicone, *Italian Anarchism*, 90–95; Ravindranathan, *Bakunin and the Italians*, 203–209. For Malatesta's account of his role in the insurrection see Malatesta, *Towards Anarchy*, 12–13.

71. Quoted in Pernicone, *Italian Anarchism*, 85.

72. Malatesta, *Method of Freedom*, 11. Similar ideas had been expressed by Malatesta at the recent October 1876 Berne Congress of the Saint-Imier International. See Peter Marshall, *Demanding the Impossible: A History of Anarchism* (London: Harper Perennial, 2008), 346.

73. The unsuccessful insurrections of 1874 were in part launched in order to out-compete Italian republican revolutionaries. See Pernicone, *Italian Anarchism*, 84–85.

74. Giuseppe Mazzini, *A Cosmopolitanism of Nations: Giuseppe Mazzini's Writings on Democracy, Nation Building, and International Relations*, ed. Stefano Recchia and Nadia Urbinati (Princeton: Princeton University Press, 2009), 111.

75. Quoted in Denis Mack Smith, *Mazzini* (New Haven: Yale University Press, 1994), 100.

76. Malatesta, *Patient Work*, 336.

77. D. M. Smith, *Mazzini*, 6–7, 10, 41, 47, 64–73, 98–101, 118–19; Martin Clark, *The Italian Risorgimento*, 2nd ed. (Harlow: Pearson Education Limited, 2009), 41.

78. Clark, *Italian Risorgimento*, 80–84.

79. Kropotkin, *Direct Struggle*, 140. One of the individuals inspired by Mazzini and Garibaldi was Bakunin who, prior to becoming an anarchist, met and attempted to work with them between 1862–64 in order to achieve Slav liberation as part of a wider democratic political revolution. Bakunin would go onto become a major critic of Mazzini and Garibaldi. See Ravindranathan, *Bakunin and the Italians*, 13–20, 57–60, 84–85, 122–26, 131–33, 147–48, 255n19; Bakunin, *Selected Writings*, 214–31.

80. Marco Pinfari, "Exploring the Terrorist Nature of Political Assassinations: A Reinterpretation of the Orsini Attentat," *Terrorism and Political Violence* 21, no. 4 (2009): 582–83; Pernicone and Ottanelli, *Assassins against the Old Order*, 7–19.

81. Quoted in Pernicone and Ottanelli, *Assassins against the Old Order*, 7–8.

82. Pernicone, *Italian Anarchism*, 11–13, 118–19, 169. The influence Pisacane had on Italian anarchism can be seen in the fact that Cafiero quotes him at length. See Cafiero, *Revolution*, 4–5, 10–11, 14, 23, 45, 47, 62, 66–67. Despite being a republican martyr, the political theory of Pisacane does not appear to have been widely known among Italian republicans in the 1860s. See Ravindranathan, *Bakunin and the Italians*, 70–73.

83. Carlo Pisacane, "Political Testament," Robert Graham's Anarchism Weblog, September, 22, 2011, https://robertgraham.wordpress.com/2011/09/22/ carlo-pisacane-propaganda-by-the-deed-1857. According to Nettlau, the earliest reprint of this text he was aware of occurred in June 1878 in the Italian anarchist journal *L'Avvenire*. See Max Nettlau, *A Short History of Anarchism*, ed. Heiner M. Becker (London: Freedom Press, 1996), 92.

84. Quoted in Pernicone, *Italian Anarchism*, 121.

85. Quoted in Pernicone, *Italian Anarchism*, 119.

86. Quoted in Cahm, *Kropotkin*, 78.

87. The following account of the Benevento Affair is a summary of Pernicone, *Italian Anarchism*, 121–26; Ravindranathan, *Bakunin and the Italians*, 225–29.

88. Quoted in Pernicone, *Italian Anarchism*, 125

89. Brousse, "Propaganda by the Deed," 151.

90. Quoted in Pernicone, *Italian Anarchism*, 126.

91. Pernicone, *Italian Anarchism*, 126–27, 140–45.

92. Cafiero, *Revolution*, 63–64.

93. Cahm, *Kropotkin*, 80–82, 100–102; Miller, *Kropotkin*, 136–37; Stafford, *From Anarchism to Reformism*, 80–83.

94. Quoted in Cahm, *Kropotkin*, 101.

95. Brousse, "Propaganda by the Deed," 151.

96. Stafford, *From Anarchism to Reformism*, 113.

97. I have decided not to collectively label these acts "terrorism." This is because although some of them were acts of terror against civilians, others were targeted attacks against specific individuals that occurred as part of an ongoing armed conflict between anarchists and the ruling classes. They were thus more akin to special operations carried out during a war. This is, in turn, consistent with how anarchists viewed themselves as militants fighting a class war.

98. Richard Bach Jensen, *The Battle Against Anarchist Terrorism: An International History, 1878–1934* (Cambridge: Cambridge University Press, 2014), 7, 23–24.

99. Andrew R. Carlson, *Anarchism in Germany*, vol. 1, *The Early Movement* (Metuchen, NJ: The Scarecrow Press, 1972), 115–16, 139–41. For the argument that they were anarchists, see ibid., 117–24, 143–48. For a critique of this view, see Cahm, *Kropotkin*, 89–90. Kropotkin denied that there was any connection between these assassination attempts and the Jura Federation. See Peter Kropotkin, *Memoirs of a Revolutionist* (Montréal: Black Rose Books, 1989), 388–89.

100. Esenwein, *Anarchist Ideology*, 65–66; Benedict Anderson, *The Age of Globalization: Anarchists and the Anti-Colonial Imagination* (London: Verso, 2013), 115n90.

101. Carlson, *Anarchism in Germany*, 284–85.

102. Carlo Cafiero, "Action (1880)," in *Libertarian Ideas*, vol. 1, 152.

103. Carlo Cafiero, "Action (1880)," 152. See also Pernicone, *Italian Anarchism*, 186–88.

104. Cafiero, "The Organization of Armed Struggle."

105. According to a police report, almost identical resolutions had been passed a year earlier on September 12, 1880, at a meeting of thirty-two anarchist militants in Vevey, Switzerland, which included Kropotkin and Reclus. See Marie Fleming, *The Anarchist Way to Socialism: Élisée Reclus and Nineteenth-Century European Anarchism* (London: Croom Helm Ltd, 1979), 172.

106. Cahm, *Kropotkin*, 152–59; Pernicone, *Italian Anarchism*, 193–94.

107. Quoted in Carlson, *Anarchism in Germany*, 252–53.

108. Quoted in Carlson, *Anarchism in Germany*, 253. Nathan-Ganz had, a few months prior, published an article on "Revolutionary War Science," meaning the use of explosives, in his paper the *An-Archist: Socialistic Revolutionary Review*. See Avrich, *Haymarket*, 57–58; Timothy Messer-Kruse, *The Haymarket Conspiracy: Transatlantic Anarchist Networks* (Urbana: University of Illinois Press, 2012), 81, 206n28.

109. Quoted in Ulrich Linse, "'Propaganda by Deed' and 'Direct Action': Two Concepts of Anarchist Violence," in *Social Protest, Violence and Terror in Nineteenth- and Twentieth-Century Europe*, ed. Wolfgang J. Mommsen and Gerhard Hirschfeld (London: The Macmillan Press, 1982), 210.

110. Carlson, *Anarchism in Germany*, 288–300.

111. Goyens, *Beer and Revolution*, 59–60, 93–95.

112. Quoted in Carlson, *Anarchism in Germany*, 254.

113. Carlson, *Anarchism in Germany*, 254–55.

114. On Italian republicans, see Pernicone and Ottanelli, *Assassins against the Old Order*, 12–14, 26–29. On Irish nationalists, see K. R. M. Short, *The Dynamite War: Irish-American Bombers in Victorian Britain* (Dublin: Gill and Macmillan Ltd, 1979); Lindsay Clutterbuck, "The Progenitors of Terrorism: Russian Revolutionaries or Extreme Irish Republicans?," *Terrorism and Political Violence* 16, no. 1 (2004), 154–81. On Russian nihilists, see Claudia Verhoeven, *The Odd Man Karakozov: Imperial Russia, Modernity and the Birth of Terrorism* (Ithaca, NY: Cornell University Press, 2009); Ronald Seth, *The Russian Terrorists: The Story of the Narodniki* (London: Barrie & Rockliff, 1966).

115. Seth, *Russian Terrorists*, 96–100; Pernicone and Ottanelli, *Assassins against the Old Order*, 35, 37–39.

116. Quoted in Jensen, *Anarchist Terrorism*, 18.

117. Nettlau, *Short History*, 148, 146.

118. Jensen, *Anarchist Terrorism*, 45–46; Skirda, *Facing the Enemy*, 43–45; Cahm, *Kropotkin*, 154–59, 320–21, notes 11 and 12. For other examples see Jensen, *Anarchist Terrorism*, 44–52.

119. Pernicone and Ottanelli, *Assassins against the Old Order*, 51–56.

120. John Merriman, *The Dynamite Club: How a Bombing in Fin-de-Siècle Paris*

Ignited the Age of Modern Terror (New Haven: Yale University Press, 2016), 71–73, 78–81.

121. Merriman, *Dynamite*, 99–105, 137–38, 145, 149–59, 180–81. For other bombings, see ibid., 172–78.

122. Esenwein, *Anarchist Ideology*, 184–88.

123. Jensen, *Anarchist Terrorism*, 31–36. For details see Pernicone and Ottanelli, *Assassins against the Old Order*.

124. On Alfonso, see Paul Avrich, *The Modern School Movement: Anarchism and Education in the United States* (Oakland, CA: AK Press, 2006), 26; Angel Smith, *Anarchism, Revolution and Reaction: Catalan Labor and the Crisis of the Spanish State, 1989–1923* (New York: Berghahn Books, 2007), 163. On Clemenceau, see Berry, *French Anarchist Movement*, 167. For other examples, see Paul Avrich and Karen Avrich, *Sasha and Emma: The Anarchist Odyssey of Alexander Berkman and Emma Goldman* (Cambridge, MA: Harvard University Press, 2012), 228–36; Avrich, *Sacco and Vanzetti*, 97–104, 137–59, 205–7; Fausto Buttà, *Living Like Nomads: The Milanese Anarchist Movement Before Fascism* (Newcastle, UK: Cambridge Scholars Publishing, 2015), 200, 221–22, 229.

125. Pernicone and Ottanelli, *Assassins against the Old Order*, 123–33; Turcato, *Making Sense*, 170–73. In response to this struggle from below the prime minister suspended import duties on grain and flour until June 30.

126. Quoted in Zimmer, *Immigrants*, 60.

127. Avrich and Avrich, *Sasha and Emma*, 91–96.

128. Quoted in Pernicone and Ottanelli, *Assassins against the Old Order*, 75. For more primary sources, see Mitchell Abidor, ed., *Death to Bourgeois Society: The Propagandists of the Deed* (Oakland CA, PM Press, 2015).

129. For example Emma Goldman, *Red Emma Speaks: An Emma Goldman Reader*, ed. Alix Kates Shulman, 3rd ed. (Atlantic Highlands, NJ: Humanities Press, 1996), 256–79; Galleani, *End of Anarchism*, 84–90; Voltairine de Cleyre, *The Voltairine de Cleyre Reader* ed. A. J. Brigati (Oakland, CA: AK Press, 2004), 173–76; Ruth Kinna, *Kropotkin: Reviewing the Classical Anarchist Tradition* (Edinburgh: Edinburgh University Press, 2016), 58–60; Clark, "Introduction," in Élisée Reclus, *Anarchy, Geography, Modernity: Selected Writings of Élisée Reclus*, ed. John Clark and Camille Martin (Oakland, CA: PM Press, 2013), 57–59; Malatesta, *Patient Work*, 124–27.

130. Louisa Sarah Bevington, *An Anarchist Manifesto*, (London: Metropolitan Printing Works, 1895), 11.

131. Avrich, *Sacco and Vanzetti*, 52.

132. James Yeoman, *Print Culture and the Formation of the Anarchist Movement in Spain, 1890–1915* (New York: Routledge, 2020), 90–98.

133. Senta, *Galleani*, 65–66, 139–41.

134. Galleani, *End of Anarchism*, 84.

135. Galleani, *End of Anarchism*, 93–95.

136. Malatesta, *Patient Work*, 58.

137. Malatesta, *Patient Work*, 127.

138. Malatesta, *Patient Work*, 264–65. See also Malatesta, *Method of Freedom*, 187–91; Errico Malatesta, *Life and Ideas: The Anarchist Writings of Errico Malatesta*, ed. Vernon Richards (Oakland, CA: PM Press, 2015), 53–58.

139. Jensen, *Anarchist Terrorism*, 36–38. For an overview of state repression in response to propaganda of the deed see Constance Bantman, *The French Anarchists in London, 1880–1914: Exile and Transnationalism in the First Globalisation* (Liverpool: Liverpool University Press, 2013), 132; Berry, *French Anarchist Movement*, 21–22, 32n22; Buttà, *Living Like Nomads*, 34–35, 39; Carlson, *Anarchism in Germany*, 127–29, 154–58, 293–94; Di Paola, *Knights Errant*, 14–17; Esenwein, *Anarchist Ideology*, 167, 188–199; Fleming, *Anarchist Way*, 213–14; Goyens, *Beer and Revolution*, 191; Merriman, *Dynamite*, 207–10; Pernicone and Ottanelli, *Assassins against the Old Order*, 77–89.

140. Kropotkin, *Direct Struggle*, 397.

Chapter 7: Mass Anarchism

1. Michael Schmidt and Lucien van der Walt, *Black Flame: The Revolutionary Class Politics of Anarchism and Syndicalism* (Oakland, CA: AK Press, 2009), 20, 124, 133–41.

2. Peter Kropotkin, *Direct Struggle Against Capital: A Peter Kropotkin Anthology*, ed. Iain McKay (Oakland, CA: AK Press, 2014), 318, 360.

3. Quoted in René Berthier, *Social Democracy and Anarchism in the International Workers' Association, 1864–1877* (London: Anarres Editions, 2015), 31.

4. Quoted in Berthier, *Social Democracy and Anarchism*, 31.

5. Michael Bakunin, *The Basic Bakunin: Writings 1869–1871*, ed. and trans. Robert M. Cutler (Buffalo, NY: Prometheus Books, 1985), 139.

6. Quoted in Nunzio Pernicone, *Italian Anarchism, 1864–1892* (Princeton: Princeton University Press, 1993), 178.

7. Maurizio Antonioli, ed. *The International Anarchist Congress Amsterdam (1907)* (Edmonton, AB: Black Cat Press 2009), 89–90. See also 83. In the original, Dunois uses the word "spontaneously." I altered the translation to "voluntarily," given how the French word "spontanément" was used by anarchists at the time.

8. Malatesta, *The Method of Freedom: An Errico Malatesta Reader*, ed. Davide Turcato (Oakland, CA: AK Press 2014), 163.

9. Malatesta, *Method of Freedom*, 163.

10. Errico Malatesta, *A Long and Patient Work: The Anarchist Socialism of L'Agitazione, 1897–1898*, ed. Davide Turcato (Chico, CA: AK Press, 2016), 158.

11. Malatesta, *Patient Work*, 158.

12. Malatesta, *Patient Work*, 148–54; Antonioli, ed. *International Anarchist Congress*, 98–100.

13. Malatesta, *Patient Work*, 153; Errico Malatesta, *Towards Anarchy: Malatesta in America, 1899–1900*, ed. Davide Turcato (Chico, CA: AK Press, 2019), 64, 73.

14. Ricardo Mella, *Anarchist Socialism in Early Twentieth-Century Spain: A Ricardo Mella Anthology*, ed. Stephen Luis Vilaseca (London: Palgrave Macmillan, 2020), 58–59.

15. Kropotkin, *Direct Struggle*, 474–75.

16. Max Baginski, *What Does Syndicalism Want? Living, Not Dead Unions* (London: Kate Sharpley Library, 2015), 18.

17. Rudolf Rocker, *Anarcho-Syndicalism: Theory and Practice* (Oakland, CA: AK Press, 2004), 60.

18. Rocker, *Anarcho-Syndicalism*, 61.

19. Rocker, *Anarcho-Syndicalism*, 61.

20. The following account is largely based on Malatesta, *Method of Freedom*, 63–65, 101–4; *Towards Anarchy*, 61–66, 73–74, 92–95, 130–35, 208–10. For the historical context of this debate, see Pietro Di Paola, *The Knights Errant of Anarchy: London and the Italian Anarchist Diaspora, 1880–1917* (Chico, CA: AK Press, 2017), 59–91; Davide Turcato, *Making Sense of Anarchism: Errico Malatesta's Experiments with Revolution, 1889–1900* (Basingstoke, UK: Palgrave Macmillan, 2012), 188–95.

21. Malatesta, *Method of Freedom*, 439–40.

22. Malatesta, *Towards Anarchy*, 63.

23. Malatesta, *Towards Anarchy*, 64, 73.

24. Malatesta, *Towards Anarchy*, 134; *Method of Freedom*, 489–90.

25. Malatesta, *Method of Freedom*, 489–90.

26. Malatesta, *Method of Freedom*, 63, 437–39; *Towards Anarchy*, 133–4; *Patient Work*, 42, 153.

27. José Peirats, *The CNT in the Spanish Revolution*, vol. 1 (Oakland, CA: PM Press, 2011), ed. Chris Ealham, 7–10, 93.

28. Murray Bookchin, *The Spanish Anarchists: The Heroic Years 1868–1936* (Oakland, CA: AK Press, 1998), 154–55, 164–65; Angel Smith, *Anarchism, Revolution and Reaction: Catalan Labor and the Crisis of the Spanish State, 1989–1923* (New York: Berghahn Books, 2007), 195, 237–49.

29. Danny Evans, private communication, June 27, 2020.

30. In 1931, the majority of delegates at the CNT's national congress voted to form national industrial federations, which would unite all the single unions in a given industry together. These were to exist in parallel to the other geographical federations that united workers from different industries together, based on their location. This decision was never implemented and was actively opposed by several anarchist delegates on the grounds that it would decrease the importance and autonomy of the local single unions. See Bookchin, *Spanish Anarchists*, 218–19; Stuart Christie, *We, the Anarchists! A Study of the Iberian Anarchist Federation (FAI), 1927–1937* (Oakland, CA: AK Press, 2008), 90–92; Peirats, *The CNT in the Spanish Revolution*, vol. 1, 33–37.

31. In 1934, Ángel Pestaña claimed that some local federations and local unions paid for two or three full-time delegates "off the record" and "under the table." I have been unable to verify this claim or discover how other members responded to these allegations. Quoted in Frank Mintz, *Anarchism and Workers' Self-Management in Revolutionary Spain* (Oakland, CA: AK Press, 2013), 54–55.

32. The higher committees of the CNT amassed far more power during the Spanish revolution and civil war of 1936–39. See Danny Evans, *Revolution and the State: Anarchism in the Spanish Civil War, 1936–1939* (Chico, CA: AK Press, 2020), 39–40, 45–49.

33. This account of how the CNT was organized is based on Bookchin, *Spanish Anarchists*, 144–46; Christie, *We, the Anarchists*, 11, 13, 73; Peirats, *The CNT in the Spanish Revolution*, vol. 1, 353n16; Evans, *Revolution and the State*, 12. For examples of CNT plenums see Peirats, *The CNT in the Spanish Revolution*, 52–53, 69–70, 255–56, 259–60.

34. Peirats, *The CNT in the Spanish Revolution*, vol. 1, 5. For the biographical details about Peirats, see Chris Ealham, *Living Anarchism: José Peirats and the Spanish Anarcho-Syndicalist Movement* (Oakland, CA: AK Press, 2015), 29–30, 141–42.

35. Quoted in Peirats, *What is the C.N.T?* (London: Simian, 1974), 19.

36. Ealham, *Living Anarchism*, 77; Agustín Guillamón, *Ready for Revolution: The CNT Defense Committees in Barcelona, 1933–1938* (Oakland, CA: AK Press, 2014), 28–29.

37. Ealham, *Living Anarchism*, 122–23.

38. Malatesta, *Method of Freedom*, 83; *Patient Work*, 155.

39. Chris Ealham: *Anarchism and the City: Revolution and Counter-Revolution in Barcelona, 1898–1937* (Oakland, CA: AK Press, 2010), 49–50; Guillamón, *Ready for Revolution*, 28–30.

40. Michael Bakunin, *Selected Texts, 1868–1875*, ed. A. W. Zurbrugg (London: Merlin Books, 2016), 49. See also, 138–41.

41. Quoted in Walther L. Bernecker, "The Strategies of 'Direct Action' and Violence in Spanish Anarchism," in *Social Protest, Violence and Terror in Nineteenth- and Twentieth-Century Europe*, ed. Wolfgang J. Mommsen and Gerhard Hirschfeld (London: The Macmillan Press, 1982), 90.

42. Quoted in Ralph Darlington, *Radical Unionism: The Rise and Fall of Revolutionary Syndicalism* (Chicago: Haymarket Books, 2013), 29.

43. Quoted in Peirats, *The CNT in the Spanish Revolution*, vol. 1, 39. Some trade unions within the CNT opposed the idea of a minimum program. See Bookchin, *Spanish Anarchists*, 218.

44. Malatesta, *Patient Work*, 281.

45. Malatesta, *Method of Freedom*, 82.

46. Malatesta, *Method of Freedom*, 181.

47. Malatesta, *Patient Work*, 182.

48.   Malatesta, *Patient Work*, 374.

49.   Malatesta, *Towards Anarchy*, 19, 23.

50.   Haia Shpayer-Makov, "Anarchism in British Public Opinion 1880–1914," *Victorian Studies* 31, no. 4 (1988): 487–516; Luigi Fabbri, *Bourgeois Influences on Anarchism* (Tucson, AZ: See Sharp Press, 2001).

51.   Quoted in Ulrich Linse, "'Propaganda by Deed' and 'Direct Action': Two Concepts of Anarchist Violence," in *Social Protest, Violence and Terror*, 215.

52.   Quoted in Kenyon Zimmer, *Immigrants Against the State: Yiddish and Italian Anarchism in America* (Urbana: University of Illinois Press, 2015), 34.

53.   Paul Avrich and Karen Avrich, *Sasha and Emma: The Anarchist Odyssey of Alexander Berkman and Emma Goldman* (Cambridge, MA: Harvard University Press, 2012), 87–90.

54.   Quoted in Avrich and Avrich, *Sasha and Emma*, 89.

55.   Quoted in Goyens, "Johann Most and the German Anarchists," in *Radical Gotham: Anarchism in New York City from Schwab's Saloon to Occupy Wall Street*, ed. Tom Goyens (Urbana: University of Illinois Press, 2017), 21–22. In response, Goldman attacked Most with a whip during one of his lectures. See Emma Goldman, *Living My Life*, vol. 1 (New York: Dover Publications, 1970), 105–6.

56.   Quoted in George Richard Esenwein, *Anarchist Ideology and the Working-Class Movement in Spain, 1868–1898* (Berkeley: University of California Press, 1989), 114.

57.   Malatesta, *Patient Work*, 319.

58.   Quoted in Pernicone, *Italian Anarchism*, 84. See also Malatesta, *Method of Freedom*, 526–29.

59.   Kropotkin, *Direct Struggle*, 150, 154.

60.   Kropotkin, *Direct Struggle*, 150.

61.   Peter Kropotkin, *Memoirs of a Revolutionist* (Montréal: Black Rose Books, 1989), 373.

62.   Quoted in Alexandre Skirda, *Facing the Enemy: A History of Anarchist Organization from Proudhon to May 1968* (Oakland CA: AK Press, 2002), 55. Kropotkin opposed the tactics of assassination and bombings within the Russian anarchist movement. See Martin A. Miller, *Kropotkin* (Chicago: University of Chicago Press, 1976), 206–07; Paul Avrich, *The Russian Anarchists* (Oakland, CA: AK Press, 2005), 59–60. For an overview of Russian anarchist's engaging in this kind of violence, see ibid., 44–55, 63–70.

63.   Malatesta, *Method of Freedom*, 176.

64.   Malatesta, *Towards Anarchy*, 49.

65.   Bakunin, *Selected Texts, 1868–1875*, 14; Malatesta, *Towards Anarchy*, 160; *Method of Freedom*, 470–71.

66.   Malatesta, *Towards Anarchy*, 49.

67.   Malatesta, *At the Café: Conversations on Anarchism* (London: Freedom Press, 2005), 82–83.

68. Kropotkin, *Direct Struggle*, 344. See also 315–33.

69. Malatesta, *Method of Freedom*, 179.

70. Malatesta, *Patient Work*, 101.

71. Malatesta, *Towards Anarchy*, 67.

72. Malatesta, *Patient Work*, 25.

73. Goldman, *Living My Life*, vol. 1, 47–48, 52–53.

74. Rudolf Rocker, *The London Years* (Nottingham, UK: Five Leaves, 2005), 25–26.

75. Kropotkin, *Direct Struggle*, 309; Malatesta, *Patient Work*, 156, 189.

76. Quoted in David Berry, *A History of the French Anarchist Movement: 1917 to 1945* (Oakland, CA: AK Press, 2009), 26.

77. Baginski, *What Does Syndicalism Want*, 11.

78. Baginski, *What Does Syndicalism Want*, 10–12, 15–16.

79. Max Baginski, "Aim and Tactics of the Trade-Union Movement," in *Anarchy: An Anthology of Emma Goldman's Mother Earth*, ed. Peter Glassgold, (New York: Counterpoint, 2000), 305.

80. Rocker, *Anarcho-Syndicalism*, 78.

81. Rocker, *Anarcho-Syndicalism*, 79.

82. Rocker, *Anarcho-Syndicalism*, 79.

83. Rocker, *Anarcho-Syndicalism*, 79.

84. Malatesta, *Patient Work*, 287.

85. Malatesta, *Patient Work*, 320.

86. Malatesta, *Method of Freedom*, 106.

87. Malatesta, *Towards Anarchy*, 55.

88. Kropotkin, *Direct Struggle*, 145–46.

89. Malatesta, *Method of Freedom*, 427.

90. Malatesta, *Towards Anarchy*, 49.

91. Malatesta, *Patient Work*, 320.

92. Malatesta, *Towards Anarchy*, 168. See also Malatesta, *The Anarchist Revolution: Polemical Articles, 1924–1931*, ed. Vernon Richards (London: Freedom Press, 1995), 80; Kropotkin, *Direct Struggle*, 293–94.

93. Michael Bakunin, *Statism and Anarchy* (Cambridge: Cambridge University Press, 1990), ed. Marshall Shatz, 114, 25. For another example, see Malatesta, *Towards Anarchy*, 98–103.

94. Emma Goldman, *Red Emma Speaks: An Emma Goldman Reader*, ed. Alix Kates Shulman, 3rd ed. (Atlantic Highlands, NJ: Humanities Press, 1996), 190–203.

95. Malatesta, *Anarchist Revolution*, 81.

96. Quoted in Caroline Cahm, *Kropotkin and the Rise of Revolutionary Anarchism, 1872–1886* (Cambridge: Cambridge University Press, 1989), 226.

97. Malatesta, *Patient Work*, 443. See also Malatesta, *Towards Anarchy*, 67–69.

98. Ealham, *Living Anarchism*, 57–59.

99. Christie, *We, the Anarchists*, 18–22; Ealham, *Anarchism and the City*, 48–51;

Guillamón, *Ready for Revolution*, 31–32; Peirats, *CNT in the Spanish Revolution*, vol. 1, 11–6; For an in-depth overview of this topic, see A. Smith, *Anarchism, Revolution and Reaction*, 210–11, 250–53, 300–301, 312, 316–17, 323–37, 343–49, 351.

100. A. Smith, *Anarchism, Revolution and Reaction*, 337.

101. Ealham, *Anarchism and the City*, 98.

102. Ealham, *Anarchism and the City*, 144–48, 163; *Living Anarchism*, 66–67. It should be noted that some of the robberies were carried out by self-described individualist anarchist affinity groups.

103. Jason Garner, *Goals and Means: Anarchism, Syndicalism, and Internationalism in the Origins of the Federación Anarquista Ibérica* (Chico, CA: AK Press, 2016), 139–45; Ealham, *Anarchism and the City*, 87–89, 100–1, 130–40, 161–64; *Living Anarchism*, 60–70; Evans, *Revolution and the State*, 7–10, 15–23; Jerome R. Mintz, *The Anarchists of Casas Viejas* (Bloomington: Indiana University Press, 2004), 177–225. It has been argued by Christie that the moderate syndicalist anarchists were not in fact anarchists or only paid lip service to anarchism. I have not been convinced by this claim. See Christie, *We, the Anarchists*, vii, 15, 26–28, 59–65, 68–73, 84–87, 93–94, 100–121.

104. Malatesta, *Method of Freedom*, 529.

105. Quoted in David Berry, *A History of the French Anarchist Movement: 1917 to 1945* (Oakland, CA: AK Press, 2009), 23.

106. Quoted in Berry, *French Anarchist Movement*, 23.

107. Malatesta, *Café*, 107, 149, 155; *Method of Freedom*, 344, 529.

108. Alexander Berkman, *What is Anarchism?* (Oakland, CA: AK Press, 2003), 114.

109. Ealham, *Anarchism and the City*, 41.

110. Luigi Fabbri, "Anarchy and 'Scientific' Communism," in *Bloodstained: One Hundred Years of Leninist Counterrevolution*, ed. Friends of Aron Baron (Chico, CA: AK Press, 2017), 16. For an overview of the class composition of anarchist and syndicalist movements around the world, see Schmidt and van der Walt, *Black Flame*, 271–91.

111. Antonioli, ed. *International Anarchist Congress*, 87–88.

112. Malatesta, *Patient Work*, 325.

113. Malatesta, *Patient Work*, 443.

114. Turcato, *Making Sense*, 163–68; Pernicone, *Italian Anarchism*, 261–67.

115. Rocker, *London Years*, 62–63.

116. Rocker, *London Years*, 90.

117. Rocker, *London Years*, 126–31.

118. J. Mintz, *Casas Viejas*, 14–16, 29–31, 79–80, 83–85.

119. Di Paola, *Knights Errant*, 34–35, 95–96, 111–13, 205.

120. John Quail, *The Slow Burning Fuse: The Lost History of British Anarchists* (London: Granada Publishing Limited, 1978), 250–51. Anarchists were able

to more effectively organize unemployed people in the United States. See Avrich and Avrich, *Sasha and Emma*, 217–23.

121. Malatesta, *Anarchist Revolution*, 81.

122. Voline, "Synthesis (anarchist)," in *The Anarchist Encyclopedia Abridged*, ed. Mitchell Abidor (Chico, CA: AK Press, 2019), 202–3.

123. Malatesta, *Towards Anarchy*, 56.

124. Malatesta, *Method of Freedom*, 176.

125. Malatesta, *Anarchist Revolution*, 110–11.

126. Kropotkin, *Direct Struggle*, 332.

127. Kropotkin, *Direct Struggle*, 348. See also Mella, *Anarchist Socialism*, 62–64.

128. Malatesta, *Method of Freedom*, 179.

129. Malatesta, *Method of Freedom*, 87.

130. Malatesta, *Towards Anarchy*, 41–42; *Patient Work*, 190.

131. Kropotkin, *Direct Struggle*, 554.

132. Goldman, *Red Emma*, 390–91, 395.

133. Goldman, *Red Emma*, 393.

134. Malatesta, *Anarchist Revolution*, 88–89.

135. Kropotkin, *Rebel*, 75; Kropotkin, *Direct Struggle*, 553–55.

136. Kropotkin, *Direct Struggle*, 578.

137. Kropotkin, *Direct Struggle*, 578.

138. Errico Malatesta, *Life and Ideas: The Anarchist Writings of Errico Malatesta*, ed. Vernon Richards (Oakland, CA: PM Press, 2015), 186.

139. Malatesta, *Life and Ideas*, 187. To compare these sections to the previous 1899 version, see Malatesta, *Towards Anarchy*, 55–56.

140. Malatesta, *Method of Freedom*, 472.

Chapter 8: The History of Syndicalist Anarchism

1.   George Richard Esenwein, *Anarchist Ideology and the Working-Class Movement in Spain, 1868–1898* (Berkeley: University of California Press, 1989), 118; Errico Malatesta, *A Long and Patient Work: The Anarchist Socialism of L'Agitazione, 1897–1898*, ed. Davide Turcato (Chico, CA: AK Press, 2016), 104; Errico Malatesta, *The Method of Freedom: An Errico Malatesta Reader*, ed. Davide Turcato (Oakland, CA: AK Press 2014), 170, 172, 338, 463.

2.   Wayne Thorpe, "Uneasy Family: Revolutionary Syndicalism in Europe From the Charte d'Amiens to World War One," in *New Perspectives on Anarchism, Labour and Syndicalism: The Individual, the National and the Transnational*, ed. David Berry and Constance Bantman (Newcastle, UK: Cambridge Scholars Publishing, 2010), 25–26.

3.   Marcel van der Linden and Wayne Thorpe, "The Rise and Fall of Revolutionary Syndicalism," in *Revolutionary Syndicalism: An International Perspective*, ed Marcel van der Linden and Wayne Thorpe (Aldershot, UK: Scolar Press,

1990), 1–2; Lucien van der Walt, "Syndicalism" in *The Palgrave Handbook of Anarchism*, ed. Carl Levy and Matthew S. Adams (London: Palgrave Macmillan, 2019), 249–50.

4. The language of "syndicalism-plus" was coined by Iain McKay, "Communism and Syndicalism," Anarchist Writers website, May 25, 2012. http://anarchism.pageabode.com/anarcho/communism-syndicalism. Thanks to McKay for suggesting this phrase to me.

5. César De Paepe, "Strikes, Unions, and the Affiliation of Unions with the International" in *Workers Unite! The International 150 Years Later*, ed. Marcello Musto (New York: Bloomsbury Academic, 2014), 128.

6. De Paepe, "Strikes, Unions, and the Affiliation of Unions with the International," 128–29.

7. Raymond W. Postgate, ed. "Debates and Resolutions of the First International on The Control of Industry," in *Revolution from 1789 to 1906* (Boston: Houghton Mifflin Company, 1921), 393–94.

8. César De Paepe, "The Present Institutions of the International in Relation to the Future," trans. Shawn P. Wilbur, Libertarian Labyrinth website, March 20, 2018, https://www.libertarian-labyrinth.org/working-translations/the-present-institutions-of-the-international-from-the-point-of-view-of-the-future-1869.

9. Eckhardt, *First Socialist Schism*, 193; Musto, ed. *Workers Unite*, 138n28.

10. Adhémar Schwitzguébel, "On Resistance Funds," in *Workers Unite!*, 138–39.

11. Julian P. W. Archer, *The First International in France, 1864–1872: Its Origins, Theories, and Impact* (Lanham, MD: University Press of America, 1997), 166–75; Robert Graham, *We Do Not Fear Anarchy, We Invoke It: The First International and the Origins of the Anarchist Movement* (Oakland, CA: AK Press, 2015), 117–19.

12. Jean-Louis Pindy, "Resolution on Resistance Funds," in *Workers Unite!*, 133.

13. Jean-Louis Pindy, "Resolution on Resistance Funds," 133.

14. Eugène Varlin, "Workers Societies," trans. Iain McKay, Anarchist Writers website, October 6, 2018. https://anarchism.pageabode.com/precursors-of-syndicalism.

15. Eugène Varlin, "Workers Societies."

16. Michael Bakunin, *Selected Texts, 1868–1875*, ed. A. W. Zurbrugg (London: Merlin Books, 2016), 56.

17. Bakunin, *Selected Texts*, 56.

18. Bakunin, *Selected Texts*, 56.

19. Quoted in Max Nettlau, *A Short History of Anarchism*, ed. Heiner M. Becker (London: Freedom Press, 1996), 122.

20. Quoted in Wolfgang Eckhardt, *The First Socialist Schism: Bakunin vs. Marx in the International Working Men's Association* (Oakland, CA: PM Press, 2016), 54.

21. Eckhardt, *First Socialist Schism*, 159–60.

22. "Resolutions of the Saint-Imier Congress of the International Workers' Association, 15–16 September 1872," in Appendix to René Berthier, *Social*

Democracy and Anarchism in the International Workers' Association, 1864–1877 (London: Anarres Editions, 2015), 182.

23. "Resolutions of the Saint-Imier Congress," 182–83.

24. "Resolutions of the Congresses of Verviers, 5 to 8 September 1877, and Ghent, 9 to 14 September 1877," in Appendix to Berthier, *Social Democracy and Anarchism*, 190–91.

25. Malatesta, *Method of Freedom*, 56. Malatesta appears to have previously opposed participating in trade unions at the 1876 Berne Congress of the Saint-Imier International. It is unclear when he changed his mind, because most of the articles he wrote in this period are currently untranslated. See Caroline Cahm, *Kropotkin and the Rise of Revolutionary Anarchism, 1872–1886* (Cambridge: Cambridge University Press, 1989), 229.

26. Peter Kropotkin, *Direct Struggle Against Capital: A Peter Kropotkin Anthology*, ed. Iain McKay (Oakland, CA: AK Press, 2014), 294.

27. Kropotkin, *Direct Struggle*, 299.

28. Kropotkin, *Direct Struggle*, 299.

29. Esenwein, *Anarchist Ideology*, 80–4. The trade union was forced to suspend its activities in 1884 in response to state repression and was replaced by a new organization in 1888. See ibid., 84–97, 117–22.

30. Paul Avrich, *The Haymarket Tragedy* (Princeton: Princeton University Press, 1984), 72–73, 89–92, 181–88.

31. Carl Levy, *Gramsci and the Anarchists* (Oxford: Berg, 1999), 19–20; Antonio Senta, *Luigi Galleani: The Most Dangerous Anarchist in America* (Chico, CA: AK Press, 2019), 18–19, 24–29.

32. Ángel J. Cappelletti, *Anarchism in Latin America* (Chico, CA: AK Press, 2017), 52, 56, 116–18, 120–1, 172–73, 203–5, 273–76; Steven Hirsch and Lucien van der Walt, eds., *Anarchism and Syndicalism in the Colonial and Postcolonial World, 1870–1940: The Praxis of National Liberation, Internationalism, and Social Revolution* (Leiden: Brill, 2010), xl–xliii; Frank Fernández, *Cuban Anarchism: The History of a Movement*, trans. Charles Bufe (Tucson, AZ: See Sharp Press, 2001), 19–29, 40–41; John M. Hart, *Anarchism and the Mexican Working Class 1860–1931* (Austin: University of Texas Press, 1978), 46–59, 75–80, 83–84.

33. Constance Bantman, "From Trade Unionism to Syndicalisme Révolutionnaire to Syndicalism: The British Origins of French Syndicalism" in *New Perspectives on Anarchism, Labour and Syndicalism*, 128–132; Constance Bantman, *The French Anarchists in London, 1880–1914: Exile and Transnationalism in the First Globalisation* (Liverpool: Liverpool University Press, 2013), 40–41; Bantman, "The Militant Go-between: Émile Pouget's Transnational Propaganda (1880–1914)," *Labour History Review* 74, no. 3 (2009): 279–80; Davide Turcato, *Making Sense of Anarchism: Errico Malatesta's Experiments with Revolution, 1889–1900* (Basingstoke, UK: Palgrave Macmillan, 2012), 36–42; Henry Pelling, *A History of British Trade Unionism*, 5th ed. (Basingstoke, UK: Palgrave Macmillan, 1992), 94–96.

34. Malatesta, *Method of Freedom*, 76–77.

35. Vadim Damier, *Anarcho-Syndicalism in the Twentieth Century* (Edmonton, AB: Black Cat Press, 2009), 13; F. F. Ridley, *Revolutionary Syndicalism in France: The Direct Action of Its Time* (Cambridge: Cambridge University Press, 1970), 20–23, 65, 74–75; Jeremy Jennings, *Syndicalism in France: A Study of Ideas* (Basingstoke, UK: Macmillan, 1990), 11; Fernand Pelloutier, "Anarchism and the Workers' Union," in *No Gods, No Masters: An Anthology of Anarchism*, ed. Daniel Guérin (Oakland, CA: AK Press, 2005), 409.

36. Kropotkin *Direct Struggle*, 317–39.

37. Jennings, *Syndicalism in France*, 24–26; Turcato, *Making Sense*, 134–35; Bantman, "The British Origins of French Syndicalism," 132–35.

38. Pelloutier, "Anarchism and the Workers' Union," 409–15. See also Paul Delesalle, "Anarchists and the Trade Unions," Libcom website, December 9, 2013, https://libcom.org/article/anarchists-and-trade-unions-paul-delesalle.

39. Quoted in David Berry, *A History of the French Anarchist Movement: 1917 to 1945* (Oakland, CA: AK Press, 2009), 24.

40. Emma Goldman, *Red Emma Speaks: An Emma Goldman Reader*, ed. Alix Kates Shulman, 3rd ed. (Atlantic Highlands, NJ: Humanities Press, 1996), 90. For Goldman's in-depth description of her visit to Paris in 1900, see Emma Goldman, *Living My Life*, vol. 1 (New York: Dover Publications, 1970), 264–80, 401. Her views on syndicalism were also influenced by her later visit to Paris in 1907. See ibid., 406–07.

41. Wayne Thorpe, *"The Workers Themselves": Revolutionary Syndicalism and International Labour 1913–1923* (Dordrecht, NL: Kluwer Academic Publishers, 1989), 25. For details see Ridley, *Revolutionary Syndicalism in France*, 63–71; Phil H. Goodstein, *The Theory of the General Strike from the French Revolution to Poland* (Boulder, CO: East European Monographs, 1984), 53–59; Émile Pouget, "The Party of Labour," Libcom website, November 19, 2010, https://libcom.org/article/party-labour-emile-pouget.

42. Ridley, *Revolutionary Syndicalism in France*, 77–79.

43. Damier, *Anarcho*-Syndicalism, 15; Wayne Thorpe, *"The Workers Themselves,"* 26–27. For an in-depth overview of reformist syndicalism, see Jennings, *Syndicalism in France*, 114–40.

44. Jennings, *Syndicalism in France*, 24, 138, 145–46; Berry, *French Anarchist Movement*, 32n37. According to Joll, anarchists only seriously influenced the CGT "for ten or fifteen years" and had little influence within the CGT after 1914. James Joll, *The Anarchists* (London: Methuen, 1969), 216.

45. Thorpe, *Workers Themselves*, 27; Jennings, *Syndicalism in France*, 137.

46. Quoted in A.W. Zurbrugg, *Anarchist Perspectives in Peace and War, 1900–1918* (London: Anarres Editions, 2018), 42.

47. Quoted in Zurbrugg, *Anarchist Perspectives*, 42.

48. Jennings, *Syndicalism in France*, 134, 137–140; Ridley, *Revolutionary Syndicalism in France*, 88–94, 180.

49. Nicholas Papayanis, *Alphonse Merrheim: The Emergence of Reformism in Revolutionary Syndicalism, 1871–1925* (Dordrecht, NL: Martinus Nijhoff Publishers, 1985), 39–41, 44–45.

50. Quoted in Jennings, *Syndicalism in France*, 30–31.

51. Pouget, "The Party of Labour."

52. Maurizio Antonioli, ed. *The International Anarchist Congress Amsterdam (1907)* (Edmonton, AB: Black Cat Press 2009), 115.

53. Antonioli, ed. *International Anarchist Congress*, 115.

54. Émile Pouget, "The Basis of Trade Unionism," Libcom website, November 19, 2010, https://libcom.org/article/basis-trade-unionism-emile-pouget.

55. For a broad overview of these movements see Marcel van der Linden and Wayne Thorpe, eds., *Revolutionary Syndicalism: An International Perspective* (Aldershot, UK: Scolar Press, 1990).

56. Damier, *Anarcho-Syndicalism in the 20th Century*, 34–37, 57–63; Cappelletti, *Anarchism in Latin America*, 165, 173-74, 284–85; Hirsch and van der Walt, eds., *Anarchism and Syndicalism in the Colonial and Postcolonial World*; Peter Cole, David Struthers, and Kenyon Zimmer, eds., *Wobblies of the World: A Global History of the IWW*, (London: Pluto Press, 2017).

57. Kenyon Zimmer, *Immigrants Against the State: Yiddish and Italian Anarchism in America* (Urbana: University of Illinois Press, 2015), 75–79, 83–87.

58. Cappelletti, *Anarchism in Latin America*, 51–65; Juan Suriano, *Paradoxes of Utopia: Anarchist Culture and Politics in Buenos Aires, 1890–1910* (Oakland, CA: AK Press, 2010), 14–16.

59. Quoted in Angel Smith, *Anarchism, Revolution and Reaction: Catalan Labor and the Crisis of the Spanish State, 1989–1923* (New York: Berghahn Books, 2007), 142n44.

60. Quoted in A. Smith, *Anarchism, Revolution and Reaction*, 129. For details about how syndicalism became the dominant position in Spain during the early 1900s, see James Yeoman, *Print Culture and the Formation of the Anarchist Movement in Spain, 1890–1915* (New York: Routledge, 2020), 198–249.

61. Pouget, "The Party of Labour."

62. Antonioli, ed., *International Anarchist Congress*, 122.

63. Quoted in Nettlau, *Short History*, 279. See also Kropotkin, *Direct Struggle*, 392, 403–11; Rudolf Rocker, *Anarcho-Syndicalism: Theory and Practice* (Oakland, CA: AK Press, 2004), 52–3; Maxim Raevsky, *Anarcho-Syndicalism and the IWW* (Edmonton, AB: Black Cat Press, 2019), 1–2.

64. Karl Kautsky, *Road to Power* (Chicago: Samuel A. Bloch, 1909), 61, 95.

65. Wayne Thorpe, "Uneasy Family," 17n2. It has been alleged by Albert Meltzer that the term was first coined by the Welsh anarchist Sam Mainwaring (1841–1907) in order to distinguish between British syndicalists, who did not think of themselves as anarchists, and syndicalists in continental Europe who self-identified as anarchists. He does not provide a source or a date for when this occurred. I have been unable to verify this claim or determine, if true,

what Mainwaring meant by anarcho-syndicalism. Meltzer claimed he was told the information by Emma Goldman. See Albert Meltzer, *The Anarchists in London, 1935–1955* (London: Cienfuegos Press, 1976), 10; Kenneth John, "Anti-Parliamentary Passage: South Wales and the Internationalism of Sam Mainwaring (1841–1907)" (PhD diss., University of Greenwich, 2001), 109–10.

66. Quoted in Cappelletti, *Anarchism in Latin America*, 64. In 1915, there was a split within the FORA between the FORA-V, which remained committed to the anarchist program of the fifth congress, and the FORA-IX, which endorsed a politically neutral program. See ibid., 66–68, 74.

67. Alexandre Skirda, *Facing the Enemy: A History of Anarchist Organization from Proudhon to May 1968* (Oakland CA: AK Press, 2002), 76–78; Paul Avrich, *The Russian Anarchists* (Oakland, CA: AK Press, 2005), 61–62, 77–78; Daniil Novomirsky, *Anarchism's Trade Union Programme*, trans. Paul Sharkey, Kate Sharpley Library website, https://www.katesharpleylibrary.net/3bk4c0. In these translations, the phrase "anarcho-syndicalism" is used. This is an error. In the original Russian only the phrase "syndicalist anarchism" appears. Thanks to Kenyon Zimmer for showing this to me.

68. Quoted in Skirda, *Facing the Enemy*, 77; Novomirsky, *Anarchism's Trade Union Programme*. In Skirda, the Russian for "revolutionary trade union" has been translated as "revolutionary syndicalist movement." To avoid potential confusion with revolutionary syndicalism in the distinct CGT sense, I have decided to alter the translation. See also N. Rogdaev, "On the Anarchist Movement in Russia," in *The International Anarchist Congress Amsterdam*, 191.

69. Antonioli, ed., *International Anarchist Congress*, 115.

70. Golos Truda, "Declaration of the Petrograd Union of Anarcho-Syndicalist Propaganda," in *The Anarchists in the Russian Revolution*, ed. Paul Avrich (London: Thames and Hudson, 1973), 71. For the history of anarcho-syndicalism in the Russian revolution, see Avrich, *Russian Anarchists*, 135–51, 185, 190–95; Thorpe, *Workers Themselves*, 98–100, 163–64.

71. The Group of Russian Anarchists Abroad, "The Organizational Platform of the General Union of Anarchists (Draft)," in Skirda, *Facing the Enemy*, 204.

72. Alexander Schapiro, "Introduction to Anarcho-Syndicalism and Anarchism," trans. Paul Sharkey, Robert Graham's Anarchism Weblog, March 15, 2009, https://robertgraham.wordpress.com/alexander-schapiro-pierre -besnard-anarcho-syndicalism-and-anarchism. For an overview of Schapiro's activity during the Russian revolution, see Thorpe, *Workers Themselves*, 238–44.

73. Thorpe, *Workers Themselves*, 53–80. The CNT as a national organization could not attend the congress because it had been made illegal in 1911 and was still in the process of reorganizing itself.

74. "The London Declaration (1913)," in Appendix to Thorpe, *Workers Themselves*, 320.

75. Damier, *Anarcho-Syndicalism*, 43–46, 64–84. For details about the CGT and World War I, including the minority within the CGT who remained

internationalists, see Jennings, *Syndicalism in France*, 161–67; Nicholas
Papayanis, *Alphonse Merrheim*, 85–110.

76. Juan Gómez Casas, *Anarchists Organization: The History of the F.A.I* (Mont-réal: Black Rose Books, 1986), 56; Stuart Christie, *We, the Anarchists! A Study of the Iberian Anarchist Federation (FAI) 1927–1937* (Oakland, CA: AK Press, 2008), 7–11.

77. Quoted in José Peirats, *The CNT in the Spanish Revolution*, vol. 1 (Oakland, CA: PM Press, 2011), ed. Chris Ealham, 10. For more information on the La Comedia Congress, see Casas, *The History of the F.A.I*, 57–60; A. Smith, *Anarchism, Revolution and Reaction*, 313–15

78. Quoted in Peirats, *The CNT in the Spanish Revolution*, vol. 1, 8–9. The CNT's commitment to achieving libertarian communism was reaffirmed at the 1924 Granollers Congress where 236 delegates voted in favor and only one against. See Christie, *We, the Anarchists*, 25.

79. Thorpe, *Workers Themselves*, 120–23; Rudolf Rocker, "Declaration of the Principles of Syndicalism," trans. Cord-Christian Casper, Academia.edu web-site, https://www.academia.edu/39134774/Rudolf_Rocker_Syndicalist_Declaration_of_Principles. For an account of his imprisonment, see Rudolf Rocker, *The London Years* (Nottingham, UK: Five Leaves, 2005), 142–215.

80. Rocker, "Declaration of the Principles of Syndicalism," 2.

81. Rocker, "Declaration of the Principles of Syndicalism," 3.

82. For an overview of the congress see Jason Garner, *Goals and Means: Anar-chism, Syndicalism, and Internationalism in the Origins of the Federación Anarquista Ibérica* (Chico, CA: AK Press, 2016), 113–27; Thorpe, *Workers Themselves*, 244–56, 313n13.

83. Garner, *Goals and Means*, 126, 306n52; Thorpe, *Workers Themselves*, 120–23, 224–26, 253.

84. Thorpe, *Workers Themselves*, chapters 3–7. For overviews of the congresses of the Comintern and RILU, see ibid., 100–106, 132–45, 181–94.

85. IWA, "Declaration of the Principles of Revolutionary Syndicalism," in *Anarchism: A Documentary History of Libertarian Ideas*, vol. 1, *From Anarchy to Anarchism (300 CE to 1939)*, ed. Robert Graham (Montréal: Black Rose Books, 2005), 418, 416. This version of the text refers to "libertarian com-munism." I have altered the translation because Rocker in fact used the term "free communism" in the 1922 declaration, the 1920 Berlin declaration, and the 1919 speech at the founding of the FAUD it was based on. This is signifi-cant because "libertarian" means anarchist, while "free communism" could potentially be supported by people who identified as syndicalists but not anarchists. See Thorpe, *Workers Themselves*, 321, 322; Rocker, "Declaration of the Principles of Syndicalism," 2.

86. IWA, "Declaration of the Principles of Revolutionary Syndicalism (1922)," 416–17.

87. IWA, "Declaration of the Principles of Revolutionary Syndicalism (1922)," 418.

88. Thorpe mistakenly claims that the Regional Workers' Federation of Brazil

affiliated. An organization with this name was founded in 1905 but changed its name to the Workers' Federation of Rio de Janeiro after the founding of the Brazilian Workers' Confederation (COB) in 1906. The COB ceased to exist in 1915. Some surviving regional federations of the COB went onto affiliate with the IWMA. Thanks to Maurício Knevitz for explaining this to me.

89. Thorpe, *Workers Themselves*, 256–67; Thorpe, "The IWW and the Dilemmas of Internationalism" in *Wobblies of the World*, 105–123.

90. Rocker, *Anarcho-Syndicalism*, 104, 115. See also Thorpe, *Workers Themselves*, 267.

91. Ole Birk Laursen, "'Anarchism, Pure and Simple': M. P. T. Acharya, Anti-Colonialism and the International Anarchist Movement," *Postcolonial Studies* 23, no. 2 (2020): 1, 7.

92. Malatesta, *Method of Freedom*, 464.

93. Luigi Fabbri, "About a Project of Anarchist Organization," Institute for Anarchist Theory and History website, n.d., https://ithanarquista.wordpress .com/about-a-project-for-anarchist-organization-luigi-fabbri.

94. Sébastien Faure, "The Anarchist Synthesis: The Three Great Anarchist Currents," trans. Shawn P. Wilbur, Libertarian Labyrinth website, August 3, 2017, https://www.libertarian-labyrinth.org/anarchist-beginnings/sebastien -faure-the-anarchist-synthesis-1828.

95. Quoted in Garner, *Goals and Means*, 151. For biographical information on Fernández, see ibid., 314n37. The phrase "anarcho-syndicalism" appears to have only become popular in Spain in the late 1920s. See Frank Mintz, *Anarchism and Workers' Self-Management in Revolutionary Spain* (Oakland, CA: AK Press, 2013), 286; Garner, *Goals and Means*, 64.

96. Berry, *French Anarchist Movement*, 150–53.

97. Berry, *French Anarchist Movement*, 152.

98. Pierre Besnard, "Anarcho-Syndicalism and Anarchism," trans. Paul Sharkey, Robert Graham's Anarchism Weblog, March 15, 2009, https://robertgraham .wordpress.com/alexander-schapiro-pierre-besnard-anarcho-syndicalism -and-anarchism.

99. Rocker, *Anarcho-Syndicalism*, 54.

100. Rocker, *Anarcho-Syndicalism*, 60.

101. Rocker, *Anarchism and Anarcho-Syndicalism* (London: Freedom Press, 1988), 5–6, 25, 31.

102. Rocker, "Declaration of the Principles of Syndicalism," 3–4; IWA, "Declaration of the Principles of Revolutionary Syndicalism," 416–18; Rocker, *Anarcho-Syndicalism*, 54.

Chapter 9: The Theory and Practice of Syndicalist Anarchism

1. Rudolf Rocker, *Anarcho-Syndicalism: Theory and Practice* (Oakland, CA: AK Press, 2004), 56–57.

2.   Pouget, "What is the Trade Union?," in *No Gods, No Masters: An Anthology of Anarchism*, ed. Daniel Guérin (Oakland, CA: AK Press, 2005), 432–33.

3.   Pouget, "What is the Trade Union?," 434.

4.   Émile Pouget, *Direct Action* (London: Kate Sharpley Library, 2003), 10–13.

5.   Errico Malatesta, *Towards Anarchy: Malatesta in America, 1899–1900*, ed. Davide Turcato (Chico, CA: AK Press, 2019), 51.

6.   Jeremy Jennings, *Syndicalism in France: A Study of Ideas* (Basingstoke, UK: Macmillan, 1990), 16–17. During the Saint-Imier International, Guillaume advocated the general strike while being wary of partial strikes for increased wages because he thought they were unlikely to succeed and could instead bring suffering to workers and sap their revolutionary spirit. See Caroline Cahm, *Kropotkin and the Rise of Revolutionary Anarchism, 1872–1886* (Cambridge: Cambridge University Press, 1989), 222–25.

7.   Paul Delesalle, "The Strike!," Libcom website, December 9, 2013, https://lib com.org/library/strike-paul-delesalle. For other examples, see Paul Delesalle, "Anarchists and the Trade Unions," Libcom website, December 9, 2013, https://libcom.org/article/anarchists-and-trade-unions-paul-delesalle; Alexander Berkman, *What is Anarchism?* (Oakland, CA: AK Press, 2003), 78–79, 197–210.

8.   Rocker, *Anarcho-Syndicalism*, 84. For the history of sabotage as a strategy see Jennings, *Syndicalism in France*, 44–46; F. F. Ridley, *Revolutionary Syndicalism in France: The Direct Action of Its Time* (Cambridge: Cambridge University Press, 1970), 120–23; Dominique Pinsolle, "Sabotage, the IWW, and Repression: How the American Reinterpretation of a French Concept Gave Rise to a New International Conception of Sabotage," in *Wobblies of the World: A Global History of the IWW*, ed. Peter Cole, David Struthers, and Kenyon Zimmer (London: Pluto Press, 2017), 44–58.

9.   Ridley, *Revolutionary Syndicalism in France*, 132–33; Nicholas Papayanis, *Alphonse Merrheim: The Emergence of Reformism in Revolutionary Syndicalism, 1871–1925* (Dordrecht, NL: Martinus Nijhoff Publishers, 1985), 20–30, 116–17, 121, 137. Nicholas Papayanis, "Alphones Merrheim and the Strike of Hennebont: The Struggle for the Eight-Hour Day in France," *International Review of Social History* 16, no. 2 (1971): 159–83. Spanish trade unionists, including anarchists, also organized a general strike for the eight-hour day on May 1, 1906, after being inspired by the CGT's campaign. See Angel Smith, *Anarchism, Revolution and Reaction: Catalan Labor and the Crisis of the Spanish State, 1989–1923* (New York: Berghahn Books, 2007), 130–31.

10.   The following account of the strike is based on Murray Bookchin, *The Spanish Anarchists: The Heroic Years, 1868–1936* (Oakland, CA: AK Press, 1998), 160–63; A. Smith, *Anarchism, Revolution and Reaction*, 292–99.

11.   It should be kept in mind that, even after this legislation was passed, workers went on strike to demand that the eight-hour day was implemented. See A. Smith, *Anarchism, Revolution and Reaction*, 302–3.

12. Nick Rider, "The Practice of Direct Action: The Barcelona Rent Strike of 1931," in *For Anarchism: History, Theory and Practice*, ed. David Goodway (London: Routledge, 1989), 87.

13. Quoted in Rider, "The Barcelona Rent Strike of 1931," 88.

14. The following account is based on Rider, "The Barcelona Rent Strike of 1931," 88–98; Chris Ealham: *Anarchism and the City: Revolution and Counter-Revolution in Barcelona, 1898–1937* (Oakland, CA: AK Press, 2010), 105–7, 112–18, 120. There had been earlier attempts by Spanish anarchists to organize tenants in 1903–4 and 1917–18. See A. Smith, *Anarchism, Revolution and Reaction*, 162, 265–66.

15. Milly Witkop-Rocker, "What Does the Syndicalist Women's Union Want?," trans. Jesse Cohn, Anarchist Library website, n.d., https://theanarchist library.org/library/milly-witkop-rocker-what-does-the-syndicalist-women -s-union-want.

16. Milly Witkop-Rocker, "What Does the Syndicalist Women's Union Want?"

17. Dieter Nelles, "Anarchosyndicalism and the Sexual Reform Movement in the Weimar Republic" (paper presented at the Free Love and Labour Movement workshop at the International Institute of Social History, Amsterdam, 2000).

18. Pouget, "What is the Trade Union?," 433.

19. Emma Goldman, *Red Emma Speaks: An Emma Goldman Reader*, ed. Alix Kates Shulman, 3rd ed. (Atlantic Highlands, NJ: Humanities Press, 1996), 91.

20. Pouget, *Direct Action*, 6.

21. Pouget, "What is the Trade Union?," 435.

22. Pouget, "What is the Trade Union?," 435.

23. Gregori P. Maximoff, *Program of Anarcho-Syndicalism* (n.p., Guillotine Press, 2015), 50–51.

24. Rocker, *Anarcho-Syndicalism*, 60.

25. IWW, "The Preamble to the Constitution of the Industrial Workers of the World (1908)," in *Rebel Voices: An IWW Anthology*, ed Joyce L. Kornbluh (Oakland, CA: PM Press, 2011), 13.

26. There are important exceptions to this generalization. The Argentinean FORA opposed the idea that the structure of the future society could be constructed within capitalism. Malatesta also argued in 1922 that trade unions were not establishing the framework of the future society due to the extent to which they were divided according to the capitalist division of labor. See Vadim Damier, *Anarcho-Syndicalism in the Twentieth Century* (Edmonton, AB: Black Cat Press, 2009), 102–4, 107–8; Errico Malatesta, *Life and Ideas: The Anarchist Writings of Errico Malatesta*, ed. Vernon Richards (Oakland, CA: PM Press, 2015), 113–14.

27. Quoted in Albert Parsons, *Anarchism: Its Philosophy and Scientific Basis* (Honolulu: University Press of the Pacific, 2003), 110. The same point was made by Albert himself. See ibid., 173.

28. Maximoff, *Program of Anarcho-Syndicalism*, 50. See also Pouget, "What is

the Trade Union?," 435; Ricardo Mella, *Anarchist Socialism in Early Twentieth-Century Spain: A Ricardo Mella Anthology*, ed. Stephen Luis Vilaseca (London: Palgrave Macmillan, 2020), 73–74.

29. Émile Pataud and Émile Pouget, *How We Shall Bring About the Revolution: Syndicalism and the Cooperative Commonwealth* (London: Pluto Press, 1990), 118.

30. Pataud and Émile Pouget, *How We Shall Bring About the Revolution*, 118.

31. Pierre Besnard, "Anarcho-Syndicalism and Anarchism," trans. Paul Sharkey, Robert Graham's Anarchism Weblog, March 15, 2009, https://robertgraham .wordpress.com/alexander-schapiro-pierre-besnard-anarcho-syndicalism -and-anarchism.

32. Besnard, *Anarcho-Syndicalism and Anarchism*.

33. Isaac Puente, *Libertarian Communism*, (Johannesburg: Zabalaza Books, 2005), 5, 17.

34. Quoted in José Peirats, *The CNT in the Spanish Revolution*, vol. 1, ed. Chris Ealham (Oakland, CA: PM Press, 2011), 104–5.

35. Martha Ackelsberg, *Free Women of Spain: Anarchism and the Struggle for the Emancipation of Women* (Oakland, CA: AK Press, 2005), 21, 80–88, 120–37; Ealham, *Anarchism and the City*, 34–48; Danny Evans, *Revolution and the State: Anarchism in the Spanish Civil War, 1936–1939* (Chico, CA: AK Press, 2020), 23.

36. Rocker, *Anarcho-Syndicalism*, 57.

37. Max Baginski, *What Does Syndicalism Want? Living, Not Dead Unions* (London: Kate Sharpley Library, 2015), 22.

38. Lennart K. Persson, "Revolutionary Syndicalism in Sweden Before the Second World War" in *Revolutionary Syndicalism: An International Perspective*, ed., Marcel van der Linden and Wayne Thorpe (Aldershot, UK: Scolar Press, 1990), 87.

39. Jerome R. Mintz, *The Anarchists of Casas Viejas* (Bloomington: Indiana University Press, 2004), 157–65.

40. A. Smith, *Anarchism, Revolution and Reaction*, 203–5, 211, 316–17, 323; James Yeoman, *Print Culture and the Formation of the Anarchist Movement in Spain, 1890–1915* (New York: Routledge, 2020), 223–25.

41. Jason Garner, *Goals and Means: Anarchism, Syndicalism, and Internationalism in the Origins of the Federación Anarquista Ibérica* (Chico, CA: AK Press, 2016), 162–69, 234–35, 243; Bookchin, *Spanish Anarchists*, 190–91. For repression under the Spanish republic, see Ealham, *Anarchism and the City*.

42. Rocker, *Anarcho-Syndicalism*, 81, 82.

43. Rocker, *Anarcho-Syndicalism*, 80–82.

44. Quoted in James Joll, *The Anarchists* (London: Methuen, 1969), 202.

45. Phil H. Goodstein, *The Theory of the General Strike from the French Revolution to Poland* (Boulder, CO: East European Monographs, 1984), 15–25; Max Beer, *A History of British Socialism*, vol. 2 (London: G. Bell and Sons, 1921), 81–90;

William Benbow, "Grand National Holiday, and Congress of the Productive Classes," Marxist Internet Archive, https://www.marxists.org/history/england/chartists/benbow-congress.htm.

46. Quoted in Goodstein, *General Strike*, 21.

47. Quoted in Julian P.W. Archer, *The First International in France, 1864–1872: Its Origins, Theories, and Impact* (Lanham, MD: University Press of America, 1997), 129.

48. Michael Bakunin, *Selected Texts, 1868–1875*, ed. A. W. Zurbrugg (London: Merlin Books, 2016), 41

49. Quoted in Cahm, *Kropotkin*, 223.

50. Quoted in Cahm, *Kropotkin*, 223.

51. Quoted in Cahm, *Kropotkin*, 223.

52. Quoted in Cahm, *Kropotkin*, 224. For more information on this debate, see David Stafford, *From Anarchism to Reformism: A Study of the Political Activities of Paul Brousse, 1870–90* (London: Weidenfeld and Nicolson, 1971), 50–51.

53. Goodstein, *General Strike*, 53–55.

54. Quoted in Jennings, *Syndicalism in France*, 16. See also, 232n25; Goodstein, *General Strike*, 57–58.

55. Arnold Roller, *The Social General Strike* (Chicago: The Debating Club No.1, 1905), 6.

56. Roller, *Social General Strike*, 7–9; Rocker, *Anarcho-Syndicalism*, 82; Goldman, *Red Emma*, 95; Pataud and Pouget, *How We Shall Bring About the Revolution*, 15, 27–28, 50–51, 91–93.

57. Lucy Parsons, *Freedom, Equality and Solidarity: Writings and Speeches, 1878–1937*, ed. Gale Ahrens (Chicago: Charles H. Kerr, 2004), 82–83.

58. Roller, *Social General Strike*, 32.

59. Pataud and Pouget, *How We Shall Bring About the Revolution*, 103–38. Quote in ibid., 121.

60. Quoted in Richards, "Malatesta's Relevance for Anarchists Today," in Malatesta, *Life and Ideas*, 271.

61. Roller, *Social General Strike*, 5–6.

62. Maurizio Antonioli, ed. *The International Anarchist Congress Amsterdam (1907)* (Edmonton, AB: Black Cat Press 2009), 134–35.

63. Quoted in Richards, "Malatesta's Relevance for Anarchists Today," 271.

64. Roller, *Social General Strike*, 7, 8.

65. Antonioli, ed., *International Anarchist Congress*, 124.

66. CNT, "The First Congress of the National Confederation of Labor," Libcom website, January 17, 2017, https://libcom.org/article/first-congress-national-confederation-labor-cnt-barcelona-september-8-10-1911.

67. IWA, "Declaration of the Principles of Revolutionary Syndicalism," in *Anarchism: A Documentary History of Libertarian Ideas*, vol. 1, *From Anarchy to Anarchism (300 CE to 1939)*, ed. Robert Graham (Montréal: Black Rose Books, 2005), 418.

68. Rocker, *Anarcho-Syndicalism*, 81; Peter Kropotkin, *Direct Struggle Against Capital: A Peter Kropotkin Anthology*, ed. Iain McKay (Oakland, CA: AK Press, 2014), 477.

69. Pataud and Pouget, *How We Shall Bring About the Revolution*, 5.

70. Pataud and Pouget, *How We Shall Bring About the Revolution*, 8.

71. Pataud and Pouget, *How We Shall Bring About the Revolution*, 1–3, 9, 12.

72. Pataud and Pouget, *How We Shall Bring About the Revolution*, 41–42, 57–58, 64, 67–84, 94.

73. Pataud and Pouget, *How We Shall Bring About the Revolution*, 80, 82.

74. IWA, "Declaration of the Principles of Revolutionary Syndicalism," 418.

75. CNT, "The First Congress of the National Confederation of Labor" (1911).

76. Quoted in Peirats, *CNT in the Spanish Revolution*, vol. 1, 110.

77. Roller, *Social General Strike*, 8.

78. Berkman, *Anarchism*, 196–97.

79. Rocker, *Anarcho-Syndicalism*, 83.

80. Rocker, *Anarcho-Syndicalism*, 83; Roller, *Social General Strike*, 10–15; Pataud and Pouget, *How We Shall Bring About the Revolution*, 48–49, 59–61, 67–77, 90–96.

81. John Merriman, *Massacre: The Life and Death of the Paris Commune of 1871* (New Haven: Yale University Press, 2014), 39–44; Jennings, *Syndicalism in France*, 138.

82. Bookchin, *Spanish Anarchists*, 133–37; A. Smith, *Anarchism, Revolution and Reaction*, 173–77.

83. Pataud and Pouget, *How We Shall Bring About the Revolution*, 164–65, 194–207.

84. Kropotkin, *Direct Struggle*, 561.

85. Bookchin, *Spanish Anarchists*, 150–52, 174–76, 190–91; Garner, *Goals and Means*, 75–78, 162–63; A. Smith, *Anarchism, Revolution and Reaction*, 264–65, 275–83, 335.

86. A. Smith, *Anarchism, Revolution and Reaction*, 92–94, 122–23. For other examples, see ibid., 281–83; Ealham, *Anarchism and the City*, 117–18.

87. CNT, "The First Congress of the National Confederation of Labor" (1911).

88. Antonioli, ed., *International Anarchist Congress*, 47–48.

Chapter 10: Organizational Dualism

1. Davide Turcato, *Making Sense of Anarchism: Errico Malatesta's Experiments with Revolution, 1889–1900* (Basingstoke, UK: Palgrave Macmillan, 2012), 80–81; Nunzio Pernicone, *Italian Anarchism, 1864–1892* (Princeton: Princeton University Press, 1993), 254–58, 272.

2. Carl Levy, *Gramsci and the Anarchists* (Oxford: Berg, 1999), 119–25; Fausto Buttà, *Living Like Nomads: The Milanese Anarchist Movement Before Fascism* (Newcastle, UK: Cambridge Scholars Publishing, 2015), 186–87, 196.

3. Wolfgang Eckhardt, *The First Socialist Schism: Bakunin vs. Marx in the International Working Men's Association* (Oakland, CA: PM Press, 2016), 2, 156–57.

4. E. H. Carr, *Michael Bakunin* (London: The Macmillan Press, 1975), 308–18; T.R. Ravindranathan, *Bakunin and the Italians* (Kingston and Montréal: McGill-Queen's University Press, 1988), 29–34, 38–40, 48–56; Pernicone, *Italian Anarchism*, 16–22; Arthur Lehning, "Bakunin's Conceptions of Revolutionary Organizations and Their Role: A Study of His 'Secret Societies,'" in *Essays in Honour of E. H. Carr*, ed. Chimen Abramsky (London: The Macmillan Press, 1974), 57, 61–63. Bakunin had previously attempted to establish a secret society of revolutionaries in 1848, which was two decades before he became an anarchist, but this attempt was unsuccessful and never went past the planning stages. See Carr, *Bakunin*, 181–86.

5. Eckhardt, *First Socialist Schism*, 2–12, 47–65, 71–78, 153–58, 243–62, 318–19, 350–51, 354–55; Ravindranathan, *Bakunin and the Italians*, 183.

6. Michael Bakunin, *Selected Writings*, ed. Arthur Lehning (London: Jonathan Cape, 1973), 92.

7. Bakunin, *Selected Writings*, 92.

8. Bakunin, *Selected Writings*, 173–74. For the evidence that this program was a draft, see Eckhardt, *First Socialist Schism*, 285, 317–19.

9. Quoted in Ravindranathan, *Bakunin and the Italians*, 160.

10. Quoted in Ravindranathan, *Bakunin and the Italians*, 160.

11. Michael Bakunin, "To the Brothers of the Alliance in Spain," trans. Shawn P. Wilbur, Libertarian Labyrinth website, March 17, 2014, https://www.libertarian-labyrinth.org/bakunin-library/bakunin-to-the-brothers-of-the-alliance-in-spain-1872. Bakunin's *Œuvres complètes* incorrectly dates the letter to June. For the correct date of writing, see Eckhardt, *First Socialist Schism*, 244, 422. For other examples of Bakunin making this argument, see Bakunin, *Selected Writings*, 93; Michael Bakunin, *Selected Texts, 1868–1875*, ed. A. W. Zurbrugg (London: Merlin Books, 2016), 215.

12. Carr, *Bakunin*, 189–224, 240.

13. Bakunin, *Selected Texts*, 210. This letter to Alerini has been misattributed within Bakunin's *Œuvres complètes* as being part of Bakunin's May 21, 1872, draft letter to Tomás González Morago. This error is repeated in Zurbrugg's edition of Bakunin. See Eckhardt, *First Socialist Schism*, 259–61, 281, 512–13n55.

14. Bakunin, *Selected Texts*, 210, 213.

15. Bakunin, *Selected Texts*, 210.

16. Bakunin, *Selected Texts*, 211–15. For the programs of the Alliance, see Bakunin, *Selected Writings*, 173–75.

17. Bakunin, "To the Brothers of the Alliance in Spain."

18. Bakunin, *Selected Texts*, 249.

19. For example, Hal Draper, *Karl Marx's Theory of Revolution*, vol. 3, *The "Dictatorship of the Proletariat"* (New York: Monthly Review Press, 1986), 55–57,

93–96; Hal Draper, *Karl Marx's Theory of Revolution*, vol. 4, *Critique of Other Socialisms* (New York: Monthly Review Press, 1990), 130, 144–47; Paul Avrich, *Anarchist Portraits* (Princeton: Princeton University Press, 1988), 13, 46, 67; Peter Marshall, *Demanding the Impossible: A History of Anarchism* (London: Harper Perennial, 2008), 263, 271–72, 276–77, 282, 286–87, 306–7; James Joll, *The Anarchists* (London: Methuen, 1969), 87

20. Bakunin, *Selected Writings*, 180.
21. Bakunin, *Selected Writings*, 178–81.
22. Bakunin, *Selected Writings*, 178. For information on Richard, see Julian P.W. Archer, *The First International in France, 1864–1872: Its Origins, Theories, and Impact* (Lanham, MD: University Press of America, 1997), 159–61, 217–8; Carr, *Bakunin*, 343–44, 349, 363, 414–15; Eckart, *First Socialist Schism*, 205.
23. Bakunin, *Selected Writings*, 180. For the two other occasions Bakunin uses the phrase in the letter, see ibid., 178, 181.
24. For an overview of Marx's usage of the term, see Draper, *The "Dictatorship of the Proletariat" from Marx to Lenin* (New York: Monthly Review Press, 1987), 11–35; Richard N. Hunt, *The Political Ideas of Marx and Engels*, vol. 1, *Marxism and Totalitarian Democracy, 1818–1850* (Pittsburgh: University of Pittsburgh Press, 1974), 284–336.
25. Bakunin, *Selected Writings*, 180.
26. Bakunin, *Selected Writings*, 182.
27. Pierre-Joseph Proudhon, *Property Is Theft: A Pierre-Joseph Proudhon Anthology*, ed. Iain McKay (Oakland, CA: AK Press, 2011), 554, 654–55.
28. Bakunin, *Selected Writings*, 193. For Nechaev's views and actions, see Ronald Seth, *The Russian Terrorists: The Story of the Narodniki* (London: Barrie & Rockliff, 1966), 31–36; Philip Pomper, "Nechaev and Tsaricide: The Conspiracy within the Conspiracy," *The Russian Review* 33. no. 2 (1974): 123–38.
29. Bakunin, *Selected Writings*, 182–83.
30. Bakunin, *Selected Writings*, 190.
31. Bakunin, *Selected Writings*, 192–93.
32. Bakunin, *Selected Writings*, 193.
33. Bakunin, *Selected Writings*, 191–92.
34. Bakunin, *Selected Writings*, 191.
35. Bakunin, *Selected Writings*, 193.
36. Bakunin, *Selected Writings*, 194.
37. Bakunin, *Selected Writings*, 172.
38. Bakunin, *Selected Writings*, 172.
39. Michael Bakunin, *The Basic Bakunin: Writings 1869–1871*, ed. and trans. Robert M. Cutler (Buffalo, NY: Prometheus Books, 1985), 164. See also, 27.
40. Bakunin, *Selected Writings*, 203.
41. Quoted in Eckhardt, *First Socialist Schism*, 244.
42. Quoted in Caroline Cahm, *Kropotkin and the Rise of Revolutionary Anarchism, 1872–1886* (Cambridge: Cambridge University Press, 1989), 145.

43. Quoted in Cahm, *Kropotkin*, 146.

44. Quoted in Cahm, *Kropotkin*, 146, 147. See also Martin A. Miller, *Kropotkin* (Chicago: University of Chicago Press, 1976), 146–47.

45. Cahm, *Kropotkin*, 106, 145, 317–18n77; David Stafford, *From Anarchism to Reformism: A Study of the Political Activities of Paul Brousse, 1870–90* (London: Weidenfeld and Nicolson, 1971), 54–55.

46. Max Nettlau, *A Short History of Anarchism*, ed. Heiner M. Becker (London: Freedom Press, 1996), 277.

47. Quoted in Nettlau, *Short History*, 280–81.

48. Malatesta, *The Method of Freedom: An Errico Malatesta Reader*, ed. Davide Turcato (Oakland, CA: AK Press 2014), 173.

49. Errico Malatesta, *A Long and Patient Work: The Anarchist Socialism of L'Agitazione, 1897–1898*, ed. Davide Turcato (Chico, CA: AK Press, 2016), 112.

50. Malatesta, Errico Malatesta, *Towards Anarchy: Malatesta in America, 1899–1900*, ed. Davide Turcato (Chico, CA: AK Press, 2019), 79.

51. Malatesta, *Patient Work*, 174–75.

52. Malatesta, *Patient Work*, 364.

53. Malatesta, *Patient Work*, 364.

54. Maurizio Antonioli, ed. *The International Anarchist Congress Amsterdam (1907)* (Edmonton, AB: Black Cat Press 2009), 122.

55. Antonioli, ed., *International Anarchist Congress*, 121.

56. Malatesta, *Method of Freedom*, 483.

57. Malatesta, *Method of Freedom*, 338.

58. Malatesta, *Method of Freedom*, 341. See also Malatesta, *The Anarchist Revolution: Polemical Articles, 1924–1931*, ed. Vernon Richards (London: Freedom Press, 1995), 29.

59. Malatesta, *Method of Freedom*, 341.

60. Errico Malatesta, *Life and Ideas: The Anarchist Writings of Errico Malatesta*, ed. Vernon Richards (Oakland, CA: PM Press, 2015), 112–13.

61. Peter Kropotkin, *Direct Struggle Against Capital: A Peter Kropotkin Anthology*, ed. Iain McKay (Oakland, CA: AK Press, 2014), 585.

62. Nicholas Papayanis, *Alphonse Merrheim: The Emergence of Reformism in Revolutionary Syndicalism, 1871–1925* (Dordrecht, NL: Martinus Nijhoff Publishers, 1985), 121–36.

63. Malatesta, *Method of Freedom*, 465. For Malatesta's later clarifications of this article, see Malatesta, *Anarchist Revolution*, 27–34.

64. Malatesta, *Method of Freedom*, 465.

65. David Berry, *A History of the French Anarchist Movement: 1917 to 1945* (Oakland, CA: AK Press, 2009), 151, 255.

66. Malatesta, *Method of Freedom*, 466.

67. Malatesta, *Method of Freedom*, 465.

68. Malatesta, *Anarchist Revolution*, 32–33; *Method of Freedom*, 397–98; *Life and Ideas*, 109.

69. Malatesta, *Life and Ideas*, 110.
70. Malatesta, *Method of Freedom*, 341–42.
71. Malatesta, *Method of Freedom*, 466–67.
72. Malatesta, *Method of Freedom*, 483.
73. George Richard Esenwein, *Anarchist Ideology and the Working-Class Movement in Spain, 1868–1898* (Berkeley: University of California Press, 1989), 118–22.
74. Antonioli, ed., *International Anarchist Congress*, 43.
75. Salvador Seguí, "Anarchism and Syndicalism," trans. Paul Sharkey, Libcom website, https://libcom.org/library/anarchism-syndicalism-salvador-seguí.
76. Juan Gómez Casas, *Anarchist Organization: The History of the F.A.I* (Montréal: Black Rose Books, 1986), 76–77, 92–97, 107–16; Stuart Christie, *We, the Anarchists! A Study of the Iberian Anarchist Federation (FAI) 1927–1937* (Oakland, CA: AK Press, 2008), 32–43.
77. Quoted in Christie, *We, the Anarchists*, 37.
78. Quoted in Christie, *We, the Anarchists*, 37, 38.
79. Quoted in Casas, *History of the F.A.I*, 110.
80. Quoted in Casas, *History of the F.A.I*, 110.
81. Jason Garner, *Goals and Means: Anarchism, Syndicalism, and Internationalism in the Origins of the Federación Anarquista Ibérica* (Chico, CA: AK Press, 2016), 214, 222–26.
82. Pierre Besnard, "Anarcho-Syndicalism and Anarchism," trans. Paul Sharkey, Robert Graham's Anarchism Weblog, March 15, 2009, https://robertgraham.wordpress.com/alexander-schapiro-pierre-besnard-anarcho-syndicalism-and-anarchism. For another example, see Gregori P. Maximoff, *Program of Anarcho-Syndicalism* (n.p., Guillotine Press, 2015), 50–52.
83. Paul Avrich, *The Russian Anarchists* (Oakland, CA: AK Press, 2005), 205.
84. Nabat, "Proceedings of Nabat," in *No Gods, No Masters: An Anthology of Anarchism*, ed. Daniel Guérin (Oakland, CA: AK Press, 2005), 487.
85. Avrich, *Russian Anarchists*, 207–8.
86. Avrich, *Russian Anarchists*, 222, 232–33, 238–39, 241; Lazar Lipotkin, *The Russian Anarchist Movement in North America* (Edmonton, AB: Black Cat Press, 2019), 119–21, 123. For a text advocating united anarchism, see ibid., 283–86.
87. Sébastien Faure, "The Anarchist Synthesis: The Three Great Anarchist Currents," trans. Shawn P. Wilbur, Libertarian Labyrinth website, August 3, 2017, https://www.libertarian-labyrinth.org/anarchist-beginnings/sebastien-faure-the-anarchist-synthesis-1828.
88. Faure, "The Anarchist Synthesis."
89. Voline, "Synthesis (anarchist)," in *The Anarchist Encyclopedia Abridged*, ed. Mitchell Abidor (Chico, CA: AK Press, 2019), 197.
90. Voline, "Synthesis (Anarchist)," 199–200.
91. Voline, "Synthesis (Anarchist)," 203.

92. Alexandre Skirda, *Facing the Enemy: A History of Anarchist Organization from Proudhon to May 1968* (Oakland CA: AK Press, 2002), 121–25; The Group of Russian Anarchists Abroad, "Organizational Platform," in Skirda, *Facing the Enemy*, 192.

93. The Group of Russian Anarchists Abroad, "Organizational Platform," 200–201.

94. The Group of Russian Anarchists Abroad, "Organizational Platform," 201. See also, 213; Nestor Makhno, *The Struggle Against the State and Other Essays*, ed. Alexandre Skirda (San Francisco: AK Press, 1996), 64–65.

95. The Group of Russian Anarchists Abroad, "Organizational Platform," 201, 207.

96. Quoted in Skirda, *Facing the Enemy*, 122.

97. The Group of Russian Anarchists Abroad, "Organizational Platform," 193, 211. See also Makhno, *Struggle*, 62–63.

98. The Group of Russian Anarchists Abroad, "The Problem of Organization and the Notion of Synthesis (March 1926)," in Skirda, *Facing the Enemy*, 188–91; The Group of Russian Anarchists Abroad, "Organizational Platform," 193.

99. Makhno, *Struggle*, 67–68.

100. The Group of Russian Anarchists Abroad, "Organizational Platform," 212.

101. The Group of Russian Anarchists Abroad, "Organizational Platform," 212. See also Peter Arshinov, "The Old and New in Anarchism: Reply to Comrade Malatesta (May 1928)," in Alexandre Skirda, *Facing the Enemy*, 240–41.

102. The Group of Russian Anarchists Abroad, "Organizational Platform," 213.

103. The Group of Russian Anarchists Abroad, "Organizational Platform," 213.

104. Skirda, *Facing the Enemy*, 131.

105. Mollie Steimer, Simon Fleshin, Voline, Sobol, Schwartz, Lia, Roman, Ervantian, "Concerning the Platform for an Organization of Anarchists," in *Fighters for Anarchism: Mollie Steimer and Senya Fleshin*, ed. Abe Bluestein (Minneapolis, MN: Libertarian Publications Group, 1983), 52–53, 58, 61–62.

106. Avrich, *Russian Anarchists*, 242–43.

107. Malatesta, *Method of Freedom*, 486–91.

108. Malatesta, *Method of Freedom*, 486–87.

109. Malatesta, *Method of Freedom*, 486.

110. The Group of Russian Anarchists Abroad, "Supplement to the Organizational Platform (November, 1926)," in Skirda, *Facing the Enemy*, 219.

111. The Group of Russian Anarchists Abroad, "Supplement to the Organizational Platform," 222.

112. The Group of Russian Anarchists Abroad, "Reply to Anarchism's Confusionists (August 1927)," in Skirda *Facing the Enemy*, 229–30.

113. The Group of Russian Anarchists Abroad, "Supplement to the Organizational Platform," 219–20.

114. The Group of Russian Anarchists Abroad, "Reply to Anarchism's Confusionists," 230.

115. The Group of Russian Anarchists Abroad, "Reply to Anarchism's Confusionists," 235.

116. The Group of Russian Anarchists Abroad, "Reply to Anarchism's Confusionists," 234.

117. The Group of Russian Anarchists Abroad, "Reply to Anarchism's Confusionists," 234.

118. The Group of Russian Anarchists Abroad, "Supplement to the Organizational Platform," 217.

119. The Group of Russian Anarchists Abroad, "Supplement to the Organizational Platform," 218.

120. Arshinov, "The Old and New in Anarchism," 240.

121. Malatesta, *Anarchist Revolution*, 107–8.

122. Errico Malatesta, "On Collective Responsibility," Institute for Anarchist Theory and History website, n.d., https://ithanarquista.wordpress.com/nestor-makhno-archive/nestor-makhno-archive-english/platform-english/on-collective-responsibility-errico-malatesta.

123. Skirda, *Facing the Enemy*, 124–28, 134–35.

124. Quoted in Garner, *Goals and Means*, 205–6.

125. Quoted in Garner, *Goals and Means*, 206.

126. Skirda, *Facing the Enemy*, 135; Garner, *Goals and Means*, 206.

127. Luigi Fabbri, Camillo Berneri, and Ugo Fedeli, "Reply by the Pensiero e Volontà Group to an Invitation to Join the International Anarchist Communist Federation," Institute for Anarchist Theory and History website, n.d., https://ithanarquista.wordpress.com/nestor-makhno-archive/nestor-makhno-archive-english/reply-by-the-pensiero-e-volonta-group-to-an-invitation-to-join-the-international-anarchist-communist-federation.

128. Lipotkin, *Russian Anarchist Movement in North America*, 127–29, 180, 191.

129. Quoted in Lipotkin, *Russian Anarchist Movement in North America*, 138.

130. Lipotkin, *Russian Anarchist Movement in North America*, 129–31, 145–49, 180, 191–92. It is sometimes claimed that anarchists in Bulgaria were the first to adopt the *Platform*. I have been unable to verify this due to how little information about the Bulgarian anarchist movement is available in English.

131. Berry, *French Anarchist Movement*, 173–76; Skirda, *Facing the Enemy*, 135–36, 143.

Chapter 11: Conclusion

1. This included, but was not limited to, racism, patriarchy, homophobia, hierarchically organized religion, authoritarian modes of education, and the oppression of nonhuman animals. It should nonetheless be kept in mind that a significant number of anarchists failed to put the theoretical opposition to

racism, sexism, and homophobia into practice or, on occasion, even support it in theory.

2.   Dark Star, ed. *Quiet Rumours: An Anarcha-Feminist Reader*, 3rd Edition (Oakland, CA: AK Press, 2012); Ruth Kinna, "Anarchism and Feminism," in *Brill's Companion to Anarchism and Philosophy*, ed. Nathan Jun (Brill, 2017), 253–84; Lucy Nicholas, "Gender and Sexuality," in *The Palgrave Handbook of Anarchism*, ed. Carl Levy and Matthew S. Adams (London: Palgrave Macmillan, 2019), 603–21; Institute for Anarchist Studies, *Perspectives on Anarchist Theory*, no. 29, *Anarcha-Feminisms* (Portland, OR: Eberhardt Press, 2016).

3.   Dana M. Williams, "Black Panther Radical Factionalization and the Development of Black Anarchism," *Journal of Black Studies* 46, no. 7 (2015): 678–703; Lorenzo Kom'Boa Ervin, *Anarchism and the Black Revolution* (London: Pluto Press, 2021); William C. Anderson, *The Nation on No Map: Black Anarchism and Abolition* (Chico, CA: AK Press, 2021).

4.   Deric Shannon and J. Rogue, "Refusing to Wait: Anarchism and Intersectionality," Anarkismo website, https://www.anarkismo.net/article/14923; J. Rogue and Abbey Volcano, "Insurrection at the Intersections: Feminism, Intersectionality, and Anarchism," in *Quiet Rumours*, 43–46. For an overview of intersectionality from a nonanarchist perspective, see Patricia Hill Collins and Sirma Bilge, *Intersectionality*, 2nd edition (Cambridge: Polity Press, 2020).

Bibliography

Primary Sources

Abidor, Mitchell, ed. *Death to Bourgeois Society: The Propagandists of the Deed*. Oakland, CA: PM Press, 2015.

Anderson, William C. *The Nation on No Map: Black Anarchism and Abolition*. Chico, CA: AK Press, 2021.

Antonioli, Maurizio, ed. *The International Anarchist Congress Amsterdam (1907)*. Edmonton, AB: Black Cat Press, 2009.

Ardouin, J., Degalvès, J., Ferrière, J., Girard, A., Grave, Jean, Janvion, E., Kropotkin, Peter, et al. "Liberty Through Education: The Libertarian School." Translated by Shawn P. Wilbur. Libertarian Labyrinth website, April 9, 2020. https://www.libertarian-labyrinth.org/working -translations/liberty-through-education-1898.

Arshinov, Peter. "The Old and New in Anarchism: Reply to Comrade Malatesta (May 1928)." In Skirda, *Facing the Enemy*, 237–42.

Ba Jin. "Anarchism and the Question of Practice." In *Anarchism: A Documentary History of Libertarian Ideas*, Vol. 1, *From Anarchy to Anarchism (300 CE to 1939)*, edited by Robert Graham, 362–66. Montréal: Black Rose Books, 2005.

Baginski, Max. "Aim and Tactics of the Trade-Union Movement." In *Anarchy: An Anthology of Emma Goldman's Mother Earth*, edited by Peter Glassgold, 297–306. New York: Counterpoint, 2000.

———. "Stirner: 'The Ego and His Own.'" *Mother Earth* 2, no. 3 (1907): 142–51.

———. *What Does Syndicalism Want? Living, Not Dead Unions*. London: Kate Sharpley Library, 2015.

Bakunin, Michael. *Bakunin on Anarchism*. Edited by Sam Dolgoff. Montréal: Black Rose Books, 1980.

———. *The Basic Bakunin: Writings, 1869–1871*. Edited and Translated by Robert M. Cutler. Buffalo, NY: Prometheus Books, 1985.

———. *The Political Philosophy of Bakunin: Scientific Anarchism*. Edited by G. P. Maximoff. New York: The Free Press of Glencoe, 1964.

———. *Selected Texts, 1868–1875*. Edited by A. W. Zurbrugg. London: Anarres Editions, 2016.

———. *Selected Writings*. Edited by Arthur Lehning. London: Jonathan Cape, 1973.

———. *Statism and Anarchy*. Edited by Marshall Shatz. Cambridge: Cambridge University Press, 1990.

———. "To the Brothers of the Alliance in Spain." Translated by Shawn P. Wilbur. Libertarian Labyrinth website, March 17, 2014. https://www.libertarian-labyrinth.org/bakunin-library/bakunin-to-the-brothers-of-the-alliance-in-spain-1872.

Bellegarrigue, Anselme. "Anarchy, A Journal of Order." Translated by Paul Sharkey. Anarchist Library website, February 21, 2019. http://theanarchistlibrary.org/library/anselme-bellegarrigue-the-world-s-first-anarchist-manifesto.

Benbow, William. "Grand National Holiday, and Congress of the Productive Classes." Marxist Internet Archive. https://www.marxists.org/history/england/chartists/benbow-congress.htm.

Berkman, Alexander. "A Decade of Bolshevism." In *Bloodstained: One Hundred Years of Leninist Counterrevolution*, edited by Friends of Aron Baron, 119–23. Chico, CA: AK Press, 2017.

———. *The Blast*. Oakland, CA: AK Press, 2005.

———. *What Is Anarchism?* Oakland, CA: AK Press, 2003.

Bernstein, Edward. *Evolutionary Socialism: A Criticism and Affirmation*. New York: B. W. Huebsch, 1909.

Besnard, Pierre. "Anarcho-Syndicalism and Anarchism." Translated by Paul Sharkey. Robert Graham's Anarchism Weblog, March 15, 2009. https://robertgraham.wordpress.com/alexander-schapiro-pierre-besnard-anarcho-syndicalism-and-anarchism.

Bevington, Louisa Sarah. *An Anarchist Manifesto*. London: Metropolitan Printing Works, 1895.

Brousse, Paul. "Propaganda of the Deed." In *Anarchism: A Documentary History of Libertarian Ideas*, Vol. 1, *From Anarchy to Anarchism (300 CE to 1939)*, edited by Robert Graham, 150–51. Montréal: Black Rose Books, 2005.

Cafiero, Carlo. "Action (1880)." In *Anarchism: A Documentary History of Libertarian Ideas*, Vol. 1, *From Anarchy to Anarchism (300 CE to 1939)*, edited by Robert Graham, 152–53. Montréal: Black Rose Books, 2005.

———. *Compendium of Capital*. Translated by Paul M. Perrone. London: The Anarchist Communist Group, 2020.

———. "The Organisation of Armed Struggle." Translated by Paul Sharkey. *The Cienfuegos Press Anarchist Review* 1, no. 3 (Autumn 1977): 101.

———. *Revolution*. Edmonton, AB: Black Cat Press, 2012.

CNT, "The First Congress of the National Confederation of Labor." Libcom website, January 17, 2017. https://libcom.org/article/ first-congress-national-confederation-labor-cnt-barcelona-september -8-10-1911.

Dark Star, ed. *Quiet Rumours: An Anarcha-Feminist Reader*. 3rd ed. Oakland, CA: AK Press, 2012.

De Cleyre, Voltairine. "A Suggestion and Explanation." *Free Society* 6, no. 29 (1900): 1.

———. *Exquisite Rebel: The Essays of Voltairine de Cleyre—Feminist, Anarchist, Genius*. Edited by Sharon Presley and Crispin Sartwell. Albany: State University of New York Press, 2005.

———. *The Voltairine de Cleyre Reader*. Edited by A.J. Brigati. Oakland, CA: AK Press, 2004.

De Ligt, Bart. *The Conquest of Violence: An Essay on War and Revolution*. London: Pluto Press, 1989.

De Paepe, César. "The Present Institutions of the International in Relation to the Future." Translated by Shawn P. Wilbur. Libertarian Labyrinth website, March 20, 2018. https://www.libertarian-labyrinth.org/ working-translations/the-present-institutions-of-the-international -from-the-point-of-view-of-the-future-1869.

———. "Strikes, Unions, and the Affiliation of Unions with the International." In *Workers Unite! The International 150 Years Later*, edited by Marcello Musto, 126–29. New York: Bloomsbury Academic, 2014.

Déjacque, Joseph. *Down with the Bosses and Other Writings, 1859–1861*. Gresham, OR: Corvus Editions, 2013.

———. "On the Human Being, Male and Female." Translated by Jonathan Mayo Crane. Libertarian Labyrinth website, April 4, 2011. https:// www.libertarian-labyrinth.org/from-the-archives/joseph-dejacque-the -human-being-i.

———. "The Revolutionary Question." Translated by Shawn P. Wilbur. Libertarian Labyrinth website, May 13, 2012. https://www .libertarian-labyrinth.org/working-translations/joseph-dejacque -the-revolutionary-question.

Delesalle, Paul. "Anarchists and the Trade Unions." Libcom website, December 9, 2013. https://libcom.org/article/anarchists-and-trade-unions-paul-delesalle.

———. "The Strike!" Libcom website, December 9, 2013. https://libcom.org/library/strike-paul-delesalle.

Ervin, Lorenzo Kom'Boa. *Anarchism and the Black Revolution*. London: Pluto Press, 2021.

Fabbri, Luigi. "About a Project of Anarchist Organization." Institute for Anarchist Theory and History website, n.d. https://ithanarquista.wordpress.com/about-a-project-for-anarchist-organization-luigi-fabbri.

———. "Anarchy and 'Scientific' Communism." In *Bloodstained: One Hundred Years of Leninist Counterrevolution*, edited by Friends of Aron Baron, 13–45. Chico, CA: AK Press, 2017.

———. *Bourgeois Influences on Anarchism*. Translated by Chaz Bufe. Tucson, AZ: See Sharp Press, 2001.

———. "Revolution and Dictatorship: On One Anarchist Who Has Forgotten His Principles." Translated by Paul Sharkey. Kate Sharpley Library, n.d. https://www.katesharpleylibrary.net/8932r8.

Fabbri, Luigi, Camillo Berneri, and Ugo Fedeli. "Reply by the Pensiero e Volontà Group to an Invitation to Join the International Anarchist Communist Federation." Institute for Anarchist Theory and History website, n.d. https://ithanarquista.wordpress.com/nestor-makhno-archive/nestor-makhno-archive-english/reply-by-the-pensiero-e-volonta-group-to-an-invitation-to-join-the-international-anarchist-communist-federation.

Faure, Sébastien. "The Anarchist Synthesis: The Three Great Anarchist Currents." Translated by Shawn P. Wilbur. Libertarian Labyrinth website, August 3, 2017. https://www.libertarian-labyrinth.org/anarchist-beginnings/sebastien-faure-the-anarchist-synthesis-1828.

Ferrer, Francisco. *Anarchist Education and the Modern School: A Francisco Ferrer Reader*. Edited by Mark Bray and Robert H. Haworth. Oakland, CA: PM Press, 2019.

Galleani, Luigi. *The End of Anarchism?* London: Elephant Editions, 2012.

Goldman, Emma. *Anarchy and the Sex Question: Essays on Women and Emancipation, 1896–1926*. Edited by Shawn P. Wilbur. Oakland, CA: PM Press, 2016.

———. *Living My Life*. Vol. 1. New York: Dover Publications, 1970.

———. *Living My Life*. Vol. 2. New York: Dover Publications, 1970.

———. *Red Emma Speaks: An Emma Goldman Reader*. Edited by Alix Kates Shulman. 3rd ed. Atlantic Highlands, NJ: Humanities Press, 1996.

Golos Truda. "Declaration of the Petrograd Union of Anarcho-Syndicalist Propaganda." In *The Anarchists in the Russian Revolution*, edited by Paul Avrich, 68–72. London: Thames and Hudson, 1973.

Group of Russian Anarchists Abroad, The. "The Organizational Platform of the General Union of Anarchists (June 1926)." In Skirda, *Facing the Enemy*, 192–213.

———. "The Problem of Organization and the Notion of Synthesis (March 1926)." In Skirda, *Facing the Enemy*, 188–91.

———. "Reply to Anarchism's Confusionists (August 1927)." In Skirda, *Facing the Enemy*, 224–36.

———. "Supplement to the Organizational Platform (November 1926)." In Skirda, *Facing the Enemy*, 214–23.

Guillaume, James. "Ideas on Social Organization." In *No Gods, No Masters: An Anthology of Anarchism*, edited by Daniel Guérin, 247–67. Oakland, CA: AK Press, 2005.

———. "Michael Bakunin: A Biographical Sketch." In *Bakunin on Anarchism*, edited by Sam Dolgoff, 22–52. Montréal: Black Rose Books, 1980.

———. "On the Abolition of the State." In *Workers Unite! The International 150 Years Later*, edited by Marcello Musto, 192–93. New York: Bloomsbury Academic, 2014.

Hins, Eugène. "Resistance Societies as the Organization of the Future." In *Workers Unite! The International 150 Years Later*, edited by Marcello Musto, 135. New York: Bloomsbury Academic, 2014.

"International Anarchist Manifesto Against War." In *Anarchism: A Documentary History of Libertarian Ideas*, Vol. 1, *From Anarchy to Anarchism (300 CE to 1939)*, edited by Robert Graham, 289–91. Montréal: Black Rose Books, 2005.

IWA. "Declaration of the Principles of Revolutionary Syndicalism." In *Anarchism: A Documentary History of Libertarian Ideas*, Vol. 1, *From Anarchy to Anarchism (300 CE to 1939)*, edited by Robert Graham, 416–18. Montréal: Black Rose Books, 2005.

IWW, "The Preamble to the Constitution of the Industrial Workers of the World (1908)." In *Rebel Voices: An IWW Anthology*, edited by Joyce L. Kornbluh, 12–13. Oakland, CA: PM Press, 2011.

Jura Federation, The. "Minutes of the Jura Federation Congress (1880)." In *No Gods, No Masters: An Anthology of Anarchism*, edited by Daniel Guérin, 281–86. Oakland, CA: AK Press, 2005.

———. "The Sonvilier Circular." In *Anarchism: A Documentary History of Libertarian Ideas*, Vol. 1, *From Anarchy to Anarchism (300 CE to 1939)*, edited by Robert Graham, 96–98. Montréal: Black Rose Books, 2005.

————. *Road to Power*. Chicago: Samuel A. Bloch, 1909.

Kautsky, Karl. *The Class Struggle (Erfurt Program)*. Chicago: Charles H. Kerr, 1910.

Kropotkin, Peter. *Direct Struggle Against Capital: A Peter Kropotkin Anthology*. Edited by Iain McKay. Oakland, CA: AK Press, 2014.

————. *The Conquest of Bread*. Oakland, CA: AK Press, 2007.

————. *Ethics: Origin and Development*. London: George G. Harrap & Co, 1924.

————. *Fugitive Writings*. Edited by George Woodcock. Montréal: Black Rose Books, 1993.

————. *The Great French Revolution*. Montréal: Black Rose Books, 1989.

————. *Memoirs of a Revolutionist*. Montréal: Black Rose Books, 1989.

————. *Modern Science and Anarchy*. Edited by Iain McKay. Chico, CA: AK Press, 2018.

————. *Mutual Aid: A Factor of Evolution*. Mineola, NY: Dover Publications, 2006.

————. "Proposed Communist Settlement: A New Colony for Tyneside or Wearside." *The Newcastle Daily Chronicle*, February 20, 1895. https://theanarchistlibrary.org/library/petr-kropotkin-proposed-communist-settlement-a-new-colony-for-tyneside-or-wearside.

————. *Words of A Rebel*. Montréal: Black Rose Books, 1992.

Lenin, Vladimir. *Collected Works*, Vol. 10. Edited by Andrew Rothstein. Moscow: Progress Publishers, 1978.

————. *Selected Works*. Moscow: Progress Publishers, 1977.

Liu, Lydia H., Rebecca E. Karl, and Dorothy Ko, eds. *The Birth of Chinese Feminism: Essential Texts in Transnational Theory*. New York: Columbia University Press, 2013.

"The London Declaration (1913)." In Appendix to Thorpe, *"The Workers Themselves*, 320.

Lum, Dyer D. "On Anarchy." In Parsons, *Anarchism: Its Philosophy and Scientific Basis*, 149–58.

————. *Philosophy of Trade Unions*. New York: American Federation of Labor, 1892.

————. "Why I Am a Social Revolutionist." *Twentieth Century* 5, no. 18 (October 1890): 5–6.

Luxemburg, Rosa. *The Essential Rosa Luxemburg: Reform or Revolution and The Mass Strike*. Chicago: Haymarket Books, 2008.

Mackay, John Henry. *The Anarchists: A Picture of Civilization at the Close of the Nineteenth Century*. Boston: Benj. R. Tucker, Publisher, 1891.

Makhno, Nestor. *The Struggle Against the State and Other Essays*. Edited by Alexandre Skirda. San Francisco: AK Press, 1996.

Malatesta, Errico. *A Long and Patient Work: The Anarchist Socialism of L'Agitazione, 1897–1898*. Vol. 3 of *The Complete Works of Malatesta*, edited by Davide Turcato. Chico, CA: AK Press, 2016.

———. *The Anarchist Revolution: Polemical Articles, 1924–1931*. Edited by Vernon Richards. London: Freedom Press, 1995.

———. *At the Café: Conversations on Anarchism*. London: Freedom Press, 2005.

———. *Between Peasants: A Dialogue on Anarchy*. Johannesburg: Zabalaza Books, n.d.

———. *Life and Ideas: The Anarchist Writings of Errico Malatesta*. Edited by Vernon Richards. Oakland, CA: PM Press, 2015.

———. *The Method of Freedom: An Errico Malatesta Reader*. Edited by Davide Turcato. Oakland, CA: AK Press, 2014.

———. "On Collective Responsibility." Institute for Anarchist Theory and History website, n.d. https://ithanarquista.wordpress.com/nestor-makhno-archive/nestor-makhno-archive-english/platform-english/on-collective-responsibility-errico-malatesta.

———. *Towards Anarchy: Malatesta in America, 1899–1900*. Vol. 3 of *The Complete Works of Malatesta*, edited by Davide Turcato. Chico, CA: AK Press, 2019.

Marx, Karl. *Capital, A Critique of Political Economy*, Vol. 1. London: Penguin Books, 1990.

———. *Selected Writings*. Edited by David McLellan. 2nd ed. Oxford: Oxford University Press, 2000.

Marx, Karl, and Frederick Engels. *Collected Works*, Vol. 5. London: Lawrence and Wishart, 1976.

———. *Collected Works*, Vol. 20. London: Lawrence and Wishart, 1985.

———. *Collected Works*, Vol. 22. London: Lawrence and Wishart, 1986.

———. *Collected Works*, Vol. 23. London: Lawrence and Wishart, 1988.

———. *Collected Works*, Vol. 24. London: Lawrence and Wishart, 1989.

———. *Collected Works*, Vol. 26. London: Lawrence and Wishart, 1990.

———. *Collected Works*, Vol. 43. London: Lawrence and Wishart, 1988.

———. *Collected Works*, Vol. 44. London: Lawrence and Wishart, 1989.

———. "Manifesto of the Communist Party." In *Marx, Later Political Writings*, edited by Terrell Carver, 1–30. Cambridge: Cambridge University Press, 1996.

Maximoff, Gregori P. *Program of Anarcho-Syndicalism*. N.p: Guillotine Press, 2015.

Mazzini, Giuseppe. *A Cosmopolitanism of Nations: Giuseppe Mazzini's Writings on Democracy, Nation Building, and International Relations*. Edited by Stefano Recchia and Nadia Urbinati. Princeton: Princeton University Press, 2009.

Mella, Ricardo. *Anarchist Socialism in Early Twentieth-Century Spain: A Ricardo Mella Anthology*. Edited by Stephen Luis Vilaseca. London: Palgrave Macmillan, 2020.

———. "Evolution and Revolution." Biblioteca Anarquista website, April 6, 2013. https://es.theanarchistlibrary.org/library/ricardo-mella-evolucion-y-revolucion

Meltzer, Albert. *The Anarchists in London, 1935–1955*. London: Cienfuegos Press, 1976.

Nabat. "Proceedings of Nabat." In *No Gods, No Masters: An Anthology of Anarchism*, edited by Daniel Guérin, 487–89. Oakland, CA: AK Press, 2005.

Nettlau, Max. "Anarchism: Communist or Individualist? Both." In *Anarchy: An Anthology of Emma Goldman's Mother Earth*, edited by Peter Glassgold, 79–83. New York: Counterpoint, 2000.

Nietzsche, Friedrich. *On the Genealogy of Morality*. Cambridge: Cambridge University Press, 2006.

Novomirsky, Daniil. *Anarchism's Trade Union Programme*. Translated by Paul Sharkey. Kate Sharpley Library website, n.d. https://www.katesharpleylibrary.net/3bk4c0.

Parsons, Albert. *Anarchism: Its Philosophy and Scientific Basis*. Honolulu: University Press of the Pacific, 2003.

Parsons, Lucy. *Freedom, Equality and Solidarity: Writings and Speeches, 1878–1937*. Edited by Gale Ahrens. Chicago: Charles H. Kerr, 2004.

Pataud, Émile, and Émile Pouget. *How We Shall Bring About the Revolution: Syndicalism and the Cooperative Commonwealth*. London: Pluto Press, 1990.

Pindy, Jean-Louis. "Resolution on Resistance Funds." In *Workers Unite! The International 150 Years Later*, edited by Marcello Musto, 132–34. New York: Bloomsbury Academic, 2014.

Pisacane, Carlo. "Political Testament." Translated by Davide Turcato. Robert Graham's Anarchism Weblog, September 22, 2011. https://robertgraham.wordpress.com/2011/09/22/carlo-pisacane-propaganda-by-the-deed-1857.

Plechanoff, George. *Anarchism and Socialism*. Chicago: Charles H. Kerr, 1912.

Postgate, Raymond W., ed. "Debates and Resolutions of the First

International on The Control of Industry." In *Revolution from 1789 to 1906*, 392–94. Boston: Houghton Mifflin Company, 1921.

Pouget, Émile. "The Basis of Trade Unionism." Libcom website, November 19, 2010. https://libcom.org/article/basis-trade-unionism-emile -pouget

———. *Direct Action*. London: Kate Sharpley Library, 2003.

———. "The Party of Labour." Libcom website, November 19, 2010. https://libcom.org/article/party-labour-emile-pouget.

———. "What Is the Trade Union?" In *No Gods, No Masters: An Anthology of Anarchism*, edited by Daniel Guérin, 427–35. Oakland, CA: AK Press, 2005.

Proudhon, Pierre-Joseph. *Property Is Theft: A Pierre-Joseph Proudhon Anthology*. Edited by Iain McKay. Oakland, CA: AK Press, 2011.

———. *What Is Property?* Cambridge: Cambridge University Press, 1994.

Puente, Isaac. *Libertarian Communism*. Johannesburg: Zabalaza Books, 2005.

Raevsky, Maxim. *Anarcho-Syndicalism and the IWW*. Edmonton, AB: Black Cat Press, 2019.

Reclus, Élisée. "An Anarchist on Anarchy." In Parsons, *Anarchism: Its Philosophy and Scientific Basis*, 136–49.

———. *Anarchy, Geography, Modernity: Selected Writings of Élisée Reclus*. Edited by John Clark and Camille Martin. Oakland, CA: PM Press, 2013.

———. "The Development of Liberty in the World." Translated by Shawn P. Wilbur. Libertarian Labyrinth website, September 2, 2016. https:// www.libertarian-labyrinth.org/anarchist-beginnings/elisee-reclus-the -development-of-liberty-in-the-world-c-1850.

"Resolutions of the Congresses of Verviers, 5 to 8 September 1877, and Ghent, 9 to 14 September 1877." In Appendix to Berthier, *Social Democracy and Anarchism*, 188–91.

"Resolutions of the Saint-Imier Congress of the International Workers' Association, 15–16 September 1872." In Appendix to Berthier, *Social Democracy and Anarchism*, 179–83.

Rocker, Rudolf. *Anarchism and Anarcho-Syndicalism*. London: Freedom Press, 1988.

———. *Anarcho-Syndicalism: Theory and Practice*. Oakland, CA: AK Press, 2004.

———. "Declaration of the Principles of Syndicalism," 1919. Translated by Cord-Christian Casper. Academia.edu website, n.d. https://www .academia.edu/39134774/Rudolf_Rocker_Syndicalist_Declaration_ of_Principles.

———. *The London Years*. Nottingham, UK: Five Leaves, 2005.

———. "Marx and Anarchism." Anarchist Library website, April 26, 2009. https://theanarchistlibrary.org/library/rudolf-rocker-marx-and -anarchism.

———. *Nationalism and Culture*. Los Angeles: Rocker Publications Committee, 1937.

———. "The Soviet System or the Dictatorship of the Proletariat." In *Bloodstained: One Hundred Years of Leninist Counterrevolution*, edited by Friends of Aron Baron, 47–56. Chico, CA: AK Press, 2017.

Rogdaev, N. "On the Anarchist Movement in Russia." In Antonioli, ed. *The International Anarchist Congress Amsterdam*, 176–95.

Rogue, J., and Abbey Volcano. "Insurrection at the Intersections: Feminism, Intersectionality, and Anarchism." In Dark Star, *Quiet Rumours*, 43–46.

Roller, Arnold. *The Social General Strike*. Chicago: The Debating Club No. 1, 1905.

Santillán, Diego Abad de. *After the Revolution: Economic Reconstruction in Spain*. Translated by Louis Frank. New York: Greenberg, 1937.

Schapiro, Alexander. "Introduction to Anarcho-Syndicalism and Anarchism." Translated by Paul Sharkey. Robert Graham's Anarchism Weblog, March 15, 2009. https://robertgraham.wordpress.com/alexander -schapiro-pierre-besnard-anarcho-syndicalism-and-anarchism.

Schwitzguébel, Adhémar. "On Resistance Funds." In *Workers Unite! The International 150 Years Later*, edited by Marcello Musto, 138–40. New York: Bloomsbury Academic, 2014.

Seguí, Salvador. "Anarchism and Syndicalism." Translated by Paul Sharkey. Libcom website, August 2, 2015. https://libcom.org/library/ anarchism-syndicalism-salvador-seguí.

Shannon, Deric, and J. Rogue. "Refusing to Wait: Anarchism and Intersectionality." Anarkismo website, November 11, 2009, https://www. anarkismo.net/article/14923.

Stalin, Joseph. *Works*, Vol. 1, *1901–1907*. Moscow: Foreign Languages Publishing House, 1954.

Steimer, Mollie, Simon Fleshin, Voline, Sobol, Schwartz, Lia, Roman, and Ervantian. "Concerning the Platform for an Organization of Anarchists." In *Fighters for Anarchism: Mollie Steimer and Senya Fleshin*, edited by Abe Bluestein, 50–62. Libertarian Publications Group, 1983.

Taber, Mike, ed. *Under the Socialist Banner: Resolutions of the Second International, 1889–1912*. Chicago: Haymarket Books, 2021.

Tucker, Benjamin. *Instead of a Book, by a Man Too Busy to Write One: A*

Fragmentary Exposition of Philosophical Anarchism. 2nd ed. New York: Benj. R. Tucker, Publisher, 1897.

Varlin, Eugène. "Workers Societies." Translated by Iain McKay. Anarchist Writers website, October 6, 2018. https://anarchism.pageabode.com/ precursors-of-syndicalism.

Voline. "Synthesis (Anarchist)." In *The Anarchist Encyclopedia Abridged*, edited by Mitchell Abidor, 197–205. Chico, CA: AK Press, 2019.

———. *The Unknown Revolution 1917–1921*. Oakland, CA: PM Press, 2019.

Warren, Josiah. *The Practical Anarchist: Writings of Josiah Warren*. Edited by Crispin Sartwell. New York: Fordham University Press, 2011.

Wilson, Charlotte. *Anarchist Essays*. Edited by Nicolas Walter. London: Freedom Press, 2000.

Winstanley, Gerrard. *"The Law of Freedom" and Other Writings*. Edited by Christopher Hill. Cambridge: Cambridge University Press, 1983.

Witkop-Rocker, Milly. "What Does the Syndicalist Women's Union Want?" Translated by Jesse Cohn. Anarchist Library website, n.d. https:// theanarchistlibrary.org/library/milly-witkop-rocker-what-does-the- syndicalist-women-s-union-want.

Yuzuru, Kubo. "On Class Struggle and the Daily Struggle (1928)." In *Anarchism: A Documentary History of Libertarian Ideas*, Vol. 1, *From Anarchy to Anarchism (300 CE to 1939)*, edited by Robert Graham, 379–81. Montréal: Black Rose Books, 2005.

Secondary Sources

Ackelsberg, Martha. *Free Women of Spain: Anarchism and the Struggle for the Emancipation of Women*. Oakland, CA: AK Press, 2005.

Adams, Matthew S. *Kropotkin, Read, and the Intellectual History of British Anarchism: Between Reason and Romanticism*. Basingstoke, UK: Palgrave Macmillan, 2015.

Adams, Matthew S., and Ruth Kinna, eds. *Anarchism, 1914–18: Internationalism, Anti-Militarism and War*. Manchester: Manchester University Press, 2017.

Anderson, Benedict. *The Age of Globalization: Anarchists and the Anti-Colonial Imagination*. London: Verso, 2013.

Archer, Julian P. W. *The First International in France, 1864–1872: Its Origins, Theories, and Impact*. Lanham, MD: University Press of America, 1997.

Arshinov, Peter. *History of the Makhnovist Movement, 1918–1921*. London: Freedom Press, 2005.

Avrich, Paul. *An American Anarchist: The Life of Voltairine de Cleyre*. Chico, CA: AK Press, 2018.

———. *Anarchist Portraits*. Princeton: Princeton University Press, 1988.

———. *The Haymarket Tragedy*. Princeton: Princeton University Press, 1984.

———. *The Modern School Movement: Anarchism and Education in the United States*. Oakland, CA: AK Press, 2006.

———. *Sacco and Vanzetti: The Anarchist Background*. Princeton: Princeton University Press, 1991.

———. *The Russian Anarchists*. Oakland, CA: AK Press, 2005.

Avrich, Paul, and Karen Avrich. *Sasha and Emma: The Anarchist Odyssey of Alexander Berkman and Emma Goldman*. Cambridge, MA: Harvard University Press, 2012.

Baker, Zoe. "Anarchism and Democracy." Anarchopac.com, April 15, 2022. https://theanarchistlibrary.org/library/zoe-baker-anarchism-and-democracy.

———. "Bakunin was a Racist." Anarchopac.com, October 31, 2021. https://theanarchistlibrary.org/library/zoe-baker-bakunin-was-a-racist.

Bantman, Constance. "From Trade Unionism to Syndicalisme Révolutionnaire to Syndicalism: The British Origins of French Syndicalism." In Berry and Bantman, eds., *New Perspectives on Anarchism, Labour and Syndicalism*, 127–40.

———. *The French Anarchists in London, 1880–1914: Exile and Transnationalism in the First Globalisation*. Liverpool: Liverpool University Press, 2013.

———. "The Militant Go-between: Émile Pouget's Transnational Propaganda (1880–1914)." *Labour History Review* 74, no. 3 (2009): 274–87.

Bantman, Constance, and Bert Altena, eds. *Reassessing the Transnational Turn: Scales of Analysis in Anarchist and Syndicalist Studies*. Oakland, CA: PM Press, 2017.

Barton, Mary S. "The Global War on Anarchism: The United States and International Anarchist Terrorism, 1898–1904." *Diplomatic History* 39, no. 2 (2015): 303–30.

Beaney, Michael. "Analytic Philosophy and History of Philosophy: The Development of the Idea of Rational Reconstruction." In *The Historical Turn in Analytic Philosophy*, edited by Erich H. Reck, 231–60. London: Palgrave Macmillan, 2013.

Beer, Max. *A History of British Socialism*, Vol. 2. London: G. Bell and Sons, 1921.

Bernecker, Walther L. "The Strategies of 'Direct Action' and Violence in Spanish Anarchism." In *Social Protest, Violence and Terror in Nineteenth- and Twentieth-Century Europe*, edited by Wolfgang J Mommsen and Gerhard Hirschfeld, 88–111. London: The Macmillan Press, 1982.

Berry, Christopher J. *The Social Theory of the Scottish Enlightenment*. Edinburgh: Edinburgh University Press, 1997.

Berry, David. *A History of the French Anarchist Movement: 1917 to 1945*. Oakland, CA: AK Press, 2009.

Berry, David, and Constance Bantman, eds. *New Perspectives on Anarchism, Labour and Syndicalism: The Individual, the National and the Transnational*. Newcastle, UK: Cambridge Scholars Publishing, 2010.

Berthier, René. *Social Democracy and Anarchism in the International Workers' Association, 1864–1877*. London: Anarres Editions, 2015.

Boehm, Christopher. *Hierarchy in the Forest: The Evolution of Egalitarian Behavior*. Cambridge, MA: Harvard University Press, 2001.

Boggs, Carl. "Marxism, Prefigurative Communism and the Problem of Workers' Control." *Radical America* 11 (1977): 99–122.

Bookchin, Murray. *The Spanish Anarchists: The Heroic Years, 1868–1936*. Oakland, CA: AK Press, 1998.

Breines, Wini. "Community and Organization: The New Left and Michels' 'Iron Law.'" *Social Problems* 27, no. 4 (1980): 419–29.

Brinton, Maurice. "The Bolsheviks and Workers' Control, 1917–1921: The State and Counter-Revolution." In *For Workers' Power: The Selected Writings of Maurice Brinton*, edited by David Goodway, 293–378. Oakland, CA: AK Press, 2004.

Buttà, Fausto. *Living Like Nomads: The Milanese Anarchist Movement Before Fascism*. Newcastle, UK: Cambridge Scholars Publishing, 2015.

Cahm, Caroline. *Kropotkin and the Rise of Revolutionary Anarchism, 1872–1886*. Cambridge: Cambridge University Press, 1989.

Campbell, Al, and Mehmet Ufuk Tutan. "Human Development and Socialist Institutional Transformation: Continual Incremental Changes and Radical Breaks." *Studies in Political Economy* 82, no. 1 (2008): 153–70.

Cappelletti, Ángel J. *Anarchism in Latin America*. Chico, CA: AK Press, 2017.

Carlson, Andrew R. *Anarchism in Germany*, Vol. 1, *The Early Movement*. Metuchen, NJ: The Scarecrow Press, 1972.

Carr, E. H. *Michael Bakunin*. London: The Macmillan Press, 1975.

Casas, Juan Gómez. *Anarchist Organisation: The History of the F.A.I*. Montréal: Black Rose Books, 1986.

Castleton, Edward. "The Many Revolutions of Pierre-Joseph Proudhon." In *The 1848 Revolutions and European Political Thought,* edited by Douglas Moggach and Gareth Stedman Jones, 39–69. Cambridge: Cambridge University Press, 2018.

———. "The Origins of 'Collectivism': Pierre-Joseph Proudhon's Contested Legacy and the Debate About Property in the International Workingmen's Association and the League of Peace and Freedom." *Global Intellectual History* 2, no. 2 (2017): 169–95.

Christie, Stuart. *We, the Anarchists! A Study of the Iberian Anarchist Federation (FAI) 1927–1937.* Oakland, CA: AK Press, 2008.

Clark, Martin. *The Italian Risorgimento.* 2nd ed. Harlow, UK: Pearson Education Limited, 2009.

Clastres, Pierre. *Archeology of Violence.* New York: Semiotext(e), 1994.

———. *Society Against the State: Essays in Political Anthropology.* New York: Zone Books, 1989.

Clutterbuck, Lindsay. "The Progenitors of Terrorism: Russian Revolutionaries or Extreme Irish Republicans?" *Terrorism and Political Violence* 16, no. 1 (2004): 154–81.

Cole, G. D. H. *A History of Socialist Thought,* Vol. 2, *Marxism and Anarchism, 1850–1890.* London: Macmillan, 1974.

Cole, Peter, David Struthers, and Kenyon Zimmer, eds. *Wobblies of the World: A Global History of the IWW.* London: Pluto Press, 2017.

Colins, Patricia, and Sirma Bilge. *Intersectionality.* 2nd edition. Cambridge, UK: Polity Press, 2020.

Cornell, Andrew. *Unruly Equality: US Anarchism in the 20th Century.* Oakland, CA: California University Press, 2016.

Cox, Laurence, and Alf Gunvald Nilsen. *We Make Our Own History: Marxism and Social Movements in the Twilight of Neoliberalism.* London: Pluto Press, 2014.

Damier, Vadim. *Anarcho-Syndicalism in the 20th Century.* Edmonton, AB: Black Cat Press, 2009.

Darlington, Ralph. *Radical Unionism: The Rise and Fall of Revolutionary Syndicalism.* Chicago: Haymarket Books, 2013.

Di Paola, Pietro. *The Knights Errant of Anarchy: London and the Italian Anarchist Diaspora, 1880–1917.* Chico, CA: AK Press, 2017.

Dobres, Marcia-Anne. "Digging up Gender in the Earliest Human Societies." In *A Companion to Gender History,* edited by Teresa A. Meade and Merry E. Wiesner-Hanks, 211–26. Malden, MA: Blackwell Publishing, 2004.

Draper, Hal. *The "Dictatorship of the Proletariat" from Marx to Lenin.* New York: Monthly Review Press, 1987.

———. *Karl Marx's Theory of Revolution*, Vol. 3, *The "Dictatorship of the Proletariat."* New York: Monthly Review Press, 1986.

———. *Karl Marx's Theory of Revolution*, Vol. 4, *Critique of Other Socialisms.* New York: Monthly Review Press, 1990.

Ealham, Chris. *Anarchism and the City: Revolution and Counter-Revolution in Barcelona, 1898–1937.* Oakland, CA: AK Press, 2010.

———. *Living Anarchism: José Peirats and the Spanish Anarcho-Syndicalist Movement.* Oakland, CA: AK Press, 2015.

Eckhardt, Wolfgang. *The First Socialist Schism: Bakunin vs. Marx in the International Working Men's Association.* Oakland, CA: PM Press, 2016.

Enckell, Marianne. "Bakunin and the Jura Federation." In *Arise Ye Wretched of the Earth: The First International in Global Perspective*, edited by Fabrice Bensimon, Quentin Deluermoz, and Jeanne Moisand, 355–65. Leiden, NL: Brill, 2018.

Esenwein, George Richard. *Anarchist Ideology and the Working-Class Movement in Spain, 1868–1898.* Berkeley: University of California Press, 1989.

Evans, Danny. *Revolution and the State: Anarchism in the Spanish Civil War, 1936–1939.* Chico, CA: AK Press, 2020.

Fernández, Frank. *Cuban Anarchism: The History of a Movement.* Tucson, AZ: See Sharp Press, 2001.

Ferretti, Federico. *Anarchy and Geography: Reclus and Kropotkin in the UK.* London: Routledge, 2019.

Fleming, Marie. *The Anarchist Way to Socialism: Élisée Reclus and Nineteenth-Century European Anarchism.* London: Croom Helm Ltd, 1979.

Frost, Ginger. "Love is Always Free: Anarchism, Free Unions and Utopianism in Edwardian England." *Anarchist Studies* 17, no. 1 (2009): 73–94.

Garner, Jason. *Goals and Means: Anarchism, Syndicalism, and Internationalism in the Origins of the Federación Anarquista Ibérica.* Chico, CA: AK Press, 2016.

Geuss, Raymond. *History and Illusion in Politics.* Cambridge: Cambridge University Press, 2001.

———. *Morality, Culture and History: Essays on German Philosophy.* Cambridge: Cambridge University Press, 1999.

Gindin, Sam. "Socialism 'With Sober Senses': Developing Workers' Capacities." *The Socialist Register* 34 (1998): 75–99.

Goodstein, Phil H. *The Theory of the General Strike from the French Revolution to Poland.* Boulder, CO: East European Monographs, 1984.

Goyens, Tom. *Beer and Revolution: The German Anarchist Movement in New York City, 1880–1914.* Urbana: University of Illinois Press, 2007.

————. "Johann Most and the German Anarchists." In *Radical Gotham: Anarchism in New York City from Schwab's Saloon to Occupy Wall Street*, edited by Tom Goyens, 12–32. Urbana: University of Illinois Press, 2017.

Graeber, David, and David Wengrow. *The Dawn of Everything: A New History of Humanity*. London: Allen Lane, 2021.

Graham, Robert. *We Do Not Fear Anarchy, We Invoke It: The First International and the Origins of the Anarchist Movement*. Oakland, CA: AK Press, 2015.

Guglielmo, Jennifer. *Living the Revolution: Italian Women's Resistance and Radicalism in New York City, 1880–1945*. Chapel Hill: The University of North Carolina Press, 2010.

Guillamón, Agustín. *Ready for Revolution: The CNT Defense Committees in Barcelona, 1933–1938*. Oakland, CA: AK Press, 2014.

Gurney, John. *Gerrard Winstanley: The Digger's Life and Legacy*. London: Pluto Press, 2013.

Hart, John M. *Anarchism and the Mexican Working Class, 1860–1931*. Austin: University of Texas Press, 1978.

Hatab, Lawrence J. *Nietzsche's 'On the Genealogy of Morality': An Introduction*. Cambridge: Cambridge University Press, 2008.

Haupt, Georges. *Aspects of International Socialism, 1871–1914*. Cambridge: Cambridge University Press, 1986.

Hirsch, Steven, and Lucien van der Walt, eds. *Anarchism and Syndicalism in the Colonial and Postcolonial World, 1870–1940: The Praxis of National Liberation, Internationalism, and Social Revolution*. Leiden, NL: Brill, 2010.

Hobsbawm, Eric. *Revolutionaries*. London: Phoenix, 1994.

Hoyt, Andrew Douglas. "And They Called Them 'Galleanisti': The Rise of the *Cronca Sovversiva* and the Formation of America's Most Infamous Anarchist Faction (1895–1912)." PhD diss., University of Minnesota, 2018.

Hunt, Richard N. *The Political Ideas of Marx and Engels*, Vol. 1, *Marxism and Totalitarian Democracy, 1818–1850*. Pittsburgh: University of Pittsburgh Press, 1974.

————. *The Political Ideas of Marx and Engels*, Vol. 2, *Classical Marxism, 1850–1895*. Pittsburgh: University of Pittsburgh Press, 1984.

Institute for Anarchist Studies, *Perspectives on Anarchist Theory*, no. 29, *Anarcha-Feminisms* (2016).

Jennings, Jeremy. *Syndicalism in France: A Study of Ideas*. Basingstoke, UK: Macmillan, 1990.

Jensen, Richard Bach. *The Battle Against Anarchist Terrorism: An International History, 1878–1934.* Cambridge: Cambridge University Press, 2014.

John, Kenneth. "Anti-Parliamentary Passage: South Wales and the Internationalism of Sam Mainwaring (1841–1907)." PhD diss., University of Greenwich, 2001.

Joll, James. *The Anarchists.* London: Methuen & Co, 1969.

Kaplan, Temma. *Anarchists of Andalusia, 1868–1903.* Princeton: Princeton University Press, 1977.

Kelly, Robert L. *The Lifeways of Hunter-Gatherers: The Foraging Spectrum.* 2nd ed. Cambridge: Cambridge University Press, 2013.

Khuri-Makdisi, Ilham. *The Eastern Mediterranean and the Making of Global Radicalism, 1860–1914.* Berkeley: University of California Press, 2010.

Kinna, Ruth. "Anarchism and Feminism" In *Brill's Companion to Anarchist Philosophy*, edited by Nathan Jun, 253–84. Leiden, NL: Brill Academic Publishers, 2017.

———. *Kropotkin: Reviewing the Classical Anarchist Tradition.* Edinburgh: Edinburgh University Press, 2016.

Kinna, Ruth, and Alex Prichard. "Anarchism and Non-Domination." *Journal of Political Ideologies* 24, no. 3 (2019): 221–40.

Kissack, Terence. *Free Comrades: Anarchism and Homosexuality in the United States, 1895–1917.* Oakland, CA: AK Press, 2008.

Kissin, S. F. *War and the Marxists: Socialist Theory and Practice in Capitalist Wars*, Vol. 1, *1848–1918.* London: Routledge, 2019.

Kuper, Adam. *The Reinvention of Primitive Society: Transformations of a Myth.* London: Routledge, 2005.

Laursen, Ole Birk. "'Anarchism, Pure and Simple': M. P. T. Acharya, Anti-Colonialism and the International Anarchist Movement." *Postcolonial Studies* 23, no. 2 (2020): 241–55.

Lehning, Arthur. "Bakunin's Conception of Revolutionary Organisations and Their Role: A Study of His 'Secret Societies.'" In *Essays in Honour of E. H. Carr*, edited by Chimen Abramsky, 57–81. London: The Macmillan Press, 1974.

———. *From Buonarroti to Bakunin: Studies in International Socialism.* Leiden, NL: E. J. Brill, 1970.

Leier, Mark. *Bakunin: The Creative Passion—A Biography.* New York: Seven Stories Press, 2009.

Leopold, David. "A Solitary Life." In *Max Stirner*, edited by Saul Newman, 21–41. Basingstoke, UK: Palgrave Macmillan, 2011.

Levy, Carl. *Gramsci and the Anarchists.* Oxford: Berg, 1999.

Linse, Ulrich. "'Propaganda by Deed' and 'Direct Action': Two Concepts of Anarchist Violence." In *Social Protest, Violence and Terror in Nineteenth- and Twentieth-Century Europe*, edited by Wolfgang J Mommsen and Gerhard Hirschfeld, 201–29. London: The Macmillan Press, 1982.

Lipotkin, Lazar. *The Russian Anarchist Movement in North America*. Edmonton, AB: Black Cat Press, 2019.

Marshall, Peter. *Demanding the Impossible: A History of Anarchism*. London: Harper Perennial, 2008.

Martin, James J. *Men Against the State: The Expositors of Individualist Anarchism in America, 1827–1908*. Colorado Springs: Ralph Myles Publisher, 1970.

McDermott, Kevin, and Jeremy Agnew *The Comintern: A History of International Communism from Lenin to Stalin*. Basingstoke, UK: Macmillan, 1996.

McKay, Iain. "Communism and Syndicalism." Anarchist Writers website, May 25, 2012. http://anarchism.pageabode.com/anarcho/communism-syndicalism.

———. "The State and Revolution: Theory and Practice." In *Bloodstained: One Hundred Years of Leninist Counterrevolution*, edited by Friends of Aron Baron, 61–117. Chico, CA: AK Press, 2017.

Meek, Ronald L. *Smith, Marx, and After: Ten Essays in the Development of Economic Thought*. Dordrecht, NL: Springer, 1977.

Merriman, John. *The Dynamite Club: How a Bombing in Fin-de-Siècle Paris Ignited the Age of Modern Terror*. New Haven: Yale University Press, 2016.

———. *Massacre: The Life and Death of the Paris Commune of 1871*. New Haven: Yale University Press, 2014.

Messer-Kruse, Timothy. *The Haymarket Conspiracy: Transatlantic Anarchist Networks*. Urbana: University of Illinois Press, 2012.

Miller, David. *Anarchism*. London: J.M. Dent and Sons, 1984.

Miller, Martin A. *Kropotkin*. Chicago: University of Chicago Press, 1976.

Mintz, Frank. *Anarchism and Workers' Self-Management in Revolutionary Spain*. Oakland, CA: AK Press, 2013.

Mintz, Jerome R. *The Anarchists of Casas Viejas*. Bloomington: Indiana University Press, 1982.

Moss, Bernard H. *The Origins of the French Labor Movement, 1930–1914: The Socialism of Skilled Workers*. Berkeley: University of California Press, 1980.

Nelles, Dieter. "Anarchosyndicalism and the Sexual Reform Movement in the Weimar Republic." Paper Presented at the Free Love and

Labour Movement Workshop at the International Institute of Social History, Amsterdam, 2000. https://www.academia.edu/23692251/Anarchosyndicalism_and_the_Sexual_Reform_Movement_in_the_Weimar_Republic.

Nettlau, Max. *A Short History of Anarchism*. Edited by Heiner M. Becker. London: Freedom Press, 1996.

Neville, Robert G. "The Courrières Colliery Disaster, 1906." *Journal of Contemporary History* 13, no. 1 (1978): 33–52.

Nicholas, Lucy. "Gender and Sexuality." In *The Palgrave Handbook of Anarchism*, edited by Carl Levy and Matthew S. Adams, 603–2. London: Palgrave Macmillan, 2019.

Nightingale, John. "The Concept of Solidarity in Anarchist Thought." PhD diss., Loughborough University, 2015.

Papayanis, Nicholas. "Alphones Merrheim and the Strike of Hennebont: The Struggle for the Eight-Hour Day in France." International Review of Social History 16, no. 2 (1971): 159–83.

———. *Alphonse Merrheim: The Emergence of Reformism in Revolutionary Syndicalism, 1871–1925*. Dordrecht, NL: Martinus Nijhoff Publishers, 1985.

Paz, Abel. *Durruti in the Spanish Revolution*. Oakland, CA: AK Press, 2006.

Peirats, José. *The CNT in the Spanish Revolution*, Vol. 1. Edited by Chris Ealham. Oakland, CA: PM Press, 2011.

———. *What Is the C.N.T?* London: Simian, 1974.

Pelling, Henry. *A History of British Trade Unionism*. 5th ed. Basingstoke, UK: Palgrave Macmillan, 1992.

Pernicone, Nunzio. *Italian Anarchism, 1864–1892*. Princeton: Princeton University Press, 1993.

Pernicone, Nunzio, and Fraser M. Ottanelli. *Assassins against the Old Order: Italian Anarchist Violence in Fin de Siècle Europe*. Urbana: University of Illinois Press, 2018.

Persson, Lennart K. "Revolutionary Syndicalism in Sweden Before the Second World War." In van der Linden and Thorpe, *Revolutionary Syndicalism*, 81–99.

Pinfari, Marco. "Exploring the Terrorist Nature of Political Assassinations: A Reinterpretation of the Orsini Attentat." *Terrorism and Political Violence* 21, no. 4 (2009): 580–94.

Pinsolle, Dominique. "Sabotage, the IWW, and Repression: How the American Reinterpretation of a French Concept Gave Rise to a New International Conception of Sabotage." In Cole, Struthers, and Zimmer, *Wobblies of the World: A Global History of the IWW*, 44–58.

Pinta, Saku. "Towards a Libertarian Communism: A Conceptual History of the Intersections Between Anarchisms and Marxisms." PhD diss., Loughborough University, 2013.

Pomper, Philip. "Nechaev and Tsaricide: The Conspiracy within the Conspiracy." *The Russian Review* 33, no. 2 (1974): 123–38.

Quail, John. *The Slow Burning Fuse: The Lost History of British Anarchists*. London: Granada Publishing Limited, 1978.

Raekstad, Paul. *Karl Marx's Realist Critique of Capitalism: Freedom, Alienation, and Socialism*. London: Palgrave Macmillan, 2022.

Raekstad, Paul, and Sofa Saio Gradin. *Prefigurative Politics: Building Tomorrow Today*. Cambridge, UK: Polity Press, 2020.

Rapoport, David C. "The Four Waves of Modern Terrorism." In *Attacking Terrorism: Elements of a Grand Strategy*, edited by Audrey Cronin and James Ludes, 46–73. Washington, DC: Georgetown University Press, 2004.

Rapp, John A. *Daoism and Anarchism: Critiques of State Autonomy in Ancient and Modern China*. London: Continuum Books, 2012.

Ravindranathan, T.R. *Bakunin and the Italians*. Montréal: McGill-Queen's University Press, 1988.

Rider, Nick. "The Practice of Direct Action: The Barcelona Rent Strike of 1931." In *For Anarchism: History, Theory and Practice*, edited by David Goodway, 79–105. London: Routledge, 1989.

Ridley, F. F. *Revolutionary Syndicalism in France: The Direct Action of Its Time*. Cambridge: Cambridge University Press, 1970.

Rocker, Rudolf. *Pioneers of American Freedom: Origin of Liberal and Radical Thought in America*. Los Angeles: Rocker Publication Committee, 1949.

Ryley, Peter. *Making Another World Possible: Anarchism, Anti-Capitalism and Ecology in Late Nineteenth- and Early Twentieth-Century Britain*. New York: Bloomsbury Academic, 2013.

Schmidt, Michael, and Lucien van der Walt. *Black Flame: The Revolutionary Class Politics of Anarchism and Syndicalism*. Oakland, CA: AK Press, 2009.

Scott, James C. *The Art of Not Being Governed: An Anarchist History of Upland Southeast Asia*. New Haven: Yale University Press, 2009.

Senta, Antonio. *Luigi Galleani: The Most Dangerous Anarchist in America*. Chico, CA: AK Press, 2019.

Seth, Ronald. *The Russian Terrorists: The Story of the Narodniki*. London: Barrie & Rockliff, 1966.

Short, K. R. M. *The Dynamite War: Irish-American Bombs in Victorian Britain*. Dublin: Gill and Macmillan, 1979.

Shpayer-Makov. Haia. "Anarchism in British Public Opinion, 1880–1914." *Victorian Studies* 31, no. 4 (1988): 487–516.

Skinner, Quentin. *The Foundations of Modern Political Thought*, Vol. 1, *The Renaissance*. Cambridge: Cambridge University Press, 1978.

———. "Interpretation and the Understanding of Speech Acts." In *Visions of Politics*, Vol. 1, *Regarding Method*, 103–27. Cambridge: Cambridge University Press, 2002.

———. "Meaning and Understanding in the History of Ideas." In *Visions of Politics*, Vol. 1, *Regarding Method*, 57–89. Cambridge: Cambridge University Press, 2002.

Skirda, Alexandre. *Facing the Enemy: A History of Anarchist Organization from Proudhon to May 1968*. Oakland, CA: AK Press, 2002.

Smith, Angel. *Anarchism, Revolution and Reaction: Catalan Labour and the Crisis of the Spanish State, 1989–1923*. New York: Berghahn Books, 2007.

Smith, Denis Mack. *Mazzini*. New Haven: Yale University Press, 1994.

Spitzer, Alan B. *The Revolutionary Theories of Louis Auguste Blanqui*. New York: Columbia University Press, 1957.

Stafford, David. *From Anarchism to Reformism: A Study of the Political Activities of Paul Brousse, 1870–90*. London: Weidenfeld and Nicolson, 1971.

Steenson, Gary P. *After Marx, Before Lenin: Marxism and Socialist Working-Class Parties in Europe, 1884–1914*. Pittsburgh: University of Pittsburgh Press, 1991.

Stepelevitch, Laurence S. "The Revival of Max Stirner." *Journal of the History of Ideas* 35, no. 2 (1974): 323–28.

Suriano, Juan. *Paradoxes of Utopia: Anarchist Culture and Politics in Buenos Aires, 1890–1910*. Oakland, CA: AK Press, 2010.

Thomas, Paul. *Karl Marx and the Anarchists*. London: Routledge & Kegan Paul, 1980.

Thorpe, Wayne. "The IWW and the Dilemmas of Internationalism." In Cole, Struthers, and Zimmer, *Wobblies of the World: A Global History of the IWW*, 105–23.

———. *"The Workers Themselves": Revolutionary Syndicalism and International Labour, 1913–1923*. Dordrecht, NL: Kluwer Academic Publishers, 1989.

———. "Uneasy Family: Revolutionary Syndicalism in Europe From the Charte d'Amiens to World War One." In Berry and Bantman, eds., *New Perspectives on Anarchism, Labour and Syndicalism*, 16–42.

Tilly, Charles. *European Revolutions, 1492–1992*. Oxford: Blackwell, 1993.

Turcato, Davide. "Anarchist Communism." In *The Palgrave Handbook of Anarchism*, edited by Carl Levy and Matthew S. Adams, 237–47. London: Palgrave Macmillan, 2019.

———. *Making Sense of Anarchism: Errico Malatesta's Experiments With Revolution, 1889–1900*. Basingstoke, UK: Palgrave Macmillan, 2012.

Van der Linden, Marcel, and Wayne Thorpe, eds. *Revolutionary Syndicalism: An International Perspective*. Aldershot, UK: Scolar Press, 1990.

Van der Walt, Lucien. "Anarchism and Marxism." In *Brill's Companion to Anarchist Philosophy*, edited by Nathan Jun, 505–58. Leiden, NL: Brill Academic Publishers, 2017.

———. "Syndicalism." In *The Palgrave Handbook of Anarchism*, edited by Carl Levy and Matthew S. Adams, 249–63. London: Palgrave Macmillan, 2019.

Verhoeven, Claudia. *The Odd Man Karakozov: Imperial Russia, Modernity, and the Birth of Terrorism*. Ithaca: Cornell University Press, 2009.

Vincent, Steven K. *Pierre-Joseph Proudhon and the Rise of French Republican Socialism*. Oxford: Oxford University Press, 1984.

Whitham, William. "César De Paepe and the Ideas of the First International." *Modern Intellectual History* 16, no. 3 (2019): 897–925.

Wilbur, Shawn P. "Joseph Déjacque and the First Emergence of Anarchism." In *Contr'un 5: Our Lost Continent*, 2016.

———. "Mutualism." In *The Palgrave Handbook of Anarchism*, edited by Carl Levy and Matthew S. Adams, 213–24. London: Palgrave Macmillan, 2019.

———. "Pierre-Joseph Proudhon: Self-Government and the Citizen-State." Libertarian Labyrinth website, June 5, 2013. https://www.libertarian-labyrinth.org/contrun/pierre-joseph-proudhon-self-government-and-the-citizen-state-2.

Williams, Dana M. "Black Panther Radical Factionalization and the Development of Black Anarchism." *Journal of Black Studies* 46, no. 7 (2015): 678–703.

Wolf, Jeremy. "Iron Law of Wages." In *The Encyclopedia of Political Thought*, edited by Michael Gibbons. Chichester, UK: Wiley-Blackwell, 2014. https://onlinelibrary.wiley.com/doi/pdf/10.1002/9781118474396.wbept0541.

Wood, Ellen Meiksins. *Citizens to Lords: A Social History of Western Political Thought from Antiquity to the Middle Ages*. London: Verso, 2011.

Woodcock, George. *Anarchism: A History of Libertarian Ideals and Movements*. 2nd ed. Harmondsworth, UK: Penguin Books, 1986.

———. *Pierre-Joseph Proudhon: A Biography*. Montréal: Black Rose Books, 1987.

Woodcock, George, and Ivan Avakumović. *Peter Kropotkin: From Prince to Rebel*. Montréal: Black Rose Books, 1990.

Yeoman, James. *Print Culture and the Formation of the Anarchist Movement in Spain, 1890–1915*. New York: Routledge, 2020.

Zimmer, Kenyon. "Archiving the American Anarchist Press: Reflections on Format, Accessibility and Language." *American Periodicals: A Journal of History & Criticism* 29, no. 1 (2019): 9–11.

———. *Immigrants Against the State: Yiddish and Italian Anarchism in America*. Urbana: University of Illinois Press, 2015.

Zurbrugg, A.W. *Anarchist Perspectives in Peace and War, 1900–1918*. London: Anarres Editions, 2018.

Index

abolition of slavery, 132–33. *See also* state abolition

abortion, 133, 288, 358

Acharya, M. P. T., 274, 355–56

action. *See* direct action

affinity groups, 4; and insurrectionist anarchism, 180–82, 353; and mass anarchism, 223, 224, 240; and militancy, 239, 240; and prefiguration, 126; and syndicalist anarchism, 293; and women's equality, 128, 355

The Alarm (paper), 41

Allemane, Jean, 141

Alliance (secret organization), 309, 310, 311–13, 314, 320, 321, 322. *See also* organizational dualism

Alliance of Socialist Democracy (Marx and Engels), 36

All-Japan Libertarian Federation of Labor Unions (Zenkoku Rôdô Kumiai Jiyû Rengôkai), 263, 274

All-Russian Conference of Anarcho-Syndicalists, 333

Amberny, Jean-Antoine, 150–51

Amsterdam Congress (1907), 261, 265, 300, 324

anarcha-feminism, 357–58

anarchism: contemporary movements, 356–59; and critique of society, 69–79; definitions and usage, 1–2, 13–44; and direct action, 130–35; and general strike, 296–306; history and context, 1–2, 3–4, 7–8,

26–29, 355–56, 359–60; insurrectionist, 171–73, 175–210, 353–55; main elements of, 2–3, 10–11, 347–49; mass, 171–73, 211–48, 353–55; and means and ends, unity of, 117–22, 351, 361–62; and organizational dualism, 307–46; and parliamentarism, 143–53; and political struggle, 168–71; and prefiguration, 122–30; and social revolution, 99–117, 359, 360–62; sources on, 4–5, 6, 8–10, 355–56; and spirit of revolt, 135–39; and state capitalism, 161–67; and state socialism, 141–43, 352–53; strategies of, 97–98, 351–52; syndicalist, 249–77, 279–306; and theory of practice, 45–60, 350–51; value system of, 61–69; and vision of future, 79–96, 348; and worker's states, 154–61

anarchism without adjectives, 2, 43, 91–92

Anarchist International, 344. *See also* platformism

Anarchist Liaison Committee of Catalonia, 331

anarcho-syndicalism: emergence of, 267–72; and IWMA, 272–74; and mass anarchism, 223; and organizational dualism, 328–32; overview, 2, 250, 266; and revolutionary syndicalism, 266, 275–77; and synthesism, 41–42, 332–33,

457

336; and trade unions, 266–76, 327–28; usage of term, 267, 268, 274–75; and women's unions, 287
Anarcho-Syndicalism (Rocker), 276
anarchy, usage of, 16, 20–22, 79, 348
Anarkhichesky Vestnik (Anarchist Herald), 333
Anderson, Benedict, 2
Andrieux, Louis, 203
Angiolillo, Michele, 205, 208
anticapitalism, 4. *See also* capitalism; state abolition
anticolonialism, 109–10. *See also* colonialism
antimilitarism, 131, 153. *See also* militancy
antiorganizationalism, 86, 126, 172, 177–78, 182, 216, 308. *See also* coordination and cooperation
anti-statism. *See* state abolition
Antwerp Congress (1873), 297
Argentine Regional Workers' Federation (FORA), 263, 264–65, 267, 269, 272, 274
Armand, E., 43
armed insurrection. *See* insurrectionist anarchism; militancy
Arshinov, Peter, 333, 335, 336, 341–42
artisans, 70–71
assassinations: and anarchism, 22, 42, 102, 207–9, 227–28; and insurrectionist anarchism, 178, 353; and mass anarchism, 239; and propaganda of the deed, 185, 186, 187, 192, 197–98, 201–3, 205–6, 209; and secret revolutionary organizations, 316; and state repression, 178, 295
assemblies. *See* coordination and cooperation; general assemblies
Association of Anarchist Federalists (AFA), 333–34, 345

ateneos (athenaeums), 116–17. *See also* trade unionism
atheism, 313
authority and authoritarianism: and anarchism, 1, 7–8, 67, 79, 84, 85–86, 348, 359; and Bakunin, 311, 314, 316, 317, 318, 320; and Black anarchism, 357; and direct action, 132, 135; and First International, 26, 27, 30, 33, 124; vs. freedom, 65, 236; and mass anarchism, 217, 219–21, 244; and means and ends, unity of, 119–20; and platformism, 338–40, 343; of state, 74, 75–76, 78; and state socialism, 159, 163; and trade unions, 325–27; and workers' state, 154, 155, 160
autonomous regions, 247. *See also* militant minorities

Baginski, Max, 4, 148–49, 215, 233, 293–94
Ba Jin (Li Yaotang), 16
Bakunin, Michael, 4; and anarchism, history of, 29, 30–31, 32, 35, 37–38, 355; and anarchism, usage of term, 36; antisemitism of, 79; on class society, 70–71; critique against, 313–16, 318; direct action of, 186, 191, 311; and economic determinism, 58; on evolutionary change, 112; and First International, 24–25, 27, 371n102; on freedom, 6, 62, 64, 65–66, 67; on general strike, 297; on humanity, 46, 47, 48, 55, 56; Marx on, 168; and mass anarchism, 212; on means and ends, unity of, 125; and organizational dualism, 308–21; on Paris Commune, 188–89; on parliamentarism, 147, 150–51; on political action, 169–70; and propaganda of the deed, 187, 190;

internationalism: and anarchism, 2, 3, 15, 108–10; and anarcho-syndicalism, 269–70; and general strike, 297, 299; and organizational dualism, 312–13, 319; and state socialism, 153; and syndicalist anarchism, 251, 252–53, 292

International Secretariat of National Trade Union Centers (ISNTUC), 268–69

International Social Revolutionary Congress (1881), 200, 202, 322

International Syndicalist Congress (1913), 268–70

International Workingmen's Association (IWMA). See First International; Saint-Imier International

International Working People's Association, 176

intersectionality, 357–59

Irish Transport and General Workers' Union, 263

Italian Anarchist Union, 216, 247, 308, 344

Italian Committee for Social Revolution (CIRS), 190

Italian Federation: and anarchism, 24, 25, 34, 36; and Benevento affair, 196; and insurrectionist anarchism, 190–91, 192–93; and organizational dualism, 323; and political struggle, 170; and state repression, 178–79

Italian Syndicalist Union (USI), 263, 269, 272, 273, 308, 328

Itō Noe, 355

Iturbe, Lola, 128

Jensen, Richard Bach, 209

Jura Federation, 25, 32, 35, 36, 124, 196, 254

Kautsky, Karl, 265–66

Kirillovsky, Yakob Isaevich, 267–68

Koenigstein, François (Ravachol), 204, 208

Kōtoku Shūsui, 355–56

Kropotkin, Peter, 4; and anarchism, 16, 29, 30, 32, 40–41, 88, 98, 236, 355; on anarchy, 89; on autonomous regions, 247; on decision making, 88; on Déjacque, 35; and direct action, 135, 197; on freedom, 66, 68; on French Revolution, 138–39; on history, 60; on *How We Shall Bring About the Revolution*, 304; on humanity, 46, 48, 49–50, 55; on London dockland strike, 256; and mass anarchism, 212, 230–31, 245, 246; on means and ends, unity of, 117, 119; on organization, 215; and organizational dualism, 322; on Paris Commune, 189; on parliamentarism, 148; on politics, 171; and prefiguration, 122, 125; print media of, 115; on propaganda of the deed, 202, 228; and Proudhon, 37; and revolutionary syndicalism, 257, 265; on schools, anarchist, 126–27; on Serreaux, 203; on social revolution, 97, 99–100, 103, 104, 106, 107, 190, 192, 228–29; on society, 78, 92–93; on spirit of revolt, 136–38; on state, 74, 76, 154, 162–63, 164, 209; on state socialism, 165–66; and syndicalist anarchism, 255; and theory of practice, 51, 59, 59–60; on trade unions, 326; and violent revolution, 101–2, 103; and World War I, 110

Kubo Yuzuru, 16

Küchler, Emil, 201

labor movement: in anarchist society, 89–92; and mass anarchism, 230,

and political neutrality, 260–62;
prehistory of, 250–56. *See also*
syndicalist anarchism

La Révolution Sociale, 203

Ricardo, David, 184

Richard, Albert, 314–15, 318

riots, 102, 133, 138, 181, 190, 205,
242, 360. *See also* direct action

Rocker, Rudolf, 4; and anarchism,
16, 41; and anarcho-syndicalism,
271–72, 276–77; and direct
action, 130–31, 233–34, 243; on
economic determinism, 58; on
freedom, 64–65; and free love,
128; on general strike, 296, 303,
304; on history and human action,
46; on human nature, 47, 49; on
parliamentarism, 146, 149, 150;
on reforms, 232; on social revolution, 102, 108; and syndicalist
anarchism, 290; and theory of
practice, 56, 58–59; on trade
unions, 215–16, 293

Roda, Maria, 129

Roller, Arnold (Siegfried Nacht), 134,
299, 300, 303, 304

Romance Federation, 124, 309

rulership and ruling classes: and anarchism, 15, 19, 22; and capitalism,
71, 73, 348–49; and collectivists,
38; and freedom, 67; and general
strike, 302; and insurrectionist
anarchism, 183–84, 210; and
parliamentarism, 147–49; and
political struggle, 170–71; and
propaganda of the deed, 187, 189,
201, 205, 209; and Saint-Imier
International, 26, 28; and social
revolution, 101–2, 103, 104; and
spirit of revolt, 137–38; and state,
17–18, 75–78, 154, 155; and state
socialism, 144–45, 162, 163; and
syndicalist anarchism, 286; and

trade unions, 325–26; and workers'
state, 159–60

Rupsch, Franz, 201

Russian Anarcho-Syndicalist
Minority, 274

Russian demonstration (1876), 196

Russian revolution (1905), 101–2

Russian revolution (1917): and
anarcho-syndicalism, 268, 270;
and Berkman, 107; and general
strike, 327; Goldman on, 117–18;
and mass anarchism, 246; and
militancy, 106; and platformism,
335, 336; and state socialism,
141, 166, 167; and syndicalist
anarchism, 282

sabotage, 131, 133, 249, 281, 284,
301. *See also* direct action

Saint-Imier Congress (1872), 25,
27, 28

Saint-Imier International: and
anarchism, history of, 2, 25,
27–29, 31, 33, 34, 39, 43; and
anarchism, usage of term, 35–36;
and anarchist society, 89, 90; and
Benevento affair, 196; collapse of,
321; and general strike, 297; and
insurrectionist anarchism, 176,
178; and organizational dualism,
322; and political action, 170; and
propaganda of the deed, 190, 191,
198; and syndicalist anarchism,
251, 254–55. *See also* First International

Salvador, Santiago, 204, 208

Schapiro, Alexander, 268, 269

schools, anarchist, 126–27. *See also*
education

Schwitzguébel, Adhémar, 29, 197,
238, 251

The Science of Revolutionary Warfare
(Most), 202. *See also* assassinations